The Transatlantic Collapse
of Urban Renewal

HISTORICAL

STUDIES OF

URBAN

AMERICA

The Transatlantic Collapse of Urban Renewal Postwar Urbanism from New York to Berlin

Christopher Klemek

THE UNIVERSITY OF CHICAGO PRESS

Chicago and London

The University of Chicago Press, Chicago 60637
The University of Chicago Press, Ltd., London
© 2011 by The University of Chicago
All rights reserved. Published 2011.
Paperback edition 2012
Printed in the United States of America

21 20 19 18 17 16 15 14 13 12   3 4 5 6 7

ISBN-13: 978-0-226-00595-9 (paper)
ISBN-10: 0-226-00595-X (paper)

Library of Congress Cataloging-in-Publication Data

Klemek, Christopher.
  The transatlantic collapse of urban renewal : postwar urbanism from New York to Berlin /
Christopher Klemek.
      p. cm. — (Historical studies of urban America)
  Includes bibliographical references and index.
    ISBN-13: 978-0-226-44174-0 (cloth : alk. paper)
      ISBN-10: 0-226-44174-1 (pbk. : alk. paper)   1. Urban renewal—North America—History—
20th century.   2. Urban renewal—Europe—History—20th century.   3. City planning—North
America—History—20th century.   4. City planning—Europe—History—20th century.
5. Urban policy—North America—History—20th century.   6. Urban policy—Europe—
History—20th century.   I. Title.   II. Series: Historical studies of urban America.
HT170.K57 2011
301.1′21609045—dc22
                                                                                              2010040490

♾ This paper meets the requirements of ANSI/NISO Z39.48-1992 (Permanence of Paper).

For my family,

                especially my two wonderful children,

                Abraham and Madeleine

Dummes Zeug kann man viel reden,
Kann es auch schreiben,
Wird weder Leib noch Seele töten,
Es wird alles beim alten bleiben.
Dummes aber, vors Auge gestellt,
Hat ein magisches Recht;
Weil es die Sinne gefesselt hält,
Bleibt der Geist ein Knecht.

Johann Wolfgang von Goethe,
Zahme Xenien (1827)

Foolish things are often written,
And also oft told,
Yet leaving everything unchanged,
They harm neither body nor soul.
But foolishness placed before the eyes,
Has a magic power;
Because it captivates the senses,
The intellect bows.

Translation by the author

Contents

Acknowledgments

From the earliest jottings through the final published form, this project was completed with the direct or indirect support of many institutions. Its principal patrons include the University of Pennsylvania, Freie Universität Berlin, the American Academy of Arts and Sciences, Florida International University, the Municipal Art Society of New York, Eugene Lang College at the New School, and the New-York Historical Society (through the particular generosity of Bernard and Irene Schwartz). Above all, the George Washington University has supplied a comfortable academic home for its author, and even furnished a faculty research grant courtesy of the Columbian College of Arts and Sciences.

A number of remarkable individuals provided encouragement and cooperation, from participating in running conversations to formal interviews. The late Jane Jacobs and her family were consistently encouraging and responsive to my inquiries in Toronto, New York, and beyond. Erik Wensberg shared a trove of New York reminiscences and connected me with other Greenwich Village resident-activists like Avreim and Carmen Greiss, Gerry and John Six, Peter and Terry Fritsch, and Eileen Bowser. Ray Matz discussed his designs for the West Village during his time at the firm Perkins and Will. In Cambridge, professor emeritus Nathan Glazer and former H.U.D. secretary Robert Wood contributed their own recollections of 1960s urban policy debates. In Toronto, former mayor John Sewell graciously sat for an extended conversation, as did architect Alan Littlewood and philanthropist Alan Broadbent. In London, architect Nathan Silver explained his community work in the 1960s. Finally, G. Holmes Perkins and Denise Scott Brown recalled the urbanist movements that emanated from postwar Philadelphia.

Several generous readers responded to all or sections of the manuscript with helpful suggestions: I appreciate the time donated by Timothy Gilfoyle, Tyler Anbinder, Edward Berkowitz, Richard Stott, Jeffry Diefendorf, Wendell Pritchett, Mark Rose, and Lizabeth Cohen, as well as the anonymous peer reviewers—even if the final product is different from anything any one of them envisaged. This project's infancy was nurtured by mentors who included Thomas Sugrue, Robert Fishman, Bruce Kuklick, Eugenie Birch, David Brownlee, Lynn Hollen Lees, George Thomas, Peter Conn, and Michael Zuckerman. The Technical University of Berlin's Center for Metropolitan Studies provided a valuable point of contact with German urban historians including Heinz Reif, Oliver Schmidt, Marcus Funck, and Alexander Sedlmaier. More broadly, this book was enriched by the many fellow scholars who exchanged insights with me on the topics it covers, including Robin Bachin, Hilary Ballon, Harald Bodenschatz, Nicholas Dagen Bloom, Robert Bruegmann, Christopher Capozzola, James Carroll, Steven Conn, Kyle Farley, Oz Frankel, Herbert Gans, Jeremy Glazer, Roberta Brandes Gratz, Owen Gutfreund, Marta Gutman, Richard Harris, Joseph Heathcott, Carola Hein, Alison Isenberg, Kenneth Jackson, Michael Katz, Lisa Keller, James Kloppenberg, Nancy Kwak, Andrew Lees, Alex Lichtenstein, Ken Lipartito, Robert MacDougall, Margit Mayer, Timothy Mennel, Eric Mumford, Carl Nightingale, Suleiman Osman, Anoo Raman, Keith Revell, Saskia Sassen, David Sawicki, Bruce Schulmann, Asif Siddiqi, Peter Siskind, Anne Whiston Spirn, Lisa Szefel, Dominic Vitiello, Alexander von Hoffmann, and Timothy White.

My colleagues in the George Washington University history department provided the material and moral support that was essential to researching and writing this book. I owe a dependable working environment to the department's staff, especially its Indispensible One, Michael Weeks, whose dedication inspires us all. Several students offered valuable research assistance at various points, namely, Michael Shapiro, Felix Harcourt, Robert Lintott, Melissa Cradic, and Cecilia Ramirez. For the scholarly excavation that such history writing entails I have depended in particularly intense ways upon the Toronto Urban Affairs Library's Judy Curry, New York Municipal Archive's Ken Cobb and Leonora Gidlund, the archivists at Boston College's Burns Library, and Kerstin Geißler of the Archiv Bezirksmuseum Friedrichshain-Kreuzberg.

In terms of the production of the book, I am consistently impressed by the painstakingly professional team at University of Chicago Press, particularly my editor, Robert Devens, editorial associate Anne Summers Goldberg, copy editor Erik Carlson, and the independent designer Richard Hendel. The press generously supplied a subvention from the Neil Harris Fund, which allowed for the reproduction of many more images than would otherwise have been possible.

Finally, it took no less than a clan of extended family members to provide the various forms of sustenance this author needed to complete his work—including countless hours of childcare, given particularly generously during summers, vacations, and holidays. For this and so much else, I am forever indebted to Joan and Gary, Ken and Carole, Courtney and Chris, Sue, John, Doug, Gabrielle, and Irene. Most of all, I am unjustifiably lucky to have Melissa Keeley, with her astonishing reserves of patience and wisdom, as my partner in urban studies and family building alike. *Ohne dich wär's unmöglich, meine Süße—Ich bedanke mich!*

To all of the aforementioned, and to many others besides, I am profoundly grateful. There is no adequate way to appreciate your generosity, but I thank you.

Introduction
The Final Frontier

July 16, 1969, could hardly be called a disappointment. But for many Americans who watched the closing of what President John Kennedy had called the new frontier, a much older one seemed to linger, as distractingly as an aching scar. "On the morning of the day Americans are landing on the moon," noted Daniel Patrick Moynihan, Harvard professor and urban affairs counselor to President Richard Nixon, "the air of victory is curiously muted [by] our seeming inability to get things done on earth, especially with respect to cities." He observed that "concern for the condition of American cities . . . has come near to being an obsession of our time."[1] Sam Bass Warner, Jr., an urban historian trained at Harvard during the late 1950s, recalled the early postwar period, when "talk of planning and building was everywhere, and hopes for a fresh start for young suburban families, for old neighborhoods, and for dowdy central business districts suffused the public consciousness."[2] But by the end of the 1960s, Warner, Moynihan and other urbanists looked in vain to find the kind of technocratic optimism expressed among their Cambridge colleagues in the early days of the Kennedy administration, such as when the founder of the Harvard-M.I.T. Joint Center for Urban Studies, Lloyd Rodwin, had fantasized back in 1961: "Suppose we could

From the San Francisco Chronicle

"There goes the old neighborhood."

Figure 0.1 New Frontier ambition meets urban crisis cynicism: Robert Graysmith's cartoon captured an ambivalent *Zeitgeist* during the first moon landing in July 1969, as technocratic visions clashed with hostile conditions on the ground—particularly in U.S. cities. (With permission from the artist.)

devise whatever technology was desired, at a reasonable cost—what kind of innovations should we then seek in order to make the future course of metropolitan development a happier one? Our technology has been reasonably successful in developing the kinds of weapons and space devices requested. Can we not count on at least a modest success in other directions as well?"[3] While Moynihan had once been inclined toward such positivist aims, the experience of the policy debacle called urban renewal had rendered him and many other urbanists "traumatized by the realization that everything relates to everything."[4] The unruly chaos of urban politics and social dynamics seemed to confute any technocratic hopes of imposing rational designs or policies on the metropolis. The omnibus quality of cities had long been a source of their strength; Walter Bagehot once explained that a city fascinates precisely because it is "like a newspaper. Everything is there and everything is disconnected."[5] Yet by the mid-1960s attempts by urbanists to connect the dots of the metropolis, and to produce policy and plans on that basis, were rapidly sinking to grief in the United States. After Kennedy's death, President Lyndon Johnson refocused attention on urban reform: "Our society will never be great until our cities are great. Today the frontier of imagination and innovation is inside those cities and not beyond their borders."[6] But the deeply held liberal assumption that government action was a big part of the answer to urban problems came increasingly into question. Even longtime housing reformer Charles Abrams bemoaned the fact that federal aid to cities had become "a contributing cause of their deterioration." The city, he announced with the title of his 1965 book, had become the frontier.[7]

By invoking these contrasting archetypes of the frontier and the city, Johnson and Abrams were prodding at scar tissue embedded deep in American culture—if not throughout the West since Augustine—just as Moynihan juxtaposed space-age ambition with earthbound failure. A frontier is essentially a military construct, defining a boundary of control, something to be defended and if possible pressed forward. In this sense, urban renewal was conceived and executed as a kind of frontier assault, drawing red battle lines around entire districts and neighborhoods, advancing against blighted slums, imposing rational new form on cities. Professional urbanist organizations, foremost among them the International Congresses for Modern Architecture (CIAM), acted like vanguard units to lead such maneuvers. However, the simplistic frontier metaphor proved counterproductive in a complicated, urbanized world—as it did in many disastrous combat situations. In the series of political and intellectual skirmishes over the goals and control of urban renewal, a recurring theme is the contrast between those who tended to see things in terms of clearly mapped divisions and those arguing for more complexity.

Discomfort with instability produced what were effectively domino theories about the advancing decay of cities, with cold war parallels extending so far as the enlistment of high-tech defense contractors like the RAND Corporation in efforts to combat urban blight.[8] Robert Fishman has posed the potent question—with reference to the fascist sympathies of CIAM leader Le Corbusier, albeit equally applicable to the comprehensive planning impulses of Lewis Mumford and others on the American side of the Atlantic—of "why so many of the best (and worst) minds of the interwar generation saw the free choices of ordinary people as leading inevitably to a horrible 'chaos' that could only be avoided by the imposition of a totalizing new order."[9] Mark Lilla similarly noted the disastrous political consequences of a tendency among intellectuals to disdain democratic process and to justify tyranny; and examining the relentless logic of large-scale state-administered projects, James Scott shows how benign intentions can tend toward disaster in the hands of a technocratic elite.[10] Likewise, in this study, the ostensible golden age of postwar urban planning emerges as a struggle to reconcile the conflicts among expertise, power, and democratic accountability.

The attempts to impose a new order on cities, and specifically a modernist vision of urbanism, via urban renewal policies eventually engendered a fierce backlash, clearly discernible by the beginning of the 1960s, that extended from North America to Western Europe. Instead of such sweeping approaches to cities, writer Jane Jacobs joined a younger generation of New Left urbanists to advocate a house-to-house approach, both for organizing grassroots resistance and for a gentler, gradual renewal of cities. Jacobs questioned the entire set of assumptions for urban intervention and called on city planners to "respect strips of chaos."[11] Urban social scientists like Herbert Gans (in the United States) and Michael Young (in the United Kingdom) suggested that the conduct of the war on urban blight was failing to win any hearts or minds in city neighborhoods. Paul Davidoff and Denise Scott Brown called for breaking down conceptual and class boundaries in the city planning profession; Philadelphia architect Robert Venturi celebrated complexity and contradiction, just as London's Townscape movement celebrated the messy urban vernacular.

Suddenly, the once vigorously contested boundary that had characterized the urban policy favored by many liberal reformers, with its clear demarcations, became a vanishing frontier, and gave way instead to a more complicated condition. Old political, conceptual, and even economic categories fell apart; old battle lines disengaged. In an endgame not without parallels in Vietnam, the American urban frontier was effectively abandoned by the 1970s, when President Richard Nixon took a declare-victory-and-retreat approach by dismantling all urban renewal programs. Among the lamentable legacies of urban renewal in the United

States was that while its proponents (including liberal public officials, academics, and planning professionals) and their opponents (many urban residents, New Left activists, and neoconservative intellectuals) fought each other along one front, their divisiveness over the means and ends of urban policy left little attention to control or harness the volatile forces of private real estate investment and disinvestment, usually labeled gentrification and blight, respectively. Ironically, gentrification ultimately did the most to close the urban frontier in the sense of slum eradication, as rehabilitation-minded citizens transcended binary attitudes about blighted neighborhoods, replacing conceptions of the older cityscape as something simply to be demolished with a more ambiguous, dynamic process. But gentrification also reinforced what Neil Smith has called a revanchist, class frontier in American cities. It seems that frontiers, urban or otherwise, remain an ineradicable presence in the landscape—at least of the United States.

So, just how distinctive was the U.S. experience? Historian Frederick Jackson Turner hailed the U.S. continental frontier as the defining element of an exceptional national character. Turner's influential frontier interpretation of American history, inflected with both irony and anxiety, emerged at the end of the nineteenth century, during the height of urbanization in the United States and Europe. The rural frontier thus fixed U.S. historians' attention at precisely the moment when it was officially declared a thing of the past, according the 1890 census. Three-quarters of a century later, Thomas Cochran noticed an analogue in the urban turn of scholarship: "That 'the owl of Minerva flies only at dusk' is often true with historians. Now that the 'classic,' densely populated city, sharply separated from the countryside, is about to disappear in the most advanced industrial nations, urban history is growing in importance."[12] Yet that emerging urban reinterpretation of American history would dislodge many of Turner's conclusions, including the distinctiveness of the U.S. experience.

Cochran was correct that U.S. historians had taken a characteristically slow route to the study of urban issues.[13] Beginning only in the 1930s, the urban paper trail was blazed initially by Harvard's Arthur Schlesinger and his student Carl Bridenbaugh. Schlesinger's *Rise of the City, 1878–1898* epitomized the bottom-up approach to studying industrial cities and, together with Bridenbaugh's *Cities in the Wilderness: The First Century of Urban Life in America, 1625–1742*, began to insist on a revision of U.S. history that emphasized the role of the urbanization. Well into the 1940s, some scholars worried about "the dangers of an urban interpretation of history," insisting that class distinctions were more explanatory of cultural change than the urban-rural dichotomy.[14] But such admonitions reflected the lingering effects of Progressive-era debates, rather than a recognition of the discipline's move toward social science history in the early cold war years.[15]

By the early 1960s, a new wave of urban historians emerged, including Oscar Handlin, Richard Wade, Sam Bass Warner, Stephan Thernstrom, and John Reps.[16] Though almost exclusively concentrated on the nineteenth century, their New Urban History focused on social issues in urban contexts and demonstrated (in the words of Warner) how the historian "might work if he wished to consummate . . . a marriage . . . between social science and equalitarian history."[17] Their insights suggested that Turner's view of the frontier as a unique force shaping the exceptional development of the United States was simply wrong. The central dynamic of American history, it now seemed clear, was not some impulse to flee the bounds of civilization, but rather the growth and development of highly stratified cities. In this respect, furthermore, the United States was not so different from Europe. So by overturning Turner's frontier thesis, a city-centered history also dislodged presumptions of American exceptionalism.

This historical revision helps to explain how such a vibrant transnational exchange of progressive policies, as Daniel Rodgers subsequently traced, could thrive between European and North American reformers by the early twentieth century. That prevailing (North) Atlanticism was acutely focused on the shared concerns of urbanized, industrial-capitalist societies like Britain, Germany, and the United States. Over the nineteenth century, the unprecedented wealth and might of these nations had been forged through their cities . . . and vice versa. To their great alarm, though, neither new elites nor old were able initially to control the disorderly forces unleashed alongside mass urbanization, despite various fitful interventions.

Beginning around the turn of the twentieth century, however, a renewed confidence appeared. It expressed the growing conviction that, given the burgeoning administrative capacities of modern systems (public and private), government could become the organizing master of the hitherto unmanageable cities—a conviction that would continue to grow right through the first decades of the cold war. Conceptually, city master plans projected order in the name of bringing renewal to cities; administratively, public authorities appropriated expansive new powers to impose programs for urban renewal. Thus, during most of the American Century—a reference, from Henry Luce onward, to that nation's growing cultural, military, and economic strength—potency was also taken to include the power to reorder the urban realm. Still, throughout this period of its national ascendency, the United States was hardly on an exceptional path; rather, it was closely tied into a transatlantic urban planning movement, with a shared vision of the urban future and shared means for realizing those ends through aggressive state interventions to remake existing cities.[18]

By the end of the 1950s similar policy instruments and objectives were in place in Berlin, London, and Toronto, as well as Boston, Philadelphia, and New York City, among many others. If, as Daniel Rodgers characterizes the early twentieth century, "the same concerns with city space, shelter, and design agitated every nation in the north Atlantic economy," I would urge that scholars extend such comparative assessments into the post–World War II period, an era of even more direct relationships and common influences.[19] During this same period, however, the underlying assumptions of European and North American planners and policymakers were subjected to divergent criticisms and revisions, which spelled the end of the transatlantic urban renewal consensus by the 1960s. While clearly inspired by international modernism, planning nevertheless functioned in specific political environments. Residents of various cities reaffirmed the traditional cityscape and rejected wholesale redevelopment. But in discrediting certain planning approaches, the confrontational political culture of Great Britain and the United States, by comparison with West Germany and Canada, created a backlash that hobbled all manner of urban initiatives. The local particulars of each urban policy crisis transformed the possibilities of planning and yielded disparate urban outcomes in those places for the rest of the twentieth century.

Looking at the first half of the twentieth century, Daniel Rodgers and James Kloppenberg have emphasized the commonalities between U.S. and European liberal reformers: "Moderate social democracy emerged in Europe for many of the same reasons, and made possible the appearance of quite similar coalitions, as those behind the more far-reaching American progressive reform measures." Yet as Kloppenberg must admit when considering Germany's descent into Nazism, similarities of intent can belie a variety of outcomes: "Those coalitions' disappearance had consequences as dramatic in England and France as in the United States. The consequences in Germany, of course, were far deadlier."[20] As the present study extends this narrative into the post–World War II Atlantic world, a whipsaw effect emerges: In the first half of the twentieth century, the reform impulse in the United States managed to persist amid changing liberal coalitions (and despite conflict), to build its achievements over successive generations. Meanwhile similar impulses in Continental Europe were rent by war and revolution. In the post–World War II period, however, it was the American liberal tradition that shredded itself, and nowhere so much so as in the city, both its original seedbed and the site of its most aggressive interventions.

■

Postwar intellectuals in the United States attempted to make sense of a radically changing American landscape, wracked by both physical and political shifts. The dialectics of suburban sprawl, downtown urban decay, and urban renewal—

hinted at by the neighborhood succession models of the Chicago school of sociology in the interwar period—were becoming visible on a large scale and preoccupied thinkers including Jane Jacobs and Lewis Mumford, Herbert Gans and Denise Scott Brown, Edward Banfield and Martin Meyerson. Their analyses and responses also engaged a set of transatlantic attitudes toward urban reform and urban aesthetics. This study follows two titanic twentieth-century concepts, modernism and liberalism, as they began to run aground in post–World War II European and North American cities. Having become tangled up together, each contributed significantly to the other's distress. In advance, however, these terms need to be untangled and defined. What precisely were modernism and liberalism?

I use the term "liberal" in its common American sense, corresponding roughly to "socialist" or "social democratic" in Britain, or sozial in Germany, by which is meant progressive, nonrevolutionary economic and political reform impulses born in reaction to the perceived volatility of industrial capitalism and mass democracy. Thus, I am not using it in Louis Hartz's narrow sense of privatist individualism à la John Locke and Adam Smith.[21] Political liberalism began to move away from the laissez faire, "classical liberal" attitude sometime in the last third of the nineteenth century and embrace corporatist, interest-group organizations, inspired in the American case by the vastly expanded, activist, bureaucratic state apparatus first glimpsed in the Civil War (and paralleled in giant business organizations).[22] This meliorist administrative state then saw its capacities expanded through successive wars and economic crises until, by the 1960s, it encompassed various social insurance measures ("welfare") within a mixed economy of regulation and private enterprise.

There are of course crucial distinctions that can be emphasized between such reformers in the United States and abroad by the early cold war period, particularly at the national level. For example, the British postwar Labour government nationalized a number of high-profile industries (coal, electricity, health care, railroads, and briefly, iron and steel) at precisely the time that the Republican-dominated Eightieth Congress checked the advance of New Deal reform. But this dichotomy is much less pronounced in the area of urban policy; even Senator Robert Taft, a staunch conservative known as Mr. Republican, supported—sponsored, no less!—the 1949 Housing Act that dramatically expanded the federal government's role in urban affairs, from the mortgage industry to public housing to slum clearance. And even as postwar Americans balked at nationalizing medicine and other sectors, they embraced a renewed round of municipalizing local services, particularly mass transportation.[23] An increased willingness to partner with and accommodate business interests would certainly characterize growth-oriented liberals in U.S. cities. But in terms of both the means and ends of urban renewal, they actually shared more than not with comparable reformers abroad.

A confidence in informed, social scientific expertise underlay much of the liberal project. Gary Gerstle traces American liberals' episodic search for realms that could be constructively affected by rational policies. Walter Lippmann's embrace of a technocratic elite after his rejection of mass democracy would epitomize this trend. By the 1920s liberals had abandoned many cultural issues, particularly race and ethnicity, as too irrational—that is, until the disaster of Nazi racism and the vilification of Soviet communism (not to mention postwar prosperity) began to make economic issues seem less pressing than racial ones. Then, of course, the civil rights movement ultimately did prove to be too explosive for the liberal coalition in the United States.[24]

But just where and how American liberalism met its demise is still under investigation. Debate continues over whether to declare the liberal political order dead or alive by the 1970s. H. W. Brands argues that the cold war was the last national emergency to provide an impetus for an activist state in the U.S., and the coming of détente revived older anti-statist attitudes.[25] Others, including Thomas Sugrue and Arnold Hirsch, have suggested that any consensus that ever existed around liberalism was already wilting under heavy fire across domestic ethnoracial divides by the 1940s.[26] Some argue that the reports of liberalism's death have been greatly exaggerated by the focus on electoral contests and can be flatly contradicted with evidence from regulatory and judicial trends in the 1970s.[27] And Francis Fukuyama maintains that liberalism is only now coming into its own on the world stage. The picture is indeed complicated, and the evidence contradictory. But I would argue that, in both halves of the twentieth century, it was cities that always offered the greatest possibilities for liberalism, while they also posed the greatest risks. This study also finds that the history of liberalism is written very differently on the walls of Berlin, London, Boston, New York, Philadelphia, and Toronto.

So what does liberalism mean in the context of city politics? Is there a distinctive urban liberalism? Liberals in Wilhelmine Germany, in contrast to their fateful failure to establish a presence at the national level of politics, emerged with a very strong base in the cities of the *Kaiserreich*.[28] Even earlier in Victorian Britain, bourgeois reformers mounted tangible challenges to Dickensian industrial cities, erecting civic centers and architectural monuments to the commonweal.[29] J. Joseph Huthmacher was probably the first to argue that early U.S. liberalism was inherently urban—that the city, with its concentration of both social outrages and an outraged electorate, provided much of the impetus for reformist (not to speak of radical) politics: "Not until the reform spirit had seized large numbers of urbanites could there be hope of achieving meaningful political, economic, and social adjustments to the demands of the new industrial civilization." Huthmacher maintained that early twentieth-century progressive reform was the product of collaboration between moralistic middle classes and pragmatic urban ethnic workers, the latter providing the real political muscle. Similarly, John Teaford sees the most fruitful reform efforts resulting from a de facto partnership—in effect a truce—between urban "machine" political organizations and those elites who would see them abolished. Only when the latter began to impose cultural assimilation policies like alcohol prohibition did the turn-of-the-century coalition collapse.[30]

Gary Gerstle notes that the New Deal's pragmatic liberals, in their search for economic stability, were once again willing to make accommodations with distasteful urban machines. That may be true from the standpoint of the White House. Yet local antiboss reform campaigns that sought to destroy corrupt machines did not end in the 1920s and 1930s, when liberal intellectuals supposedly turned away from cultural issues toward economic ones. Nor did the ongoing suburbanization of urban elites dissipate this antiboss impulse. Instead, it was just after World War II that such movements made their electoral breakthroughs, including the Young Turks in Philadelphia and those around Robert Wagner, Jr., in New York or John Hynes in Boston.

By that time civic reformers were also armed with the corpus of urban renewal legislation compiled during the New Deal, and a city planning agenda hatched in interwar Europe. City planning would become the liberal technocratic panacea par excellence. Where Americanization, prohibition, and other cultural programs had foundered in the 1920s, this time reformers were poised with funding, new legal authorities, and an electoral mandate to impose a rational order on the urban polity.

The urge to improve cities is probably as old as urban settlement. But what sort of urban policies did mid-twentieth-century liberals enact? Public and private infrastructural solutions to the engineering problems of industrial cities (sanitation, transportation, energy) were well developed by the end of the nineteenth century. Despite industrial building booms, however, housing conditions remained the main preoccupation of American and European civic reformers into the twentieth century. In the United States, Progressive-era housing initiatives reached legislative fruition with the New Deal (especially the Wagner-Steagall Housing Act of 1937), but there they also mixed with Depression-response measures to stimulate stagnating urban economies. By the post–World War II period, these were further complicated by calls to rescue downtown central business districts from the effects of suburbanization and to mitigate the impact of industrial relocation. In the

United States, a series of state and federal appropriation acts and enabling legislation from the 1930s through the 1960s assembled immense resources and authorities to address this convoluted agenda. The creation of the U.S. cabinet-level Department of Housing and Urban Development marked its high water in 1965, yet this entire decades-long regime of city-targeted programs can be referred to collectively as urban renewal.

Liberal urban reform from the New Deal through the Great Society became consummately enshrined in the impulse of urban renewal, which included numerous legislative and administrative initiatives at the municipal, state, and federal levels. This regime, with its iconic comprehensive plans and zoning resolutions, encompassed a broad alliance of policymakers (elected officials and civil servants), policy-oriented intellectuals (liberal social scientists), designers (architects and planners), and members of the business community (from the real estate, construction, and banking sectors). Contributors included many of the best and brightest in their fields, all of whom were trusted and underwritten (both financially and electorally) by a coalition of voters consolidated by President Franklin Roosevelt (and often referred to as the liberal consensus). The ambitious urban renewal program, fueled by an unprecedented fiscal mandate, also yoked noble social goals to an innovative aesthetic vision, or *Leitbild*, to use a particularly apt German term (literally "guiding image").

In particular, the aspects of urban renewal concerned with slum clearance and housing construction were heavily influenced by a (primarily) European planning and design movement that went under various pseudonyms: *Neues Bauen*, the International Style, functionalism, and, above all, modernism. Its association with urban reform was in part a testament to the fact that many of the European workers' housing projects, funded either by associations or the government, were completed in the formative 1920s, when the movement was sweeping into vogue. In Germany, at least, the provision of cheap housing seemed the ideal application for modern industrial materials, and such projects resonated with the radical ideals of many modernist designers. Not only were the German housing experiments available as models to those formulating housing policy from the Depression onward, but, what's more, Nazi persecution of leftists had brought many of the designers of those projects to Britain, the United States, and Canada (often in that order), where they gained positions of great influence in universities and on various commissions. With them came the notion that not only did progressive housing need to look different, but the entire city structure should be reorganized according to the "functionalist" principle of segregating land uses. So what precisely did this so-called functionalist modernism mean?

Modernism in architecture is marked aesthetically by the end of the stylistic

eclecticism that characterized the turn of the twentieth century and institution-
ally by the eclipse of the École Nationale Supérieure des Beaux-Arts in Paris as
the center of influence. But it is characterized perhaps most of all by an impulse
to express industrial construction processes (by then actually generations old),
as well as the style of industrial structures (e.g., factories and grain elevators).
All narratives of elite architectural history, which view architects as a species of
artist, must admit that the great majority of structures were until very recently
designed by engineers, anonymous builders, or amateurs and often either disre-
garded approved academic styles in the interest of expediency or else followed the
dictates of vernacular taste.[31] Nevertheless, the generation of architects coming
to prominence after the World War I vigorously embraced Louis Sullivan's maxim
that "form follows function," inspired by the sleek iconoclasm of Frank Lloyd
Wright, the industrial craftsmanship of Peter Behrens, and the workers' city envisioned by Tony Garnier. After some expressionist experiments, the circle of European practitioners that included Walter Gropius, Ludwig Mies van der Rohe, J. J. P.
Oud, and Charles-Edouard Jeanneret (a.k.a. Le Corbusier) rejected all decorative
elements that might conceal the modern, industrial nature of their structures.
By the mid-1920s proponents of this unornamented functionalism, as it was increasingly called, were seeking to limit the shape of architecture to rectilinear
prisms and its materials to iron, glass, and concrete. Since such a palette did not
leave much room for regional distinctions, adherents dubbed this approach the
International Style and promoted it via the International Congresses for Modern
Architecture.[32] Just how much embellishment could be tolerated within the stric-
tures of the dogma and still be rationalized as functional would be the subject of
perpetual debate.

Functionalism, while a less-than-clear concept in modernist architecture
(Gropius would revise it up until his death), was both explicit and rigid in terms of
modernist urban planning. The 1933 Athens Charter of CIAM decreed the segregation of the four functions of work, residence, transportation, and leisure. This
vision of urban functional reorganization, in addition to having an elegant clarity,
simultaneously promised to beautify the tangled cityscape and alleviate the social
ills of the industrial metropolis. It may well be said that "architecture is art's am-
bassador to the real world."[33] But the application of functionalist principles put
city planners at pains to bridge the realms of the rarefied atelier and the rough as-
phalt. After all, how a building looked was still largely an aesthetic question. Certainly the search for cheap industrial building methods for the mass production
of housing did give a social flavor to some modernist projects, yet the Levitt and
Sons' suburban developments (among many others) were simultaneously achieving the same ends using traditionalist ornamentation: mass-produced housing

clad in kitschy versions of Cape Cod and ranch styles. So matters of architectural taste could remain just that. But any design proposal that moved beyond the individual building, site, or client to take in a block, neighborhood, or (in the case of master plans) an entire city was bound to become much more deeply entangled with questions of economics, sociology, and, above all, politics.

Following about a generation of widespread acceptance, functional segregation first became a major point of contention when, in the 1950s and early 1960s, Jane Jacobs and some of her allies abroad began arguing forcefully in favor of its opposite: functional (and social) diversity as the lifeblood of the city's form and economic vitality. Given the suburban exodus, functionalist planners could point in their defense to the tendency throughout the West of increasing numbers voting with their feet (or streetcars or automobiles, etc.) in favor of a de facto segregation of residence from work and everything else. Jacobseans, on the other hand, had the advantage of defending the existing (if dwindling) conditions of the traditional cityscape, with its marbling of retail, residence, and industry, rather than trying to promote any radical reorganization. But those who agreed with Jacobs would face an uphill battle against both demographic trends and zoning statutes, which had given the force of law to a functionally segregated city vision. Theirs was unquestionably a rear guard action at midcentury. However, it anticipated the widespread revival of urban living in the late twentieth century.

At the broadest levels, three cascading sets of questions animate this study: First, precisely how did functionalist urban renewal, a phenomenon now broadly reviled, occur so ubiquitously in the West, and why did it take the specific, almost unvarying forms that it did? Answering this starts from transnational intellectual influences, then leads to national political circumstances, and ends in various local urban contexts. Across these multiple levels, one is struck by an extraordinary convergence of forces—electoral mandates, professionalized expertise, even popular culture—that seemingly overdetermined this reform impulse, and reinforced its power. (I will refer to this concatenation—much broader than any single policy or program—as the urban renewal order, with obvious debts to Steve Fraser and Gary Gerstle's term for a closely related phenomenon: the New Deal order.)[34] Second, once the interlocking strength of the urban renewal order is understood, it is then just as imperative to ask how and why it ended so abruptly and so soon, within barely a single political generation. Finally, it is illuminating to inquire whether the United States followed an exceptional path with respect urban renewal—from its origins to its legacies—or instead one shared with comparable urbanized nations. All of these questions highlight a novel dimension of my method, that is, addressing the transnational and comparative context for developments in the United States.[35] The reader will thus notice a primary though never exclusively American focus, the relative proportion of that emphasis being calibrated to place U.S. urban history in the foreground of a wider field.

■

Let me reiterate that the postwar urban renewal policies—even the crises they experienced—were remarkably similar in Berlin, London, Toronto, and the American cities of the northeast corridor. And yet Philadelphia-based urbanist Witold Rybczynski, writing recently about visits to Paris in his book *City Life*, could see little but dissimilarities abroad. For him, the striking contrast reflected less a vibrant Continental urbanity than the absence of the shadow of urban crisis—that seemingly ubiquitous concatenation of crime, social problems, physical decay, disinvestment, and abandonment that fell over so many U.S. cities beginning in the 1960s. Rybczynski, like countless North Americans visiting European cities in the late twentieth century, was forced to confront a glaring question: Why aren't our cities like that?[36]

Somehow things didn't turn out at all uniformly in the cities of Europe and North America, in spite of all the transatlantic parallelism and the shared impulses, concerns, and agitations. The twentieth century may well have begun on a course of convergence, urbanistically speaking, but it ended more divergently than ever before. This book seeks to explain the origins of that now popularly accepted divergence, and locates it a generation later than the obvious caesuras of global depression and war. Part I provides important background, establishing the strength of the international urban reform vision as it came to be institutionalized by midcentury: the interlocking foundations of its intellectual cachet, political power, and academic and professional influence. Part II then tracks the convergence within a transatlantic conversation among postwar urbanists (architects, planners, and policy intellectuals). It is focused around Jane Jacobs' influential critique of the urban renewal establishment, both examining the American roots of that critique and following its influence internationally, from German sociological debates to Britain's *Architectural Review*. Next, part III looks at anti-renewal politics, focusing specifically on Jacobs' own activism in New York and Toronto, partly confirming but also complicating her anti-renewal ideas. Finally, part IV is devoted to the professional ethics and aesthetics which emerged from the backlash against urban renewal, looking at the shift toward grassroots advocacy planning among architects and urbanists, visible in various examples from Philadelphia to Berlin. In the end, the urban reform vision was displaced in the United States by a paradigm of urban crisis, signifying the close of an era whose conclusion lacked the transnational coordination of its beginning, and with it the demise of any shared transatlantic urban ideal.

Such major transatlantic conceptual shifts, indicative of an evolving Leitbild but also of changes in the planning process, were visible by the mid-1960s: In New York, Jane Jacobs and her neighbors developed community-planned housing for the West Village to avoid dislocation, while advocacy planners like Paul Davidoff assisted Harlem residents to get control of their neighborhood's development. In Berlin, the private Entstuckung of Wilhelmine apartment blocks, whereby landlords had for decades stripped the neoclassical embellishments off their buildings to approximate better the modernist aesthetic, was being lamented as folly. It was a sign of just how far (and fast) the reputation of modernist pioneer Walter Gropius had fallen that upon his death in 1969 an obituary took pains to note that the Bauhaus founder and longtime Harvard architecture chair was not "irrelevant."[37] A growing self-doubt on the part of urbanists meant that the unexamined questions underlying planners' physical determinist motivations could now be readdressed:

> What form should the city follow—still the CIAM functionalist Leitbild? Or something more complex? Newer . . . or older?
> What mechanism should determine urban form—planning commissions, community planning boards, the marketplace?
> How does form matter—can it solve perennial questions of housing, safety, growth, economic vitality? Can or should the city be art?
> How should social science relate to social policymaking in a democracy—particularly with respect to complicated urban issues?

Britain, although never completely enamored of dogmatic International Style, had thoroughly embraced total planning in the immediate postwar period. Yet the country's bipartisan consensus ended by the late 1970s in an anti-planning backlash. Similarly, the rejection of liberal urban programs fueled the rise to power of antireform mayors in Philadelphia, New York, and Boston. In the United States these failures were more dangerous not only because of the anti-statist or anti-urban suspicions they reinforced, but also because of the country's explosive racial dynamics. Rather than alleviating or even simply neglecting them, urban renewal exacerbated and inflamed racial tensions. Progressive housing policies and aid to cities came to symbolize the antithesis of the ideals that motivated them. City planning based on functional segregation had the effect of intensifying racial segregation, whether through the "race moats" that were discerned in downtown beltway proposals like Philadelphia's South Street expressway or through the "second ghetto" that was constructed, albeit in perfect conformity with the CIAM Leitbild, on Chicago's South Side and in too many other African-American neighborhoods.

The mistakes were not fundamentally different in German and Canadian cities, but the legacies were. In the former case, a confidence in government intervention remained unshaken by urban renewal's failures. West Berlin had been perhaps the most purist in its application of modernist principles (at least following the immediate postwar years of reconstruction expediency) and yet experienced the least controversy from citizens eager to inhabit new apartments in the 1960s and 1970s. Even after moderating its renewal approach, at the very end of the period under examination here, the city retained a strong planning apparatus as capable of implementing sensitive, neo-traditional schemes as it had previously been at clearing old districts. In Toronto, the politicization of planning only served to invigorate civic democracy through the inclusion and reconciliation of various groups. The confrontational clashes—by Canadian standards—of the late 1960s and early 1970s resolved into a reformed, proplanning consensus similar to that of Berlin. Ironically, given these cities' social democratic reputations, one should note the role of moderate conservatives interested in pursuing social progress. Such "Red Tories," including Berlin editor-publisher Wolf Jobst Siedler and especially Toronto mayor David Crombie, were pivotal in criticizing and reformulating urban planning in those cities. Like the rejection of technocratic planning expertise that occurred across the political spectrum in Britain and the United States, the German and Canadian moves toward a more responsive urban policy also transcended party. But these proved far less corrosive to the authority of established administrative institutions than their Anglo-American counterparts.

Particularly in the United States, the chastening of planners for insensitive designs and urbanists for social scientific hubris was purchased at a high cost: a major opportunity for improving urban life was missed. The move from physical determinism to a more radically democratic model, such as the maximum feasible community participation mandate of the Model Cities program, and toward market economics, including embrace of suburban tendencies, meant that the New Deal and Great Society vision was lost, at least in cities. Sobered by a sense of intractable urban crisis, a relatively small, though influential, circle of Boston intellectuals dismantled the very local and federal planning initiatives they had advocated. In Philadelphia we find a failed rapprochement between designers and social science/social justice planners. Here was the abandonment of the last great attempt to find a middle way between total planning and complete surrender to the "creative destruction" of the market, especially the real estate industry. Bureaucratic tyranny was checked at the expense of the whole liberal urban program.

This larger urban tragedy explains the nagging sense of impotence that Daniel Patrick Moynihan saw muting any Apollonian victory culture in the summer of

1969. Paradoxically, an urban policy based on the certainties of modernist planning and social scientific expertise left Americans with a widespread sense of bewildered resignation toward their cities. Sam Bass Warner, Jr., noted this ironic legacy in The Urban Wilderness of 1972: "Americans have no urban history. They live in one of the world's most urbanized countries as if it were a wilderness in both time and space. . . . The giant cities of our country have always seemed to me, as they have to most Americans, vast incomprehensible places."[38] Urban renewal in the United States set up polarizations that not only undermined those initiatives but also foreclosed alternative solutions and future possibilities, leaving little conceptual or political space for the constructive reform of liberal programs. To compare internationally the outcomes and legacies of this crucial arena of liberal reform is to see the reverse trajectory of that enumerated by historians of the early modern period, with its errands into the wilderness eventually resulting in a transatlantic system. The American story in the twentieth century began with the comforting idea of an ordered Atlantic world of shared urban patterns, only to conclude overawed before an incomprehensible urban wilderness. Via its ill-fated urban policy engagement, the United States ultimately came closer to exceptionalism than even in the age of the mythic Turnerian frontier.

Part I Interlocking Foundations of the Urban Renewal Order

The staggering effects of industrialization on cities became evident in Europe and North America over the course of the nineteenth century, bringing unprecedented transformations in urban form, economy, politics, and society. From Great Britain (a densely urbanized nation) to Canada (with only a handful of large cities sprinkled across a vast continent), reformers searched for ways to channel disruptive urban forces and, increasingly, to refashion the industrial cityscape completely. The most influential comprehensive response initially saw full expression during the 1920s in German-speaking cities like Vienna, Frankfurt, and especially Berlin. Elements that in some cases occurred or even originated elsewhere first came together there: a popular sense of cultural break, thanks to the Great War and its aftermath, radical modernist designs for replanning the urban landscape, and progressive public patrons willing to support them.[1]

Within a decade and a half, the ascent of Hitler had eclipsed some aspects of this constellation in Germany, particularly the more iconoclastic aesthetics and their leftist associations. But even Nazi urban planners like Albert Speer shared their predecessors' aversion to the metropolis as it stood. The Allies' victory in World War II swept away the Nazi regime in turn, but it also demolished Europe's urban centers more extensively than even the most extreme critics had dreamed. Modernist city planning, via the influence of exiles, returned with Germany's occupation. By the 1950s German planners had put an aggressive program in effect to deconcentrate urban centers, reorganize them according to segregated functions, and make them "automobile ready." Berlin in particular was to be modernized as a liberal capitalist show window of the cold war, and there was little room in the future thus envisioned for the "quaint and phony" vestiges of the older city.

Though ideologically apart from the turbulent politics of Berlin during the first half of the twentieth century, Britain's colossal capital, London, stood by the end of World War II at the center of a restructuring of British society along social democratic lines. These included the implementation of aggressive planning legislation to clear slums and decentralize the population, to construct modern housing, and to build highways. Interwar British design had initially expressed its own idiosyncratic style of modernism. Yet under economic pressures and shifting

Figure 0.2 Meyer's Court, 1910: an iconic image by Berlin muckraking photographer Willy Römer, showing children in the interior courts of an apartment block on Ackerstraße in the Wedding district. Such vivid exposés fueled urban reform impulses on both sides of the Atlantic. (Photo credit: Bildarchiv Preussischer Kulturbesitz/Art Resource, NY.)

professional fashions, its forms came by the 1950s to closely resemble the urban renewal visions afoot in Berlin. By 1965 these aims, shared across the ideological spectrum, were being executed on a vast metropolitan planning scale that dictated the course of the greater London region.

Wartime dislocations and postwar open immigration brought British and German influences across the Atlantic. Like Britons, Canadians also reacted against the hitherto laissez-faire development of their cities. Toronto led the way in 1947, adopting slum clearance and modernist public housing projects similar to those in Europe. And Torontonians also responded to the unplanned sprawl of the early twentieth century by creating a 1953 metropolitan government, analogous to the Greater London Council. But rather than implement an antigrowth boundary like the London greenbelt, Metropolitan Toronto used its far-reaching powers to pursue pro-growth policies that coordinated the schools, infrastructure, and transportation demands of booming suburbs. Thus, in a Canadian hybrid, expansive European-style regional public authorities were put to American-style privatist ends.

If we examine, for comparison, the northeast corridor of the United States—that megalopolis of cities whose industrial development matched Europe's—we can perceive the emergence, from roughly the 1930s through the 1960s, of four interlocking pillars within the American urban renewal order. First, Americans' tastes in architecture and urban design moved from the Beaux-Arts toward modernism, as seen in both public and private commissions, and throughout popular culture from world's fair exhibitions to Hollywood movie sets. By the 1950s, U.S. corporate headquarters and government buildings alike were announcing that the once radical modernists' aesthetics had gone mainstream.

A second converging element was the professionalization and credentialing of experts in disciplines of "urbanism": modernist architecture, planning, urban design, and related social science. Rooted, like parallel developments in other fields, in the expansion of postwar universities (particularly graduate education), this undergirded the rising social prestige of technocratic elites, a significant number of whom set themselves to solving the "problem" of cities. At Ivy League centers of advanced research, cities became a growing focus of disciplinary interest. Urbanist experts, disdainful of cities' drift hitherto, were nevertheless optimistic about mastery through comprehensive analysis and planning. They saw themselves as agents for fundamental change in the nature of urban life.

In a third key component, during this period Uncle Sam came to town, as it were: Within the context of the expanding reach of federal government, and given the demographic dominance of cities for a generation already, Washington began taking increasing responsibility for urban affairs. Congressional appropriations for overlapping programs aimed at construction stimulus, slum clearance, housing provision, and road building mounted from 1934 through 1968. This urbanizing policy trend reached its pinnacle under Democratic legislative and executive dominance in 1960s with the initiation of various task forces and programs, culminating in the 1965 creation of an executive cabinet department tasked with cities.

Washington's urban turn meshed with the fourth development, the advancement of ambitious redevelopment schemes by local public entrepreneurs, Robert Moses preeminent among them, who took advantage of new federal largesse and expanded statutory powers. But well beyond any single swashbuckling official, the real epochal shift at the municipal level can be seen in a wave of midcentury regime changes that positioned progressive reformers—usually anti-machine elites—who took modern city planning as their banner. Examples include New

York mayor Robert Wagner (son of the senator who framed pioneering urban renewal legislation), Boston mayors John Hynes and John F. Collins, and Philadelphia's Young Turk reform movement, especially the architect-reformer who shaped that city's planning for three decades, Edmund Bacon.

These four distinct elements constituted the pillars of an urban renewal order in the United States—no less than in Germany, Britain, and Canada (see table A1 in the appendix). Each interconnected tightly with the others, and frequently even combined in the person of a single individual. Many urbanists, particularly planners, moved among academic, federal, and municipal posts, often holding them concurrently. It was not rare to find a technocratic city expert in the position of not only designing projects, but also helping to author enabling legislation, campaigning for mayoral candidates who would support such, implementing plans as appointed municipal officials, and all the while training a new professional class to do the same. With urbanists thus helping stimulate the demand for their own expertise, the urban renewal order was rapidly built up into a seemingly impregnable edifice on the political landscape.

1 Atlantic Crossings of the Urban Renewal Order
From Interwar Berlin, via Wartime London, to Postwar Toronto

"A Passionate Hatred of the Metropolis":
Berlin (Anti-)Urbanism from Weimar to Reconstruction, 1919–65

The urban renewal order began as an idea, or rather a clutch of ideas, swimming between fin de siècle Europe and North America. Scholars have mapped several important intellectual tributaries feeding the modernist movement in urbanism by the early twentieth century. Robert Fishman profiled the three perhaps most essential forces, each with headwaters in disparate reaches: Ebenezer Howard (a Londoner), Frank Lloyd Wright (an American writ large), and Le Corbusier (an adopted Parisian from Switzerland)—the last of whom would be a wellspring for the ideas promulgated around the world by an influential professional organization, formalized in 1928 as the Congrés Internationaux d'Architecture Moderne (CIAM).[1] Yet it was in German-speaking cities during the 1920s, particularly Vienna, Frankfurt, and Berlin, that modernist urbanism was first implemented on a large scale.[2] The explanation for such an ambitious civic program of *Neues Bauen* (an early German term for the style, literally "new building") lay in the power of organized labor and working-class politics in those cities—both through the unions themselves, as private patrons of construction projects for their members, and via municipal public housing programs and subsidies undertaken by labor-dominated city governments.[3] In addition to progressive public policies, however, the radically modernist style of these projects' architecture offered a distinctive aesthetic complement to the bold socialist impulses they embodied. Major Berlin examples included the work of CIAM members Martin Wagner, Bruno Taut, Hugo Häring, Hans Scharoun, and Walter Gropius (among others) on projects at the Hufeisensiedlung (1925–33), Onkel Toms Hütte (1926–31), and Siemensstadt (1929–31). These Weimar-era experiments foreshadowed the urban renewal order that flourished two decades later on both sides of the Atlantic, wherein bold professional urbanists realized aggressive modernist redevelopment projects through a practical alliance with progressive governments.

By the eve of Hitler's accession to the German chancellery in 1933, Berlin was "with little doubt the architectural capital of the world."[4] The pathbreaking and

Figure 1.1
A sketch circa 1910 by Heinrich Zille, chronicler of working-class Berlin. The woman scolds children playing in the barren court of a typical apartment block: "Get away from those flowers; play with the trash cans!" (Courtesy of Villa Grisebach.)

influential Bauhaus design school—founded by Gropius though by then under the direction of Ludwig Mies van der Rohe—moved from the provinces (Dessau) to the metropolis, and the city bristled with radically new ideas that were about to shape the world. Yet there was an uneasy relationship between the old Prussian capital and many of those it hosted; in truth, Berlin's urbanists possessed a visceral loathing of the urban industrial setting they inherited.[5] Werner Hegemann's 1930 monograph, which translated roughly to *Petrified Berlin: History of the World's Largest City of "Rental Barracks"*—a reference to the ubiquitous five-story apartment blocks that housed most of the city's industrial workers (see fig. 1.2)—epitomized intellectuals' excoriation of Germany's largest (and Europe's most dense) city as it had developed within the Paris-inspired framework of an 1862 master plan

Schöneberg, Prager Platz, Motzstraße 1900—1910

Eines der vielen hoffnungslosen westlichen Wohnviertel der wilhelminischen und Haberland-Zeit, die in freiem Felde eng verbaut wurden, als stünden sie in einer Festung. Links »Renaissance«, im Vordergrunde rechts neumodischer »Barock«.

Neuzeitlicher Wohnungsbau

Gehag Siedlung Britz im Osten Berlins, 1927. Architekten: Martin Wagner und Bruno Taut.

Figure 1.2 Werner Hegemann assailed Berlin as a petrified city, choked by its dense, nineteenth-century apartment blocks, which he derided as "rental barracks." In this illustration from his influential 1930 book, he contrasts a typical built-up area of the city (Schöneberg), with a prototype of modernist urbanism: the low-density horseshoe project designed by Martin Wagner and Bruno Taut for a housing cooperative in the Britz district. (Source: Werner Hegemann, *Das steinerne Berlin: Geschichte der größten Mietkasernenstadt der Welt* [Berlin: Gustav Kiepenheuer, 1930]. Used with permission of Birkhäuser Basel.)

by James Hobrecht.[6] That disdain for Berlin's civic status quo permeated every city planning proposal from the architectural avant-garde. With an iconoclastic shock value akin to that of Le Corbusier's 1925 Voisin plan to raze central Paris for superblock towers, Ludwig Hilberseimer's 1928 photo collage imagined rows of wall-like, twenty-story, six-hundred-meter-meter-long high-rises (fig. 1.3)—a scheme which would have completely obliterated eighteen blocks on either side of Friedrichstraße, Berlin's busiest commercial thoroughfare. Similarly, Cornelis van Eesteren, a Dutch architect affiliated with the Bauhaus, won a 1925 competition with his (unexecuted) design to replan Unter den Linden's baroque promenade for high-rise superblocks and high-speed traffic. These specific proposals were never built, but they were emblematic of influential urbanists' approach to large industrial cities like Berlin, and they delineated a powerful *Leitbild*.

The early twentieth-century urbanist community was agitated by various transatlantic trends, each grasping for some control over the seemingly chaotic, often disturbing implications of massive urban growth. For example, the possibility of purifying civic spaces, almost instantaneously, via aesthetic unity made a formidable impression on visitors to the White City at the 1893 Chicago World's Fair. A more practical mechanism emerged when New York City enacted the United States' first comprehensive zoning law in 1916.[7] A Progressive-era initiative with radical roots as well as conservative real estate applications, zoning gradually took hold among liberal reformers as a way to legislate against residential overcrowding and industrial blight.[8] Of course, the advent of zoning codes and City Beautiful redevelopment schemes in the Progressive-era United States both bore the unmistakable imprint of Paris, that European "capital of the nineteenth century" (as Walter Benjamin hailed it), with its Beaux-Arts streetscapes enforced by a powerful centralized planning authority. Meanwhile, the first European design generation to come of age in the twentieth century, though it still embraced the strong hand, would renounce the Parisian design ideal, purging both its historicist facades and the densely built blocks behind.

The direction of modernist urbanism was evident in Hilberseimer's drawings as early as 1924 (fig. 1.4), four years before he established a city planning program at the Bauhaus (he would continue to teach the subject at Illinois Institute of Technology after 1938). His rationalistic designs for a high-rise city emphasized separation, both of urban uses and individual structures, as well as an austere stylistic homogeneity. The advantages were implicit: high-rise apartments would have more light and air, automobiles more speed and less congestion, children and other pedestrians more open space, away from the hazards of traffic. Not least, from the standpoint of such affecting presentation sketches, modernist towers would command dramatic vistas. Hilberseimer's contemporaries (Gropius, van

Eesteren, Le Corbusier, and others) would codify and formalize the vision of a functionally reorganized and aesthetically redesigned city over the next decade in the doctrinal councils of the CIAM organization. Functionalism, as its inflexible creed came to be called, had radical implications for how cities should look and operate. To realize it in any existing city, enormous swaths of the built environment would need to be cleared out of the way, an eventuality that was more than acceptable to those captivated by this vision of the urban future.[9]

As the symbol of continental Europe's most urbanized nation, Germany's capital had been the subject of intense concern for architects, planners, politicians, and reformers since the nineteenth century. Andrew Lees, who surveyed attitudes toward cities in the United States, Great Britain, France, and Germany during this period, concluded that the Germans exhibited the most pervasive anti-urban hatred, as well as the most polarization of attitudes toward cities. To explain why this animosity toward the metropolis was so much worse in Germany than elsewhere, Lees noted an ominous byproduct of that country's rapid industrialization: "the tenacious grip of pre-modern attitudes and values among powerfully entrenched social groups."[10] By the 1920s, such dispositions were being exacerbated by the fact that attitudes toward the city were often politically linked, and were thus buffeted by the vehemently polarized climate of Weimar politics. For if, as Lees contended, "acceptance of the city was most pronounced among men and women closer to the ideological center," then this moderate position was increasingly rare in a period renowned for their absence. The Weimar Republic, like its mercurial capital city, was (to borrow Barbara Miller Lane's apt description) "compounded of extravagant artistic creativity and extreme political instability."[11] Particularly in the wake of World War I and the Bolshevik revolution, political radicalism became endemic to Berlin's avant-garde architects. Most influential among these was Bauhaus design school founder Walter Gropius, the scion of an influential Berlin architectural family.

The Nazi takeover of Germany forced the Bauhaus to close—a gesture emblematic of the regime's very real break with the leftist cultural ferment of the Golden Twenties. Yet Hitler and the architects and planners patronized during the Third Reich embraced many of the industrial modernist design ideas taught at the banned school, even as they rejected its radical ideology and its most avant-garde aesthetics.[12] Thus, emphasizing the continuity of such developments in her classic study, *Architecture and Politics in Germany 1918–1945*, Barbara Miller Lane argues that Hitler's notorious politicization of architecture and design must be traced back to the preceding decade. While the Nazis did see architecture as the most consummately political of the arts, such a view was not particular to their totalitarian vision, but rather inherited from the cultural environment of the Weimar

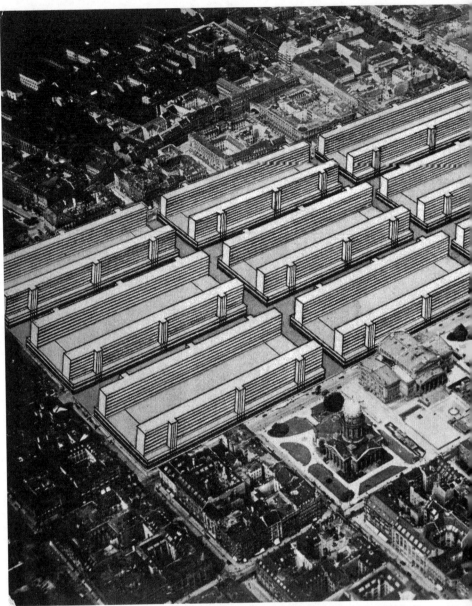

Figure 1.3 Ludwig Hilberseimer's provocative 1928 proposal for Berlin's central Friedrichstadt district envisions modernist urbanism dropped by a deus ex machina to eradicate the old cityscape. Around this time, Hilberseimer began teaching city planning at the Bauhaus design school founded by Walter Gropius. (Ludwig Hilberseimer, Berlin Development Project, Friedrichstadt District: Office and Commercial Buildings, Bird's Eye Perspective View, 1928.

Photocollage of ink on paper mounted on aerial photograph, 17.2 ×
25 cm. Gift of George E. Danforth, 1983.1804.2. Reproduction, The Art
Institute of Chicago. Photography © The Art Institute of Chicago.)

Figure 1.4 By the mid 1920s, European urbanists fashioned a guiding vision (*Leitbild*) that was carried worldwide over the next three decades by individuals and organizations (especially the International Congresses for Modern Architecture, or CIAM) and eventually commanded a transnational consensus among professional architects, planners, and policymakers. In pointed contrast to existing cities, Ludwig Hilberseimer's striking 1924 sketches for a rationalized, modernist urban utopia were clean, devoid of clashing architectural ornamentation or any comingling of activities. Key elements included the segregation of expressways from pedestrian skyways and sleek slab towers that seemed to float, isolated from each other and detached from the streetscape. (Ludwig Hilberseimer, Highrise City [*Hochhausstadt*]: Perspective View: North-South Street, 1924. Ink and watercolor on paper, 96.5 × 148 cm. Gift of George E. Danforth, 1983.991. Reproduction, The Art Institute of Chicago. Photography © The Art Institute of Chicago.)

Republic. Many of the leaders in the modernist design movement were driven into exile, primarily for what they had striven to symbolize politically. (Nazi reactionary conservatives, in effect, took the Bauhäusler at their revolutionary word.) But the Nazis not only retained the politicization of architecture from the Weimar intellectuals, they also embraced the anti-urban strains. "Whatever their differences," notes Lane, the new modernist designers held at least this one point in common with the conservative architects who denounced them: "they all shared a passionate hatred of the metropolis."[13]

This widely held dream of eradicating the nineteenth-century character of Berlin and other European cityscapes would largely come true—albeit cataclysmically—through the deus ex machina of World War II. By the zero hour of 1945, fascist repression and the violent upheavals of the 1930s and 1940s had scattered the community of modernist architects and planners who rose to prominence during the Weimar period. As many found their way into positions at prestigious universities in the United States, their radical politics often moderated by American political culture and corporate clients, these urbanists nevertheless remained connected via the CIAM organization.[14] At a series of conferences, the group formalized its tenets into what came to be called the Athens Charter (drawn up in 1933, first published in Vichy France a decade later), which declared that cities needed to be decongested and reorganized into four functionally segregated zones: work, residence, transportation, and leisure. Over the next decade, this "functionalist" recipe—linked to the modernist architectural style favoring freestanding, unadorned boxes—was evangelized as the sole possibility for enlightened city building. After the war, the reconstruction of a Europe knee-deep in rubble offered unprecedented opportunities for the application of CIAM's principles, just as these ideas were reaching the apex of their institutional influence.[15]

At the end of World War II, the fate of Germany's cities lay in the hands of the conquering powers, especially the United States and the Soviet Union. The wartime strategies of all the belligerents had escalated the effects of the conflict on urban targets to the point that many cities were effectively razed—not to speak of the human toll.[16] In Germany, air raids caused between 400,000 and 600,000 civilian deaths, in addition to nonfatal causalities of 650,000 to 850,000. Roughly half the built-up areas in large cities (those with prewar populations of at least 100,000) were destroyed. Berlin lost one-third of its housing, and while not the most extensively damaged, as the largest target it amassed many times more rubble than any other city—enough in fact to fill the Great Pyramid twenty times over.[17] Having suffered intensely during the German invasion of Russia, the Soviets proved more interested in exacting reparations than promoting reconstruction (at least initially).[18] For its part, the American occupation initially followed the Joint Chiefs of Staff directive 1067, essentially calling for the repastoralization of the industrial belligerent, though such a punitive approach was reversed once Germany's strategic position in the emerging cold war became clear.[19] But even after the more constructive Marshall Plan became U.S. policy, the American military government contributed little substantively toward the physical and aesthetic rehabilitation of German cities. Jeffry Diefendorf cites the absence of any "consistent, high-level American policy" on urban reconstruction, concluding that the U.S. occupation authorities were far less interested in planning than the French or British.[20]

Nevertheless, the Americans could not long ignore the massive housing crisis created by widespread destruction, combined with the influx of refugees and displaced persons. In response, they urged large-scale construction of cheap, mass-produced housing. And although the United States offered little material support directly to architects and city planners, the occupation did offer a mechanism for the reintroduction of some German émigrés who found asylum across the Atlantic, and their influence decidedly shaped the course of reconstruction.

Of those modernist exiles, none found more fertile ground than Walter Gropius did in the United States.[21] As chairman of the Department of Architecture at Harvard from 1937 until 1952, Gropius had a decisive impact on American urbanism, through his own pedagogy and via his equally influential students like Marcel Breuer, Philip Johnson and I. M. Pei.[22] Simultaneously, acting as a kind of cultural go-between, Gropius became the central figure advocating the modernization of German housing and planning under the American occupation.[23] His 1947 visit under the auspices of the U.S. military government, while noted at the time primarily for his impolitic pronouncements about redesigning Frankfurt to replace Berlin as the western capital of a divided Germany, nevertheless "left a deep impression on many German planners."[24] A less renowned though no less intriguing planner-in-exile was Hans Blumenfeld, who toured Germany in 1949 and advised the U.S. military government. Blumenfeld was a German communist who fled to Russia during the 1930s, and then on to Philadelphia's planning commission in the 1940s; McCarthyism finally drove him to Toronto in the 1950s.[25]

Ultimately, however, Germans would largely be left to undertake the reconstruction of battle-ravaged cities on their own (fig. 1.5). The German architecture and planning professions proved highly unified throughout the initial postwar decades. The CIAM-derived disposition that opposed the nineteenth-century urban form remained coherent and dominant throughout the period—albeit with some gradual alterations to the idealized models they pursued. Gerhard Rabeler, a city planner in postwar Münster, distinguished four waves of ideas and images influencing the German planning profession during the first decade and a half of reconstruction (1945–60): The initial phase, lasting from 1945 until the currency and constitutional stability of 1949, was characterized by an emergency posture as well as wide-ranging discussion. In the second phase, corresponding to the first half of the 1950s, debates over whether to use restoration techniques or entirely new construction for bombed centers resulted in the dominance of an ideal of "deconcentrated und reorganized cities."[26] By the mid 1950s, economic momentum, the transition from manufacturing to service industries, and personal mobility had engendered a more regional planning perspective (phase 3). West German planner Hans Bernhard Reichow's widely read 1959 call for highway modernization ("automobile-ready cities") was pivotal.[27] Finally, in the early 1960s, a fourth phase saw the emergence of a modest reaction to the aggres-

Figure 1.5 A German planning brochure announces, "We're building the new city"—the "we" acknowledging that postwar reconstruction was undertaken without direct involvement of the Allied occupation. The cover, featuring an idealized model of a redevelopment project for Berlin's Kreuzberg district, embodied all the elements of CIAM functionalism: deconcentrated and reorganized land use including ample open space between buildings for recreation, segregation of residential areas from other uses, particularly the automobile-ready streetscape. Urban renewal projects took on heightened importance in West Berlin, as prominent demonstrations of urban reform in that cold war display window. (*Wir bauen die neue Stadt: Die städtebauliche Neugestaltung der Luisenstadt* [Berlin: Bezirksamt Kreuzberg, 1956]. Source: Bezirksmuseum Friedrichshain-Kreuzberg, Archiv.)

sive decentralization, with critiques calling for more density and urbanity.[28] (This last development, and others related to it, will be examined in chapter 3.)

Prior to 1971, the Federal Republic had no dedicated planning law at the national level. The Christian Democratic Union (CDU) government considered a federal statute as early as 1962, with a mind toward stimulating the economy by means of urban renewal programs. A recession around 1966–67 added impetus to this initiative, but it was only after the Social Democratic Party (SPD) took power in 1969 that the deliberations entered their final stages and eventually produced a federal urban planning act (discussed in chapter 12).[29] Focusing on the prevention of speculation, the SPD opposition initially seized renewal as a campaign issue at a May 1965 housing and planning congress in Bremen, "Healthy Housing in Healthy Communities: A Residence for Every Citizen." This was the first substantive conference on the topic by any of Germany's parties, followed a week later by the CDU's response, "Germany Tomorrow: Urban and Regional Planning" in Saarbrücken.[30] Since the federal act was finally passed so late in this slow political game (1971), it simply grandfathered many of the renewal processes which had already begun during its ten-year incubation.[31]

Despite such partisan dickering, German planners and urbanists did not lack opportunities and resources for redeveloping their cities. In the absence of federal legislation, the individual states had passed construction codes shortly after the war, such as Berlin's 1949 zoning (amended in 1956). Postwar German urbanism seemed less ideologically explosive, as the radical and reactionary politics of the 1920s and 1930s certainly got cooled by the deluge of war, then submerged beneath the jockeying of occupying great powers. Yet by the 1960s, many cities in the young Federal Republic were strikingly, even drastically, modern—and none more so than the tragically divided one sometimes referred to as the "display window" of the cold war.

According to John Burchard, an architectural engineer and M.I.T. professor who toured occupied Germany in 1945 and again in 1963 (at the invitation of Boston's consul general from the Federal Republic of Germany, funded by the German Academic Exchange Service), Berlin was praiseworthy among those cities "which having suffered great damage are content to be new cities along new lines." In general, Burchard was struck by the Herculean achievements of German urban reconstruction. As far as picturesque old German towns went, Burchard granted the pleasantness of "the few medieval ones like Rothenburg which went untouched in the war and remain untouched by modern life." But he attacked as "too sentimental and too short-sighted" those cities like Munich, Hanover, and Frankfurt that were "caught up in modern life but trying too hard to restore . . . or preserve their past" and therefore in danger of becoming "only ghastly reminders of another era."[32]

With a purist's desire for authenticity that was typical of the CIAM school of thought (he had been loosely affiliated with the organization since 1939),[33] Burchard subscribed to a German medieval ideal in terms of urbanism, yet he nevertheless insisted that only modernist approaches were appropriate for modern times. Burchard was particularly interested in the ways Germans wrestled, not altogether successfully, with the juxtaposition of old and new, and with accommodating the automobile. Burchard's argument against restoring "quaint and phony" older styles, however, is undermined by the fact that he, like the tourists for whom it was intended, was fooled by the painstaking reconstruction of Rothenburg, a town which (few spellbound visitors realize) lost almost one-third of its historic center to bombing.[34]

Nevertheless, Burchard's sensibilities mirror architectural discussions on both sides of the Atlantic about the place of older structures within the modernized city. Stuttgart-based Wilhelm Westecker, attempting a similar "midterm evaluation" of reconstruction in more than thirty West German cities, found much to celebrate and almost nothing to criticize among the historic reconstructions and modernist redevelopments.[35] His approbation was typical, since by and large, public or professional criticisms of the late 1950s tended to focus on the unfulfilled promises and missed opportunities of postwar planning (especially transportation) rather than challenge its goals.[36] Despite regime change, war, and other upheavals, those goals remained consistent with the ones that had been articulated by Bauhaus and CIAM leaders since the 1920s: out with the old cityscape; in with a modernist, functionalist city (fig. 1.6). And after decades of debates and proposals, Berlin's postwar urbanists were finally in a position to realize these visions.

Modernism Is from MARS; Planning Is from County Hall: The British Urban Renewal Order, 1943–65

Berlin had provided an urban setting where modernist urbanism underwent some of its earliest conceptual experiments during the first decades of the twentieth century, fierce controversies through its middle years, and particularly widespread application in the postwar period. It is worthwhile now to compare the parallel emergence of an urban renewal order in Britain, a country fatefully connected to Germany by the international crises of the twentieth century's first half.[37] Their ideological paths, of course, were far from parallel. And domestic British politics followed their own idiosyncratic logic: Just after victory over Germany in 1945, conquering hero Winston Churchill found his Conservative Party tossed off the government benches in favor of a Labour slate headed by Clement Attlee. Building on the social solidarity engendered in the war (and despite continued rationing), the Labour government spent the next five years constructing the framework of a British welfare system, underpinned by Keynesian economic theory and the specific blueprints laid out by Oxford economist William Beveridge in his 1942 report *Social Insurance and Allied Services*.[38]

The urbanist equivalent of the Beveridge report took form almost simultaneously, as University College London town planning professor Patrick Abercrombie drew up highly influential plans for London and its region. As an acolyte of Ebenezer Howard's Garden City movement (see fig. 1.7), Abercrombie's war-

Figure 1.6 In the post–World War II period, planning officials in Berlin, influenced by visiting urbanists (including exiled German modernists), rejected the inherited cityscape as "quaint and phony" vestiges inappropriate for modern times. This brochure from the Kreuzberg borough office in Berlin criticized various aspects of the untidy cityscape—from mixed uses to architectural ornamentation—declaring: "Not like this!" Such out-with-the-old proselytizing cleared the way for new, CIAM-inspired urbanism. (*Wir bauen die neue Stadt: Die städtebauliche Neugestaltung der Luisenstadt* [Berlin: Bezirksamt Kreuzberg, 1956]. Source: Bezirksmuseum Friedrichshain-Kreuzberg, Archiv.)

time proposals foresaw not the reconstruction of the status quo ante bellum but rather the decentralization of the capital through relocation of population and industry to satellite "new towns" out beyond a protected greenbelt which would prevent contamination of the English countryside by unplanned sprawl of the dreadful metropolis (fig. 1.8). Concretely, Abercrombie's London plan would guide the city's development into the 1970s, by which time more than a million former Londoners would find their homes and jobs relocated outward. Symbolically it formed the template for national urban policy (fig. 1.9). The 1947 Town and Country Planning Act obliged all municipalities to undertake similar surveys and plans and also established a new national ministry. This planning strategy seemed in harmony with the postwar zeitgeist. In fact, similar centrifugal policies had been encouraged at least since the extension of suburban rail connections in the 1920s.[39]

Yet idealistic policymakers were faced with extreme pressures in the aftermath of a destructive war: London's housing shortage (with origins well before World War II) would last for decades, perhaps Europe's worst case.[40] In 1946, working-class Londoners from the East End provocatively took to squatting in empty town-houses in the tony West End, rather than be left homeless. Exacerbated by the fact that wartime restrictions on private construction remained in effect for years, the government never met the demand for housing. Aneurin Bevan, Labour's minis-ter of health from 1945 to 1951, is primarily remembered as the architect of Brit-ain's socialized health service, but he also had the portfolio addressing the acute housing shortage. He did so with moderate, human-scaled bungalows, in what has been described as a golden age of public housing.[41]

The style of housing, in addition to the shortage of it, became a major theme of postwar British planning debates. With characteristic distance from European revolutions, modernist urbanism did not really obtain a foothold in the United Kingdom until (as noted by a fixture of the British architectural establishment, J. M. Richards) "a full dozen years after it had been launched on the Continent" in the wake of World War I.[42] Belatedly, the Modern Architectural Research Group (MARS) enlisted British talent in the international modernist movement for the

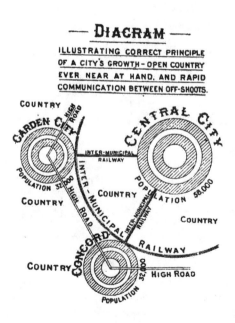

Figure 1.7 A turn-of-the-century movement spearheaded by the unassuming London clerk Ebenezer Howard produced a distinctly British response to the growth of industrial cities. Howard rejected the density and sprawl of the metropolis for a modest balance of town and country, which he dubbed the Garden City. He envisioned the planned decentralization of work and residences, limiting the size of new towns and satellite settlements, and imposing green belts of parkland to insulate them from the open countryside. Howard's vision had spawned model Garden Cities at Welwyn and Letchworth by 1920s and became influential in the British planning movement generally. (Ebenezer Howard, *Garden Cities of To-Morrow* [London: Swan, Sonnenschein & Co., 1902].)

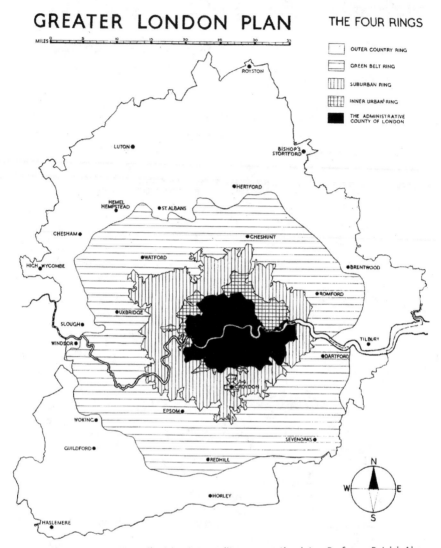

GREATER LONDON PLAN

MILES

THE FOUR RINGS

OUTER COUNTRY RING

GREEN BELT RING

SUBURBAN RING

INNER URBAN RING

THE ADMINISTRATIVE
COUNTY OF LONDON

ROYSTON

LUTON

BISHOP'S
STORTFORD

HERTFORD

HEMEL
HEMPSTEAD · · ST. ALBANS

CHESHAM

CHESHUNT

WATFORD

HIGH WYCOMBE

BRENTWOOD

ROMFORD

UXBRIDGE

SLOUGH

TILBURY

WINDSOR

DARTFORD

CROYDON

EPSOM

WOKING

SEVENOAKS

GUILDFORD

REDHILL

N
W   E
S

HORLEY

HASLEMERE

Figure 1.8 Translating Howard's vision into reality a generation later: Professor Patrick Abercrombie prepared a plan on behalf of the Minister of Town and Country Planning's Standing Conference on London Regional Planning, proposing a greenbelt growth boundary to prevent London's interwar suburbs from sprawling out into the open country. Over subsequent decades, more than a million Londoners would be relocated via slum clearance programs from the dense core into eight satellite new towns, modeled on the Garden City idea, built beyond the greenbelt. As Abercrombie's policy framework blended with CIAM aesthetic influences, postwar Britain became the most hospitable climate for modernist urbanism since Weimar Germany. (*Greater London Plan 1944* [London: His Majesty's Stationery Office, 1945]. Courtesy of the Library of Congress.)

Figure 1.9 Influential planner Patrick Abercrombie (*pointing*) presents a model for the reconstruction of Plymouth, England, to officials in 1944. Abercrombie's wartime planning studies for the London region became templates replicated across Britain and incorporated into national policy. The 1947 Town and Country Planning Act obliged all municipalities to undertake similar surveys and plans, and established a new national ministry. (Source: Plymouth and West Devon Record Office 1418/2010. Picture courtesy of *The Plymouth Herald*.)

fourth CIAM, a legendary convention which took place on a Mediterranean cruise in the summer of 1933.[43] The MARS group was particularly interested in slum clearance and contributed heavily to the CIAM research project which became the official statement of functionalist urbanism: *Can Our Cities Survive? An ABC of Urban Problems, Their Analysis, Their Solutions, Based on the Proposals Formulated by the CIAM.*[44]

When the MARS group developed a utopian plan for the radical reconstruction of London into a "decentralized linear city," the idea withered in the face of Abercrombie's widely embraced master plan.[45] Thus, the older, indigenous British planning tradition, as founded by Ebenezer Howard and enacted by Abercrombie, competed for a time with the modernist movement as promulgated by CIAM and its local affiliates. Prominent Edwardian architect Sir Reginald Theodore Blomfeld lamented in 1934 that "Modernismus" had "invaded this country like an epidemic."[46] Particularly during the war years, British antipathy toward ideas so tied up with continental (especially German) influences lingered. But modernism could also be construed (by the British right or left wing) as the enemy's enemy, since both the Nazi and the Soviet governments had denounced the style from 1933 onward as either Jewish-Marxist, on the one hand, or decadent bourgeois capitalist, on the other.[47] What's more, many leaders of the movement, including Walter Gropius and Arthur Korn came to Britain as exiles from those very regimes and became outspoken advocates there. By the late 1940s, the British Town and Country planning tradition of Howard and Abercrombie was being rapidly subsumed under the modernist vision of CIAM and MARS. By then, Britain (particularly its civil service) offered the most hospitable official platform for modernist urbanism since the "red cities" of Germany and Austria twenty years earlier. As *Architectural Review* editor J. M. Richards observed (with some consternation) in 1947, "From the point of view of propaganda, the MARS group now finds itself in a powerful position because members of the group occupy key positions in many government departments and other influential organization, and are able to play their part there in propagating CIAM ideals."[48]

In fact, austerity and construction controls on the private building industry, combined with the dramatic expansion of government projects, had led almost half of Britain's architecture professionals to shift into public service by 1948, particularly with the London County Council (LCC). World War II destroyed roughly one-third of the city, and since the LCC was charged with both reconstruction and (after 1950) public housing, it attracted the best young architectural talent and hosted key planning debates.[49] The first major public illustration of postwar British urbanism came at the Festival of Britain, held on London's South Bank waterfront for the centennial of the Victorian Crystal Palace exposition of 1851. The event, planned by the Labour-dominated local and national government after 1947, prominently featured CIAM-influenced design; among other projects was the first high-profile public building commission since the war: MARS member Leslie Martin and Robert Matthew's Royal Festival Hall.

Notwithstanding such a showcase for Labour's vision of urban renewal, in 1951 Winston Churchill managed a comeback for the Conservatives, who recaptured Downing Street for nearly a decade and a half, during which time they pursued (relatively) more market-oriented urban policies. The Conservative national government removed wartime building controls, producing a London office boom from about 1954 to 1964 characterized by bold, modernist projects, above all (literally) the city's first skyscrapers, including Shell Oil's Upstream Building, Post Office Tower, the Empress State Building (all 1961), and Centre Point (1963). Ironically, by restricting the construction of housing on inexpensive land at the city's periphery, Abercrombie's greenbelt strategy had put so much pressure on real estate prices in London proper during the 1950s (a 60 percent rise between 1958 and 1963) that the public planning authorities could hardly afford to carry out his vision.[50] Despite such soaring prices, Conservative home ownership policies enjoyed long-term success. Despite persistent social inequalities, rising levels of private home purchase, perhaps more than any other single factor, helped to make the postwar period a generally prosperous one. The party touted such developments with Harold Macmillan's successful 1959 campaign slogan, "You've never had it so good."[51]

Thus, by the end of the 1950s, London and other British cities had a more robust private real estate sector than Berlin or other West German counterparts, at least for housing. Paradoxically, it was under Conservative leadership, particularly while the future prime minister Macmillan was minister of housing and local government from 1951 to 1954, that the British government accelerated its public housing program, moving away from Bevan's more conventional housing toward large-scale redevelopment projects of prefabricated modernist high-rises.

With respect to stylistic debates, Nichola Bullock suggests that the postwar competition for scarce resources had two countervailing effects in Britain. First, as in Germany, it initially led to privileging patch-up reconstruction over radical redevelopment schemes (to the chagrin of CIAM champions). But for new developments, scarcity also tipped the question of aesthetics toward the construction efficiencies inherent in a spare modernism. Bullock concludes that by 1955, both in public and private construction—from downtowns to new towns, from office towers to schools buildings—modernism had become mainstream.[52]

Not only Labour but particularly Conservative administrations vastly expanded the public role in housing, planning, and redevelopment. Like the administrations of cities and towns across the country, London County Council was controlled by Labour, as were the borough councils. The LCC nevertheless partnered with Conservative national governments to pursue numerous redevelopments, which historian Peter Sheppard has termed the period's *grands projets*, that aggressively discarded many received elements of London's urban fabric.[53] Traffic modernization projects included the 1961–62 underpass at Hyde Park Corner, improvements to Regent Street, and a regional ring road system. Examples of tower housing built by the LCC range from the well-crafted 1958–59 Alton Estates in Roehampton, Surrey, to the dangerously shoddy 1968 Ronan Point in Newham, East London. (With twenty-one thousand inhabitants, the multistage Roehampton development was the largest of many housing projects undertaken by the LCC.)[54] Most ambitious was the City of London's transformation—from the 1950s to the 1980s—of a Smithfield bomb site into the massive Barbican Centre: a supercompound of luxury tower housing, galleries, cinemas, theatres, conference facilities, a concert hall, library, botanical conservatory, museum, and the Guildhall School of Music, all connected by skywalks.

The above list represents only a selection of the concretely realized examples. In spite of all the private and public sector housing activity, however, a 1965 survey of London residential conditions reported that they were probably the worst in Europe.[55] Yet British urbanists were apparently undeterred by quips that a planning region "is an area safely larger than the last one to whose problems we found no solution."[56] For in that very year, the London County Council (dating from 1889) was abolished and replaced with the Greater London Council, encompassing a population twice as large, an area four times the size, with more and larger boroughs. It marked the final consolidation, on a metropolitan scale, of London's urban renewal order.

Metro Middle Way: Toronto's Transatlantic Urbanism, 1947–69

Crossing the Atlantic (albeit still within the British Commonwealth of Nations), the urban renewal order also arrived in Canada by the end of World War II, again offering administrative remedies to the conditions that preceded it. Mindful of the privations of the Great Depression, Canadian policymakers pursued economic expansion and physical growth, including the modernization of highway transportation. At the same time, they sought to assert control over the haphazard development of individual suburban homesteaders and private builders through regional planning and zoning. And beginning with the 1947 Regent Park project in Toronto, there were slum clearance initiatives aimed at both eradicating older residential areas deemed eyesores and confronting housing shortages with modernized public housing blocks (figs. 1.10, 1.11).

In comparison to the United States, Canada during the first half of the twentieth century suffered both a weaker mortgage market and fewer federal housing initiatives (either for financing or construction). No federal public housing program existed until 1956; Toronto's non-property-owners were only enfranchised in 1957.[57] This laissez-faire approach led Richard Harris to characterize it as "more American than the United States." Canada certainly seemed to bear more similarities to the U.S. experience than that of Britain or Germany.[58]

However, the Canadian national mood was undergoing a fundamental shift toward comprehensive planning. During the Depression, Toronto liberals (many from the University of Toronto's Faculty of Social Work, including Albert Rose, Harry Cassidy, and Charles Hendry) joined the League for Social Reconstruction to promote reform via slum clearance and public housing. A number of major studies advanced the cause, including the 1934 Bruce Report (of the Committee on Housing Conditions in Toronto), the 1935 book *Social Planning for Canada*

REDEVELOPMENT PROJECT **TORONTO**

Figure 1.10 The cover of a 1962 brochure promotes the expansion of redevelopment in Toronto with a study in contrasts: delinquent youth in the street of dark, Victorian row houses are juxtaposed against children playing wholesome games in bright, open park space around modernist housing. (*South Regent Park: A Study* [Toronto: Metropolitan Toronto Housing Authority, 1962]. Image courtesy Toronto Public Library. Copyright permission: City of Toronto)

Figure 1.11 Design for Regent Park, Canada's first urban renewal project, proposed in 1947 and built over the following decade. The plan to redevelop six blocks of Toronto's Cabbagetown neighborhood reflects the influence of the international urbanist *Leitbild*, including typical functionalist elements like consolidation of the old street grid into superblocks, the clearing of open space between modernist apartment buildings, and the segregation of residences from traffic and other activities. Because the project actually predated the commitment of federal resources, it was primarily financed locally through a referendum driven by liberal reformers. (Source: Housing Authority of Toronto, *Regent Park Housing Project: Canada's Premier Housing Redevelopment Project* [1951]. Image courtesy Toronto Public Library.)

(including Humphrey Carver's "Housing Programme"), and the 1944 Curtis Report (of the Advisory Committee on Reconstruction). Eventually, the call for major public intervention in cities was answered by national legislation beginning with the Housing Act of 1944 and the creation of the Canadian Mortgage and Housing Corporation in 1946.[59]

Such indigenous developments were reinforced by the permissive immigration policies Canada adopted from 1947 onward, as the influence of British and German planners ushered in more drastic changes. Jacqueline Tyrwhitt, one of the most doctrinaire members of the British CIAM organization from 1940 onward, set up the planning program at the University of Toronto in 1951 and pro-

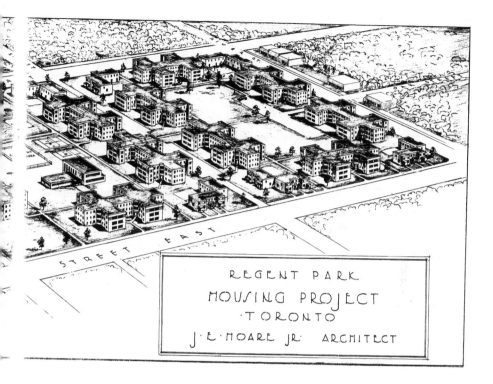

REGENT PARK
HOUSING PROJECT
·TORONTO·
J·E·MOORE JR· ARCHITECT

moted the Toronto chapter of CIAM.[60] The City of Toronto hired a development commissioner and chief planner from Britain. Such transplants brought with them the enthusiasm generated by the British Town and Country Planning Act and Abercrombie's London plans.[61]

Canadian urbanism remained a sort of Euro-American hybrid, particularly with respect to regional planning. In Toronto, growth was the unquestioned goal of postwar civic leaders. This required transportation modernization (highway construction, but also commuter rail), as well as the provision of new utilities and schools to promote suburban construction. Postwar Toronto promoted rather than restricted suburban growth, in contrast to London or West Berlin—their growth boundaries provided by a pastoral greenbelt and a militarized border wall, respectively. In distinction to the United States, as well, pressures from the top of Canada's federal system pushed urban policymakers toward metropolitan-scale solutions to sprawl-related questions. Central-city Torontonians sought the annexation of the expanding suburban periphery, thereby taking on the infrastructural burdens of these growing communities, though at the same time consolidating control downtown. Nonetheless, in 1953 a provincial panel reaffirmed the autonomy of the thirteen suburban municipalities, while it simultaneously

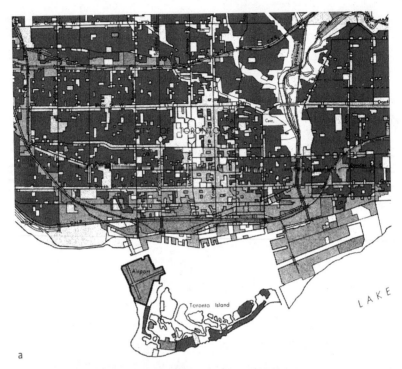

a

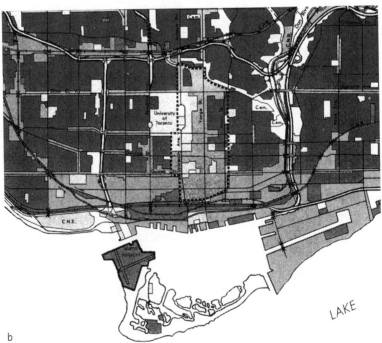

b

c

Figure 1.12 Toronto metropolitan planning facilitated U.S.-style suburban growth via a British-style regional planning authority—but notably without the growth boundaries of Abercrombie's London plan—and simultaneously envisioned comprehensive changes for the older urban core, whereby the low-rise cityscape would give way to high-rise office and apartment construction. Map details from the 1959 official plan illustrate the vision of moving away from the existing mix of residential and nonresidential uses (*a*), toward zones restricted for greater homogeneity of land uses, along the lines of CIAM functional segregation (*b*). Finally, a network of expressways was to penetrate the old downtown and connect it with the suburbs (*c*). (*The Official Plan of the Metropolitan Toronto Planning Area* [Toronto: Metropolitan Toronto Planning Board, 1959]. Copyright permission: City of Toronto.)

inserted a new layer of government between the local and the provincial, binding the urbanized region into the Municipality of Metropolitan Toronto (whose government was known locally as Metro). A jurisdiction modeled on the London County Council and "the first metropolitan government on the continent since New York in 1898," Metro was in practice a theater of rivalry between the city of Toronto and its suburbs, with the provincial authorities mediating between them.[62] In short, Metro became emblematic of Toronto's third way.

It was a political coup for Frederick Gardiner, the man appointed to head this massive apparatus with its expansive powers. "On the day in 1953 when Fred Gardiner took control of the Municipality of Metropolitan Toronto," explained *Globe and Mail* journalist Robert Fulford, he fused the newly amalgamated jurisdiction with his own ambitions to become "the most powerful local politician in the city's history." Fulford compared Gardiner to the 1958 expressway that would bear his name: "big, ugly, aggressive and effective."[63] According to the German émigré (and uncannily ubiquitous) city planner Hans Blumenfeld, Gardiner combined all the positive characteristics of New York's legendary power broker Robert Moses without any of the negative ones. Since Blumenfeld was responsible for much of the regional planning under Gardiner, his assessment of the man certainly benefits from proximity.[64] But given that Blumenfeld was also an outspoken apologist for both Stalin and the Berlin Wall, his particular perspective merits more explication.

Arriving in Toronto two years after Metro was established, Blumenfeld found in post–World War II Canada the realization of dreams the urbanist had nurtured since his days in Germany before the First World War. Blumenfeld's life story reads like the apotheosis of the transatlantic urban renewal order. By the time he became assistant director of the Metropolitan Toronto Planning Board in 1955, the sixty-three-year-old had already cut a broad swath across many of the most important hubs of planning in Europe and North America (to many of which this study will return). Raised in Hamburg, Blumenfeld experienced a temporary interruption in his training as an architect to serve in World War I, after which he worked under Joseph Frank in the United States and Adolf Loos in Austria. A lifelong socialist, Blumenfeld moved to the Soviet Union in 1930, where he planned industrial towns (Vladimir and Kirov) as well as projects in Moscow, until he was expelled in the Great Purge of 1937. He resettled in the United States, working first in New York City (with a stint designing for the 1939 world's fair), then as research director at the Philadelphia Housing Association (1941–44), and ultimately as senior land planner (1945–48) and chief of the Division of Planning Analysis (1948–52) at the Philadelphia City Planning Commission. The U.S. Department of Defense engaged him to tour Germany as a visiting expert in city planning in 1949. He returned to Philadelphia as a consultant from 1953 to 1955, and was invited to teach at the University of Pennsylvania. But these opportunities were foreclosed by the loss of his residence permit following a McCarthy-era interrogation.[65] It was then that he received the invitation to work under Gardiner at the Metropolitan Toronto Planning Board.

Metro's greatest achievements would be in the provision of regional public services, including water supply, sewage disposal, and school construction.[66]

Gardiner vigorously championed the highway program, whose centerpiece was an expressway across Toronto's waterfront, which he named after himself. Toronto also became the first North American city to construct a new subway system since the Depression. The culmination came in 1959, when Blumenfeld and other Metro urbanists produced, in the words of Toronto historical geographer James Lemon, "the most massive planning document ever" (fig. 1.12).[67]

Although both Blumenfeld and Gardiner stepped down from Metro in 1961, their stewardship left a clear legacy. Gardiner had wanted to encourage Toronto's growth in every direction, including vertically. An office boom doubled the region's capacity over the course of the 1960s.[68] Gardiner's regional planning body encouraged the suburbanization of the region's population, but Metro's preemption also left the central city cramped for growth. By the early 1960s, Toronto city officials, outnumbered on the Metro council, had become somewhat desperate to preserve the city's own economic interests in the face of policies and trends that facilitated the shift of jobs and residences just beyond its tax borders. In response to its now-fixed horizontal boundaries, the Toronto city council aggressively pursued the city's vertical growth, approving a series of high-rise apartments (both public and private) and office projects. Most prominent of these was Viljo Revell's massive modernist city hall complex, which opened in 1965 on the site where one of Toronto's poorest slums, "the Ward," had just been cleared. Thus, by the mid-1960s, an urban renewal order—albeit a distinctly Canadian hybrid—extended from the center of the city of Toronto out to the suburban edge of Metro's regional jurisdiction.

2 Assembling the Four Pillars
An Urban Renewal Order Takes Shape
in the United States, 1934–65

Daniel Rodgers ends his study of transatlantic progressive impulses—a preponderance of them in the area of urban reform—with the conclusion that a long period of exchange and convergence, stretching back to the late nineteenth century, broke down upon the rise of totalitarianism and the outbreak of World War II. Rodgers thus finishes his far-reaching book with the stage set for a revival of American exceptionalism, a renewed cultural and intellectual isolationism that was supposed to have settled over the cold war era. Yet, to look at the field of urbanism, the transatlantic convergence was never more apparent than in the decades immediately after the war—in its *Leitbilder*, its political programs, and even its leading figures. The emergent urban renewal order represented a culmination, an intense revival, of that older transnational conversation.

Many recurring themes and developments have already become evident in the elaboration of an urban renewal order in Germany, Britain, and Canada. Nowhere were these interwoven trends more conspicuous than in that chain of the most European of American cities, which Jean Gottmann collectively dubbed Megalopolis—an archipelago of old mercantile ports that became manufacturing centers on the north Atlantic seaboard stretching between Boston and Washington. During a transformative thirty-year period from the 1930s to the 1960s, European modernists-in-exile intersected with indigenous U.S. developments, including (1) a shift in design tastes, popular and official, toward the modernist aesthetic, (2) the enshrinement of expert authority in the field(s) of urbanism, (3) a massive federal policy revolution, and (4) urban political reform movements. In the context of the United States, then, it is possible to observe in detail how the urban renewal order came to rest upon these four interlocking pillars. This chapter will examine each component in turn, as well as the relationship between them.

1. Domesticating Modernism: From MoMA to Main Street

A diffuse aesthetic shift that occurred from officialdom to popular culture was an important first step in determining the kind of urbanism that was to shape U.S. cities in the twentieth century. As late as the 1930s and 1940s, leading American design schools still promulgated Beaux-Arts-inspired curricula, and patrons from banks to New Deal government agencies draped their new buildings with neoclassical ornamentation. Yet bold, iconoclastic, and indisputably modern construction was not alien to U.S. shores. The champions of European modernism (especially Gropius and Le Corbusier) freely acknowledged the influence of American design ideas—from the trademark horizontality of Frank Lloyd Wright's prairie houses and the signature verticality of Daniel Burnham's skyscrapers to the austere, anonymous, but no less striking grain silos and factories that pervaded the landscape by the early twentieth century.

Americans' implicit early embrace of modern design was brought out into the open and celebrated during the years of economic depression and war. Not incidentally, the modernist movement was also then shedding its radical European roots. True, some early modernist housing projects in the United States were sponsored by leftist trade unions (following the German example), such as the Carl Mackley Houses, designed in Philadelphia by German-born architects Oskar Stonorov and Alfred Kastner for a hosiery workers federation in 1933–35.[1] Yet it was depoliticized—or perhaps even conservatively repoliticized—examples of modernism that moved into the American mainstream.

A 1932 architectural exhibition at the Museum of Modern Art, often credited with legitimizing (and rebranding) the International Style for the United States, stripped the European movement of its radical manifestos to present it as pure abstraction—just as the museum had done with many leftist artists. The exhibition, curated by Philip Johnson and Henry-Russell Hitchcock, focused primarily on individual architects (Walter Gropius, Mies van der Rohe, Le Corbusier, J. J. P. Oud, Frank Lloyd Wright, and others) and the extent of their influence internationally (primarily in the U.S. and Europe). However, one of the exhibit's five rooms was organized around the theme of housing and examined the possibilities for modernism on a larger urban scale (fig. 2.1). Members of the Regional Planning Association of America, particularly Lewis Mumford, Catherine Bauer, Clarence Stein, and Henry Wright, provided text panels that scorned the densities in Manhattan and then presented possibilities for "drastic changes." Images juxtaposed conventional row housing in Queens with the Garden City–inspired Sunnyside Gardens project nearby. At the center of the room was a scale model of a super-block housing project recently designed by Otto Haesler for Kassel, Germany.[2]

Meanwhile, 1930s Hollywood played a more lowbrow role in normalizing the new aesthetic, projecting sleek moderne sets as backdrops for Depression escapist fantasies on silver screens nationwide. And in a very direct form of propaganda, Lewis Mumford and other U.S. adherents of the Garden City movement developed a documentary film for the 1939 New York World's Fair (The City) that condemned contemporary urban conditions and hailed New Deal resettlement experiments like Greenbelt, Maryland. The world's fair presented many dramatic visions of its theme, "Building the World of Tomorrow"; particularly prescient

Figure 2.1 A gallery devoted to the theme of housing from *Modern Architecture: International Exhibition* at New York's Museum of Modern Art in 1932. Lewis Mumford and other U.S. adherents of the regional planning movement shaped the presentation of the CIAM *Leitbild* alongside British Garden City influences. Photographs of negative examples from New York's Lower East and Upper East Sides (labeled "slum" and "superslum") faced a model of Otto Haesler's Rothenberg-Siedlung in Kassel, Germany. Another panel contrasted the back alley of Queens row houses to public spaces in the Sunnyside Gardens planned community. (Digital image © The Museum of Modern Art/Licensed by SCALA/Art Resource, NY.)

was the "Futurama" exhibit in the General Motors pavilion (fig. 2.2). The automobile corporation hired Norman Bel Geddes to design a model city of the future featuring functionally segregated high-rise towers interspersed with expressways, thereby promoting urban redevelopment to thousands of visitors. By the 1940s commercial designers like Viennese émigré Victor Gruen were making modernist retail environments familiar elements in old downtown commercial districts and new suburban shopping centers.[3] These models and small-scale experiments soon had larger counterparts in the built environment.

Ironically for an aesthetic once steeped in revolutionary rhetoric, corporate America adopted the mantle of modernism and provided its most prestigious patronage, beginning with the Philadelphia Savings Fund Society Building (Howe and Lescaze, 1929–32) and continuing after a hiatus with Portland's Equitable

Figure 2.2 Visitors to the 1939 New York World's Fair ride through the "Futurama" model in the General Motors exhibit, designed by Norman Bel Geddes. Photograph by Margaret Bourke-White. (Source: Harry Ransom Humanities Research Center, The University of Texas at Austin. Photo © Estate of Margaret Bourke-White/Licenced by VAGA, New York, NY.)

Building (Pietro Belluschi, 1944–48) and New York's Lever House (Gordon Bunshaft, 1952) and Seagram Building (Mies van der Rohe, 1954–58).[4] An important prototype for the kind of office buildings that came dominate Manhattan and other American cities was the United Nations headquarters in New York (1947–53). Designed by an international committee of distinguished modernist architects, it was a landmark of the International Style.

Whatever stylistic term was used, by the 1950s modernism in general was being recast as part of the U.S. heritage. Frank Lloyd Wright was rehabilitated as a national treasure, an icon of American individualism; a younger avant-garde of abstract expressionist painters like Jackson Pollock became part of the CIA's cold war propaganda campaigns; staunch anticommunist writer Ayn Rand portrayed a modernist architect as the paradigmatic individualist in the face of collectivization with her 1943 novel The Fountainhead (filmed by Warner Brothers in 1949).[5] The unadorned style also came to define U.S. government construction, which had shed its Beaux-Arts and even whimsical Depression-era deco designs for a plain Main Street modernism that would become the dominant aesthetic vocabulary of countless post offices, schools, and other public buildings of the postwar era (as well as many overseas embassies). Even if it could never quite become "100 percent American," given its transnational heritage, modernism cultivated a convincing Yankee accent.

2. On Expert Authority: The Academy and the Professionalization of an Urbanist Establishment

The second cultural development that significantly shaped the urban renewal order in the United States was the professionalization of experts in an array of fields loosely united under the term "urbanism." A word previously used in Romance languages to describe city planning in particular, it was transliterated more broadly by University of Chicago sociologist Louis Wirth in 1938 to describe his study of urban life generally, encompassing characteristic forms of physical (then called ecological) structure, social organization, and collective behavior. Wirth hoped that an objective social scientific theory could contribute answers "concerning such problems as poverty, housing, city planning, sanitation, municipal administration, policing, marketing, transportation, and other technical issues."[6] Indeed, by the 1930s urbanism was fast coming to signify the analysis and amelioration of city problems.[7] Le Corbusier and other members of the primarily European CIAM group proposed making Wirth an honorary member for his conceptual contribution to their struggle.[8]

The creation of an urbanist establishment, so to speak, was certainly just one part of a larger trend toward the enshrinement of technocratic expertise in American life. In many areas, new or expanded graduate programs and advanced degrees emerged to confer legitimacy through professional training and, ultimately, exclusive credentialed authority. In the fields of modernist urbanism, the first important centers for such professionalization emerged in the mid-twentieth century, first at Harvard University and Massachusetts Institute of Technology (M.I.T.), then at the University of Pennsylvania. Such developments require locating an intellectual history within specific culturally prestigious institutions, namely, elite centers of higher education, which act as a kind of fulcrum for the influence of particular ideas upon society at large.[9] To put it another way, Ivy League universities began credentialing modern urbanists—planners, city architects, and urban designers—before most Americans even knew they needed such services (beyond a handful of high-profile turn-of-the-century City Beautiful projects). It was in large part through this very process of professionalization that urbanists obtained powerful authority in mid-twentieth-century American life.

Harvard had already established the most influential school of modernist architecture and planning in America by World War II.[10] The Graduate School of Design (encompassing architecture, landscape architecture, and city planning programs) was consolidated in 1936 under Dean Joseph Hudnut, who was charged with overhauling the curriculum.[11] After generations of emulating the historicist atelier system of the École des Beaux-Arts in Paris, American schools of architecture, planning, and related design fields were revolutionized by the arrival of that newer European style wave, functionalist modernism. The exile to America of leading proponents of the Continental approach began transforming the training at Harvard and (gradually) elsewhere in the late 1930s.[12] Hudnut's first major appointment was to hire Bauhaus founder Walter Gropius as chair of the department of architecture, a post from which he promulgated the functionalist ideas developed in the German *Neues Bauen* movement and the CIAM network generally.[13] Gropius and fellow Harvard professor Martin Wagner (formerly the city planning director of Berlin) would play an influential role in U.S. urbanism via the so-called Harvard Bauhaus.

Citing urban decay and inadequately planned development, Dean Hudnut together with Harvard's Graduate School of Public Administration convened a Conference on Urbanism in early 1942, at which "two-score workers in the field of urban problems" were asked, "What kind of cities do we want?" The conference, subtitled "The *Problem* of the Cities and Towns" (emphasis mine), promoted broader federal engagement to ensure more open space and freedom of movement in urban areas. The proceedings concluded with an epilogue by Gropius and Wagner, "The New City Pattern for the People and by the People." In their opinion, "the people have already demonstrated by unmistakable action—that is, by their 'flight from the city'—that they do not approve of the current methods of building up their living space." They continued:

> But how do we know the desires and preferences of the people? Or have we the means available to detect them? Have the town-fathers and realtors of the past been the proper persons to represent the people's desires and preferences? Who is guilty of the "crimes" committed in the past in planning and building, the people or their agents? Obviously both have failed to understand how much is at stake and so have failed to state clearly what they wish and prefer. It is not too much to hope, however, that as soon as better public enlightenment regarding planning is effected, people will be able to make better use of their constitutional rights. They will then demand that their representatives put in power those "composers" and "conductors" who can best fulfill their desires for an improved way of life in their communities. For the average man, once enabled to see the potentialities within his grasp, will insist on public competition, thus empowering the badly needed man of vision to supersede the speculator. Isn't it strange that our economic system, based so squarely on competition and on selection of the best, has so far failed to apply these principles within the realm of planning and town-building?[14]

Such was the frank elaboration of an audacious vision by two exiled German urbanists. Their rhetoric juxtaposed allusions to some of the more alarming corners of recent European political culture (from the "crimes" of a show trial to the "conductors" of a community's general will) alongside an awkward attempt to graft such impulses into American democratic capitalism.

Meanwhile, Hudnut remained strangely silent at the conference. In fact, he was gradually coming to oppose such heavy-handed visions of urbanism. Following a bitter struggle for control of the school throughout the late 1940s and early 1950s, in 1953 Gropius installed Catalonian architect Josep Lluís Sert not only as his successor as chairman of architecture, but also to replace Hudnut as dean of the entire Graduate School of Design (a position he would hold until 1969). As the president of CIAM, Sert shared Gropius' views on urbanism, which he had articulated in the organization's 1942 statement of principles (published by Harvard), *Can Our Cities Survive?* (fig. 2.3).[15] Hudnut was thus marginalized during an early institutional battle for the direction of U.S. urbanism, but as historian Jill Pearlman notes, he simultaneously planted "the seeds of a new post-modern urbanism that took root two decades later."[16]

By the early 1950s, the University of Pennsylvania had also added its own major contribution to U.S. urbanism, notably by institutionalizing advanced urban social science research alongside the design fields. The university had a

Figure 2.3 Cover designed by Herbert Bayer for José Luis Sert, *Can Our Cities Survive? An ABC of Urban Problems, Their Analysis, Their Solutions, Based on the Proposals Formulated by the C.I.A.M. International Congresses for Modern Architecture.* The book represented the culmination of two decades of urbanist conferences, with contributions from group chapters in many countries, including extensive discussion of urban planning by the British MARS group. It was published in various editions during the 1940s by Harvard University, as Bauhaus founder Walter Gropius, former Berlin planning director Martin Wagner, and Spanish-born CIAM president Sert consolidated control over urbanist training at the influential "Harvard Bauhaus"—as its graduate school of design became informally known. (© 2010 Artists Rights Society ARS, New York/VG Bild-Kunst, Bonn.)

distinguished history in architecture, having been the foremost American school of the Beaux-Arts approach from the turn of the century through the 1920s. But eventually stagnation set in, and an adherence to that older method prevented the embrace of new functionalist design principles. In 1950, under pressure from students, University of Pennsylvania president (and Minnesota's former liberal Republican governor) Harold Stassen lured the American modernist architect George Holmes Perkins from Harvard to revamp the School of Fine Arts.[17]

Perkins envisioned a comprehensive interdisciplinary training ground for architects, planners, and other designers (including landscape architects), like the one Walter Gropius had brought from the Bauhaus to Harvard. Renowned urban historian and cultural critic Lewis Mumford joined Perkins' faculty as the school's resident long-hair intellectual. But Perkins' most fateful hire—analogous to Harvard Dean Hudnut's recruitment of Gropius—was New Deal planner Robert Mitchell. Rather than a European lineage, Mitchell brought a connection with important intellectual impulses emanating from the University of Chicago, where in the 1930s he had taught alongside urban sociologists Louis Wirth, Robert Park, and Ernest Burgess. In the years initial postwar years, the University of Chicago's venerable sociology tradition was evolving into a school of planning that emphasized social scientific analysis of urban issues, particularly through the teaching of Rexford Tugwell, a Penn-trained economist who had served in Franklin Roosevelt's brain trust, as a New Deal administrator and then governor of Puerto Rico.[18] In Philadelphia, Mitchell seized the opportunity to weave the insights coming out of Tugwell's Chicago school together with traditional physical planning approaches and lobbied Perkins to agree to an Institute for Urban Studies as the research arm of Penn's planning department. Two urbanists on the Perkins faculty described the goals and methods of school: "At Penn, the economics of housing have been interwoven with physical, social and psychological considerations, yielding a much fuller understanding of housing problems and issues at all geographic scales."[19] From the University of Chicago, John Dyckman, Martin Meyerson, and Edward Banfield were all lured to Penn's Institute for Urban Studies. Its first graduate was Herbert Gans, a doctoral student who had followed his mentor Meyerson from Chicago. After completing his dissertation in 1957, Gans remained affiliated with the institute while he undertook a participant observation study of an urban renewal neighborhood in Boston's West End, which eventually became very influential when later published as The Urban Villagers.[20]

By the late 1950s, even the venerable institutions of Cambridge were scrambling to keep up with Penn's innovations in urbanism. Certainly, Harvard and M.I.T. already boasted the two oldest graduate planning programs in the United States (established in the mid 1930s), and architecture had been taught there from the late nineteenth century on. However, these were programs that led primarily to the master's degree, and more advanced research in the urbanist fields would be needed to remain competitive for faculty and students. For this, a new generation of urbanist scholars was recruited. In 1957, Martin Meyerson left the University of Pennsylvania to become the first Frank Backus Williams Professor of City Planning and Urban Research at Harvard. The New York native had come to Harvard following undergraduate studies at Columbia to obtain the master's degree in city planning (graduating 1949). Meyerson then worked with the planning commissions of Philadelphia and Chicago and taught at the planning programs of both the University of Chicago and the University of Pennsylvania before being tenured by Harvard at the age of thirty-four.[21] Similarly, M.I.T. established the Center for Urban and Regional Studies as part of a new Ph.D. program in city and regional planning in 1958.[22] Lloyd Rodwin was named its first director. Rodwin, a Brooklyn native educated at City College, worked under Charles Abrams and took a master's degree in land economics from Wisconsin and then a Harvard Ph.D. in regional planning in 1949.[23] He became professor of land economics in the Department of City and Regional Planning at M.I.T.

The culmination of these trajectories was the creation in 1959 of the Joint Center for Urban Studies, as a cooperation between Harvard and M.I.T., spearheaded by Rodwin and Meyerson. Meyerson became the first director of the Joint Center, Rodwin the chair of its faculty committee. While still at the University of Pennsylvania, Meyerson began to publish as director of the American Council to Improve Our Neighborhoods (ACTION), an initiative funded by the Ford Foundation, which enlisted the participation of Edward Banfield and James Rouse, to complement the Eisenhower administration's urban renewal programs.[24] At the Joint Center, together with Rodwin, Meyerson promulgated a vision of planning as an interdisciplinary endeavor that was moving from its utopian origins toward social scientific maturity, even technocratic certainty. In a characteristic project to demonstrate how "artistic intuition and technical capacity can work together," Serge Chermayeff and Christopher Alexander received a grant from the Joint Center to write *Community and Privacy: Toward a New Architecture of Humanism*. The book, dedicated to Walter Gropius, acknowledged the "continuing encouragement and help" of Martin Meyerson and the use of an IBM 704 at the M.I.T. Computation Center—though it is unclear what role the computer actually played in their designs.[25]

Social scientists, at Harvard, M.I.T., Penn, and beyond, were able to enlist themselves in urban public policy debates as a result of a turn toward issues of the city occurring in several academic disciplines. Sociology was the first to train its methodology on the systematic analysis of urban subjects, beginning with work of Wirth and his colleagues at the University of Chicago in the 1920s, such that by the 1950s courses were regularly dedicated to the topic and complemented by an extensive literature.[26] Harvard economist Walter Firey sought to explain urban land use in Boston in the 1940s, and William Alonso carried this discussion forward at the Joint Center.[27] Richard Moier introduced a "communications theory of urban growth."[28] M.I.T. professor Kevin Lynch was then in the process of developing a survey planning approach that integrated the subjective impressions of individuals as they moved through the city, which he articulated in a pair of influential Joint Center publications.[29]

Harvard economist Raymond Vernon produced the New York Metropolitan Region Study, published by Harvard University Press from 1959 to 1961, under the general editorship of Max Hall. According to later Joint Center director Robert Wood, "this three-year, nine-volume study, including twenty-year projections of key economic indices for the New York region, represented an intellectual breakthrough by which Vernon and his associates made the study of urban areas academically respectable in the social sciences." Additionally, the study brought the Joint Center together with the Ford Foundation, whose director of public affairs, Paul Ylvisaker, held a Harvard Ph.D. and had worked for Philadelphia mayor Joseph Clark, Jr.; the foundation subsequently supported Boston "gray areas" programs to combat juvenile delinquency and other urban social problems.[30]

The Cambridge-based American Academy of Arts and Sciences offered the Joint Center an opportunity to present the cutting edge of social scientific urbanism in the Winter 1961 issue of its journal, Daedalus. Of the eleven contributors to the special issue "The Future Metropolis," edited by Rodwin and Lynch, only two were not affiliated with Harvard or M.I.T. (Yale political scientist Karl Deutsch and a former planning colleague of Meyerson from Penn, John Dyckman). Taken as a group, the collection embodied the Joint Center's founding vision of urbanism as a field of progressive, interdisciplinary study: Lynch on urban forms, Gyorgy Kepes on iconography, Deutsch on communication, Rodwin on cities in developing nations, and Morton and Lucia White on the intellectual history of anti-urbanism. Lynch and Rodwin declared in their editors' introduction that "on the whole these papers are optimistic." Martin Meyerson's concluding essay, "Utopian Traditions and the Planning of Cities," while acknowledging the static rigidity of past social and physical utopias (including Le Corbusier's), suggested that "utopians now have the task of devising institutions and the material organization of society to free men from the restrictions under which they previously operated" and that "both leaders and citizens could be encouraged to participate in utopian thinking and thus to help resolve policy as to long-term urban development.[31]

For all the broad interdisciplinarity of its research methodology, the specific subjects of planning study and practice at the Joint Center were initially confined primarily to two: Boston and Venezuela—regions seemingly at opposite ends of the process of urbanization and industrialization. Rodwin's interest had always run toward international planning projects, and, under the auspices of the Joint Center, he encouraged training planners to work in developing nations. In 1961, the Joint Center initiated a decade-long consultancy relationship to the Venezuelan project of Ciudad Guyana. Meyerson brought colleagues from the University of Pennsylvania to the project, including Wilhelm von Moltke and James Kise.[32]

Meanwhile, the Joint Center focused sustained attention on its own backyard. The very first projects prepared for the Joint Center included a report on the politics of Boston by Martha Derthick and a study by Rodwin on the city's housing. The Joint Center's Richard Bolan compiled a set of transportation and physical planning analyses of the Boston metropolitan area. Alexander Ganz prepared an economic development program. Through the late 1960s, the Joint Center explored the legal and economic feasibility of introducing computer-based information systems for health and welfare in the area.[33]

All these studies, unlike others that would come out of the Joint Center later in the 1960s, assumed a salutary contribution of analysis. Meyerson was eager to demonstrate "strong support for the application of social science to Boston's urban problems and for scientific evaluation of new programs." Meyerson served personally on the advisory committee to Action for Boston Community Development (ABCD), an ambitious antipoverty program hatched by civic reformers Edward Logue and John F. Collins, with business, philanthropic, and social work leaders. Meyerson convened the group's "first formal meeting to consider a strategy for community development in Boston" at the Joint Center on November 30, 1960.[34] Like the Joint Center, the ABCD initiative would be funded through the Ford Foundation. Ultimately, however, it was not to be private charities or universities but rather the vast resources of the federal government that would provide the most sweeping opportunities for urbanists.

3. Governing a Nation of Cities: Urbanism Comes to Washington

In addition to reinforcing the shift of American tastes toward modernism, the consolidation of urbanism in graduate training and advanced study programs at U.S. universities lent prestige and professional credentials, which were quickly translated into institutional influence well beyond the ivory tower. Opportunities for urbanists on a vast new scale materialized in the corridors of power from the national capital to city halls, as the legislative and administrative outlines of the urban renewal order took shape between the 1930s and 1960s. Within this larger political narrative arc, a growing national government took belated interest in the cities of a highly urbanized nation, fitfully engaging its ever-expanding federal authorities with urban affairs.

Mark Gelfand has traced the gradual evolution of federal urban policy from neglect toward sustained support, a long struggle to overcome the states' rights and agrarian vestiges ingrained in U.S. political culture.[35] After much local and some federal experimentation in the early twentieth century, the exigencies of the 1930s and 1940s—namely, economic crisis, wartime coordination, and postwar stimulus—catalyzed expansive federally funded programs to address urban problems. Many of these entailed multilayered intergovernmental schemes, administered locally in cities via authorities created by state governments to disburse federal appropriations. While various initiatives emerged out of a long series of congressional acts between 1934 and 1968, the U.S. urban renewal order primarily proceeded along three (at times overlapping) fronts: housing provision, slum clearance, and road building. This suite of programs built cumulative momentum both under Democratic presidents like Franklin Roosevelt and Harry Truman in the 1930s and 1940s and under Republican Dwight Eisenhower, a strong advocate of highway modernization, in the 1950s.

President John Kennedy was a cold warrior known for being "more interested in what happened in Havana, Berlin, and Saigon than what took place in New York, Chicago, or Los Angeles."[36] Nevertheless, he was also a sophisticated urbanite who presided over the final ratification of the federal government's urban reorientation—de facto and de jure—thanks to steps begun in his brief administration and completed under President Lyndon Johnson. Kennedy delivered "the first message specifically on cities that any president had sent to Congress."[37] Noted during the 1960 campaign for assembling an advisory board of "wise men" (policy experts drawn primarily from his alma mater, Harvard, second-generation historian Arthur Schlesinger, Jr., among them), Kennedy also included among his advisers many Joint Center urbanists, such as M.I.T. planning professor Robert Wood.

Despite Lyndon Johnson's aversion to the Ivy Leaguers, their influence expanded under his administration. In support of his 1964 Great Society initiative, Johnson convened three task forces. Wood headed the task force on "Metropolitan and Urban Problems," while Harvard planning law professor Charles Haar was in charge of a related environmental task force. Martin Meyerson, as a member of the advisory groups, urged the creation of an Urban Institute, modeled on the RAND Corporation in foreign policy, "to provide an autonomous capacity for timely and forthright evaluation within a context of sympathetic concern for urban issues."[38] These advisory groups produced many tangible policy initiatives, including the Model Cities program, whose task force included Haar, Wood, M.I.T. planner Bernard Frieden, Penn's Chester Rapkin, and Philadelphia renewal administrator William Rafsky. Most significantly, Kennedy, Johnson, and their advisers initiated an executive cabinet department for urban issues (essentially an elevated version of the Housing and Home Finance Agency), which was realized with the establishment of the Department of Housing and Urban Development (H.U.D.) in 1965.

By 1967 the fledgling H.U.D.—then just two years old and headed by its first secretary Robert Weaver—was distributing recruitment pamphlets proclaiming "Help Wanted: Urbanists." They extolled the "breadth of the H.U.D. programs" and career opportunities "for the talented college graduate who seeks a role in shaping the future of the city." The department summoned this new breed of urbanist, who was to be "a creation of the urban age—and reflect the Nation's determination to revitalize its cities and suburbs." They should possess "the essential skills to handle . . . urban planning, slum clearance, model cities, mass transportation systems, beautification projects, or community centers." Of course, the department admitted, "urbanism is not yet a profession—but it is coming because it is needed. . . . The challenge of relieving blighted neighborhoods, offering hope and guidance for the poor, providing training for the undereducated, and a place in the community for the minorities is very great indeed." As if summoning the urban renewal order's own breed of superhero, the brochure concluded: "The urbanist, in brief, is needed wherever urban problems exist."[39] Here, at the very least, was a heroic self-description of the federal government's activist posture vis-à-vis the nation's cities.

4. Urbanism as Reform: Planning, Renewal, and Urban Regime Change

Such federal policy shifts linked up not only with the movements in academic circles but also with reform impulses erupting at the level of city politics. In *The Contested City*, John Mollenkopf traces how political entrepreneurs had fashioned pro-growth coalitions in many large U.S. cities by the late 1950s, allying such bizarre bedfellows as Republican business elites, Democratic urban machines, and reform-oriented professionals. In addition to providing an alternative political analysis to the irreconcilable interpretative camps that saw either static urban power elites or pluralist power structures, he also explains the motivations behind the unlikely alliances supporting urban renewal at the local level.[40] New nationwide urban programs certainly provided opportunities for various entrepreneurial partnerships to be formed between the public and private sectors, cemented with federal money and a certain back-room style. As Joel Schwartz has aptly observed, "The melding of public spirit and private gain resembled traditional urban boosterism, except that never before did boosters find so much public domain up for grabs, or thanks to postwar politics and social science, so many rationales for their operations."[41]

New York's Robert Moses was the first star in the firmament of this U.S. urban renewal order. Emerging out of Progressive-era reform milieus, Moses made his name realizing public works (parks, roads, bridges, and much more) on ever larger scales, first under Democratic governor Al Smith in the 1920s, then under Republican mayor Fiorello La Guardia during the 1930s, and eventually reporting to practically no one but himself. By the arrival of the 1949 Housing Act, he had become the undisputed master of "write-down" redevelopment, enabling the

Figure 2.4 U.S. urban renewal: housing. Approved in 1934 and dedicated by Eleanor Roosevelt in 1936, the aptly named First Houses was the first project of the New York City Housing Authority (created by the state in 1934 to qualify for federal financing) and moreover the nation's first low-income public housing project. Attacking an area notorious for crowded conditions since the nineteenth century, the redevelopment at East Third Street and Avenue A entailed partial demolition (every third structure) of the site's tenements in order to open up space between buildings. First Houses also demonstrated the early outlines of the urban renewal order on the ground in the United States, as money from New Deal Washington first made its way into local slum clearance projects. (La Guardia and Wagner Archives, La Guardia Community College/The City University of New York. © New York City Housing Authority.)

clearance of vast swaths of New York real estate for various new construction projects, from Stuyvesant Town to Lincoln Center.[42]

Robert Moses, his uncommon (and often unsavory) personal qualities sensationally profiled in Robert Caro's *The Power Broker*, was indeed an exceptional public sector entrepreneur who found himself in the exceptional conditions of New York in the era of urban renewal.[43] Moses was never the whole story, though, insufficient even to explain the dramatic public works in his own city. Joshua Freeman has argued that New York City represented an island of social democratic policies by the late 1950s, standing outside a national consensus that extolled marketplace solutions to social needs. To demonstrate that New York was a laboratory

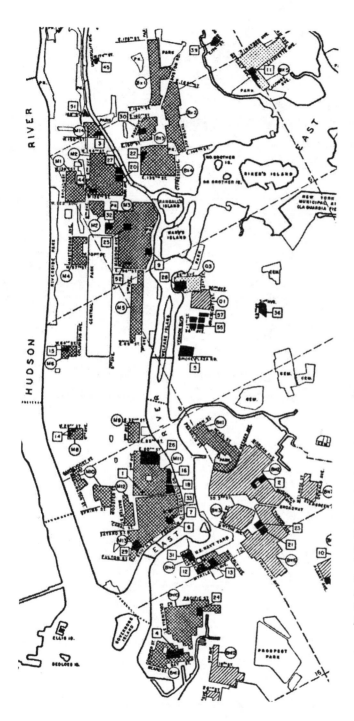

Figure 2.5 U.S. urban renewal: slum clearance. In the decades following the modest one-acre experiment of First Houses, New York's slum eradication program expanded tremendously. This City Planning Commission master plan adopted in 1949 indicates over forty approved projects, and vast swaths of the city as "sections containing areas for clearance, redevelopment, and low-rent housing." Such designations were required in order to qualify for federal urban renewal funds, as set forth under Title I of the 1949 Housing Act. (Courtesy NYC Municipal Archives.)

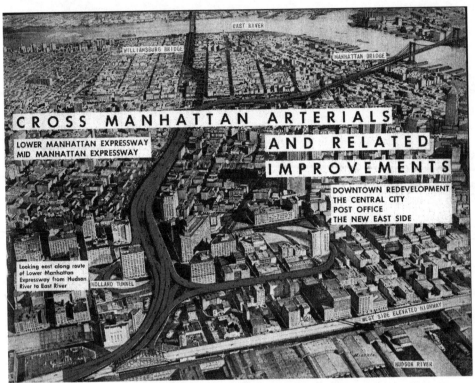

Figure 2.6 U.S. urban renewal: highways. The modernization of transportation infrastructure for an automotive age simultaneously served multiple ends in cities, including the eradication (or isolation) of undesirable areas, the segregation of traffic into dedicated expressways, and the linking of the urban core with suburbanizing regions—though there was disagreement about whether this would produce centrifugal or centripetal effects. Highway construction also served many masters: This rendering appeared on the cover of the 1959 pamphlet *Cross Manhattan Arterials and Related Improvements*, published under the auspices of various agencies, including the Triborough Bridge and Tunnel Authority, the City of New York, the New York State Department of Public Works, the U.S. Department of Commerce, the U.S. Bureau of Roads, the Port Authority, and the "City Construction Coordinator"—the latter being the pamphlet's author, Robert Moses. Already by this time, however, highways through New York's neighborhoods were becoming lightning rods for Moses' "bulldozer approach" to planning, and citizen opposition eventually halted the proposed Lower Manhattan Expressway along Broome Street. (Courtesy of MTA Bridges and Tunnels Special Archive.)

for progressive urbanism, Freeman cites the City University system, a municipal arts center (the City Center in Shriner's Hall on 55th Street), public transit, and broadcasting. President Roosevelt's 1944 Economic Bill of Rights may have faltered in Washington, but New York was again exceptional, offering public insurance (HIP), a labor-liberal tenant movement to maintain rent controls (and prevent gouging during housing shortages), and high-standard publicly subsidized housing, exemplified by Co-Op City, Penn South, Chelsea, and various trade union projects. As in Weimar-era Berlin, New York's strong labor unions played a role in support of movements for social housing going back to the 1920s, but they also became key constituencies in the postwar urban renewal coalition, promoting jobs on city projects—even as members increasingly moved to the suburbs.[44]

By the late 1950s, the urban renewal order in New York was already entering its second generation. The son of a legendary senator who co-sponsored New Deal housing legislation, new mayor Robert Wagner saw planning initiatives as vitally important—he made televised appeals to promote them—because they symbolized reform of both the corrupt old machine politics and of the insensitive destruction associated with the increasingly unpopular Robert Moses.[45] Rife with paradoxes, though, Wagner seemed to look forward and back simultaneously. During his administration, New York's planning commission undertook the first comprehensive modernization of the city's zoning codes since 1916, clearing regulatory obstacles for more of the fashionable modernist tower-in-plaza office buildings (fig. 2.7). Yet he also moved to provide legal protection to certain areas, an effort that culminated in 1965 in the passage of New York's groundbreaking historic preservation statutes. In the early 1960s, officials like City Planning Commission chairman James Felt and Housing and Redevelopment Board director J. Clarence Davies assured New Yorkers that urban renewal in that city was moving beyond the bulldozer approach. Thus, roughly three decades after its beginnings in the 1930s, the urban renewal order in New York appeared politically well entrenched, relatively progressive, and responsive to both elites and average citizens—at least rhetorically.

In comparison to New York, urban renewal in Boston had a relatively late start. No redevelopment authority existed until 1957, as the state legislature was unsympathetic to James Michael Curley's Irish machine politics throughout the New Deal and 1940s and thus unwilling to charter one. There had, however, been a planning competition in 1944, a highway plan in 1948, and a general plan for the city, which appeared in 1950. When reformist mayor John Hynes unseated Curley in 1949, the stage was set for urban renewal. Beginning in 1954, public relations executive John T. Galvin held prominent "citizen seminars," devoted to the city's development, at Boston College.[46]

Unfortunately, Boston's renewal efforts under Hynes proved disastrous in the court of public opinion. Notorious to this day are two federally funded efforts: construction of the central artery and clearance of the West End neighborhood.[47] The 1959 election of Hynes' successor John F. Collins coincided auspiciously with the ascension of Boston's John F. Kennedy to the White House the

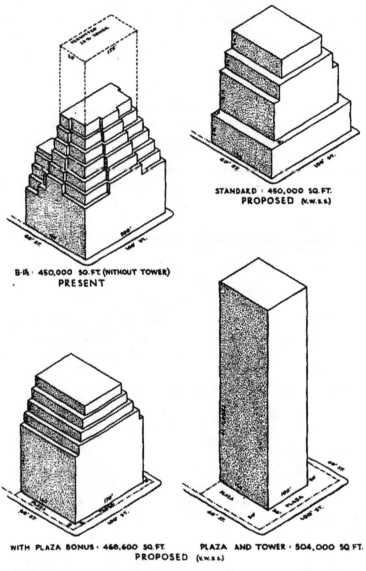

B-I½ : 450,000 SQ.FT (WITHOUT TOWER)
PRESENT

STANDARD : 450,000 SQ.FT.
PROPOSED (N.W.S.S.)

WITH PLAZA BONUS : 466,600 SQ.FT.
PROPOSED (K.W.S.S.)

PLAZA AND TOWER : 504,000 SQ FT.

200' × 150'   BLOCK FRONT

Figure 2.7 U.S. urban renewal: statutory reform. Under Mayor Robert Wagner, New York began moving away from Robert Moses' take-no-prisoners urban renewal and even enacted historic preservation statutes. Yet Wagner also institutionalized the modernist *Leitbild* into the city's zoning code, when the City Planning Commission undertook its first comprehensive updating of that regulatory framework since 1916. This diagram shows how new height incentives will favor "plaza and tower" designs over the "wedding cakes" produced under old zoning rules. The reform also emphasized segregation of land uses (in the words of Planning Commission chairman James Felt, "a proper district for all uses . . . no more unrestricted or undetermined districts—everything has a place"). All new private buildings were governed by New York's new zoning regulations, which took effect in 1961, thus extending modernization pressures even to areas not targeted for slum clearance by city agencies. (Courtesy NYC Municipal Archives.)

Figure 2.8 International Style comes to Avenue of the Americas: The culmination of shifts in taste among academic architects and corporate clients, as well as the codification of the CIAM modernist *Leitbild* into zoning codes, is visible on Sixth Avenue south of West Fifty-first Street by the early 1970s. In the wake of New York's 1961 zoning reform, office buildings in midtown Manhattan—designed for U.S. corporations like Time and Life, Exxon, and McGraw Hill by a handful of U.S. architects, particularly Max Abramovitz and Wallace Harrison—cumulatively echoed the unbuilt Highrise City Ludwig Hilberseimer imagined in Berlin fifty years earlier. (Ezra Stoller © ESTO. All rights reserved.)

next year. Boston's business leaders formed a coordinating committee, known as the Vault since the sixteen Brahmin met each month in Ralph Lowell's bank. In 1960 Collins recruited Edward Logue from his renowned work at the New Haven redevelopment authority to head Boston's own agency.[48] The Boston Redevelopment Authority, created in 1957 under Kane Simonian, would under Logue subsume the powers of both the Boston Housing Authority and the City Planning Board. With Logue's energy and knowledge of federal programs (he helped write the 1960 urban renewal platform for the Democrats), Boston leaped from seventeenth to fourth place in financed projects (behind much larger New York, Philadelphia, and Chicago).[49] A primary focus of the Collins-Logue-Vault team was redeveloping Scollay Square into a "hub" area around a new city hall. Logue and Collins also sought to shift the emphasis toward rehabilitation in response to Hynes' blunders.

But of all the postwar urban reform crusades, Philadelphia's was where the impulse crystallized most single-mindedly around city planning and urban renewal, albeit with a distinctive style. By the early twentieth century, Philadelphia's elites had so emphatically fled from aging neighborhoods and commercial and industrial areas that the Paoli local commuter line of the Pennsylvania Railroad came to symbolize wealthy suburban enclaves anywhere: "the Main Line" entered the American vocabulary as an archetype.[50] The city's government meanwhile was left under the control of a neighborhood-based political machine, so scandalous in its corruption that Lincoln Steffens gave Philadelphia pride of place in his 1903 muckraking exposé The Shame of the Cities. Sociologist E. Digby Baltzell spent his career scrutinizing the failures of the Philadelphia elite (which produced him), arriving at the conservative conclusion that their Quakerish tolerance of diversity led to a disastrous abdication of political leadership.[51]

Philadelphia's elites, however, did not stay away for long. Just as these stereotypes were becoming widespread in popular culture and scholarship (as exemplified by The Philadelphia Story, a 1929 play with numerous stage and screen adaptations), a circle of such scions was undertaking precisely the kind of political engagement of which Baltzell and his literary counterparts despaired.[52] These Young Turks, as they dubbed themselves, were well-educated professionals early in their careers, flush with New Deal enthusiasm and the specific goal of sweeping the Republican machine out of city hall, as well as revitalizing Philadelphia's cultural and economic life generally. Walter Massey Phillips, a twenty-eight-year-old Princeton and Harvard educated lawyer, acted as the spearhead of this movement, allying himself with Joseph Clark, Jr., the son of a wealthy Philadelphia lawyer and tennis champion, and Richardson Dilworth—both Ivy League lawyers with political ambitions.[53] Over the decade after Phillips founded the City Policy

Committee in 1940, he and his assembled allies achieved investigations of corruption, the revision of Philadelphia's city charter in 1951, and the following year the election of the city's first Democratic administration since 1884, with Clark as mayor, Dilworth as district attorney, and Phillips as city representative and director of commerce.[54]

Before the end of World War II, Phillips and the others adopted modern planning as the symbol of their reform movement, convincing the city of the need to create a viable planning commission to help ease the transition to peacetime production, and, rather perceptively, to counter the effects of decentralization on the city's core.[55] Thomas Gates, the president of the University of Pennsylvania (and partner at both J. P. Morgan and the Drexel and Company investment banks), had supported Phillips' initiative, and Edward Hopkinson, Jr. (also a senior partner at Drexel and Company as well as a prominent university trustee), became the chairman of the new planning commission. During the war, Phillips founded the Citizens' Council on City Planning (1943). By 1949, Clark had served both as that organization's director and as a member of the advisory commission for Independence National Historical Park, an influential planning project.[56] During the following ten years (1952–62), while Clark and subsequently Dilworth held the mayoralty, the city became widely noted for a Philadelphia renaissance of improved city services, professional reform, and—above all—aggressive city planning.[57]

For the key role of executive director, the City Planning Commission hired Robert Mitchell, then wartime head of the Urban Section of the National Resources Planning Board (NRPB). Mitchell's selection had important implications for the kind of planning envisioned for Philadelphia. As noted previously, Mitchell had taught at the University of Chicago, where, under the influence of renowned sociologists like Louis Wirth, he turned away from the European-influenced slum clearance projects he had worked on with the Public Works Administration and began instead to focus on neighborhood conservation. He was among the first to suspect that CIAM-style self-contained housing projects concentrated social ills rather than insulating residents from dilapidated areas: "How wrong we were, disregarding the social and cultural aspects of neighborhoods."[58] With the NRPB Mitchell had gained attention by implementing such strategies in Baltimore (in the Waverly neighborhood) and Chicago (in the Woodlawn neighborhood), and the Philadelphians seemed to be endorsing this delicate approach.

Mitchell assembled a staff that included Martin Meyerson, Edmund Bacon, and German émigré Oskar Stonorov. Stonorov urged Mitchell and Phillips to mount an exhibition that would "dramatize planning and Philadelphia's potential" to the general public.[59] In 1947, they staged such an exhibition in Gimbel's department store, in time to harmonize with the aggressive anti-corruption themes of

Dilworth's first (unsuccessful) mayoral campaign (figs 2.9 and 2.10).[60] Phillips parlayed the publicity by founding yet another organization, the Greater Philadelphia Movement (1947), intended to circumvent the conservative Chamber of Commerce and rally support from the private sector for the implementation of the planning proposals dramatized in the Gimbel's demo. Shortly after the exhibit, however, Mitchell left the planning commission for Columbia University (though he returned to teach at the University of Pennsylvania three years later). The task of implementation would fall to the Gimbel exhibit's co-designer, Edmund Bacon.

Edmund Bacon came from a family of "Quakers unbroken for nine generations back to William Penn."[61] After studying architecture at Cornell (later apprenticing with Eliel Saarinen), and working on WPA projects in Flint, Michigan, Bacon returned to Philadelphia and joined the Young Turks' circle.[62] Phillips initially arranged for Bacon to become the director of the Philadelphia Housing Association in 1940. The housing movement in Philadelphia predated Phillips' reform-through-planning crusade by more than a generation. There Bacon encountered a venerable tradition of Progressive-era philanthropic organizations, including the Octavia Hill Association, founded in 1896 by Helen Parrish, a pupil of that eponymous London housing reformer. That group in turn led to the creation of the nation's first citizen housing agency in 1909, renamed in 1917 the Philadelphia Housing Association. The young planning movement thus intersected with Philadelphia's older urban improvement traditions, but with crucial distinctions. As the debate for the city's postwar priorities developed, "housers" continued to call for the improvement of slum conditions while most planners preferred to focus on the revitalization of the city's commercial core.[63] Bacon was no houser. For him, the primary utility of his position as director of the housing association (which Bacon called "a do-good organization where nice elderly ladies got together and had tea and tried to figure out how to improve the housing of the poor") was to lobby for a planning commission, organizing neighborhood support and pressuring the city to fund the agency.[64]

Following military service in the Pacific, Bacon returned to the city with a new prominence, beginning when Stonorov invited him to co-design the 1947 *Better Philadelphia Exhibition*, and culminating in his promotion to director of the City Planning Commission in 1949. Through implementation of the state's enabling legislation, Philadelphia's planning commission was positioned early to capitalize on the large federal redevelopment grants available after the passage of the congressional housing acts of 1949 and 1954. (Though, as in Pittsburgh, federal funds would prove less significant than local private investment, when allied with powerful city agencies.) Over the twenty-one years that Bacon headed

Figure 2.9 Public exhibitions were a regular vehicle for the promulgation of modernist urbanism. In Philadelphia, city planning and urban renewal were explicitly allied to a political reform movement, as elite Democratic insurgents wrested control from an entrenched Republican neighborhood machine. This display from *The Better Philadelphia Exhibition: What City Planning Means to You*, held in Gimbel's department store in 1947, featured a rotating model depicting neighborhoods before and after proposed redevelopment. Accompanying brochures encouraged visitors to turn the tables of politics as well, by voting for reformers to transform their city. (Ezra Stoller © ESTO. All rights reserved.)

Figure 2.10 A detail from one display at the 1947 *Better Philadelphia Exhibition*, depicting Philadelphia's typical nineteenth-century row houses lifted away by a deus ex machina—the guiding hand of the city planner?—to reveal a superblock of modernist housing projects, and declaring, "We must get rid of neighborhood nuisances for . . . new housing." (Ezra Stoller © ESTO. All rights reserved.)

the agency, especially during the years when he had the support of Mayors Clark and Dilworth, Philadelphia executed a series of bold projects, attracting nation-wide attention.[65] Primary among these were the construction of an office complex, Penn Center, on the site of the old Pennsylvania Railroad terminal, the development of an urban shopping mall, the Gallery, on east Market Street, and the gentrification of a colonial neighborhood near Independence Hall, Society Hill (fig. 2.11). Bacon assessed his auspicious circumstances thus: "By some historical accident there has been set into motion here the convergence of an extraordinary series of creative forces, which are in process of changing the face of the city. I believe that this experience, the product not of one person but of the interaction of many, is rich with ideas that are applicable to other cities in all parts of

Figure 2.11 "The image has the power." Empowered to transform the inspiring imagery of the Gimbel's exhibition into concrete reality, Philadelphia planning director Edmund Bacon transformed urban renewal from a symbolic banner of reform into tangible results. Bacon, with a model of center city Philadelphia in 1966, looks over Independence Hall toward Society Hill, the historic neighborhood he transformed with a blend of redevelopment and rehabilitation. One of three Society Hill towers designed by I. M. Pei is visible at the left side of the picture, and the elevated Delaware Expressway (I-95) appears in the foreground. (Temple University Libraries, Urban Archives, Philadelphia PA.)

the world where there is a desire for a finer physical expression of man's inner aspirations."[66]

Bacon's conception of planning differed significantly from that of his predecessor at the commission. The social scientist Mitchell had wanted to examine urban processes, such as traffic, while the designer Bacon was focused primarily on the beautification and aesthetic modernization of his hometown. Bacon's zeal to redesign the city after his fashion—including a penchant for detailed, provocative proposals—brought him into conflict with various camps. In 1957, when he published plans in the Philadelphia press indicating the demolition of several blocks of the city's central business district, even members of Phillips' Greater Philadelphia Movement, Bacon later recalled, "questioned my sanity and were appalled by my lack of understanding of the value of the dollar." In the case of Penn Center, he was censured by the American Institute of Architects and the American Institute of Planners on account of designing for private property without a client, program, or comprehensive plan. Bacon dismissed such objections, saying: "Unless the leaders oppose your idea at the beginning, it isn't worth having." Conceiving of himself as a visionary artist working at the scale of the entire city, Bacon remained confident of the transformative power of civic design: "My method frequently is interpreted as requiring the planner to be arrogant and overbearing. Yet it is the image, not the planner, which has the power. For this to work, the planner must be able to create the image in the first place, and must trust the image to achieve its own fulfillment."[67]

This emphasis on design as reform was evident already from the time of Bacon's 1932 Cornell senior thesis, which called for the eradication of Philadelphia's ornate Second Empire–style city hall (disdained by Philadelphia elites as a gaudy symbol of corruption long before its completion in 1901) in favor of a new civic center. Bacon was convinced that he could demonstrate urban design's utility as the linchpin of comprehensive urban recovery, visually articulating physical solutions to complicated social problems.[68] By late 1964, the same week in fact that heralded Lyndon Johnson's landslide election, Bacon's face was featured on the cover of *Time* magazine (fig 2.12). As New York was for the New Deal and Fair Deal, Philadelphia—once "corrupt and contented"—became a standard bearer in the Great Society's urban renewal order.[69]

The Sum of Its Parts

The tight connection between the four pillars of the urban renewal order was at times quite remarkable—conceptually, procedurally, and just as often interpersonally. Consider, for instance, the urbanists assembled in Philadelphia under the University of Pennsylvania's dean G. Holmes Perkins, a bewildering

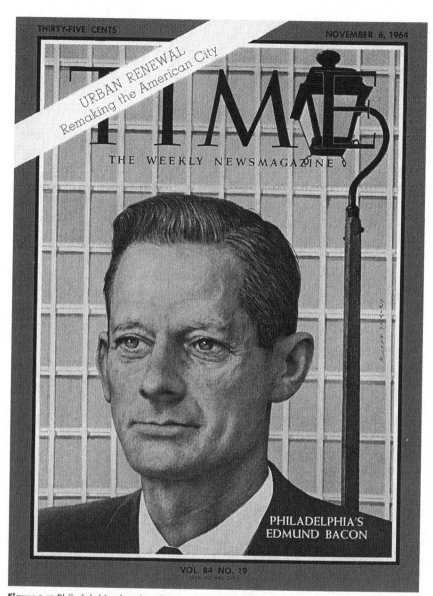

Figure 2.12 Philadelphia planning director Edmund Bacon as the poster boy for urban renewal in the United States, featured on the cover of *Time*, the same week that President Lyndon Johnson won a landslide mandate for his Great Society reelection platform. For urban programs, local and national resources—as well as the guiding vision—were never more focused than during this high-water mark. (© 1964 TIME, Inc. All rights reserved. Used by permission and protected by the Copyright Laws of the United States. The printing, copying, redistribution, or retransmission of the Material without express written permission is prohibited.)

who's-who of figures exerting influence at the local, national, and even international level. Perkins himself was perfectly fitted for the role of modernizing the university's School of Fine Arts, so that it could provide conceptual support to the city's renewal programs. In 1945, five years before he accepted that academic post, Perkins drafted the pathbreaking Pennsylvania state redevelopment legislation that paved the way for Philadelphia's redevelopment authority, with its powers of eminent domain. In addition to directing the city planning department at Harvard, he attended international conferences of CIAM in the 1930s, led the Urban Development Division of the National Housing Agency during the World War II, and worked on Patrick Abercrombie's comprehensive new town program in postwar Britain. While at Penn, he served on reformer Walter Phillips' Citizens' Council on City Planning (1953–55), as president of the Philadelphia Housing Association (1954–55), and as chair of the City Planning Commission (1958–68) while its director was Edmund Bacon (who simultaneously taught for Perkins at Penn). Perkins credited his own "Puritan/Pilgrim heritage," particularly his "belief in public service," for creating a tight town-gown relationship in the hope that "working contacts with the city [would] enhance faculty and students alike."[70]

Beyond Perkins, the interconnected web grows much denser. Many on his faculty were Philadelphians, ideologically united by New Deal influences, including their sense of the role of aesthetic reform in alliance with liberal (though not radical) politics. Many had worked in New Deal agencies, and Perkins' subsequent consultancy on U.N. projects for developing nations, in addition to other faculty endeavors (like architecture professor Louis Kahn's designs for India and Bangladesh) bore the imprint of Vice President Henry Wallace's notion of "a New Deal for the world."[71] Perkins invited Robert Mitchell back to Philadelphia, within three years of his leaving the directorship of the City Planning Commission to teach at Columbia University, and charged him with setting up Penn's planning program. Mitchell thereby brought to the school not only a relationship to Philadelphia's reform-via-planning experiments, which Bacon was executing, but also a connection with important intellectual impulses emanating from the University of Chicago's school of social scientific urbanism. Perkins then managed in 1951 to attract a young Martin Meyerson, who was on Mitchell's original staff of the Philadelphia Planning Commission in the 1940s prior to moving to Chicago. Under the auspices of the Institute for Urban Studies, Meyerson completed his collaboration with former University of Chicago colleague Edward Banfield and developed ideas of "rational planning" before both men moved on to Harvard's Joint Center for Urban Studies.[72] Britton Harris, who was a proponent of "regional science" in his work with the Chicago Housing Authority and in Puerto Rico, was lured from Chicago to Penn in 1954. William Wheaton, whose training had encompassed Princeton, Harvard, and Chicago, joined the Penn planning department in 1951, two years after he had been a principal writer of the 1949 Housing Act. Others were tapped from Mitchell's Columbia University sojourn, including economist William Grigsby and Chester Rapkin, a traffic and land use specialist who completed his Columbia Ph.D. and then joined the Penn planning department in 1954. Rapkin would be instrumental throughout the 1950s in the Eastwick redevelopment project—the largest urban renewal area in the United States—and then as framer of the Model Cities program in 1965–66.[73]

Four distinct transformations, then, comprised the urban renewal order: converting mainstream tastes to modernist prescriptions for the redesign of cities, professionalizing urbanist expertise, marshaling urban-oriented policy and appropriations at the federal (and state) level, and winning power at the city level for reformist administrations. Ultimately, however, the tight interlocking of these elements proved the most fateful development of all. Until every one of the components was present for each individual country, the redevelopment of its cities could not proceed in any ambitious way. Once all the parts were mutually reinforcing—as they were by the early to mid 1950s in the United States, United Kingdom, West Germany and Canada—that firm edifice would prove very difficult to topple (see table A1 in the appendix). Nevertheless, questions arose almost immediately upon completion.

Part II Converging Critiques of the Urban Renewal Order

The urban renewal order was a formidable juggernaut, but its dominance also brought scrutiny and, gradually, a reevaluation of its assumptions. Some of the earliest critiques came from architects and designers who felt uneasy about the results of modernist urbanism, particularly the loss of a certain human-scale perspective and detail. German urbanists increasingly questioned the sufficiency of a rigid functional segregation and the assumptions of decentralization at the expense of a vital urban core. In the words of Werner Hebebrand, "a city has to be more than just functional, and it is precisely this 'more' that gives it the glitter and radiance." In the case of Berlin, new redevelopments contrasted unfavorably against the civic and humane virtues embodied in the nineteenth-century urban fabric.

In the United Kingdom, such reservations found expression in a celebration of British urban vernacular. Particular small-scale elements, ignored by the didacticism of modernist planning, came to embody a sense of civic vitality and historical complexity. Decentralization policies, for example, threatened both the cosmopolitanism of the city and the distinctiveness of the countryside. Beginning in the late 1940s, Britain's *Architectural Review* championed the "happy accidents" produced by "a *laissez-faire* environment" over the visual ideal imposed by an insufficiently sensitive official planning apparatus. By lovingly scrutinizing the vanishing minutiae of their British "townscape," its contributors were perhaps the first to forcefully point to the gap between promise and reality in modernist redevelopment. Soon thereafter, the English architectural couple of Peter and Alison Smithson led a coup within the preeminent international organization of modern urbanists, challenging the cardinal tenets of functional segregation and questioning the value of new constructions when compared with the older cityscapes they obliterated.

Across the Atlantic, a successor school of urbanism was coalescing in Philadelphia, where the teachings of Lewis Mumford, Louis Kahn, and Robert Venturi moved design beyond modernism's rigid formalism and ahistorical functionalism. And in that city of shrines to American history, a variation on the urban renewal order emerged, which preserved a place for older cityscape within redevelopment areas. Planner Edmund Bacon's approach was notable for several reasons, including his partial shift in scale from the bird's-eye perspective to renewal on a house-to-house basis. Bacon used public urban renewal authorities to take control of blocks designated slums of obsolete structures, and then, to attract private investment, he recast them as desirable for upscale rehabilitation. By thus luring the Main Line suburban elites back to the colonial Society Hill neighborhood, Bacon thereby preserved more residential architecture than any previous urban renewal project. Yet his process still dislocated just as many poor residents; it could even be said that planned gentrification was also born in that historic Philadelphia neighborhood.

As transatlantic émigré architect Denise Scott Brown would discover, design professionals were not the only members of the urbanist establishment voicing serious objections to the urban renewal order. Urban social scientists also linked the circles of critical architects in places like Berlin, London, and Philadelphia. In the later 1950s, when U.K. and U.S. sociologists began looking at the human effects of urban renewal in London's East End and Boston's West End, they found reason for dismay in the pernicious aftermath of relocation and redevelopment. German social scientists expressed even broader misgivings about the authoritarian implications of technocratic planning, as well as the often inhuman scale of modernist urbanism. Theirs was an attempt to identify some legitimate basis upon which to build, literally, in a fledgling democracy. Urban sociologists in West Germany focused their discussion around the concept of the "public sphere," as a way to get at something worth preserving in a society undergoing rapid structural transformations. At least for some of them, this idea engendered a renewed respect for older urban patterns.

The combined weight of this transnational collection of criticisms, misgivings, and reservations amounted to a nagging unease within the urbanist community during the 1950s. But they did not significantly affect public, or more precisely, official support for urban renewal policies. And though they prefigured practically all the major objections that would ever be made of the urban renewal order, they were practically unknown beyond the academic, professional conversations of which they were a part. That changed when journalist Jane Jacobs examined urban renewal.

Married to an architect, employed by a leading architectural journal, and patronized by influential figures—particularly *New Yorker* architecture critic Lewis Mumford, *Architectural Forum* editor Douglas Haskell, *Fortune* editor William H. Whyte, Jr., and the Rockefeller Foundation's Chadbourne Gilpatric—Jacobs certainly had one foot firmly in the establishment camp. But she was also an untrained amateur with an anti-authoritarian streak and no intention of deferring to credentialed urbanists. Starting from 1956 with a series of speeches and articles,

Jacobs assailed the urbanist establishment with increasingly harsh criticisms of the dubious expertise professed by planners and the counterproductive effects of redevelopment programs. Then in 1961 she published a broadside attack on the entire urban renewal order with *The Death and Life of Great American Cities*. In it she blasted the tenets of modernist urbanism and advocated in their place a complete moral inversion, celebrating the underrated hodgepodge of dense, variegated, honeycombed, gradually accumulated urbanity.

Though her points were in line with many objections voiced by professionals during the 1950s, the urbanist establishment, including former supporters, fiercely attacked Jacobs, denouncing her for ignorance, oversimplification, and reactionary intentions. Jacobs' blunt irreverence pushed U.S. urbanists into a defensive position, causing them to close ranks and defend the status quo more rigidly than during the debates of the previous decade. Jacobs' best-selling book came just as popular opposition was beginning to achieve critical mass. Urbanists' alarmed response reflected their awareness that the foundations of the urban renewal order were in fact weakening; for those invested in it, condemning Jacobs became a desperate, and ultimately futile, last stand.

At the same time, the reception of Jacobs' books outside the United States provides a telling contrast. Her ideas were even more in conflict with the popular, strong planning regimes entrenched in both Great Britain and West Germany by the early 1960s. Yet Europeans took her not as a reactionary anti-planner, but rather as a complement to indigenous conversations. On the one hand these included popular critics, often conservatives, whose attacks on urban renewal paralleled her own. On the other hand, by the mid 1960s, Jacobs was also embraced by powerful exponents of the European urban renewal order, including high-profile public officials. Despite the transatlantic influence of modernist orthodoxy, Jacobs' critique proved less heretical abroad than in the United States. Whereas American planners denounced her vision as naive, she shared some core concepts with urbanists in Europe. (Surprisingly, Jacobs saw her closest intellectual compatriots in the British journalist Ian Nairn and German planner Rudolf Hillebrecht.) This partly explains why the popular embrace of such attitudes subsequently proved so much more disruptive for the urban renewal establishment in the United States than elsewhere.

3 Aesthetic Critiques
The Urbanist Establishment
Rediscovers the Old City

Beyond MARS: British Skepticism and London's Townscape

The popular response to wartime devastation in Europe proved a stubborn fact for housing reformers, modernist architects, functionalist planners, and other proponents of the urban renewal order who shared an aversion to traditional urban patterns. Simply put, Europeans clung to the conventional city even after destruction seemingly compelled its abandonment. As early as 1951, Josef Wolff pointed out that the German population's dogged return even to bombed-out urban areas ("an unexpected referendum of the people") should have prodded planners out of their technocratic fixations on modernizing traffic and shown them that old cities were not so bad after all: "A real sense of home had also developed in the old, much abused city structures. Shouldn't that have made the conscientious planner wonder whether his theories about the deficiencies of the old cities were right? Shouldn't it have forced upon him the heretical notion that those cities weren't as bad as their reputation?"[1]

Such heresies lingered in certain corners of the transatlantic urbanist establishment. Growing worries appeared among the British MARS affiliate—particularly from the postwar leader J. M. Richards, who was deeply involved with CIAM from 1946 to 1949—that the functionalist "ideals express themselves in an idiom which is by no means accepted or understood by the man in the street. . . . Modern architecture . . . may be in danger of becoming an art of the kind that is appreciated only by connoisseurs of a private cult." Richards, increasingly critical of MARS' focus on Le Corbusier, thought British urbanism should be less concerned with international CIAM dogma than specific local contexts, "the impact of contemporary conditions upon architecture," and, especially, popular taste.[2]

At the same time that Richards expressed these reservations about the appeal and applicability of the modernist movement, he edited one of Britain's oldest—and most unorthodox—journals of urbanism. The *Architectural Review* was founded in 1897, during the heyday of stylistic historicism. The magazine retained a staunchly independent streak throughout the twentieth century, rather than becoming a doctrinaire mouthpiece for CIAM modernism, as was the case at most major professional architecture and planning journals. As late as the mid-1930s, long after the German *Bauwelt* was purged of all but Bauhaus-inspired designs, the *Architectural Review* was still eclectic, and even the newest British projects it featured seemed more art deco than stark functionalist. And when editors like Richards or Nikolaus Pevsner eventually affiliated with MARS, they never became completely intoxicated by the dream of the modern; their journal continued to devote as much attention to historic and vernacular architecture as new projects; even the design and layout retained a playful, antiquarian clutter.[3]

The *Architectural Review* championed ideas at odds with functionalist urbanism, including the concept of multiple use—first taken up by the journal in 1949, though closely identified with Jane Jacobs much later—defending the value of mixing functions in a building or area.[4] With self-conscious deliberateness the *Review* thereby established itself as a haven for an unfashionable aesthetic sensibility, which ran under the banner Townscape. Architectural historian Joan Ockman once dismissed the Townscape movement as a "singularly British combination of modern architecture and national sentimentality," whereby modernist architects in the government employ were forced to "make the best of a difficult situation, mixing pared-down functional principles with 'people's detailing' and other accommodations to an English sense of coziness."[5] Yet more than a watered-down adaptation of continental modernism, the *Architectural Review* pursued a vision of distinctiveness and intellectual legitimacy for postwar British design.

When air raid damage prompted discussion of reconstruction plans for London, the *Review* responded with a statement of principles that clearly distanced it from CIAM and MARS. A 1943 picture essay emphasized the city's populist tradition of rowdy, bustling street life, rather than analytic clarity of master plans or architectural icons. Its argument urged modesty in approach, human scale, and above all warned against idolizing Paris. Planners had labored far too long (as they saw it, at least since the rise of Beaux-Arts training) under the impression that every other city was a failed Paris, awaiting the imposition of monumental vistas. London's grandeur, they argued instead, was built up from minute, unexpected glimpses, and functional chaos rather than forced order. (The editors took pains to reappropriate the term "functional" from CIAM lingo, and to reendow it with a connotation of timeworn practicality.) The history of Parisian Beaux-Arts urbanism offered a kind of proxy war in debates about contemporary urban renewal. At a time when New York's Robert Moses wrote admiringly of nineteenth-century Parisian planner Georges-Eugène Haussmann, the contrarian *Review* was rejecting Haussmann's legacy as a cautionary tale of reform's unintended consequences and tyranny against the common man—with clear analogies to contemporary Britain and the United States—rather than a paragon of modernization.[6] Even when featuring then-dominant opinions of Lewis Mumford and other advocates for the decentralization of urban regions, the *Review* took pains to present alternative viewpoints. J. M. Richards' 1941 essay "Regionalism Re-examined" argued that such regional planning strategies would preserve neither the cosmopolitanism of the city nor the distinctiveness of the surrounding region.[7]

Another exponent of the *Architectural Review*'s idiosyncratic perspective was longtime director and chairman Hubert de Cronin Hastings, who wrote under the pen name Ivor de Wolfe. Rather than focusing on outrages upon the face of Britain, he sought to emphasize the unique strengths implicit in his country's traditions. In 1949, de Wolfe's recommendation for how planners should handle the jumbled bric-a-brac of elements in the English vernacular landscape "is that you love, or try to love them instead of trying to hate and rid yourself of them in one way or another." This was meant, so he claimed, not as "a pretext for whimsy," but as an attempt "to make a new kind of whole" by concentrating "on the urge of the parts to be themselves." He characterized the English design tradition, represented by the eighteenth-century Picturesque visual philosophy—and contrasted with French rationalism (embodied by Le Corbusier) and German romanticism (seen, at a stretch, in Frank Lloyd Wright)—as inherently more empirical: "a dislike which amounts to an inability to see wholes or principles and an incapacity for handling theory [together with] a passionate preoccupation with independent details, parts or persons, an urge to help them fulfill themselves, achieve their own freedom; and thus, by mutual differentiation, achieve a higher organization." De Wolfe urged the systematic "collection of individual examples of civic design," to build a better appreciation of the English townscape, noting that such an a posteriori approach had eminent precedent in politics: "How significant and idiosyncratic—how radical—this simple act is, is seen when we remind ourselves that that is exactly the method that has been followed in the creation of this country's greatest contribution to civil organization—the common law. One looks to see an English, a radical, modern aesthetic growing in the same way out of innumerable individual judgments."[8]

Ironically, given this paean to the distinctiveness of the English constitution, the *Review*'s Townscape approach came into sharpest relief when it was applied to the United States, the subject of a 1950 special edition. The editors proceeded from an analogous supposition about the relationship between national character and the built environment: "The picture a nation creates of itself out of, and upon, its landscape is a more realistic self-portrait than many of us like to admit." Their definition of landscape was broad-minded enough to include "townships, roads, railways, electricity grids, clearings, afforestation schemes, backyards, real estate ventures, wastes, wilds, ornamental parkways, ribbon developments"—in short, *everything* "whether created consciously or unconsciously, by acts of commission or omission." These elements constituted "a realization in three dimensions of that society's form-will—a realization of its will to shape life in a certain way." Looking on these terms at "the mess that is man-made America," the *Review* suggested (and not necessarily disapprovingly) that "the American community rejected a visual ideal, in favour of a *laissez-faire* environment—a universe of uncontrollable chaos sparsely inhabited by happy accidents."[9]

While the magazine's criticisms of Britain were directed largely against an insensitive official planning apparatus, the American cityscape encountered by the *Review* was still poised on the eve of large-scale urban renewal, and therefore few such public interventions were as yet available to criticize. Instead, the private Rockefeller Center project (1926–40) received the most attention in terms of the perils of redeveloping cities. The editors concluded that such superblock planning "clearly does not produce the cities which we or the U.S. really want," and that the embrace of this technique obscured "the need for thinking out the kind of cities we really want."[10] Coming at a time when high-rise superblocks for public housing and urban renewal were just beginning to appear in the United States and Britain, these criticisms would prove prescient of the widespread dissatisfaction that ultimately accompanied their large-scale application by the 1960s.

De Wolfe, reacting against the rational, technocratic conception of MARS and CIAM (of which he had been an early member in the 1930s), emphasized "town planning as a visual art," which was then dubbed "townscape" by the *Review*.[11] Consequently, the role of the *Architectural Review*'s art editor, Gordon Cullen, another MARS member, who came to the magazine in 1947, was crucial.[12] In a series of articles between 1951 and 1960, Cullen collected photos and sketches of elements in British towns and countryside under the series title "Townscape," edited into a book of the same name in 1961. With a subtle mix of description and prescription, Cullen's studies accentuated anecdotal detail and the joy of visual complexity in traditional cityscapes seen from the pedestrian viewpoint, as compared with the monotony of modernist redevelopment schemes (fig. 3.1). His sensibility was not anti-modernist, though, but rather what many at the *Architectural Review* liked to think of as empiricist. In practice, this meant affirmation of the popular vernacular, including (in anticipation of Pop Art) even the more unrestrained adornments of capitalist commerce, notably electric signage: "the most valuable contribution of the twentieth century to urban scenery . . . startlingly conspicuous everywhere you look but almost ignored by the town planner." The very "visual incongruity" of this "normal element of city life" was taken as "something the townscaper should hasten to accept as a valuable aid. It is wrong to say that publicity degrades public taste. Public taste is already vulgar and also has the one merit of vulgarity, i.e. vitality."[13]

Architectural Review staff writer Ian Nairn decried the combined outcomes of

Figure 3.1 The *Architectural Review*'s Townscape philosophy celebrated British vernacular urban design, particularly via the illustrations of Gordon Cullen, like this one advocating a picturesque, human-scaled vision of London's public realm. Note that Cullen depicts modernist buildings integrated into the Georgian neighborhood fabric and also emphasizes the varied textural details from flagstone pavers to bollards. (Source: "Legs and Wheels," *Architectural Review* 104, no. 620 [August 1948]: 77. Reproduced with permission estate of Dr. Gordon Cullen, Commander of the British Empire, honorary Fellow of the Royal Institute of British Architects.)

British government planning and private development, in a series of articles later collected into books.[14] In the column "Outrage" and subsequently "Counter-attack," Nairn and Cullen assembled examples of neglect and misguided beautification efforts into a scathing portrait of what they termed Subtopia—a rapidly emerging British landscape characterized by withering town centers and sprawling suburban fringe. As one contemporary noted, the series "provoked so much attention—and second thoughts—from architects, planners, and citizens that a Counter-attack Bureau has been set-up to handle the flood of inquiries."[15]

Cullen's strengths as an illustrator no doubt contributed to the *Architectural Review*'s popularity—a fact that irritated urbanists of the high modernist persuasion. To architectural theorist Joseph Rykwert in 1955, for instance, Cullen was emblematic of an "artistic, woolly" approach that those in the modernist camp saw as irrelevant: "The weakness at the foundations of the *Review* is a concern for surface and a neglect for structure."[16] Similarly, a 1954 letter to the *Review* from architect Alan Colquhoun lamented the journal's lack of focus on structure and function as per CIAM and suggested that "it is because this fact has been lost sight of that so much of postwar British architecture is effete and superficial."[17] There is room for debate about the *Review*'s impact, whether positive or negative, on practice in Britain at the time; Rykwert maintained that, despite being "probably the most striking architectural publication appearing anywhere in the world," its appeal was primarily to the layman. His impression that "many British architects never see it"—an assertion albeit belied by the advertisers—implied a "failure to register an influence on the bulk of current architecture." In any case, it is indisputable that the *Review*'s aesthetic focus and skepticism toward aggressive reconstruction was out of step with the urbanist establishment.

The Townscape critique attracted attention across the Atlantic, as well. John Burchard, architectural engineer and dean at M.I.T., worried that the Townscapers' criticisms exaggerated the negative in modernist designs through their blunt juxtapositions of promise and reality: "The problem of telling the truth in architectural photography is a difficult one these days. On the one hand, few buildings now stand in serene park-like surroundings unchallenged by unsightly or incompatible buildings, untarnished by urban litter. This is part of the architectural ambiance, without a doubt, but since we learn not to see it in life, photographs that emphasize it may well over-state the case for *Outrage*. On the other hand, architectural photographers with their cumulus clouds and dramatic trees may not tell the truth either."[18]

Others Americans were more enthusiastic: "Few men have so perceptive an eye for details" that make up the human scale, wrote *Fortune* magazine editor William H. Whyte, Jr., "something all designers of downtown projects praise in theory and most obliterate in the projects, [and] the quality the city most desperately needs." Whyte commissioned Cullen and Nairn to contribute a pictorial essay for the conclusion of his 1958 "Exploding Metropolis" series, to complement an early article by Jane Jacobs (fig. 3.2). Whyte thus imported the *Architectural Review*'s trademark sensibility and—tempering it with Yankee optimism—asked Cullen and Nairn "to look at the townscape of our own cities, to sketch not the horrors known so well, but the strengths, so easily overlooked."[19] From her New York vantage point, Jacobs realized that the *Architectural Review* staff was "also exposing the unworkability and joylessness of anti-city visions," just as she was beginning

Figure 3.2 Pedestrians and transportation coexisting in the Loop, Chicago's central-city neighborhood: This visual appreciation of the American townscape by Gordon Cullen, presenting an intricate series of visual revelations, accompanied a 1958 essay by Jane Jacobs. (Reproduced with permission estate of Dr Gordon Cullen, Commander of the British Empire, honorary Fellow of the Royal Institute of British Architects.)

to do.[20] With such shared realizations, a transatlantic critique of the urban renewal order began to emerge.

Return to Center: Reaffirming the German City

Clearly, a reevaluation of the means and ends of the urban renewal order extended beyond Britain and the *Architectural Review*. During the West German boom period of the late 1950s and early 1960s, there emerged a distinct, albeit still modest, reaction against aggressive decentralization. Some skeptics proposed that planners redirect these growth dynamics inward, rather than pursue rigid deconcentration schemes that diluted the city's intensity. In 1960, economist and sociologist Edgar Salin celebrated the humanistic urbanity of antiquity and earlier German cities, which, although not literally appropriate for industrial mass culture, provided a model for planners to cease promoting decentralization and instead prevent the hollowing out of a vital core: "It is not the dissolution of the city that creates a new form, but rather only a strengthening of the core can enable new life to radiate out into the furthest districts."[21] Gerhard Rabeler observed, however, that Salin's ideas were often translated into reactive oversimplification: "An unreflective ideology of deconcentration was replaced with an equally unreflective ideology of urbanity and densification."[22]

Wilhelm Wortmann similarly affirmed the metropolis in the face of what he called "overblown pastoralism," calling in 1961 for the preservation of urban lifestyle, including concentration around public transit nodes. He rejected the deconcentration-reorganization model as an anachronistic response to the city before the second industrial revolution, which had never envisioned the possibility of self-renewal.[23] And after studying an urban renewal area in 1963, planning professor Peter Koller of Berlin's Technical University warned the city council against destructive and "technocratic conceptions."[24] In another Berlin government study (begun around 1963 though not published until 1967), Werner March praised the "power of the solid enclosed blocks to unite and encourage community."[25] Werner Hebebrand's 1964 city planning seminar for the national German industrial federation in Regensburg called for the rebuilding of cleared areas and questioned CIAM functionalism as an end in itself: "A city has to be more than just functional, and it is precisely this 'more' that gives it the glitter and radiance."[26]

By the mid-1960s, some of these retrospective ideas had found modest accommodation in professional architectural and planning journals like West Berlin's *Bauwelt*, whose editor, Ulrich Conrads, reprinted Martin Wagner's 1931 appreciation of Greek revival architect Karl Friedrich Schinkel.[27] Or, when the occasion of the 250th anniversary of Karlsruhe's radial baroque city plan provided an opportunity "to confront building past with building present," the journal celebrated the incorporation of the classical facade from the bombed-out 1817 margrave's palace into a 1963 bank building.[28] Of course, neither emphasizing the historical sensibilities of a CIAM pioneer like Wagner nor preserving an exceptional architectural monument in Baden-Württemberg brought modernist urbanism into serious question.

The journal did, however, vociferously attack one model project of modernist reconstruction right in the center of West Berlin: the new campus for the Technical University.[29] Meanwhile, at that same institution, architectural historian Ernst Heinrich was cultivating an appreciation of Berlin's vernacular architecture, calling for contextual sensitivity in renewal as well as the preservation of entire streets and squares.[30] This unorthodox sensibility found its way into the journal *Bauwelt* via his acolytes Johann Friedrich Geist and Dieter Huhn. In an iconoclastic essay they provocatively suggested that the creator of Berlin's 1862 master plan— oft-maligned city architect James Hobrecht—might in fact deserve a memorial for shaping the city's effective pattern of housing, commerce, and public spaces over the subsequent century. "Does [Hobrecht] deserve a monument? Those who blame him for what they call the fatal, petrified Berlin would reject such a monument; they would renovate. But another answer is also possible: Those who say that the hallmark of the city is not the density of concentration alone, but its solid enclosed blocks, would not hesitate to approve his monument."[31]

Their discussion swung between concrete observations of Berlin (documented with photographs) and "ideal types" of the public sphere, invoking "the shared public space," "the public realm," and the bounded town square that had delimited the first "public grounds." All these terms bore the imprint of contemporary German sociologists Jürgen Habermas and Hans Paul Bahrdt (about whom more shortly). In their discussion of urban bulwarks for the public sphere, Geist and Huhn fixed upon the ideal type of the nineteenth-century apartment house as a site occupied by all social classes, echoing what Hobrecht termed "commendable mixing."[32] They decried the dissolution of mixed apartment districts with the "break-up and reorganization of the population by income class." And they rejected the trend toward "solitary houses," where "the relatively insignificant difference between the cabins of a summerhouse colony and an assemblage of luxury buildings lies only in the number of residents: both thoroughly reflect clear, anti-urban contours." Above all, the authors lamented the loss of Hobrecht's cityscape at the hands of uncomprehending modernists, who simplified facades into structural walls, designed new housing projects without any privileged squares, and insured that "a green preservative is spread around every city building." In their eyes, the treatment of corners provided a telling contrast between the constructions—and implicit civic sensibilities—of the nineteenth and twentieth centuries:

> The distinction between the old and new development of corner lots is so striking and so consistent that it is impossible to take as coincidental. This fact seems symptomatic. . . . The cause must therefore be the consequence of general attitudes. In the nineteenth century the corner was a privileged site. It was the natural place for pubs, shops, or exceptional apartments. Architects competed by applying bay windows, towers, and colossal formations. The corner was emphasized in striking manner. The reverse is just as conspicuous today: no shops, no pubs, an all-around embarrassment—a few shy balconies, otherwise parking spaces, garbage dumpsters, shrubbery, prohibition signs, perhaps gas stations. Houses shun the corners as if they were indecent. Sidewalk slabs and curbs are the last remaining markers. What does this mean?[33]

German urbanists appeared to be in the midst of a reformation in the mid-1960s, self-critical and at times even suffering from a crisis of confidence. In a widely reprinted talk delivered at the Munich Seminar of the Institute for Housing and City Planning in April 1965, Berlin professor of architectural history Julius Posener wondered, "Is the city dying from city planning?" Bauwelt editor Conrads invoked parallels to the turn of the century, when Camillo Sitte and Theodor Goecke also saw themselves in the midst of a transitional period.[34] No less than that patriarch of German modernist urbanism Walter Gropius confessed to an interviewer in 1964 that his functionalist movement had been misinterpreted, to the detriment of more humane considerations: "It isn't all practical," he said. "We must consider psychological function as well as structural function. We may have two buildings that are equally practical but psychologically different—one gives a feeling of beauty, the other of drabness or ugliness." Apparently without irony, the architect and namesake of the mammoth six-hundred-acre Gropiusstadt housing project—just breaking ground in Berlin at the time, but notorious a decade later as the bleak backdrop for disaffected young drug addicts—suggested that "little kicks of contrast" could enable buildings "to stimulate human beings who will use them."[35]

Bacon's Rebellion: Preservation and Urbanism in "the Philadelphia School"

The conceptual transition occurring among urbanists may be best embodied by a man at the center of the U.S. urban renewal order. Philadelphia planning director Edmund Bacon turned out to be something other than the rigid modernist, anti-traditionalist planner that his calls for reform through redesign might suggest. Bacon was certainly driven to subordinate Philadelphia's "multiplicity of wills" to his own "design idea."[36] Yet his uncompromising vision for the centuries-old city also included a place for its older elements. He was, more accurately, an unabashed gentrifier of historic urban neighborhoods, as illustrated by his most ambitious, and most successful, project: the reinvention of Society Hill through managed preservation.

The extremism of Bacon's Society Hill project lay instead in his desire to counter the suburbanization of Philadelphia's elites. Such people, he believed, "had been reacting to the disadvantages of the congested Victorian industrial city, and the idea was universally and uncritically held that the only proper aspiration for a decent, healthy, upcoming, normal American family was the suburban environment." But he felt capable of swiftly reversing this trend. "At one swoop," Bacon believed, his Society Hill project "smashes the image of the core surrounded by a ring of the lowest income group moving outward in an ever widening circle leaving a sea of devastation in its wake. It smashes the picture of the city abandoned by the whites to become a ghetto of only one race."[37]

Bacon wanted to change the social composition of the neighborhood, to replace its (predominantly Polish) working-class residents with those wealthy enough to rehabilitate the homes to their past grandeur. At the same time, he wanted to avoid the ravages of speculative development, which might rush in at the sign of redevelopment. To steer between those opposing shoals, he sought to handpick residents who were willing to offer total commitment to the neighborhood. This meant they had to possess the means to reach Bacon's standards of restoration, which generally meant money, although a few of the prior residents managed to meet the stringent requirements with their own sweat equity. But money alone was not what Bacon sought; already since the 1930s various Philadelphia philanthropists had donated endowments for the restoration of old family homesteads, creating urban house museums they could visit from their suburban estates. Instead, Bacon insisted that the Main Liners move back to the city.[38]

This goal entailed changing both attitudes and facts on the ground. Bacon relied on the power of his vision to change perceptions, explaining that "the planner must create the image of the vital, viable, cultural-residential core in terms that stir the passions of people and motivate politicians." Bacon was explicit about his desire to effect a "return to city living on the part of the middle and upper income groups," and he aggressively promoted that vision in order artificially to create a demand for Society Hill properties among Philadelphia's suburban elite, personally leading tours for influential social-register women to stimulate their interest in the area.[39]

Bacon's design approach differed significantly from other urban renewal and slum clearance programs and could be described as a pro-urban pedestrian-level perspective—in contrast to the typical bird's-eye viewpoint of most planning. His was renewal on the house-to-house scale, seeking to reattract individual wealth by surgically expunging the perceived negative aspects of the Victorian cityscape (clashing stylistic embellishments, converted storefronts) and restoring Society Hill to an idealized Georgian residential glory. He recognized that successful interventions, beyond government programs, required the cumulative investment of myriad residents. At the same time, he believed in the power of his vision, as a planner bolstered by statutory powers, to shape and control these forces. Jane Jacobs would later attack Bacon for being an aesthete, uninterested in whether his designs actually attracted people—but she was not exactly right; for him it was merely a question of which people. Bacon's image of the city's direction had undisguised social ramifications; it was both supported by and supportive of the elites that had brought him and his allies into power.

In 1957, Mayor Richardson Dilworth—like Bacon, a fellow Young Turk elite reformer—made the symbolic gesture of moving into the refurbished Society Hill neighborhood himself. Bacon saw his greatest coup when two of the most prestigious families—that of C. Jared Ingersoll, director of U.S. Steel, and that of Henry M. Watts, Jr., chairman of the board of the New York Stock Exchange—agreed to purchase and inhabit neighboring properties. Real estate and banking dynamics turned in the neighborhood's favor after it was seen as a good risk (ca. 1961) and became a seller's market by 1965. From an economic standpoint, Bacon's scheme was successful, ultimately doubling the area's tax revenue. Society Hill's renewal was undertaken with federal and state legislation and financing from 1957 onward, although private investment ($165–$180 million) outpaced public funds ($43 million) at a 6:1 ratio. National renewal averages were closer to 3:1.[40]

Bacon felt vindicated in other, less quantifiable ways as well. In 1966—the year Congress passed the National Historic Preservation Act—he told a Princeton audience that "we are on the threshold of cracking the suburban ideal."[41] He would remain convinced that Society Hill had "produced a new brand of people—affluent but passionately convinced that suburbs are wrong and cities are the place to bring up children."[42] Ultimately, although the project manifested a relatively moderate approach physically—726 out of 2,197 buildings would be retained—it entailed a much more radical (or perhaps reactionary) social reorganization of the city. Paradoxically, Bacon's preservation project dislocated as many families as if the entire neighborhood had been razed (fig. 3.3).[43]

■

Figure 3.3 A scene illustrating Edmund Bacon's attempt to reconcile preservation and modernism in Philadelphia's Society Hill neighborhood. This 1967 walking tour on Spruce Street encounters a refurbished 1759 tavern juxtaposed against I. M. Pei's 1963 Society Hill towers. Society Hill entailed more preservation than any previous urban renewal area, retaining over seven hundred older structures—even while the project also demolished twice that number. The project deliberately displaced the neighborhood's working-class residents in order to lure wealthy suburban families back to the city. (Temple University Libraries, Urban Archives, Philadelphia, PA.)

Bacon's particular planning approach coincided with an influential conceptual transition taking hold on the University of Pennsylvania campus (where he was also a faculty member). Rather than a bastion of orthodox modernist design or a think tank for Philadelphia's urban renewal programs, the university's School of Fine Arts proved to be a volatile powder keg, which ultimately brought both of these into question. The independent path which the Philadelphia school was to take became evident in dean G. Holmes Perkins' immediate hiring priority and first trophy acquisition: independent scholar and *New Yorker* urbanism critic Lewis Mumford, who would serve as the program's elder sage and philosopher, offering courses in urban history, contemporary architecture, and civic design for a decade beginning in 1951.[44]

Mumford had a complex and always critical relationship to modernist design, sometimes acting as a national cheerleader, at others times rebuking its arrogance. According to his biographer Robert Wojtowicz, Mumford "consistently rejected [modernist urbanism's] ahistorical polemics, its stylistic clichés and its international pretensions," and his appointment thus signaled the University of Pennsylvania's break with the more orthodox modernist design schools.[45] Mumford despaired about the disregard of history in modernist architectural training: "Instead of drawing on the history of twenty centuries the student now draws upon the history of twenty years," he noted apropos of Gropius' architectural program at Harvard. "Under the original guise of functionalism, a new formalism has developed; and the organic development of modern forms, through a deeper insight into the entire architectural complex, is now threatened with arrest."[46]

As an antidote, Mumford utilized both the antiquities collections of the University of Pennsylvania's museum of anthropology and archaeology and the contemporary planning projects underway in Philadelphia to research his 1961 magnum opus, *The City in History*, which received the National Book Award the following year.[47] Mumford saw Bacon as "one of the best planners in the country" and lauded his vision for its balance of modern and historic, urban and pastoral:[48] "The civic nucleus of Philadelphia, though weakened by the suburban exodus, has begun, through the art museum, the library system, the universities, and not least through the historic precinct itself, to exert its attractive power throughout the Delaware Valley. This should lead, not merely to the inner renewal of the city, but to the maintenance of the green matrix and the changeover from the clotted conurbation of the past to the new urban and regional grid."[49]

The distinctive reputation of Perkins' School of Fine Arts coalesced by the mid-1950s and began attracting students both for its social scientific approach to planning and for pure design. The University of Pennsylvania architecture program became a magnet when in 1955 Louis Kahn, an architect with a mystic-artist persona, returned from Yale's faculty to teach at his alma mater. Kahn was joined by Robert Venturi, a Princeton-educated architect from the Main Line, apprenticed in Kahn's practice. The designs and ideas of these two Philadelphia natives, Kahn and Venturi, challenged the strict modernist orthodoxy and signaled the stylistic independence of the "Philadelphia School" of architecture (as it was nicknamed in the April 1961 issue of *Progressive Architecture*).[50] Yet there existed within Penn's School of Fine Arts an irreducible tension between those, like Kahn and Venturi, who focused on physical form and those, like Robert Mitchell and his planning department, who examined the economic and social aspects of urbanism. These tensions played out in the figure of Denise Scott Brown, an urbanist pulled by both poles. But before we can examine these any further, we must first return to Britain to trace the transnational route, conceptual as much as geographic, that brought her to Philadelphia. That story begins with a reformation led by a teacher at London's Architectural Association and his wife.

CIAM's Defiant British Children:
The Smithsons' Independent Group, 1953–60

Professionals within the urbanist establishments of the United States, West Germany, and Britain began to question the urban renewal order in various ways. Most direct was the critique hatched right from within the CIAM organization by two young British architects, Peter and Alison Smithson. The married couple worked in the Schools Division of the London County Council for a brief period in 1950, where they were among a group who rejected the Townscape picturesque in favor of Le Corbusier–inspired functionalism.[51] At barely thirty years old, the Smithsons attracted attention when their Miesian design won the architectural competition for a new school building in Hunstanton (1950–54). They were then inducted into the CIAM circle via membership in the British affiliate (MARS). The aging founders of the CIAM movement, including Le Corbusier himself, viewed the Smithsons and their cohort as generational successors and handed over increasing responsibility for the preparation of conferences. But rather than carrying on the organization, these young arrivals—particularly the polemical Smithsons—rebelled and effectively dismembered it.[52]

In 1951, concurrent with the Festival of Britain, the eighth CIAM conference was hosted in the London suburb of Hoddesdon by the British MARS group, which insisted on "the core" or "the heart of the city" as the primary theme—a pointed emphasis upon something never favorably addressed by the organization's four-functions schema (work, residence, transportation, leisure). Yet the British conference hailed the civic nucleus as "the element which makes the community a community."[53] This urbane turn was continued at the ninth CIAM conference, held in Aix-en-Provence in July 1953. Alison and Peter Smithson's "urban re-identification" poster display (such displays were called "grids") directly attacked the functional segregation enshrined in CIAM's Athens Charter (fig. 3.4). On one heretical panel, for instance, a photograph of London row houses festooned with flags was captioned: "In the suburbs and slums the vital relationship between the house and the street survives, children run about, people stop and talk, vehicles are parked and tinkered with: in the back gardens are pigeons and pets and the shops are round the corner: you know the milkman, you are outside your house in your street."

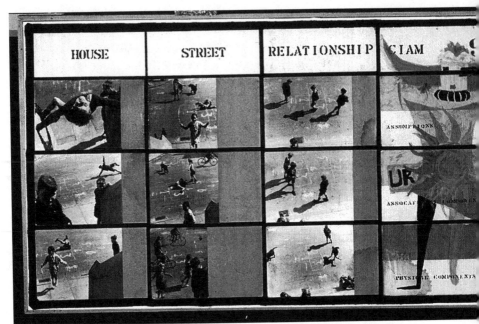

HOUSE	STREET	RELATIONSHIP	CIAM

Figure 3.4 Poster display by Alison and Peter Smithson at the ninth Congress for Modern Architecture in 1953, emphasizing "urban reidentification." Photographs of London street life represented city dwellers' relationships at the level of house, street, district, and city. The British architectural couple led an internal critique of the CIAM organization's founding principles—particularly the functional segregation of work, residence, transportation, and leisure—and provoked its disbanding by the decade's end. (Courtesy of Dirk van den Heuvel. © The Smithson Family Collection, London, with permission.)

All of this amounted to an implicit denunciation of insular modernist projects; the Smithsons essentially rejected the fundamental CIAM segregation of functions in favor of what architectural scholar John R. Gold called a more integrated "hierarchy of human associations—house, street, district, and city." [54] Similarly, Eric Mumford noted that, while certainly still members of the modernist movement, "they seemed to be suggesting a way of reconfiguring the city without losing the vitality of working-class street life, which the Smithsons were among the first to recognize as possibly superior to the kind of existence being brought into being by CIAM architects." [55]

The Smithsons' populist panels betrayed the influence of young British artists with whom they affiliated, a group loosely centered around the Institute of Contemporary Art. The Independent Group, as they were known, was organized in 1952 by Mary and Reyner Banham and shared a fascination with popular cul-

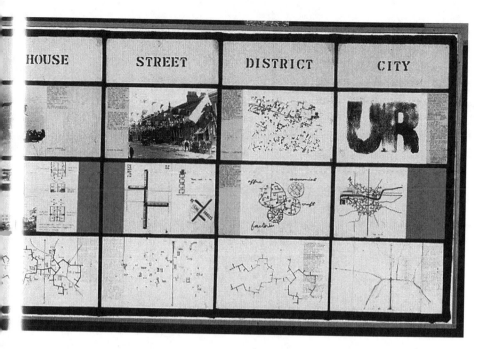

| HOUSE | STREET | DISTRICT | CITY |

ture, especially American mass media.[56] This proto-pop-art clique was character-ized by "a neo-Dadaist interest in the 'as found' aesthetic" and shared with the Townscape movement an effort to render the mundane more visible.[57] (Smithson claimed he took from Jackson Pollock the sense that a "freer, more complex yet quite comprehensible idea of 'order' might be developed.")[58] For their part, the architects designed a series of exhibitions for the group. The Smithsons drew particular inspiration from another couple, photographer Nigel Henderson and his wife, Judith Stephan, an urban anthropologist. Architecture scholar Helena Webster concluded that "the Smithsons' contact with the Hendersons, who were carrying out sociological studies in the East End of London at the time, steered their reading of the city towards a form which reflected the structure of human association."[59] A photograph of the Smithsons lounging with Henderson and sculptor Eduardo Paolozzi in the middle of Livingston Street, Chelsea, was used as the poster for the 1956 exhibit, "This Is Tomorrow."

Despite having completed only one major building, the Smithsons exerted considerable influence given Peter's teaching position at the Architectural Associ-ation. The leading London school was (and is) housed in several of the Georgian townhouses on Bedford Square just around the corner from the British Museum in Bloomsbury. Between 1955 and 1960, Smithson pushed the institution to inculcate in students a greater sensitivity to the context of their designs. One Architectural Association student in particular, a young South African emigrant named Denise Scott Brown, absorbed the London mix of sociologically informed planning, the vernacular civic design approach of Townscape, and the popular culture preoccupations of the Independent Group. She carried these with her across the Atlantic to Philadelphia and her eventual partnership with Robert Venturi, after Peter Smithson encouraged her and her husband Robert Scott Brown to enroll at the University of Pennsylvania and study under Louis Kahn.[60]

The Smithsons and a Dutch group led by Jacob Bakema (known collectively as Team X because they were planning a tenth CIAM conference for 1956) continued to push for more contextual building. They drew upon Sir Patrick Geddes's premodernist, Garden City distinctions of a variation across "valley section" and asserted that CIAM was "wrong to build the same house" everywhere. The founding generation resisted: Le Corbusier accused the "young" of "debilitating negations and verbal dilettantism"; Gropius complained "they think they are asked to do the same as us" in challenging authority.[61] Yet by the time the conference convened in Dubrovnik, Team X's symbolic patricide had enough momentum that CIAM president Sert resolved to continue the group's work only informally through his capacity as dean of Harvard's Graduate School of Design. In Otterlo in 1959, the CIAM leadership recognized that it no longer occupied the avant-garde position, and the organization officially ceased to exist. The *Architectural Review* published a picture of the Smithsons and other Team X members holding a drawing of a cemetery cross and wreath labeled "C.I.A.M."[62]

Ironically, the Smithsons' own architecture displayed a severe, modernist rigor, beginning with their school at Hunstanton in 1950. Still displaying a stylistic puritanism a decade latter at the last CIAM congress in Otterlo, Peter Smithson attacked the historical revivalism of Ernesto Rogers.[63] Though definitely not in that magazine's Townscape mold, Reyner Banham championed the couple in the pages of the *Architectural Review* as "New Brutalists" for their uncompromising, ungilded aesthetic (likening it to that of Philadelphia's Louis Kahn). Whereas *Architectural Review* editor Nikolaus Pevsner understood Britain as "the most compromising, the most adaptable, the most practical of all nations," Banham detested the picturesque sensibility, whether he encountered it expressed in the opinions of the *Review*, in the teachings at the Architectural Association, or from architects working under the London County Council.[64] Banham saw the Smithsons as rigorous antidotes to wayward tendencies in British urbanism, alongside architect James Stirling and theorist Colin Rowe. In a 1959 interview, Peter Smithson portrayed himself as restoring the pure founding principles of modernism, in order that "a genuine aesthetic of machine building technology should arise . . . a rather brutal approach." Alison Smithson concurred: "If you considered yourself in the same tradition as the original masters, and in that way reacting upon what we found things were in the forties, buildings which were built as if they were not made of real materials at all but some sort of processed materials such as Kraft Cheese; we turned back to wood and concrete, glass and steel, all the materials which you can really get hold of."[65]

For all their identification with the traditional London by-law streetscape, the Smithsons' proposals throughout the 1950s sought not to preserve it but rather to find a modernist analogue, usually in the form of raised pedestrian skyways, or "streets in the air."[66] This was evidenced in their unrealized proposals for the 1952 Golden Lane and 1957 Berlin Hauptstadt projects.[67] The latter retained, if only to supersede, conventional street patterns—common in practice but still disdained in design circles and civil engineering alike. Only the Smithsons' second major commission made concessions—in scale if not style—to the streetscape. For the new offices they designed for *The Economist* Group in London's West End (1960–64), their Brutalist aesthetic was considerably buffed up with Portland-stone facing slabs and other decorative elements, and the project stepped down to harmonize with the neighboring Boodles clubhouse and other buildings along St. James's Street. In distinction to the Golden Lane and Berlin Hauptstadt proposals—both for bomb sites —the *Economist* buildings entailed extensive demolition of Victorian structures. Nevertheless, reviewing the project for the *Architectural Review*, Gordon Cullen approved of the Smithsons' "flexibility in the solution of neighborly problems," since their new building "observes the proprieties and remains invisible. Meanwhile, the unity of the street is maintained."[68] This was an exception for the time and even for the Smithsons; as late as their 1972 (completed) Robin Hood Gardens housing estate, the couple was proposing Corbusian solutions for London's townscape. But even if their walk did not always appear to fulfill their heretical talk, the Smithsons opened up the conceptual space (through their writing, teaching, and agitation within Team X) for even the doctrinaire mainstream of architects and planners to move beyond the CIAM charter. Young Architectural Association student Denise Scott Brown would be swept up in a transatlantic wave to do just that. She soon discovered, however, that it was not designers but rather social scientists who presented the thorniest critiques of the urban renewal order.

4 Policy Objections
Social Scientists Question the Urban Renewal Order

From East End (London) to West End (Boston): Urban Sociology's Unwelcome Conclusions

Born into a prosperous Jewish family in South Africa, Denise Scott Brown (née Lakofski) came to the University of Pennsylvania to study with Louis Kahn. She was attracted by Kahn's affinity with the ideas she encountered at London's Architectural Association, particularly those of Peter Smithson. Though disappointed to learn upon arrival that Kahn did not teach planning, she was convinced by adviser David Crane, who shared Scott Brown's African roots and had in 1957 just received Penn's joint master's degree in civic design from the Departments of Architecture and City Planning, to stay in the program and try to synthesize these two fields.

The Congo-born Crane would work various influences on Scott Brown: He convinced her to pursue the master's in city planning and combine it with her interest in architecture (she would obtain a master of architecture in 1965), thereby pointing the way for her lifelong commitment to civic design—a field sometimes described as the architect within planning. Yet he also advised her that despite her talent she would find her "place would be behind her husband," fellow student Robert Scott Brown. Following her first husband's sudden death in a car accident in 1958, Crane played matchmaker to connect her with Robert Venturi.[1]

That first semester in Philadelphia, however, Scott Brown's conception of the city was ignited by instructor Herbert Gans' analyses of urban forces. Gans was fast emerging as the leading American exponent of a social scientific critique that complemented aesthetic revisions within the urbanist establishment. But while Gans' own sociological research took place in Levittown, Pennsylvania, and Boston's West End, his ideas, ironically enough, could be traced right back to the London that Denise Scott Brown had just departed.

Prior to World War II, British urban sociology was not in the same league as that of the Chicago school in the United States, and cities were almost exclusively a topic for gloomy, elitist urban critics.[2] But social conditions in London during the 1950s screamed for more careful examination.[3] An influx of Caribbean immigrants led to a pogrom through Notting Hill in August 1958. Both the housing situation and the policies for its amelioration aggravated such tensions. And while modernist architects and planners paid much lip service to sociology as a discipline that informed their work, almost no research had actually been done into the human effects of such already extensive relocation schemes.

Into this breach stepped Peter Willmott and Michael Young. Young, trained as a lawyer at the London School of Economics, became the Labor Party's director of research and drafted the social welfare platform which carried Clement Attlee to Downing Street in 1945. With the return of Tory government in 1951, Young entered a doctoral sociology program at London University, where his dissertation, "The Rise of Meritocracy," coined a new term to attack the national standardized testing system that promised social equality but actually reinforced privilege.[4] Young then founded the Institute of Community Studies and began to examine urban poverty together with Peter Willmott. They decided to study the London County Council's relocation of one entire community from a traditional East End neighborhood into high-rise housing on London's periphery. As Willmott put it, "In the programs of urban redevelopment under way in the United States [and] Britain, one fact above all is striking. Hardly anything is known about the social consequences—about what redevelopment means to the people whose homes are being demolished."[5] Their observations, published in 1957 as *Family and Kinship in East London*, suggested that the cost-benefit ratio was unfavorable. These arguments were of course unwelcome among advocates of urban renewal programs just getting up steam.[6]

Some of the richest soil for U.S. social scientists' similarly disillusioning encounters with the urban renewal order was in Boston, a city saturated with academic institutions. As early as 1953, a study by the Housing Association of Metropolitan Boston concluded that "all types of official action by themselves would not check blight and improve living standards in residential neighborhoods, unless there was active citizen participation in the effort." It suggested the promotion of neighborhood rehabilitation and conservation as a better alternative. In a project supported by the Urban Renewal Administration (Demonstration Branch), the Housing and Home Finance Agency, and the Massachusetts Department of Commerce, the housing association undertook a study from 1954 to 1957 of "demographic-ecological" considerations.[7] The final report noted that "urban renewal action in American cities has been mainly of the total redevelopment-clearance type." Yet the populations concerned were too large to relocate and could not afford relocation in any case. The housing association concluded that future projects must emphasize rehabilitation with "spot-redevelopment." Rehabilitation, furthermore, was an approach that necessitated citizen participation, so this too would have to become "more characteristic of well administered renewal programs."[8] The housing association study cited Boston's West End and Philadelphia's Eastwick as typical cases of the disregard for the site inhabitants by planners, all too happy to develop projects among themselves and announce plans as faits accomplis. Alas, "citizen-residents were not as happily pleased to accept, let alone applaud the project plans as the professional administrators had hoped. In their eagerness to rush ahead without being slowed down by consulting with local citizens, they had probably made haste wastefully."[9] Mounting opposition threatened to produce an "extreme example of citizen-participation-in-reverse."[10]

An extreme example of urban renewal was precisely what Boston's West End became. This was not, however, as a result of the residents' anticipated resistance, but rather for the unanticipated effects of the project's completion. The West End became the most closely documented urban renewal project in the country through the involvement of three young researchers: Marc Fried, Herbert Gans, and Chester Hartman. All were affiliated with Harvard Medical School and the Center for Community Studies of the Department of Psychiatry at Massachusetts General Hospital. First proposed in 1950, their project entailed "a centrally located, 48-acre neighborhood of some 7,500 persons that was demolished in 1958–1959 to make way for a luxury apartment house complex." It would provide "one of the few sources of comprehensive, independently gathered and analyzed data on the effects of slum clearance and relocation."[11] Directly inspired by the Young and Willmott's work on relocated working-class residents in East London, the researchers studied the neighborhood and its former inhabitants for over a decade, before, during and after the renewal process. Hartman assessed the residents' housing improvements ("disappointingly small") following West End clearance and relocation.[12] Fried counted the "psychological costs of relocation," or, as he termed it, "grieving for a lost home."[13] Perhaps most compelling was Gans' evocative participant-observation study of the neighborhood—documented between October 1957 and May 1958, just as demolition commenced—which formed the basis of his influential 1962 book *The Urban Villagers*.[14] Reviewing Gans from Britain, Willmott noted, "The point of view of the local people in districts like the West End is ignored, partly because they cannot express it clearly in the places where it would need to be heard, partly because little is done, from the other end, to find out what it is. In consequence, they suffer."[15] Through such studies, U.S. and U.K. urbanists collectively questioned the logic—just as the international movement against the Vietnam War did a few years later—of destroying a village in order to save it.

Authoritarians in the Public Sphere: German Urbanists and the Problem of Democratic Planning

In West Germany similar calls were emerging by the mid-1950s—like that from the president of the German Academy of City and Regional Planning in 1955—

for more urban studies by economists, sociologists, geographers, and medical researchers.[16] Around 1960, Wolfgang Hartenstein and his colleagues at the Institute for Applied Social Science in Bad Godesberg undertook several sociological studies. Essentially public opinion surveys, they sought to explore "motivations, opinions, and behavior," taking Hamburg as their "sociological microcensus."[17] The studies were commissioned by the city council with the support of city *Baumeister* Rudolf Hillebrecht, who saw sociology as the servant of good planning, complementing more statistical analyses.[18] Topics included political consciousness and attitudes toward the Nazi past, but there was also an entire study devoted to "traffic sociology." They observed a growing enthusiasm for the emancipating independence of the automobile, but also an aggressive quality in the power play of "armored car" drivers in a perceived competition for individualized mobility. The study urged traffic planners to take these sociopolitical risks into consideration alongside technical data.[19]

To psychologist Alexander Mitscherlich, the Hamburg public opinion studies revealed darker undertones. He castigated the residually authoritarian family structure as a poor foundation for democracy: "It should not be forgotten that our democracy twice owed its life not to a popular uprising against autocratic or terrorist forms of government, but rather to wartime defeats."[20] Mitscherlich received medical and academic degrees from Heidelberg, where he joined the faculty during World War II as director of the Psychosomatic Clinic. He later turned his attention to urban questions and produced a widely read 1965 monograph entitled *Our Inhospitable Cities: An Incitement to Unrest*.[21] Mitscherlich disputed the ancient reputation that cities were the source of all evils, noting how remarkably "city firm" the civic loyalties of the German population remained even in the wake of their communities' complete destruction. Taking cities as inevitable for modern industrial societies, Mitscherlich concerned himself with how they might be rendered more humane. Mitscherlich saw hope for giving succor to civilization's discontents—returning to a late Freudian social-psychological project, if in a decidedly less pessimistic posture than that of its Viennese originator—through relatively simple improvements in the civic experience, though he cautioned that this was not a matter of formal regional planning alone. From his methodological point of view, these were ultimately questions of socialization and individualization. For Mitscherlich, that process shifted so conclusively onto the dwelling that he declared: "Show me your residence and I'll tell you who you are." Given such stakes, Mitscherlich criticized postwar architecture, "most of which naively reflects the rigid, practically caste-ridden societal norms," citing (in a rare concrete example) its failure to provide children with the kind of unregimented space for play that was needed to generate personal attachments and a sense of place. Yet while he acknowledged that these were rather more fundamental questions than architecture could address, he forcefully condemned the "weak-spirited, insufficient solution of building and planning housing at such a scale, in such mindless rows, and with such deficient 'side space' for play and relaxation, without vibrant meeting places—not to speak of internal deficiencies—as has been the case with us since the end of the war."[22]

Mitscherlich was by no means the only German social scientist in the 1960s attempting to educe the relationship between urban form and democratic society. German sociologists were particularly attentive to urban issues.[23] A 1960 article in *Bauwelt*, entitled "Neighborhood or Urbanity," introduced the sociologist Hans Paul Bahrdt to the discussion of urban quality of life.[24] Many of his major works subsequently focused on the contributions sociology might make to urbanism. In his 1961 book *The Modern Metropolis: Sociological Reflections on City Planning*, Bahrdt introduced the concept of "the public sphere" (*Öffentlichkeit*—literally "publicness") into the discussion, tracing the roots of modern metropolitan life to medieval free cities, whose markets provided a public sphere (of individuals truncated into economic actors) distinct from the responsibilities of professional or private life. Looking at the recent history of cities, Bahrdt noted the gradual impoverishment of the street as a public space from a site mixing various means of transportation with other activities into one dominated by the needs of cars alone. Consequently, while Bahrdt did not intuitively disdain the traditional block pattern of, say, Hobrecht's Berlin—if anything he lamented the erosion of its urban public space—his observation of social usage in a motorized era led him to ultimately reject such older forms as inappropriate: "Traditional city planning forms were once by and large sensible. The city's rules of life were visible in them. But because we use them differently today, they have become meaningless." Finally, while he endorsed many of the dominant planning ideals (automobile readiness, functional reorganization, transit segregation, etc.), Bahrdt called on city planners to create the conditions for balanced public and private spheres.[25]

Bahrdt's concept of the public sphere became a touchstone for social scientific critiques of planning throughout the period. The name generally associated with this idea, however, is Jürgen Habermas, as a result of his 1961 *Habilitationschrift*, translated in 1989 as *The Structural Transformation of the Public Sphere: An Inquiry into a Category of Bourgeois Society*.[26] Both Bahrdt and Habermas had studied in Göttingen in the early 1950s.[27] Habermas' theory of the public sphere looked to a later period, namely, the democratic revolutions of the eighteenth century and the industrial capitalist developments that subverted them in the nineteenth. Habermas was also primarily concerned with the media and political institutions, rather than the urban locus as per Bahrdt. Habermas and his collaborators at Frankfurt's

Institute for Social Research were concerned with sociological diagnoses of the authoritarian, anti-democratic tendencies latent in postwar German society. By the mid-1960s, Habermas was engaged in a prolonged debate with Herbert Marcuse regarding the implications of technology and technocratic sensibilities for democratic society.[28] The terms and ideas of Bahrdt, Habermas, and Marcuse penetrated multiple social scientific discussions of West German planning during the 1960s—the concept of "structural transformation," for example, even turns up in the title of practitioner Rudolf Hillebrecht's 1964 book *The Consequences of Economic and Social Structural Transformation for City Planning*.[29] Bahrdt, however, was the initial presence, and the only one of the three to address himself directly to the planning profession and its organs.

Yet Bahrdt was not alone in making a social scientific critique of Germany's urban renewal order. Young Freiburg political scientist and sociologist Hans Oswald took a similar perspective. Oswald's 1966 book *The Overrated City: A Contribution of Communal Sociology toward City Planning* argued that residents of industrial cities were attached to "translocal" structures and organizations, weakening the socialization of the immediate community. Neighborhood planning (in the Garden Cities tradition) and anti-urban critiques generally, according to Oswald, were out of touch with these administrative changes that distinguished modern urban reality from the medieval ideal, and they only served to intensify democratic apathy. Working on a planning project that sought to transform suburban developments into a Palatinate village, Oswald was struck by the planners' unreflective physical determinism, so uninformed by "real life in cities": "In my work I encountered a series of problems and difficulties with practitioners. It was amazing how many unexamined assumptions about modern society lay in the proposals of city planners. In some places it is taken as a matter of course that it is possible and even imperative to revitalize preindustrial neighborhoods through a certain building type. It is amazing how little most of those responsible for city planning know about the actual life of those cities. The literary statements of famous architects and planners demonstrate that this experience is not confined to isolated cases."[30]

Also in 1966, Alexander Mitscherlich left Heidelberg for Frankfurt's Sigmund Freud Institute, where he encouraged young researchers like Heide Berndt to explore psychoanalytic and sociological approaches to the city. With a strong awareness of American sociological urbanists, including Herbert Gans, Marc Fried, David Riesman, Jane Jacobs, and Kevin Lynch, as well as Bahrdt, Habermas, and Marcuse, Berndt concluded that functionalism had ceased to be a functional architecture. Architects now needed "to develop an aesthetically novel and highly psychically differentiated formal language." While noting that "a revival of eclecticism stimulates only the fetishistic artistic pleasure," she suggested that "satirical application" of older styles could bring today's materials to life—an idea that anticipated the work of so-called postmodern architects decades later.[31] Influenced by both Mitscherlich and Bahrdt, she adapted the methodology of the latter's 1957 study of conceptions of society among the working class for her own 1965 thesis, published in 1968 as *Conceptions of Society among City Planners*.[32] Later, she took up Bahrdt's critique of the deficient public sphere in modernist planning. She lamented planners' impoverished proposals for the public realm, which amounted merely to "unstructured open space between monumental buildings." For Berndt, the most vivid illustration was municipalities' inability to construct generous public facilities, such as subways: "Urban access systems that once anchored the public realm through representative spaces are increasingly confined to merely technical transport functions." The constraints were certainly fiscal, but such explanations made the losses no less detrimental.[33]

Such sociological critiques of the urban renewal order presented difficult questions to its adherents. They pointed at weaknesses in the social assumptions the modernist movement held dear. In 1965 the German architectural establishment welcomed a translation of Christian Norberg-Schulz's 1963 *Intentions in Architecture* as a contribution from what Siegfried Gideon called CIAM's third generation, who would gently revise (and thereby reinforce) the pioneers of modernism. A practicing architect, Norberg-Schulz advanced an argument drawing heavily on architectural history as well as semantics and other theoretical fields to investigate the meaning of buildings for their users. Dissatisfied with the schism within the architectural profession and with the specter of unplanned chaos, Norberg-Schulz characterized the Bauhaus as a cleansing impulse, but one he sought to place on a better foundation of psychological and sociological understanding.[34] By then, this was an attempt to salvage a set of urbanistic principles under heavy suspicion.

5 Outsider's Revolt
Jane Jacobs and Outright Rejection from beyond the Urbanist Establishment

Jacobs' Ladder: Storming the Urbanist Establishment

By the mid-1950s, the urban renewal order had engendered a core of professional critiques. Housing reformers such as Catherine Bauer and Charles Abrams, originally leaders calling for federal urban renewal legislation, were now openly critical of the outcomes.[1] Architect and planner Percival Goodman and his brother Paul had urged the democratization of the planning process since their 1947 book *Communitas: Means of Livelihood and Ways of Life*.[2] No sooner had Walter Gropius and his colleagues seemingly consolidated the legacy of modernist urbanism at the "Harvard Bauhaus" than a swarm of challenges materialized. Harvard design school dean and CIAM president Josep Lluís Sert and other members of the founding generation were irritated by the British delegation to the ninth congress of CIAM in 1953 at Aix, where Peter and Alison Smithson scuttled the proposal for a universal charter of habitat with their emphasis on old-style urban neighborhoods. Nagging doubts from within the urbanist establishment were soon joined by the forceful attacks of unsympathetic outsiders.

Responding to such challenges, Sert organized an urban design conference at Harvard in 1956, inviting architects, planners, and influential figures in urbanism (Edmund Bacon, Victor Gruen, Charles Abrams, Pittsburgh mayor David Lawrence, Richard Neutra, Gyorgy Kepes, Hideo Sasaki, Garrett Eckbo, and M.I.T. and Havard faculty members Reginald Isaacs, Frederick Adams, and Lloyd Rodwin).[3] Sert also invited *Architectural Forum* to send a representative; when the New York journal's editor canceled, he sent as a substitute a forty-year-old assistant editor named Jane Jacobs to address the influential gathering—though at the time her responsibilities with the magazine "consisted mainly of writing captions."[4] Within five years of that conference, the unknown Jacobs overshadowed nearly every figure in American urbanism.

At a minimum, Jane Jacobs' work for the *Architectural Forum* had brought her into contact with the leading practitioners of postwar urbanism. Gradually she began covering various urban renewal projects. In 1954, Jacobs wrote a series on Edmund Bacon's celebrated work in Philadelphia, which she praised on the basis of sketches he provided. But upon visiting the completed projects later, she concluded that those paper plans belied a horrible reality, and she felt deceived.[5] She observed an unsettling social phenomenon in Philadelphia's renewal developments: "Everything that had been there was bulldozed. Everything was new but the streets were deserted. There was no one around. Everyone was over on the other, older, street." When she pointed this out to Bacon, she remembered, "it was absolutely uninteresting to him. How things worked didn't interest him. He wasn't concerned about its attractiveness to people. His notion was totally aesthetic, divorced from everything else."[6]

Jacobs described the experience as "a revelation." Thereafter she was suspicious of design proposals, which "always looked so seductive" but often failed to anticipate the disastrous social and economic results of their implementation.[7] Precisely because of what she identified as his fixation on appearances in Philadelphia, Jacobs would regularly credit Bacon in particular for inspiring her to develop what became the most vigorous attack on the urban renewal order.

Jacobs was trained as neither architect nor scholar; in fact, she held only a high school diploma, augmented by a few semesters of continuing education courses at Columbia University. But in her first public appearance before the credentialed opinion makers of transatlantic urbanism she proved unbowed, seizing the opportunity to pose an outsider's dissent to the prevailing verities of the urban renewal order. In her 1956 Harvard address she condemned modernist projects because, "in most urban development plans, the unbuilt space is a giant bore," then proceeded to the unorthodox suggestion that architects should strive to make their outdoor spaces "at least as vital as the slum sidewalk." She argued that social impoverishment was as profound a danger as the substandard housing that planners sought to eradicate. She complained: "We are greatly misled by talk about bringing the suburb into the city." Further, she urged planners to "respect strips of chaos" such as "the plaza, the marketplace, and the forum." In conclusion, she suggested that planners would do well to "look at old lively parts of the city" and dispense with their elitist antipathy toward commercial activities. Architects should pay more attention to designing laundries, mailrooms, and other unnoticed places of informal contact. Jacobs thus chastened urbanists to stop styling themselves as heroic artists, treating the cityscape as an easel to display buildings. Instead, designers needed to become sensitive to the social use of space.[8]

Jacobs' Harvard performance caught the attention of the eminence grise of American urbanism, Lewis Mumford, who declared her "analysis of the functions of the city is sociology of the first order; and none of the millions being squandered by the Ford Foundation on 'Urban Research' will produce anything that has a minute fraction of your insight and common sense." Encouraging her to reach a wider audience, he noted, "Your worst opponents are the old fogies who imagine that Le Corbusier (1922–25) is the last word in urbanism."[9] A wider audience was soon provided by *Fortune* editor William H. Whyte, Jr. Whyte brought Jacobs together with the ideas emerging from Britain's *Architectural Review* (represented by Gordon Cullen and Ian Nairn) for a contribution to *Fortune's* series "The Exploding Metropolis."[10] Her *Fortune* piece, in turn, attracted the attention of the Rockefeller Foundation, which offered Jacobs a grant to turn her ideas into a book.

The Rockefeller Foundation sponsored a conference on urban design at the University of Pennsylvania in the fall of 1958, again convening many opinion makers of American urbanism, including figures from the Penn School of Fine Arts (Perkins, Mumford, Kahn) as well as others affiliated with Harvard or M.I.T. (Kevin Lynch, I. M. Pei; see fig. 5.1). Jane Jacobs was by then in the midst of researching her book, and the Rockefeller Foundation supported the conference in part to stimulate her work. Jacobs was attracted to the approach of Lynch, which emphasized the subjective experience of city dwellers. She was not, however, receptive to the Joint Center's vision of urbanism. Rodwin and Meyerson met with Jacobs and encouraged her to adopt a methodology that involved survey samples of resident perceptions in housing projects. But she preferred her own critical point of view to one with social scientific authority, which, she felt, legitimized urban renewal.[11]

Figure 5.1 In the late 1950s, architectural journalist Jane Jacobs waded into middle of the urbanist establishment with a controversial critique of urban renewal and modernist planning generally. A group photo from the 1958 conference on urban design criticism, sponsored by the University of Pennsylvania and the Rockefeller Foundation, shows her (*in profile with purse on shoulder*) alongside many leading figures, including (*from left to right*) William Wheaton, Lewis Mumford, Ian McHarg, J. B. Jackson, David Crane, Louis Kahn, G. Holmes Perkins, Arthur Holden [assistant to Dean Perkins], Catherine Bauer Wurster, Leslie Cheek, Jr. [Chadbourne Gilpatric is obscured], Mrs. Eric Larrabee, Kevin Lynch, Gordon Stephenson, Nanine Clay, and I. M. Pei. (Photo courtesy of Grady Clay.)

Articulating the rationale behind her book, Jacobs explained that the urbanist establishment struck her as "intellectually very moribund," with little self-criticism of its basic assumptions and orthodoxies or curiosity about how big cities really work. In her view, current conceptions of urbanism were based on "two dominant and very compelling mental images of the city." On the one hand was "the image of the city in trouble, an inhuman mass of masonry, a chaos of happenstance growth, a place starved of the simple decencies and amenities of life, beset with so many accumulated problems it makes your head swim." In direct contrast, "the other powerful image is that of the rebuilt city, the antithesis of all that the unplanned city represents, a carefully planned panorama of projects and green spaces, a place where functions are sorted out instead of jumbled together, a place of light, air, sunshine, dignity and order for all." Jacobs countered that both of those conceptions was "disastrously superficial. Both of them neglect—they simply overlook—the most fundamental part of any useful image of the city—the way people use the city. And so these powerful mental pictures have become hindrances and blocks to intelligent observation and action."[12]

To break though these habits of thought, Jacobs set to work gathering "contrary data from real life," drawing examples from cities across the United States and paying particular attention to Boston, Philadelphia, and New York. Rather than facilitating social progress, she saw urban renewal projects destroying neighborhoods' natural propensity for "spontaneous unslumming." Jacobs was convinced of the "regenerative forces inherent in energetic American metropolitan economies" (the dynamism of "urbanization combined with industrialization"), especially if they could be freed from obstacles like a lack of financing and unfair competition from government-subsidized mortgages in the suburbs. When this unslumming process succeeded (as Jacobs believed it had in Boston's North End, San Francisco's North Beach, or her own West Village), it did so because those with means to leave chose instead to stay in a former slum, thereby increasing the neighborhood's "range and prosperity of enterprises." They did so, however, for reasons of personal affection, often connected to the "genuine exuberance and interesting range of diversity" in the public life of the sidewalks and other institutions. The only major countervailing factor to such regeneration appeared to be intolerance for racial or ethnic diversity, which, as she saw it, arose spontaneously.[13]

Yet the debilitating effect of racial flight was actually not the only development that dampened Jacobs' confidence in the automatic market processes of urban improvement. She was also troubled by the specter of oversuccess. Just as problematic as an exodus from the neighborhood was a rush of popularity. The "self-destruction of diversity" resulted when an area's magnetism priced out the very characteristics which made it desirable. Jacobs interpreted this "killing with kindness" as the "malfunction" of an economic process which begins as salutary.

While she was harsh on the effects of government urban renewal programs, Jacobs' lingering concerns about the volatility of the urban real estate market in particular left room for a vision of more constructive public intervention. Her essentially moderate position proposed government "windbreaks, so to speak, which can stand against the gusts of economic pressures." These might take the form of zoning and taxing for diversity (like historic preservation, but less stagnant, considering building ages, sizes, and rates of replacement) or strategic placement of public construction ("to anchor diversity by standing staunch in the midst of *different* surrounding uses, while money rolls around them and begs to roll over them").[14] Rather than leaving many urban neighborhoods pinned between a "drought" of private lending and cataclysmic "floods" of federal urban renewal money, government could offer rent subsidies and guaranteed mortgages to stimulate the provision of low- and moderate-income housing provided by private enterprise (and thereby avoid the stigma associated with public housing). "Conventional credit will reappear too in a blacklisted district," she predicted, "if the federal government will guarantee mortgages as generously as it does for suburban development and new [urban renewal] projects."[15]

After almost two and a half years of work, Jacobs completed her manuscript at the end of 1960. *The Death and Life of Great American Cities* opened with sweeping criticisms of most incursions into the urban fabric, from monumental civic centers of the City Beautiful era to contemporary modernist housing projects. Jacobs lumped them all together as totalitarian for their intolerance of the fundamental complexities of contemporary urban life. She then described a healthy urban order in terms of four "generators," or conditions, for diversity: (1) primary mixed uses, (2) small blocks, (3) buildings of various kinds and ages, and (4) population density (concentration). Most of her book is devoted to explicating these qualities and their social and economic virtues. Significantly, each of these four tenets stood in deliberate contrast to the fundamental axioms of modernist urbanism: zoning against mixed uses, pedestrian superblocks, demolition, and open-space clearance. From Jacobs' standpoint, the urbanist establishment was overly aesthetic, superficial in its approach to urban problems, and blind to "the order that underlies the superficial chaos of cities." Above all, the urban renewal order was too totalizing. As a corrective, Jacobs included some suggestions regarding community organizing and shifting power toward the neighborhood level.

Jacobs' search for more sensitive, inclusive alternatives in design and politics make her a significant harbinger of broad shifts in the postwar United States, against government, technocratic experts, and other established authorities. Iron-ically, during this same period, Ayn Rand offered a widely read libertarian version of the Architect as Heroic Artist, in the protagonist of her best-selling 1943 novel *The Fountainhead*: Howard Roark would rather destroy his buildings than see his artistic vision compromised. A staunch free-market conservative, Rand was eager to testify before the House Un-American Activities Committee against her fellow screenwriters while she worked at the Hal Wallis studios during the late 1940s. By contrast, in 1952 Jacobs left the State Department's Overseas Information Agency in the wake of a series of McCarthy-era interrogations about her union activities on behalf of the United Public Workers of America. Thus, a more apt anteced-ent to Jacobs' condemnation of all top-down planning—conflating revolution-ary, left-liberal, and fascist or ultra-conservative ideologies—is the sweeping cautionary analysis in Hannah Arendt's 1951 *Totalitarianism*. But more than any previous text, Jacobs' book crystallized a mounting popular reaction against one of the mid-twentieth century's signature liberal policy regimes, the urban renewal order.

A Death and Life Experience: Ressentiment and the Reception of Jacobs' "Half-Brick" in the United States

The Death and Life of Great American Cities appeared in the fall of 1961 and was widely excerpted in the U.S. national press. Many of Jacobs' core ideas—about the shortcomings of urban renewal projects or the underrated worth of old urban neighborhoods—echoed numerous critiques already voiced within the urbanist establishment over the previous decade. In spite or perhaps precisely because of this, that establishment forcefully resisted her book. By 1962 Jacobs was being en-ergetically attacked by the most powerful urbanists of the time, including Robert Moses, Edward Logue, Edmund Bacon, Holmes Perkins, and even her erstwhile supporter Lewis Mumford.

Moses wrote a letter to her publisher, Random House, to condemn the book. "Aside from the fact that it is intemperate and inaccurate, it is also libelous," he charged.[16] Other tempers flared when the *Saturday Evening Post* adapted a section of Jacobs' book for its column "Speaking Out: The Voice of Dissent" under the stinging title "How City Planners Hurt Cities."[17] The *Post's* editor received an im-mediate response from University of Pennsylvania dean Holmes Perkins, who expressed shock "not because I would in any way oppose the expression of a contrary opinion" but because he felt Jacobs' "statements run quite counter to the facts." Referring to an urban renewal proposal she criticized in Boston, he assured the editor that the city's redevelopment authority's "program stated the North End is one of the most lively neighborhoods of Boston. It has a flavor and way of life which should be preserved, not destroyed. A clearance project for the North End would be an outrage and the city would never be the same." He concluded: "The Boston group are justly up in arms about this. I wish to protest the article with my whole heart."[18] Likewise, Boston Redevelopment Authority director Edward Logue sent a letter insisting, "Just to keep the record very straight, we have no plans whatsoever for clearance in the North End."[19]

Jacobs urged her editor not to relent, utterly unconvinced by the statements of Perkins and Logue: "No matter how fervent the planners' protestations of love and understanding for the North End and intent to 'preserve it,' the use of urban renewal tools can only harm the North End." After all, she noted, current federal urban renewal regulations militated against preservation, since eligibility for funds required that administrators "cite as flaws the very qualities that make the North End healthy and lively, i.e. mixed uses, obsolete street patterns, lack of open spaces, etc." They had thus already certified the area as a slum, blighted, deteriorated or deteriorating. More revealing, she noted, was that Logue, "who is supposed to be so enlightened about the North End, and in whose hands its future is entrusted, is the same Ed Logue who told me that the best thing that could happen to San Francisco would be another fire, if it hurt nobody but wiped away everything existing, because replanning and rebuilding of San Francisco is needed from the ground up."[20]

Many in the urbanist establishment highlighted Jacobs' lack of credentials—and her gender—as a sampling of reviews demonstrates: Declaring that "Mrs. Jacobs clearly knows so little about planning that she continually, or intentionally, confuses it with architecture and, especially, with public housing and site design," the executive director of the American Society of Planning Officials, Dennis O'Harrow, said she would cause "a lot of harm," and denounced her as an irresponsible demagogue: "Mrs. Jacobs has presented the world with a document that will be grabbed by screwballs and reactionaries and used to fight civic improvement and urban renewal projects for years to come." Pittsburgh housing administrator Alfred Tronzo dismissed her for "star-gazing from the second floor window of a Greenwich Village flat—while anxiously awaiting the 3 a.m. closing of the neighborhood pubs as an omen that all is well in the land." Roger Starr of New York's Citizens Housing and Planning Council accused her of living in a naive fantasyland straight out of Grace Moore's Hollywood musicals: "She describes her folksy urban place on Hudson Street with such spirit and womanly verve that she has made a considerable number of readers believe it really exists. She has even set herself to wondering why the rest of the world isn't like Mooritania and how it could be made more so."[21] *American City* magazine similarly mocked her praise for old neighborhoods:

The author is particularly enamored of an area called the North End in Boston. Here, apparently, is the full flowering of the American Way of Life. Here is the place where European tourists should stop to learn of the benefits of a democratic society based on the freedoms granted in the Constitution and the Bill of Rights. Let Khrushchev see the North End and he would immediately stop this nonsense that communism will bury us. . . .

The author might have included a few pictures of this New England Paradise. But she has not an illustration in the entire volume. Apparently she reasons that a thousand words are better than one picture.[22]

Many dismissed her critiques as unrealistic—a New York planner noted, "Some of us perhaps wish we really had the extensive powers ascribed to us by Mrs. Jacobs"—or at least misplaced: "The vast power and actual activity of administrators, politicians, real estate men, developers, legislators, lawyers, engineers who dabble in planning, and others who maintain their real stranglehold on our cities, appears somehow very insignificant in this book."[23] Despite their dismissals, Jacobs' challenge to the legitimacy of newly credentialed professional expertise seemed to stir genuine disdain and alarm in the urbanist ranks: "It is wrong-headed, patchily informed, often just silly, and so romantically sentimental about the crowded and muddled type of city that serious planners may be disposed to discount the entertainment value that made it a best-seller."[24] One housing administrator quipped that *Death and Life* proved "the old adage that a half-truth is similar to a half-brick, because it can be hurled further." A reviewer noted: "It is the only book that we know of which is quoted in context both by liberals and conservatives. It has the further distinction of winning kudos both from the *Saturday Evening Post* and the *Reporter* magazine. It is an exciting book, but scarcely constructive."[25] An official agreed that the book "is going to do a lot of harm, throw a lot of monkey wrenches in the machinery. But we are going to have to live with it. So batten down the hatches, boys, we are in for a big blow!"[26]

Most treacherous, given the encouragement he offered earlier, was Lewis Mumford's *New Yorker* review, condescendingly titled "Mother Jacobs' Home Remedies for Urban Cancer," which portrayed her as an amateurish housewife.[27] In private, Mumford was even more angry: "In asking for a comment, you are in effect suggesting that an old surgeon give public judgment on the work of a confident but sloppy novice, operating to remove an imaginary tumor to which the youngster has erroneously attributed the patient's affliction, whilst over-looking major impairments in the actual organs. Surgery has no useful contribution to make in such a situation, except to sew up the patient and dismiss the bungler."[28]

Inconsistently, reviewers accused Jacobs of being both uninformed *and un-*

original. O'Harrow wrote: "Every valid criticism of urban development that she makes has been made by planners for years. If she had bothered to seek out real planners, she would have known this."[29] Such an acknowledgment highlights the urbanist establishment's particular sensitivity to Jacobs' attack because it came (and brashly) during an insecure moment of reform and transition. Historian Robert Fishman attributes Mumford's venom to his recognition that "Jacobs' blunt and irreverent treatment of the regionalist tradition [expressed] some of his own growing self-doubts."[30] Rather than coming at the these questions from deep left field, as many of the reviews implied, Jacobs was articulating and popularizing ideas that had already taken hold in certain quarters.

A public demonstration of these incongruities occurred when Jacobs joined Edmund Bacon and Edward Logue at a panel discussion in the Museum of Modern Art on February 11, 1962. Bacon defended Philadelphia's Benjamin Franklin Parkway (an older City Beautiful design also criticized by Jacobs) and, declaring that Jacobs was blind to his accomplishments, invited listeners to come to Philadelphia to see for themselves. (Jacobs promptly seconded the motion that everyone go and see what he had done.) Bacon attacked Jacobs' tendency to romanticize older areas, saying she overlooked the existence of true slums. He cited Philadelphia crime statistics to dispute her correlation of crime rates with open space. According to an observer, "his main point was that her conclusions did not follow from facts at all—that she rarely backed up her statements with statistics, and that many examples which she used were actually the opposite of what she said they were." Jacobs answered that "her main reason for the book was to find out how a city works—what 'urbanity' is." She endorsed more renewal and more planning, but only if "based on a new attitude which is sensitive to the real values of the city—which understands 'urbanity.' We should not plan to *allow* diversity, we must *generate* diversity. We should look at the city to see what we like, not what we don't like. We should put in that which is missing, not take out that which we don't like." Jacobs denounced the work of Bacon (and I. M. Pei) in Philadelphia's Society Hill and opposed its extension as a model for Logue's Boston projects in the North End.[31]

Logue, for his part, joined Jacobs in criticizing planning as currently practiced for being "too much a branch of the Fine Arts. That most planners care more about what their colleagues think of their plans than the public." He endorsed rehabilitation and community participation in renewal. But he also lashed out at Jacobs. Logue reported on a visit he made to Jacobs' celebrated West Greenwich neighborhood, relating how "he had visited Hudson Street the previous evening (at 8:00 p.m.) and aside from the truck traffic gash that ran through it, he saw very few 'eyes' looking out on the street—only two of ten stores were open (a pizza

Figure 5.2 Jane Jacobs and her daughter (*standing*) chat with neighbors in front of their New York home at 555 Hudson Street, evoking the civic culture of the sidewalks she celebrated in *The Death and Life of Great American Cities* (1961). A dense mixture of residential and commercial uses (including the famous White Horse Tavern on the corner) occupies various old buildings. The photograph accompanied a 1961 *New York Times* story about residents' opposition to the proposed redevelopment of fourteen blocks of Manhattan's West Village neighborhood. (With permission: Ernest Sisto/The New York Times/Redux.)

parlor and the White Horse Bar), a store at the prime location was vacant (she said that this was a sculptor's studio). Furthermore he said that it was a drab area, which did not seem well maintained, that there were papers on the streets, that the buildings were ugly and unkempt, and finally that he did not think this would become the model for urban America."[32]

Jacobs responded that "the West Village was not used in her book because it was an exceptional example, but because it was a good average area of no outstanding quality which had the diversity and urbanity that she believed in" (fig. 5.2). Such modesty aside, Jacobs' critique was pointed enough to rattle the urbanist establishment. Its response, a defensive one, recommitted to the urban renewal order and probably stiffened internal resistance to change. But Jacobs had also illuminated some open secrets, turning a closed discussion into a public debate. Thereafter, the fate of the urban renewal order would depend less on expert authorities and academic debates and more on the political mobilization of nonprofessional citizens.

Urbanists Abroad: Placing Jacobs in the Transatlantic Urban Conversation

Writing in the *Observer* in 1965, expatriate Paul Mandel offered "A Love Letter to London" in which he implored his British readers to appreciate what their traditions (in distinction to dutiful American planners and a "Germanic sense of sterility and order") had preserved:

> Many of the Londoners I know take for granted the pleasantness and diversion that a perfectly ordinary walk in their city can supply. Not we Americans. A countrywoman of mine, an articulate New Yorker named Jane Jacobs has for years been defending almost alone the charm of cities and the variety and warmth they can generate. . . . Well London I claim, is Jane Jacobs's land, the place she's been talking about all along. London is one city still where the planners and traffic engineers haven't been able to wreck the surprise of coming around a corner and finding a tiny bombed out church or a busy bookmaker's or a window full of dressed pheasants, or four people playing tennis on a March morning.[33]

And while Mandel noted that London's planners "are *trying* to wreck it"—citing Dunstan House obscuring St. Paul's Cathedral, speculation in Hempstead, and highway construction—he felt the city might take comfort from "the fortunately congenital inefficiency of its changers and fixers."

But while those in the Townscape movement had established a skeptical view of the urban renewal order, and a decade had passed since the Smithsons had celebrated "the cycle of street activity," many British urbanists were just as hostile to Jacobs' ideas as the planning establishment in United States.[34] *Town and Country Planning* published a dismissive 1962 reply to *Death and Life*, entitled "Manahatta Plies Her Nails," concluding that "the Americans seem to us to be even further from success in tackling the planning and other governmental problems of urban agglomerations than we are." With undisguised disdain, the review referred "students of comparative futility" to an explanation of why Americans like Jacobs opposed metropolitan planning, as articulated by the U.S. Housing and Home Finance Agency's Milton P. Semen: "We Americans have never gotten over our taste for diversity and diffusion of power in government—another term for checks and balances—or our deeply ingrained suspicion about the desirability or even the safety of vesting too many responsibilities and too much power in any one monolithic political structure."[35] In sharp contrast to Jacobs, most British planners supported government-mandated decentralization of cities. The American woman thus smacked of political traditions largely unfashionable in the era of robust government programs under Labour prime minister Harold Wilson.

True to form, the *Architectural Review* was more sympathetic. The publication's director and chairman Hubert de Cronin Hastings (a.k.a. Ivor de Wolfe) immediately welcomed Jacobs' message in exuberant terms as "a warm but high wind across the Atlantic and (one hopes and believes) a hot handshake" for the proponents of the British Townscape movement. He declared *Death and Life* "a far more important work than Lewis Mumford's pretentious *City in History*," as well as "a must for all who believe the urban consequences of those odd bedfellows, Ebenezer Howard and Le Corbusier, to be the spawn of the devil working through his chosen vessels." The *Review* seconded Jacobs in warning Britons against elaborate redevelopment schemes that segregated pedestrians from automobiles, urging them instead to bring cars to heel on shared city streets.[36]

All that said, the *Architectural Review*'s affinity for Jacobs also obscured a fundamental difference in their point of view. The *Review*'s neo-Picturesque visual philosophy affirmed the haphazard received vernacular as an appropriate stylistic complement to British democracy. Jacobs' attacks on prescriptive modernist planning focused primarily on its being out of touch with the economic, political, and social dynamics of cities. Jacobs was uninterested in the aesthetic debate. For her, attractiveness was defined functionally as the ability to attract lively use. Robust functional diversity was fundamentally more important to her than superficial stylistic distinctions. Nevertheless, any district that exhibited the kind of complex diversity of uses that she advocated would almost unavoidably possess buildings of various ages and styles. Jacobs certainly acknowledged this, but she did not share Townscape's concern with the aesthetic or symbolic value of such a mix.

Such distinctions notwithstanding, Jacobs quickly became a touchstone in Britain. When Camillo Sitte's long-forgotten 1889 masterpiece on urban design, *Der Städtebau nach seinen künstlerischen Grundsätzen* (City planning according to artistic principles), reappeared in a 1965 English translation, the *Journal of the Royal Society of Arts* equated it with *Death and Life*: "Sitte's book was probably to his readers at the end of the nineteenth century what [Jacobs'] is to her readers today. Both have protested that too many people were indifferent to the qualities of what existed and had destroyed the achievements of the past without putting in their place anything of equal value in design or social purpose."[37]

The editors of *Architects' Journal* nominated Jane Jacobs Woman of the Year in 1962. By the time of a convention of the Royal Institute of British Architects in 1967, no less than the parliamentary secretary of housing and local government, Wayland Kennet, declared himself an admirer of Jacobs, describing her as "one of the most original minds of our generation, a breath of fresh air, always three jumps ahead of most of us and always one jump ahead of any of us."[38] Over just five years, Jacobs had burrowed into the very core of the British urban renewal order.

■

When *The Death and Life of Great American Cities* appeared in German in 1963, it resonated with other outsider critiques of the urban renewal order.[39] The following year, Berlin editor-publisher Wolf Jobst Siedler and photographer Elisabeth Niggemeyer published a paean to a city they saw being destroyed by modernist planning: "The Slain City: A Farewell to the Putto and the Street, the Square and the Tree."[40] This collection of pictures and essays (most originally published during the late 1950s) became a coffee table manifesto, juxtaposing images of lively, old, pre-renewal West Berlin cityscapes with those of barren modernist redevelopments (figs. 5.3, 5.4). Niggemeyer agreed to the polemical project in part because she "had just read Jane Jacobs," whom she would later visit in New York.[41]

Explaining the motivation for this "exercise in ironic melancholy" during a television interview years later, Siedler recalled how relieved he was, returning home to war-ravaged Berlin as a twenty-year-old soldier in 1947, to find the city's characteristic streetscape at least skeletally intact.[42] His greatest shock and disappointment was to come with the "second destruction," when urban planners subsequently undertook a systematic "demolition for reconstruction." There was no question for him that "modern city planning did more to alter the face of old Berlin than the American fifth bomber fleet."[43]

Siedler, like Jacobs, was often dismissed as too conservative or even reactionary, which was not altogether inappropriate. For example, he approved *Die Zeit's*

Figures 5.3 and 5.4 A sympathetic portrait of Berlin's traditional streetscape, contrasted with a bleak housing redevelopment, both from the Charlottenburg district in the early 1960s. The two photographs by Elisabeth Niggemeyer illustrated a 1964 paean to the postwar city facing what author Wolf Jobst Siedler called a "second destruction" at the hands of modernist urban renewal, *The Slain City: A Farewell to the Putto and the Street, the Square and the Tree.* (Source: Wolf Jobst Siedler and Elisabeth Niggemeyer, *Die gemordete Stadt: Abgesang auf Putte und Straße, Platz und Baum* [Berlin: Herbig, 1964]. Used with permission of Elisabeth Pfefferkorn-Niggemeyer.)

description of him as Germany's only left-wing Tory, or, in his own words, more old conservative than neoconservative.[44] Yet Jacobs also found a receptive audience among German social scientists and even practicing planners. Hans Paul Bahrdt readily acknowledged Jacobs' "unmistakable influence" throughout his work. He honored her in his 1967 *Humane City Building: Reflections on Housing Policy and City Planning for a Near Future*, which he described as a "political pamphlet, polemicizing against the state of affairs" and arguing for "humane thought and action." As he explained it, Jacobs had much to teach academic social scientists: "Even though she is not a trained sociologist, Jacobs has in our opinion given urban sociologists a lesson in exactly how to practice their discipline. The first three chapters of her book are almost exclusively concerned with the sidewalk." Bahrdt devoted a section of the book to what he termed "Points of Confusion in J. Jacobs," in which he defended her from those who misinterpreted her work while he blamed her sweeping condemnation of all planning approaches for much misunderstanding. Her "grandiose book" would have made fewer enemies and a more constructive contribution "if she at least sketched out the variety of different recipes necessary for the stabilization of urban diversity" in assorted cities. (His own appendix included a set of proposals for transportation systems, residential districts, and a hypothetical city plan.) In general, Bahrdt's approach to the planning process was less confrontational than Jacobs'. In his concluding chapter, "Planning as Political Negotiation," he asserted that "objectivity and politicization are not contradictory," tried to reconcile "expert knowledge with the public sphere of politics," and urged cooperation between planners and sociologists.[45]

Moving beyond his earlier analyses into a more politicized posture, Bahrdt defended the goal of an "urbanized city" not only against the attacks of "the now gradually fading conservative civilization critique" but also from "certain modernists who believe that modern communication and transportation technologies have rendered irrelevant the concentration of human settlements in the historically developed form of the city." In response to influential planner Rudolf Hillebrecht's pronouncement that "no one should be forced to live in monuments"—that is, heavily ornamented buildings like those of Stalinist Moscow or East Berlin—Bahrdt retorted that since the functionalism of the Bauhaus had degraded to an equally formulaic pose, it was hardly different in this respect from nineteenth-century "facade thinking" or fascist pseudomonumentality.[46] Recognizing people's "urge for self-expression," Bahrdt thought that "representation in architecture and planning should be affirmed"—though only in subordination to individual housing, neighborhood, and transportation designs.

By the 1960s, at a time when renewal projects were just beginning to gather momentum, Rudolf Hillebrecht (fig. 5.5), planner of postwar Hamburg and

DER SPIEGEL

13. JAHRGANG · NR. 23
3. JUNI 1959 · 1 DM
AUSGABE BERLIN
POSTVERLAGSORT BERLIN

VERKEHR AN DER LEINE
Hannovers Stadtplaner Rudolf Hillebrecht (siehe „Städtebau")

Figure 5.5 Das Wunder von Hannover. Germany's national newsmagazine, *Der Spiegel*, featured Rudolf Hillebrecht as the face of urban renewal in the 1959 cover story "The Miracle of Hannover." After working under Albert Speer during the Nazi years, Hillebrecht became the most influential city planner in postwar Germany, overseeing reconstruction of Hamburg and Hannover. He also chaired Berlin's planning advisory board from 1957 to 1979. Like Robert Moses, Hillebrecht promoted auto-ready urbanism, constructing major traffic arteries into city centers, yet at the same time he encouraged social scientific planning studies and protected historic urban cores. (Source: *Der Spiegel* 23, no. 13 [June 3, 1959].)

Hannover and chair of Berlin's powerful planning advisory board from 1957 to 1979, unquestionably possessed "the highest national and international reputation of any of the German planners."[47] Economic resources were finally available to realize redevelopment proposals rooted in prewar functionalist dogma that had been on German planners' drawing boards since the early postwar years. Having already rebuilt areas destroyed during the war in keeping with modernist principles, German urbanists turned in earnest toward eradicating the surviving remnants of the nineteenth-century cityscape.[48] By and large, challenges to the prevailing planning paradigm—as when Siedler decried the second destruction—were effectively rebuffed by the professional establishment.

Hillebrecht responded to *Death and Life* with an essay, "From Ebenezer Howard to Jane Jacobs; or, Was It All Wrong?"[49] His influential answer was that no, it was not all wrong, and excessive esteem for older structures and related legal frameworks were nineteenth-century atavisms that jeopardized effective planning. Hillebrecht spoke at hundreds of meetings to counter public suspicion of planning, rooted in a lingering resentment of wartime controls and Nazi excesses, which made large-scale urban projects difficult in the immediate postwar period.[50]

Like his counterparts in the United States, Hillebrecht was a confident, forceful planner who initially spoke out against *Death and Life* as anti-planning. But he was also an urban thinker with a complex, and distinctly German, set of influences. He had trained with Walter Gropius at the end of the Weimar period but then went on to work also under the Nazi Albert Speer. As a city planner in the period of postwar reconstruction, Hillebrecht directed transportation modernization, pushing arterial roadways through Hamburg and Hannover to produce auto-ready cityscapes.[51]

Yet Hillebrecht was also careful to incorporate citizen participation into his planning; he had commissioned public opinion surveys and viewed sociology as the servant of good planning.[52] Most notably, he strove to maintain a dense, residential, mixed-use, pedestrian-friendly core at the center of any regional plan. This focus on *Nachbarschaftsplanung* (planning around a vibrant neighborhood) can be found as far back as various wartime plans, was discussed extensively by scholars like Bahrdt and Hans Oswald, and may have even predisposed German urbanists toward Jacobs' ideas.

Thus, it is not inexplicable that Hillebrecht eventually sought out Jacobs, visiting her Greenwich Village home and inviting her to tour his German projects. In early 1967, Jacobs accepted his invitation (her first trip overseas) and actually liked what she saw there. After touring Hillebrecht's work in Hannover, she told an audience of British architects that he, together with the *Architectural Review*'s Ian Nairn, were practically the only people "who really understand infilling as a very

Figures 5.6 and 5.7 A 1958 model for the Kreuzkirche neighborhood housing project in Hannover and an aerial photo of the completed redevelopment (the church at left) and environs in 1966, about the time that Jane Jacobs visited and lauded that city's urban renewal planning. Garden City influences, and even nearby traffic modernization, were integrated into a dense older cityscape. (Model © Landeshauptstadt Hannover, Stadtvermessungsamt, 1958. Photo courtesy of Historisches Museum Hannover.)

viable, functional way of planning."[53] Writing to her family in January 1967, she enthused: "In Hannover I actually see the kind of planning, all built, actually executed! that I have recommended! But this is not because of my book. It is because of Prof. Hillebrecht, the planner from here who came to see us in N.Y. He did it beginning in the late 1940s and early 1950s."[54]

This uncanny bond between Hillebrecht and Jacobs, who offered no illustrations, seldom commended designs, and balked at the work of most American planners, is a rare insight into her vision of a constructive role for planning. The approach to Nachbarschaftsplanung which made such an impression on Jacobs can be seen in Hannover's Kreuzkirche neighborhood. When Hillebrecht organized Germany's first major postwar building exhibition in 1951, he invited Hamburg planner Konstanty Gutschow to replace a damaged area with a mix of housing, including two-story row houses surrounded by five-story apartment blocks.[55] It is not immediately obvious why this kind of development impressed Jacobs, as the inner portion of the site, centered on a reconstructed church, resembles a superblock. Yet seen within the context of the old city in an aerial photograph from 1966, it does demonstrate awareness of the traditional streetscape, particularly reinforced by the perimeter buildings, and self-consciously affirms "urbanity" (Urbanität), as was characteristic of numerous postwar German planners (figs. 5.6, 5.7).[56] While this was certainly not the only planning model afoot in Germany (other portions of the 1951 Hannover exhibition went much further toward the superblock), it was a significant school of thought largely missing from the postwar planning Jacobs had encountered in the United States.

In Britain and Germany Jane Jacobs appears strikingly different from the almost reactionary anti-planner, the outsider and opposition figure perceived by U.S. urbanists. Those other nations gave her a consistently more positive reception, which suggests a faithful if fundamentally different interpretation of her ideas. In those contexts Jacobs appears less extreme, her ideas somehow less radical, less disruptive. British and German urbanists had either anticipated or were flexible enough to absorb such ideas, while the American planning establishment proved more rigid and doctrinaire, at least in its initial confrontation with Jacobs. As U.S. urbanists would soon discover, however, Jane Jacobs was just a harbinger of the much larger wave of popular opposition that urban renewal order was engendering.

Part III The Transatlantic Collapse of the Urban Renewal Order

American cities led the way in political backlash against the urban renewal order. The first phase of the revolt took shape around opposition to freeways. Neighborhood groups in New York and San Francisco organized to oppose specific road proposals in the mid-1950s. By 1959 they had defeated arteries planned for Washington Square and the Embarcadero. In the mid-1960s, Philadelphia's crosstown expressway proposal stirred up a vigorous resistance from residents of the South Street corridor, galvanizing accusations of racist planning. As with many comparable U.S. cases, these movements began with grassroots opposition from those directly affected by plans. Their ad hoc coalitions drew together long-term minority residents with white middle-class gentrifiers and gradually gained sympathy among some of the civic elite, including influential members of the media and legal professions. Eventually, publicity catalyzed a general opinion shift, wherein citizens stopped deferring to the authority of planning experts. While many opposition groups began by attacking the planning process directly via hearings, they ultimately succeeded in applying political pressure to elected officials by making dramatic appeals in the court of public opinion. As the 1960s progressed, more mayors abruptly began to overrule the elaborate highway proposals of their planning commissions, and these policy reversals indicated a major urban power shift.

Parallel anti-expressway movements erupted outside the United States. These also had grassroots origins and saw eventual success when elected officials swung behind the highway opponents' positions. Opening salvos in 1959 halted major projects in both London (the Piccadilly redevelopment) and Toronto (the Rosedale crosstown artery), and these emergent urban coalitions gained clout fighting freeways over the following decade. In 1971 a Conservative Ontario provincial government reversed the road-building agenda for central Toronto in response to public pressure; in London in 1973, the Labour Party made the issue central to its campaign platform and proceeded to enact a freeway moratorium upon election to the council majority.

The second wave of popular resistance against the urban renewal order challenged its broad slum clearance agenda. In principle, this came down to contesting the rhetoric of blight, defending maligned neighborhoods by redefining their characteristics as worthy of preservation. In practice, it was often a gritty fight by threatened residents against an entrenched redevelopment machine using every available professional, political, and legal means. Nowhere was this more clear than in the battle waged by New York's West Village neighborhood to lift its designation as a "blighted" slum eligible for redevelopment—terms of debate codified by city officials via new 1961 zoning laws that encouraged sharper segregation of property uses (residential, commercial, etc.), clearance to eradicate obsolete structures, and specific redevelopment proposals featuring high-rise construction.

Coincidentally, West Village resident Jane Jacobs was well prepared to defend the virtues of her community against its detractors, thanks to the arguments honed in her book. More important, she built upon the organizing tactics of the anti-road movement, successfully begun in Greenwich Village just a few years earlier. But the position of Jacobs' West Village community group was complicated by several countervailing pressures. Aside from the city's slum clearance proposal, the neighborhood faced two contradictory trends. First was disinvestment, in the form of dilapidating structures, the flight of white working-class residents, fears of minority immigration, and deindustrialization. At the same time, the community suffered affordability pressures due to speculators and some early signs of gentrification. Instability, much of it traceable to the uncertain aftermath of a collapsing centuries-old Manhattan waterfront transshipment economy, was their volatile lot.

Nevertheless, more than anything previous, the fight against a slum clearance proposal drew the neighborhood together and gave residents pride in a distinct community identity. Theirs proved a fierce battle for survival, confronting the urban renewal order directly with a multilevel strategy—vigorous grassroots organizing, legal challenges in court, effective use of public relations, savvy alliance building, and pressure on elected officials—which cumulatively staggered the "clearance-for-profit" approach pioneered by Robert Moses. Those citizens succeeded in driving a wedge, from the bottom up, into the alliance between planning experts, politicians, and private developers. The momentum of that success dovetailed with New York's nascent historic preservation movement (which had emerged separately out of concern for architectural treasures like Pennsylvania Station and Jefferson Market Courthouse) to enact districtwide protections.

In the wake of ad hoc freeway revolts and the emergence of pro-neighborhood groups like the West Villagers, the final phase in the fall of the urban renewal order was its rapid, systemic collapse on both sides of the Atlantic.

London witnessed a progression from anti-roadway and pro-neighborhood protests to a broad political sea change. A redevelopment proposal for the Covent Garden neighborhood (prepared in 1965–68) provoked grassroots resistance from residents. The resulting controversy touched off a crisis of faith throughout London's planning establishment, spurring hearings and even protest resignations across the spectrum, from of a leftist planning officer to a Conservative borough representative. Authorities withdrew the plan in 1973 in favor of a new approach emphasizing preservation, at least as far as the neighborhood's architecture was concerned. This occurred against a backdrop of structural weakening for long-standing political coalitions; in particular, Labour dominance of the capital city was diluted by the amalgamation of the Greater London Council to include conservative, outlying areas. After Labour politicians regained control of the council on an anti-freeway platform in 1973, local leaders in both parties signaled a turn away from the urban renewal order. Legislation from the national government also moved toward neighborhood improvement after Labour's return to power in 1974. The election of Conservative prime minister Margaret Thatcher in 1979 ushered in an unequivocal ideological break with strategic planning, urban and otherwise.

In New York as early as 1962, media portrayals and project reversals suggested a shift in the balance of power in the politics of planning. At the same time, federal legislative changes, incorporating more rehabilitation and resident participation, reflected pressures filtering up from the grass roots to Washington. While perhaps intended to blunt opposition, in practice the effect of these national policy responses was that highway and redevelopment projects increasingly bogged down, strengthening the hand of critics of the urban renewal order. After a rapid denouement, renewal regimes definitively fell in U.S. cities: The Young Turk reform movement was marginalized from Philadelphia government, starting with a schism within the Democratic Party (during the 1963 primary), through the first election of a Republican district attorney in fifteen years (Arlen Specter in 1966), to the rise of Mayor Frank Rizzo and the resignation of Edmund Bacon (1970–71). In Boston, Louise Day Hicks' emergence and near mayoral victory in 1967 as an angry neighborhood defender reflected common trends.

This new neighborhood empowerment, however, was criticized as incapable of anything but opposition and basic self-preservation, unable to advance any positive agenda. That criticism was not entirely fair, but as various local and national elements gave way to the backlash, few alternatives to urban renewal order appeared. This incoherence was at least partially an effect of that perennial wedge of U.S. politics, race. The divisive mayoral insurgencies of Frank Rizzo in Philadelphia and Louise Day Hicks in Boston activated racial resentments among working-class whites, just as successful Republican congressional candidates and even the campaign of presidential nominee Richard Nixon began doing between

1966 and 1968.[1] And though racial positioning and rhetoric were entirely absent from Jacobs' pro-neighborhood arguments, as the 1960s wore on even the New York liberal coalition she confronted was fractured by the animosities of a racially divisive teachers' strike, as well as violent undertones of rising street crime and fears of large-scale rioting. Racism proved a ubiquitous, corrosive presence in U.S. urban politics, breaking down old coalitions but simultaneously inhibiting the formation of sound new ones.

By contrast, novel political configurations were precisely what materialized in Canada. Having exiled herself to Toronto in 1968, Jane Jacobs might have thought she had stepped through the looking glass: Conservative ratepayers' (i.e., property owners') groups forged a citywide, cross-class partnership with radical tenant organizers to protect Toronto neighborhoods from intensive private overdevelopment and insensitive public projects. This unlikely alliance, growing from 1969 to dominate the city council and mayoralty by 1972, gave a rebuke to the prevailing Metro planning priorities. As in the United States and Britain, an insurgent movement had pushed aside the urban renewal order. In a crucial distinction, however, Toronto's opposition unified behind a new civic coalition with an alternative urban Leitbild and eventually, a mandate to execute it.

6 The First Wave of Resistance
Freeway Revolts

Greenwich Village community activists held a ribbon-tying ceremony under the Washington Square arch on November 1, 1958. In a photo op staged with a cute factor ample to attract several newspapers, a pair of three-year-olds—the daughters of neighborhood leader Jane Jacobs and New York University law professor Norman Redlich—posed holding the knot. That political street theater celebrated the defeat of Robert Moses' proposal to bisect the square with a large traffic artery. And by closing even the smaller existing road, it further underscored the community's reappropriation of the park for exclusively pedestrian uses.[1] Given that large-scale urban expressways were the last component of the urban renewal order to be constructed, it is paradoxical that the first major wave of grassroots resistance arose in opposition to them. Highway acts trailed housing and slum clearance initiatives, with the significant, fully funded road-building legislation arriving only in the mid-1950s. By that time, rates of automobile ownership in the United States had been greater than one vehicle per every five people already for three decades—theoretically high enough for the entire nation to be on the road simultaneously.[2] A further irony, then, is that a nation of car drivers was the first to balk at urban freeways. Nonetheless, an American movement to preserve urban neighborhoods against planned destruction rallied under this banner for its earliest symbolic victories. Everywhere they broke out, from the 1950s through the 1970s, freeway revolts marked the beginning of the end for the urban renewal order.

In the United States the opening shots were heard on opposite coasts. Jane Jacobs' experience with anti-roadway battles in New York during the 1950s proved central to her conception of how power works in cities, in terms both of the analysis presented in her writing and of her subsequent political organizing. In San Francisco, public outrage at a highway plan mounted in 1955–56, with thousands mobilized in opposition, via well-organized neighborhood associations. The highway project along that city's Embarcadero waterfront was halted after the first mile of elevated roadway was completed in 1959.[3] Thereafter, anti-highway resistance erupted in city after city—from Boston to Baltimore, Nashville to New Orleans—with mounting success over the course of the 1960s.[4]

Philadelphia was emblematic of the explosive political mixture that often included a general disillusionment with planning experts, new assertiveness from a growing black urban population, and the defection of former reform allies (both

elite and populist). In 1945, while Robert Mitchell served as the original director of the Philadelphia City Planning Commission, he sketched a transportation
scheme that included a ring of highways around the central business district. As
the construction of this highway loop subsequently worked its way around "center city" Philadelphia (clockwise from the west side) under his successor Edmund
Bacon, resistance grew at each stage and these pressures transformed the design
of the roads. It also galvanized opposition to the planning commission: In the
early 1960s, road protesters began carrying signs reading: "Fry Bacon."[5]

The Schuylkill Expressway was a classic, limited-access highway, bulldozed
through Fairmount Park along the eponymous river's banks; Philadelphia's first
modern highway, despite planners' intentions, neither beautified the city nor al-
leviated congestion.[6] Next, a northern connector across Vine Street made some
minimal accommodations to the existing cityscape, with a handful of cross
streets bridging the depressed expressway.[7] The better-than-expected success of
Society Hill gentrification put pressure on the final two beltway links—ultimately
altering the course of both—as they would have girdled the neighborhood's real
estate expansion. With allies including Vice President Hubert Humphrey, the new
residents of the rebranded Old Philadelphia district eventually insured that the expressway running along the Delaware River on the city's east side was depressed
and covered (at least as it passed their neighborhood) so as to impede riverfront
views and access minimally. At a time of increasing resistance, this alteration set a
national precedent for the accommodation of highways to the existing cityscape,
as well as for the federal government's financial interest in the aesthetic and social
impact of their construction.[8] New York officials immediately seized on the idea
to tunnel the controversial Lower Manhattan Expressway.[9]

In January 1957, as the Society Hill project began, Philadelphia Redevelopment
Authority's William Rafsky proposed to close the beltway loop with a southern
arterial across Lombard Street. But just as with the Delaware riverfront expressway, Society Hill's influential new residents were loath to have an ugly expressway
across their backyards and pushed to move it southward. Bacon insisted that the
highway not be routed across Washington Avenue, the main trucking arterial of
South Philadelphia, in the interest of preserving the industry located there. Finally, South Street was selected.

The final link in the inner beltway quickly became emblematic of the sharp
contrast between Bacon's showy center city projects and the deteriorating conditions in the residential neighborhoods beyond.[10] South Street had long been
a symbolic borderline, ethnically and politically, going back to the colonial period, when it formed the southern boundary of William Penn's "greene count-
rie towne." But the rapid socioeconomic transformation of Society Hill, paired

Figure 6.1 Philadelphia residents scrutinize highway proposals at a city planning presentation on May 29, 1964. (Temple University Libraries, Urban Archives, Philadelphia PA.)

with the Crosstown Expressway proposal, turned South Street into a flashpoint for Philadelphia's urban renewal order. In 1964, real estate broker George Scott dubbed South Street Philadelphia's Mason-Dixon Line, separating rich from poor. This characterization was picked up by George Dukes, a member of the Rittenhouse Community Council and other groups, who called it a race moat inside which affluent center city residents were pulling up the drawbridge on the rest of Philadelphia's neighborhoods. Dukes joined Alice Lipscomb of the Hawthorne Community Council to lead an anti-expressway group, the Citizens Committee to Preserve and Develop the Crosstown Community (CCPDCC).[11]

Lawyers and planners had been the core of Walter Phillips' Young Turks reform drive, supporting the renewal plans of the 1940s and 1950s through their influence in the planning commission, the mayor's office, and the Greater Philadelphia Movement. By the middle to late 1960s, however, *opponents* of the city's plans were finding support within a younger generation of sympathetic law and

Figure 6.2 Opponents of the Crosstown Expressway picket Philadelphia's city hall on May 22, 1968. Neighborhood leader Alice Lipscomb (*left*) and others carry signs reading "People! Not Planners," "No Mason Dixon Line," and "We Don't Want an 'Effective Buffer Zone.'" (Temple University Libraries, Urban Archives, Philadelphia PA.)

planning professionals. Primary among these was Robert Sugarman, a twenty-nine-year-old lawyer with the high-powered Philadelphia firm Dechert, Price and Rhoads.[12] That firm's willingness to offer Sugarman's services pro bono to an anti-expressway group may have stemmed from its position as counsel to the beleaguered Penn Central Railroad, probably the largest and most dramatic corporate casualty of pro-automobile policies.[13] From the boardrooms to the grass roots, the ground was clearly shifting beneath the pillars of the Philadelphia urban renewal order.

The New York road battles are particularly salient because of the involvement of internationally prominent figures like Jane Jacobs and Robert Moses, the latter significant not only as Gotham's master builder, but a key policy advocate in Washington and consultant to many other cities. In the mid-1950s, residents of

Greenwich Village banded together as the Joint Emergency Committee to Close Washington Square Park to Traffic and delivered Robert Moses one of his first defeats. Building a strong coalition which included Assemblyman William F. Passanante, Manhattan borough president Hulan Jack and Tammany leader Carmine G. DeSapio (the latter a Greenwich Village resident), they turned a defensive position (opposition to a road-widening scheme) into an offensive counterproposal (that the square be closed to traffic altogether). "Mr. Moses predicted that if the community got its way, the citizens would soon be back begging him to reopen the road and build a highway, but the mess they were in would serve them right and teach them a lesson," Jacobs recounted. Nevertheless, in 1958, "the community, by exerting rather tough political pressure abruptly, got the park road closed, first on a trial basis and then permanently" (see fig. 6.3).[14]

Figure 6.3 In one of the earliest salvos of the freeway revolts, in 1958 Greenwich Village residents defeated Robert Moses' proposal to bisect their neighborhood park square with a large traffic artery. As a celebration—and a savvy public relations tactic—the community held a ceremonial ribbon tying, and cheered the "last car through Washington Square." The episode marked West Village resident Jane Jacobs' emergence alongside many established New York activists as a "public character" (her term) in neighborhood life—and on the radar of public officials. (Claire Tankel collection, Greenwich Village Society for Historic Preservation.)

The Washington Square episode marked Jacobs' emergence as a "public character" in neighborhood life—and on the radar of public officials.[15] In 1960, she chaired the Save the Sidewalks Committee and, together with Greenwich Village Association president Anthony Dapolito, confronted the borough president over a street-widening plan.[16] This string of increasingly high-profile victories for Jacobs culminated in the defeat of the Lower Manhattan Expressway, the central link in Robert Moses' vision for a metropolitan highway network since it was first proposed in the New York Regional Plan of 1929. By the fall of 1962, it was clear that the Board of Estimate, City Planning Commission, and Bureau of Relocation were proceeding with the $100 million proposal for an elevated highway extending along Broome Street.[17] Jacobs was named chairman of the Joint Committee to Stop the Lower Manhattan Expressway. When the Board of Estimate finally met in December to decide the expressway issue, its unanimous rejection of Moses' plan was a dramatic indication of the new influence a neighborhood activist like Jacobs now commanded. As the Village Voice pointed out, "She has turned her causes into hot-potato issues and is lately the terror of every politico in town. She has mustered public support and sympathy to the extent that now even the mayor bends to Jacobs decree or completely loses face."[18]

Highway construction, of course, extended beyond the purview of mayors; the defeated Lower Manhattan Expressway, for example, was later resurrected as a New York state highway proposal. Jacobs' opposition tactics almost resulted in a prison sentence during that additional round, after she was arrested at a 1968 hearing of state transportation officials. In an affidavit cited by the New York Times, the hearing's chairman "said he saw Mrs. Jacobs urge more than ten persons to the stage and engage in violent and tumultuous conduct. He also said he saw her tear and destroy minutes of the meeting and damage a stenographic machine."[19] Jacobs, for her part, claimed merely to have led a "peaceful march," to which the chairman made no objection, down the aisle and across the stage. Facing jail for up to four years, the fifty-one-year-old mother of three plead not guilty, saying that the charges "bear no relation to what happened," and alleged that the district attorney's office repeatedly altered an official's statement to support the desired charges. "The inference seems to be," she told the New York Times, "that anybody who criticizes a state program is going to get it in the neck." Such intimidation notwithstanding, the opposition succeeded in once again insuring that no expressway would be built across Manhattan (below the George Washington Bridge, at least). Following her arrest, residents from Greenwich Village and beyond rallied behind their embattled leader, including a benefit at the Village Gate jazz club for the Jane Jacobs Legal Defense Fund.[20] Jacobs' legal struggles dragged on for months, but by the time they concluded with an inconsequential fine, a severe penalty had already been exacted from the community: Jacobs decided to move her entire family, including two conscription-age sons, to Canada. For their new home, they chose Toronto, only to discover another round of freeway revolts just getting underway abroad.[21]

■

An analogous, if slightly delayed, anti-expressway movement unfolded outside the United States. In Britain, resistance to the urban renewal order appeared at least as early as the 1959 plan to redevelop London's Piccadilly Circus, which was postponed and eventually dropped. Shortly thereafter appeared Europe's "first systematic study of urban traffic problems," Colin Buchanan's 1963 report *Traffic in Towns*, which concluded that pro-car policies were seriously threatening urban quality of life in Britain.[22] A more systemic freeway revolt was manifested citywide by the late 1960s, under the banner of "Homes before Roads," and gained traction within the Labour ranks by 1971. When that party won control of the Greater London Council in 1973, the new official policy became "Stop the Motorways"; that year the motorway box was dropped from the Greater London Development Plan.[23] This shift abruptly halted work on the West Cross Route, notably leaving the section of the M41 begun near the Shepherd's Bush area of London with an elevated highway spur to nowhere. All of this paralleled the opposition in the United States and, above all, in Canada.

For if Jacobs expected that Canada would offer her some peace to do her writing, she was soon disappointed. It must have seemed like a cosmic joke when, shortly after moving to Toronto, and having just been released on bail after her arrest at the New York state highway hearing, Jacobs learned of a Metro Toronto expressway project slated to be built along Spadina Road, just a few blocks east of the new home of her family on Albany Avenue (fig. 6.4). Her adopted neighborhood, known as the Annex, centered on the commercial strip along Bloor Street, with proximity to the University of Toronto giving the area a bohemian reputation. The highway proposal was in an uncertain state, but Jacobs took heed: "variously described to us as elevated, no, depressed; six lanes wide, no eight; with a subway underneath, no, without; to be built soon, no not for a long time. Whatever it was it was not imaginary." Jacobs was not inclined to give planning officials any benefit of the doubt: "In the mind's eye," she conjured, "one could see the great trees and jolly Edwardian porches falling before the onslaught."[24]

Controversy had dogged Metro Toronto's highway planning from the outset. Planner Hans Blumenfeld was exasperated when the exclusive Rosedale neighborhood forced the city council to kill a crosstown expressway project in 1959. But that was a minor prelude to the kind of organized citywide resistance that

Figure 6.4 Proposed expressway along Spadina Avenue, looking south at the Harbord Street crossing, just a few blocks from Toronto's Annex neighborhood and the Albany Avenue home of Jane Jacobs. (Source: *Functional Design Report South from Eglinton Avenue: William R. Allen Expressway and Rapid Transit Line* [Metropolitan Toronto Roads and Traffic Dept., 1970]. Image courtesy Toronto Public Library. With permission: City of Toronto.)

coalesced around the north-south Spadina portion. Though Metro transportation planners' original conception for the Spadina freeway only called for demolishing "a few" houses, and included a subway easement, the provincial government eventually expanded the proposed road width and extended it through the University of Toronto campus and the Annex neighborhood.[25]

Upon hearing the rhetoric of Metro traffic department director Samuel Cass, who cited Los Angeles as the ideal to which Toronto should aspire, Jacobs publicly attacked such conceptions for their naïveté: "Toronto, it seems, retains illusions about inner city expressways that have been shattered elsewhere." With her already well-honed anti-expressway arguments, she exhorted readers of Canada's national press to examine the comprehensive costs, including diversion of public transit expenditure, and to avoid "getting hooked on an addictive drug." If American cities had already reached a point of no return in their road building, Toronto, in its unspoiled innocence, still had a choice. Playing on the string of Canada's imagined inferiorities, she goaded her hosts: "As a relatively recent transplant from New York, I am frequently asked whether I find Toronto sufficiently exciting. I find it almost too exciting. The suspense is scary. Here is the most hopeful and healthy city in North America, still unmangled, still with options. Few of us profit from the mistakes of others, and perhaps Toronto will prove to share this disability. If so, I am grateful at least to have enjoyed this great city before its destruction."[26] Jacobs frequently emphasized this theme, whereby she lauded Toronto for being one of the last remaining Great American Cities but then challenged its citizens, by way of cynical prediction, for being in danger of throwing this all away.

The proposed expressway through central Toronto galvanized citywide opposition, spearheaded by the Stop Spadina Save Our City Coordinating Committee (SSSOCCC). Metro's Blumenfeld, exiled in turn from Germany, Russia, and the

Figure 6.5 "People Not Cars"—the freeway revolt comes to Canada: a Spadina expressway protest at the University of Toronto in March 1970. Faculty member Marshall McLuhan cowrote a film with Jane Jacobs to criticize the proposed road. (Photo by Barrie Davis. With permission: *Toronto Globe and Mail.* Source: City of Toronto Archives, fonds 2, series 8, file 22, item 001.)

United States for his leftist views, felt particularly stung when roadway opponents accused him specifically, in a 1970 publication entitled "The Bad Trip," of having of intentionally manipulated the metropolitan transportation report in favor of private vehicles.[27] Meanwhile, Jacobs the Toronto newcomer joined a high-profile Canadian intellectual, the University of Toronto's Marshall McLuhan, and together they wrote the script for a movie about the anti-expressway campaign. In early 1970, Jacobs offered a set of public lectures, in which she quipped, "We could have car manufacturers, oil companies, land speculators and luxury apartment developers do our planning. They could do it for free, and it would be just the same as we have now. We would save a lot of money that way." *Globe and Mail* journalist Robert Fulford observed how Jacobs placed what had seemed like merely provincial concerns into "the context of a long-running international argument," thus helping Toronto "to sharpen its ideas about itself [and] to see its problems as a reflection of cities everywhere."[28]

She also brought a New Yorker's brass against Metro Toronto's officials. At one public hearing, after attacking every member of the Metro transportation committee with what were described as "scathing verbal broadsides," denouncing their hearing as "a sham, a charade," she declared: "This is the first really controversial issue facing this Metro government and the inadequacies don't bode well for the city. The politicians have fallen back on expediency while mouthing principles." The committee accused her of rabble rousing and asked her how she expected to get any sympathy from them. "I'm not asking you to be sympathetic with me. I don't give a damn," Jacobs answered. "You don't give a damn about anything," exclaimed one of committee member. "Yes I do," Jacobs replied, "I love this city."[29]

Within a year, Jacobs and her allies had replicated the defeat of the Lower Manhattan Expressway proposal. In the spring of 1971 the same provincial government (under Premier William Davis) that had originally expanded the Spadina highway scheme to such controversial proportions abruptly backed down and embraced the opponents' slogan: "Cities are for people, not for cars!" Blumenfeld saw it as pure election year demagoguery.[30] But in so doing, the province had suddenly intervened in the transportation policy of Metro Toronto on behalf of the central-city constituents, symbolically placing their reservations ahead of pro-suburban highway development. The broad urban coalition that had mobilized against Canada's urban renewal order became impossible to ignore and thereby reclaimed a measure of clout in the metropolitan power struggle.

7 The Tide Shifts
Neighborhood Protectionism

From Anti-highway to Pro-neighborhood

Grassroots efforts to stop the construction of highways through cities formed the first significant wave of challenges to the urban renewal order beginning in the 1950s. By the 1960s, this freeway revolt had spread to many American cities and beyond. Robert Moses had predicted, during the policy discussions that preceded the U.S. national highway program, that the portions of the network in dense urban areas would be the most likely to stir resistance. After all, unlike rural and suburban ones, these urban freeways came at the expense of large numbers of residences and businesses, negatively impacting those least likely to use the new roads, and igniting a cultural clash over an urban versus a suburban vision of American life. It, too, was a clash between residents who saw themselves as unwarranted casualties—a contingent sometimes dismissed as NIMBY ("not in my backyard") obstructionists—and planning policymakers who saw some local sacrifices as necessary for infrastructure meant to serve the larger public good.[1]

However, these sacrifices were not equitably distributed, but rather levied quite regressively, with poor and minority urban communities facing disproportionately higher numbers of demolitions. In fact, Moses and other advocates did not shy away from linking urban highway construction to another agenda within the urban renewal order: the eradication of areas that planners deemed obsolete or "blighted." Often planners selected highway routes to obliterate or isolate undesirable areas. Yet this approach usually masked deliberate destruction as the side effect of a larger public works project. At the same time, though, many slum clearance proposals did explicitly condemn neighborhoods on the basis of the supposed undesirability of their inherent characteristics. It would take longer for residents to develop the conceptual and tactical resources to challenge slum clearance schemes and defend neighborhoods on their own terms, to affirm their worthiness in the face of a rhetoric of blight. Yet this did happen, and by the early 1960s, pressure from residents in New York neighborhoods like Gramercy, Bellevue, and the West Village had forced a shift in rhetoric from public officials, halted several specific slum clearance proposals, and facilitated the expansion of historic preservation statutes to protect entire neighborhoods. Unofficially, this heralded a larger cultural sea change in attitudes toward old neighborhoods, evident by the 1970s in phenomena like the revival of Brooklyn's "brownstone belt" and a growing enthusiasm for fixing up homes in Victorian districts more gener-

Figure 7.1 Neighborhood self-defense. Redevelopment proposals connected with the expansion of Columbia University's Manhattan campus, including construction in Morningside Park, sparked a racially charged opposition from residents in neighboring Harlem. (The university also purchased the Delano Village housing project to house Harlem Hospital staff.) In 1968, a group of young African-American urbanists founded the Architects' Renewal Committee in Harlem (ARCH) and helped organize community opposition to Columbia's plans. This episode pitted some of the most powerful advocates of urban renewal—a major urban university and city planning officials—against community defenders, and it ultimately spilled over onto the campus as a precipitating issue for that year's explosive student sit-in. (*West Harlem Morningside: A Community Proposal* [Architects' Renewal Committee in Harlem, Inc.; and West Harlem Community Organization, Inc.; September 1968].)

ally. (Incidentally, these trends were reflected, respectively, in two popular public television programs born during the period, *Sesame Street*, in 1969, and *This Old House*, in 1978.) Even the "ghetto" self-help philosophies promoted by some black urban leaders at the time exhibited related themes of neighborhood defense and uplift (fig. 7.1).[2]

The Late-Phase Urban Renewal Order in New York

An instructive example of precisely how the tide turned against the urban renewal order, in the key context of New York's city politics, is provided by Jane Jacobs and her West Village neighbors' efforts to protect their community. Partly in response to mounting opposition, the federal government issued new urban renewal guidelines (and accompanying funding) in 1959 to create more avenues for citizen participation. Cities were thenceforth required to undertake more comprehensive analysis of their planning means and objectives, and to insure the participation of site residents in any redevelopment project. "And we mean by that," clarified Federal Housing and Home Finance Agency head Robert Weaver in 1961, "not just a passive acceptance of what is being done, but the active utilization of local leadership and organizations which can profitably assist in the community's efforts."[3]

In response to the 1959 federal guidelines, New York City Planning Commission chairman James Felt initiated a three-year Community Renewal Program (with a $1.5 million federal grant) across eighty residential neighborhoods citywide. By 1960, six neighborhoods were designated to demonstrate the application of spot rehabilitation as a response to blight. The initiative dovetailed with the city's new zoning statutes, which officially took effect in December 1961. Like Mayor Robert Wagner, Chairman Felt saw the new codes as "a testament to what can be accomplished through united civic effort," insuring "that New York would once more have the finest zoning code in the nation." It would provide "a firm foundation to support the City's comprehensive planning program."[4]

Felt was upbeat regarding "renewed citizen interest all over town—in Brooklyn Heights, in Dongan Hills, in Greenwich Village, in Bayside, in Cobble Hill, in Riverdale. People want to develop their community with good taste and respect for its traditions." Citizen participation, however, was welcome only up to the point when it became citizen obstruction. Felt tried to remind community members that "this approach also calls for responsible citizenship as well. Urban renewal—which represents New York's golden opportunity to overcome immediate urban problems—has found itself the subject of some misguided criticism of late. I say misguided, because well-meaning, sensible citizens rebelling against our architecture, our technology, our mores and our culture in general have sought to single out urban renewal as the villain. While I realize that local officialdom is considered fair game, let us remember that this is an indictment of our urban way of life, which had been accepted by the public all these years."[5]

Although his commitment to the professed ideals of citizen participation later came into question, Felt was unwavering in his conviction that all areas must be brought into line with the new zoning code, and specifically that the promiscuous mingling of industrial, retail, and residential uses should be prohibited under the "application of sound land use principles." With respect to such principles, the West Village was a major offender. In addition to "a mixture of old 3- and 4-story buildings of the town-house type, most of which have been excellently rehabilitated in the past decade," Felt could not ignore the "run down and deteriorated," "old-law tenements," or the "indiscriminate mixture of warehousing, truck terminals, garages and loft buildings." He concluded that the "mixture of land uses, the character of the non-residential activity, the heavy commercial traffic it generates and the presence of the elevated freight line to the west, have unquestionably blighted this area."[6]

Thus, in early 1961, as part of the new Community Renewal Program, the Wagner administration initiated the approval process for a federally funded study of the West Village. In May, the City Planning Commission published its recommendation to designate the West Village "as an area appropriate for Urban Renewal" and amend the master plan to depict the neighborhood as a "predominantly non-residential area characterized by blight and suitable for clearance, replanning, reconstruction or rehabilitation for predominantly residential use" (fig. 7.2).[7] Many West Village residents took the blight designation as a signal of ill intent, although Chairman Felt also reassured them that the commission's was no bulldozer approach, and instead would "seek to use renewal as a tool to stabilize and protect our neighborhoods, not disrupt or destroy them. Wherever possible, we hope to extend the blanket of renewal protection to areas where, with a minimum amount of neighborhood disruption, we can provide the assistance to fix up homes, to alleviate blighting conditions and to create a sound residential environment. The conservation and rehabilitation of our existing housing supply is the backbone of our urban renewal program."[8]

That spring, Chairman Felt could hardly have known how ironic his selection of Jane Jacobs' home turf was, since her controversial paean to its functional diversity would not yet be published until a few months later. He assumed he was being sensitive to the residents' wishes, in a bold, modernized style, when he proposed "to explore the technical and economic feasibility of decking over this westward [industrial] section, thus providing a residential break-through to the river which has been strongly urged by the community." As the subsequent months demonstrated, both Jacobs and Felt were obsessed by the West Village, and for essentially the same reason—its unzoned eclecticism—so their clash over it was practically inevitable. To Jacobs, it was irreplaceable; to Felt it was unacceptable.

If the administration's new rhetoric was credible, however, there was initially room for optimism on both sides. Urban renewal officials at the beginning of the 1960s appeared intent on distinguishing themselves from the just-concluded era

Figure 7.2 New York City Planning Commission map of land use in Manhattan's West Village in 1961, presenting the mix of residential and nonresidential activities as a justification for designating the area for urban renewal, particularly in light of the city's stringent new zoning codes. (Courtesy NYC Municipal Archives.)

of Robert Moses. Far from intending to demolish the West Village, the director of the Housing and Redevelopment Board, J. Clarence Davies, insisted that an objective neighborhood study had "no preconceived notion of what kind of a program would be suggested for the area other than the general objective" of "furnishing middle-income housing primarily on industrial and commercial sites." Furthermore, he reassured alarmed residents, any planning "would be done only after consultation with any and all representatives of the neighborhood groups. . . . It is our stated objective and we have always had as a set policy the conservation of good housing and the approach of this Board has not been, nor will it ever be, the bulldozer approach." As evidence of good intentions, Davies invited skeptics to examine the (upper) West Side Urban Renewal Project: "I think if you will examine our practices and policies, as well as our record, you will be able to reassure yourself not only of our good intentions, which have been much maligned, but of our practices which should go a fair ways toward dispelling the hysterical attitude of opposition which has been deliberately created."[9] In March 1961, the Housing and Redevelopment Board unveiled a redevelopment plan for the West Village by renowned architect Victor Gruen, whose work Jacobs had praised, but it failed to mollify her opposition.[10] Such comments and actions from planning officials betrayed defensiveness, as Jacobs and other community members began publicly to question their intent.

Davies warned that the private market—not public officials—was doing more than any other force to destroy the unique qualities of Village life, and that the city's renewal agency was the residents' only recourse: "I think it should be obvious to you that, if the Village area is left alone and if no middle-income housing is projected by the Board, which is the only way it can be, eventually the Village will consist solely of luxury housing which we, of course, would be powerless to prevent." He cautioned concerned residents that "this trend is already quite obvious and would itself destroy any semblance of the present Village that [Jacobs and her allies] seem so anxious to preserve."[11]

Jacobs' Anxious Grassroots Insurgency

West Village residents had in fact expressed anxieties about market trends for some time. Jane Jacobs and her neighbors bitterly fought the contention that their area was blighted and in need of redevelopment. Yet, at the same time, they had to acknowledge the neighborhood's instability. From the perspective of the West Village in the 1950s and 1960s, three distinct forces kept the community in flux and even threatened to destabilize it: real estate pressures, complications flowing from the neighborhood's diverse and changing composition, and government renewal proposals.

First were the inflationary pressures of the real estate market, especially a rash of luxury housing speculation. In 1960, Jacobs (and her family) picketed the governor's New York City office "to protest real estate changes in Greenwich Village" that favored speculators.[12] "These real-estate grabbers," Jacobs later remarked. "You'd think there was oil under the ground here."[13] Accordingly, many Villagers were "greatly concerned with getting more middle income housing, in particular to help accommodate the many families, which have been displaced by the luxury buildings and conversions."[14] Collaborative overtures to the administration by various Village organizations were rebuffed, prior to the city's own comprehensive renewal proposal, at which point the threat of private real estate development became one of the planners' primary arguments in favor of their West Village scheme. Subsequently, while the West Village community organization argued countless rounds of negotiation with the city agencies, a real estate developer, William Zeckendorf, Sr., acquired parcels along the former high line rail freight corridor. Even Lewis Mumford publicly acknowledged Jacobs' analysis, his high-profile excoriation of her book notwithstanding, of the destructive effects from such "cataclysmic finance, known medically as the Zeckendorf syndrome."[15] Only through the support of a more sympathetic mayor, John Lindsay—and the city's condemnation powers—did the Villagers fend off this large-scale private redevelopment threat.[16]

Over the course of the 1950s, the process of gentrification (*avant la lettre*) was already recognized in the West Village, especially by longtime residents. The neighborhood's Irish community was in the process of transition, with many opting for the suburban feel of Staten Island. Many of these families felt as economically (and culturally) threatened by the arrival of young professionals like Jacobs as she might have felt toward subsequent luxury developments. One Irish worker, who was exceptionally active alongside Jacobs in neighborhood organizations and thus bridged these old and new constituencies, found it difficult to overcome suspicions about the intentions of the newcomers when mobilizing his childhood associates against urban renewal. A number even relished the prospect of obtaining modern housing in a project similar to those on Manhattan's East Side. James Kirk, for example, a business agent for the United Weighers' Association of the Port of New York, former president of the Greenwich Village Association, and a sixty-two-year resident, organized a petition with two hundred signatories to challenge Jacobs' assertions of outside builder influence. In a letter to Mayor Wagner he explained, "We applaud the action of the Planning Commission. . . . We want to prevent the continuation of the conversions into luxury apartments which are causing the working people of this neighborhood to be evicted." In the view of these older residents renewal would be a "blessing" and "courageous action."[17] Despite these dynamics, however, many (including those who moved out) remained closely tied to neighborhood institutions like the Catholic church.[18]

The West Village also possessed a set of commercial and industrial operations that manifested a complex relationship to city initiatives and resident mobilization. Some in business there feared the encroachment of loft conversions and tenement rehabilitation into their sphere and endorsed the planners' separation of uses as a means of protecting their workplaces and jobs. The proximity of residences to these works sites was certainly nothing new for the older working-class community, but the sensibilities of more bourgeois neighbors were expected to bring noise and other environmental complaints that could restrict the making and moving of goods. Indeed, Jacobs, who saw the maintenance of such mixed uses as crucial to neighborhood stability, tried simultaneously to train the trucking operations to be clean, courteous neighbors. In her battles with the renewal agency, though, Jacobs did manage to rally support from the Central Labor Council, Artists' Equity, and the International Longshoremen's Association—who later offered to financially sponsor an alternative housing plan developed by the community.[19]

As in many parts of New York City in the period, Puerto Rican immigration also played a role in the West Village. Some surmised that the minority presence was a major factor in the city's decision to redevelop the area.[20] It may have also influenced the decisions of some white working-class residents to leave. Perhaps since they were also newcomers (in comparison to the Irish), however, Puerto Ricans also proved more receptive to organizing by the likes of Jacobs.

The West Village, like much of New York City, was certainly changing demographically. But within that fluidity it also possessed an exceptional—and exceptionally consistent—ethos. Namely, it tapped into the bohemian mystique attached to Greenwich Village as a whole, which famously attracted the most diverse collection of lifestyles from around the world. It was perhaps the consummate self-consciously tolerant community. In 1963, Jacobs, Ed Koch (then leader of the Village Independent Democrats), parent groups, and the National Association for the Advancement of Colored People fought the school board's transfer of fifty-five children from an African-American orphanage out of the Village's Public School 41, "thus depriving the remaining children of the desirable experience of attending a racially mixed school."[21] This progressive self-conception extended to many constituencies in the Village; even working-class Irish Catholic residents had made their peace with the long-standing presence of homosexual bars and black intellectuals.[22] This tolerance of diversity unquestionably shaped the vision of the urban ideal Jacobs expressed in her writing.[23]

Fighting against urban renewal in the trenches of city politics, however, convinced Jacobs that the large neighborhood or district was also the fundamental unit of urban democracy, a political theory she developed in *The Death and Life of Great American Cities*.[24] When William H. Whyte, Jr., first noticed Jacobs in the mid 1950s, he instantly recognized that "her real work was extracurricular; fighting Robert Moses and his projects was her major activity. She proved every bit as combative as Moses himself."[25] Her speeches, essays, and books became an extension of the battles she fought, and her community experiences formed the substance of much of her writing. By the early 1960s, the urban renewal vision championed by Moses successor James Felt constituted another existential threat to the West Village community as Jacobs and many of her neighbors understood it.

The West Village urban renewal plan was announced just three weeks after Jacobs finished the manuscript of *Death and Life* and returned to her job at the *Architectural Forum*. Jacobs saw the coincidence as uncanny, since "both the city's selection of the area and its schemes for converting it into inane anti-city were about as neat a case study as could well be imagined of the intellectual idiocies and ignorance of city workings that I had been writing about."[26]

Jacobs was convinced that the new policies articulated by urban renewal officials like Felt and Davies were simply disguising rather than replacing the clearance-for-profit approach associated with Robert Moses. She joined other intellectuals, including sociologist Nathan Glazer and historian Staughton Lynd, as well as leaders of community groups, in signing a petition to challenge the rhetoric of urban renewal's new, more human face, and declaring that this "totally ignores the facts of the Title I projects actually being implemented." Denouncing the Seward Park Extension, Riverside-Amsterdam Projects, West Side Urban Renewal Project, and Cadman Plaza Project in Brooklyn Heights, they urged instead that "upgrading and renewal should be used to benefit the existing community and its residents." "If the new Board really believes in the conservation of neighborhoods and neighborhood character, in the preservation and renewal of communities, in spot renewal rather than mass clearance of buildings and people; if it really intends to begin modern, professional planning for human beings and their needs as well as for the future of this city, it has had and still has a chance to show its good faith by drastically restudying these five ill-conceived, unprofessional, and obsolete projects at present under way. Until then, there can be no talk of a new policy."[27]

Drawing on experience from previous battles, neighborhood activists organized resistance as soon as the West Village urban renewal proposal was announced and grew increasingly strident. Thirty neighbors formed the Committee to Save the West Village, named Jacobs chair, and promptly petitioned the Housing and Redevelopment Board for a one-month period to disprove the contention that their neighborhood was blighted.

Jacobs and the committee proved remarkably effective at this task. Reasons for the Villagers' eventual defensive victory can found on many levels, not the least of which were resourcefulness and shrewd tactics. The Villagers capitalized on a useful set of skills, including those of publicists, journalists, clerical workers inside city government (acting as moles), an articulate spokeswoman who assailed the arcane details of urban renewal policy in public hearings, and even, when necessary, the neighborhood's beatniks and folk singers, with their vigilant countercultural protest posture. Jacobs counted on the strength of "hundreds of people [who] work on the committee and its various sub-committees, and we've had to become experts in everything from how to organize and run torchlight parades to how to analyze typewriter type and collect legal evidence." Despite the fact that she was a professional writer and magazine editor, a reporter for the New York Herald Tribune in March 1961 cast the group's leader as a "down to earth . . . mother who's bringing up three children" and emphasized the committee's grassroots support: "Everyone in the neighborhood is working on the Save the West Village Committee. Mrs. Jacobs took us on a tour of the streets and we couldn't go two steps without children appearing with handfuls of signed petitions. The local printer replenished her supply, and the local coffee house proprietor reported on the television show that had filmed their meeting in this shop this morning."[28]

The group thus utilized and fortified what would later be called the available social capital of the community, with supportive clergy opening their churches for meetings, printers and other merchants donating services, and children distributing flyers as well as keeping an eye out for surveyors. Yet this supposedly homespun insurgency also played hardball city politics, publicly attacking agency heads for corruption or challenging Gotham's mayor with scathing ultimatums. Furthermore, in order to open multiple fronts simultaneously, Jacobs and her neighbors augmented their pressure on elected officials with a judicial strategy that included a suit against the city in state court.[29]

Jacobs and the other organizers managed to cobble together a coalition of important allies with a stake in the West Village. These included Greenwich Village Association president Anthony Dapolito, Carmine DeSapio—the last Tammany boss (and himself a neighborhood resident)—as well as his challenger and political successor, reformer Edward Koch of the Village Independent Democrats. Future mayor John Lindsay, then U.S. representative for the Seventeenth Congressional District, also weighed in on the Villagers' behalf. Although faced with hostility from major institutions including the New York Times editorial board and professional associations directly invested in urban renewal, the fight to stop renewal of the West Village had the sympathy of many journalists and intellectuals. This responsiveness in part reflected professional connections of various West Village residents, including the committee's vice chair, publicist Rachelle Wall, and, of course, Jacobs. The 1961 release of her book, with its associated media controversy, added all the further publicity that her publisher Random House could generate.

A Dirty Fight to the Finish

When an ostensibly independent advisory group, the Citizens Housing and Planning Council, endorsed the West Village renewal proposal in the New York Times, Jacobs attacked the group for having sought no consultation with the proposal's strong and vocal opponents before offering its endorsement. Worse, she alleged, the council had actively colluded with city officials to manipulate the public, through the creation of a puppet organization to support the plan. Jacobs also intimated that the organization's directors used its name to promote projects from which they stood to benefit. For her, this represented a gross abrogation of the democratic process: "In this case the citizens have actually been deprived of the first, most important and most fundamental of such hearings, and the taxpayers left unguarded with respect to the most basic findings necessary in considering the use of public urban renewal funds."[30]

Rejecting the backroom style of politics, Jacobs opted for aggressively confrontational, even moralizing tactics. For example, in a law suit, Jacobs v. City of New York, she alleged that the city's proposal was illegal, since the blighted designation was removed in 1954 (and affirmed in the official 1959 map), and since state law required a public hearing before any status revision ("a safeguard against arbitrary action, or against stamping as blighted or deteriorating a place which, in fact is not . . . as in this case.").[31] When the New York Supreme Court supported the Villagers' claims, ruling that the city's actions were "without warrant in law," Justice Henry Clay Greenberg added sympathetically, "The legal question aside for the moment, it is obvious that, as a matter of simple justice, equity and public decency, there is considerable merit to the plaintiffs' position."[32] Armed with this decision, Jacobs and the Committee to Save the West Village submitted a petition to Mayor Wagner calling for the removal of Felt, Davies, and any other personnel connected with these "acts, [which] we believe tend to discredit their office."[33]

The Wagner administration could not ignore the pressure from a group "out to get the plan killed and in a somewhat dramatic fashion" (in the words of one staffer), and was forced to confront the issue. Despite some sympathy from insiders like Hortense Gabel, assistant to the mayor for housing ("on the merits the protesting groups have some arguments in their favor"), the administration's main impression was that the Villagers were "demagogic in the extreme and have impugned the integrity by rumor and innuendo [of officials] . . . vilified to an unpardonable degree by extremists."[34] Mayor Wagner, consequently, did not even bother to respond to Jacobs, despite her title as chair on the petition, but rather addressed himself to H. Marshall Scolnick (the first male member of the committee listed), in a dismissive tone:

> I have been around government for a long time, and I just cannot accept this unique approach that public officials of unquestioned honesty and ability should be removed from office, by the appointing power, because there is controversy over the wisdom of some plan they have projected. . . .
>
> Under no circumstances will I countenance even a hearing on removal charges. I am sure that, if you were in government, you would realize the chaotic implications of such a step. The timid official would practically have to take a public opinion poll before proposing any program in the field at all.[35]

Again the committee chose confrontation over conciliation. "We do not accept your denial of our petition as representing your informed and considered judgment. Your letter of explanation makes it perfectly clear that you have misunderstood the petition itself and misinterpreted our motives in presenting it." The mayor had, they explained to him, confused the methods and goals of the urban renewal proposals: "There are other means at our disposal for discussing the merits of their proposals. . . . We believe these *means* to be unjust, deceptive, and designed to circumvent the protection given us by the law against the willful acts of government agencies." They warned Wagner that his proposed solution of Board of Estimate proceedings would constitute a "further illegal act," and concluded in characteristically provocative style: "We strongly urge that you personally reread our petition in the light of this letter and reconsider your decision. We hope to hear from you soon for if days go by and we do not hear from you what are we and other citizens of New York to think?—That you are closing the door to reasonable consideration of our problem and forcing us once again to go to the courts for protection?"[36]

The letters from Jacobs and the Committee to Save the West Village implied Wagner's coresponsibility for his administration's planning policies—even as they demanded he take action against his appointees—and they offered little incentive for his cooperation other than the upholding of democratic principles. Yet Wagner did cultivate his reputation as a corruption fighter, and the Villagers' indelicate approach yielded a dramatic change in the mayor's public position. Two months later the mayor's office issued a statement, indicating that he was "deeply concerned and sympathetic with the people of the West Village neighborhood in their desire to conserve and to build constructively upon a neighborhood life which is an example of city community life at its healthiest." More substantively, however, he announced his support for their position by recommending the West Village proposal "be withdrawn . . . and that this action be taken as soon as possible so as not to leave an integral portion of Greenwich Village in a state of limbo."[37]

Yet despite Jacobs' emerging position as the most outspoken activist-critic in American urbanism—or perhaps because of it—the city agencies were essentially unwilling to engage her as a bargaining partner. When U.S. representative John Lindsay and others wrote to ask Davies why the community was not consulted and urged him to leave the basic planning decisions to neighborhood groups, Davies confirmed that "obviously the wishes of the community are and must be the basic elements of whatever neighborhood plan would be created." At the same time he denounced the "air of hysterical suspicion" and the "hysterical outburst which our request for survey and planning funds has evoked" from the West Village: "Quite obviously our choice must be that of representing all of the citizens and opposition of a small group, while all must be considered, must not be allowed to stand in the way of a program."[38]

The officials found plenty of justification for dismissing Jacobs and her neighbors as hysterical obstructionists. When the planning commission announced its decision to move ahead with the controversial proposal despite Mayor Wagner's recommendation, a "near-riot" ensued: "[Jacobs] and her fellow Villagers rose from the audience in such a manifestation of community wrath that police had to be called to clear the room."[39] Chairman Felt attempted to maintain order: "This is the most disgraceful demonstration I have ever seen. We cannot operate on the basis of disorderly conduct." One unidentified woman insulted the chairman: "You belong with Khrushchev. How dare you assume such authority? Who the hell do you think you are making decisions in the interest of builders?" State assemblyman Louis DeSalvio also spoke up: "By this reprehensible and strange decision you have sent the urban renewal program of this city, state and federal government back to the dark ages of Robert Moses, and his arbitrary and inhuman procedures." As officers forcefully ejected Stephen Zoll from the chamber, the Macmillan publications editor and Christopher Street resident cursed the chairman: "You have made a deal. Your name will be remembered with horror."[40]

Such a mob scene did little to ingratiate the Villagers, instead giving fuel to their opponents, who would portray Jacobs and her allies as outside the circle of reasonable partners. Milton Bergman, chairman of the Citizens Union issued a public statement strongly condemning the "riot tactics of the West Villagers" as an "attack on democratic processes." It was all the more deplorable, he said, "because the disorderly conduct appears to have been deliberately organized and led by supposedly intelligent and civic-minded people and not just a case of people's emotions getting out of hand." He commended the planning commission "for sticking to its honest conclusions as to what the public interest requires. It is employed to give expert planning advice, not to act merely as a barometer of public opinion—certainly not of public uproar. . . . We call on the citizens of our city to exercise responsible restraint and not to endanger our democratic institutions by this kind of revolutionary abuse."[41]

In the planning commission's analysis, the plan's opponents were motivated not (understandably) out of ignorance or confusion, but rather based their actions "on two premises which, whether explicitly or implicitly stated, provided the basic theme for most of their statements, arguments at meetings, letters to editors and the impressive number of articles, columns and editorials they placed or inspired in various periodicals." The first premise, "common to almost all the opposition statements," held that "neither the City Planning Commission nor the Housing and Redevelopment Board nor, by implication, any public officials, mean what they say, can be believed or can be trusted to do what they say they intend to do." The second premise, "less widely shared but still pervasive, was that any public intervention for renewal is *per se* harmful, that all public renewal and housing programs are by nature destructive and that only local residents, if left to their own efforts without the interference of government, can bring about the renewal of the city." Chairman Felt labeled this the laissez faire theory of urban renewal: "To accept this is to abandon our cities to the very process which created the slums of the past and necessitated housing and urban renewal programs. . . . If, in past efforts, the City has neglected the sense of community and human scale, we are now moving toward correction of those faults."[42]

Despite such rebuttals of the Villagers, though, Felt, Davies, and other officials in fact gave few indications that their pronouncements of a new democratic renewal approach extended much beyond rhetoric. Indeed, a pattern of secretive and misleading tactics seemed to confirm Jacobs' worst suspicions. Ominously, just as the new community participation program was being launched, Felt appealed to the mayor's office for approval to remove the seals from the City Planning Commission's vehicles, since they drew "a great deal of unnecessary attention from the public, and often lead to unwarranted conclusions."[43]

During the year prior to the city renewal declaration, Village organizations attempted to enlist the Housing and Redevelopment Board to help construct Mitchell-Lama (i.e., rent-subsidized) housing on available sites, which Jacobs noted at the time, "would require little or no relocation, and which would have enthusiastic community support." Yet the board and its representatives were not only uninterested in such collaboration; Jacobs and her allies found the agency could "only be described as uncooperative to the point of total obstructionism." Instead, from Jacobs and other residents' perspective, the community's call for affordable housing that "the Village area quite desperately needs" was met with "the most expensive and the slowest means for obtaining the smallest net increase in housing units, which could well be devised."[44]

Not only had the agency rejected the community partnership initiated by residents, but also the West Village urban renewal proposal—the first under the new guidelines—actually circumvented its own procedures by requesting study funding prior to public hearings. That the agency made the mistake of doing so in Jacobs' own neighborhood, immediately causing "bitter controversy and neighborhood hostility," meant that the proposal never escaped what Mayor Wagner called a "climate of suspicion."[45] Years later, when Davies asked Jacobs what made her think that the clearance of the area was a foregone conclusion, she pointed to the amount his board had requested. Knowing the percentage of study money within a typical renewal budget, she knew they must have envisioned a massive project.[46] Jacobs would find many occasions to suspect that so-called planning studies were being used as a formality in the introduction of preconceived and essentially unalterable projects.

Mayor Wagner's sincerity was repeatedly brought into question. Just weeks after his recommendation that the proposal be withdrawn, the planning commission moved undeterred to seek $350,000 in federal funds for a preliminary West Village renewal study. The commission held that its failure to pursue a project which it believed was needed would "indeed constitute a surrender of independence and a dereliction of responsibility." A mayoral statement on this flanking maneuver affirmed the authority of Felt and his agency: "Occasionally we may differ. However, the City Planning Commission is an autonomous body and as such should function objectively and independently." In fact, a confidential memo handwritten by Felt to Wagner suggests that the "independent" announcement and response were carefully coordinated.[47]

Further election year pressure from Village residents succeeded in convincing the Housing and Redevelopment Board to renounce any intention of implementing the proposal. But after the election, the City Planning Commission's designation of the area as a slum still stood on the master plan, opening the way for a pronouncement by Chairman Felt declaring his intent to revive the West Village project in 1962. The West Village Committee immediately responded with further appeals to Mayor Wagner: "We are bewildered at Felt's New Year optimism that he can eventually act counter to your promise and we are naturally alarmed when he continued thus to intensify the already cruel anxiety and damage to which we are subject."[48]

Again, Wagner acquiesced to the citizens' pressure. Then, suddenly, in late March 1962, yet another "far-from-innocuous study proposal" emerged, under the auspices of a Department of Marine and Aviation plan for an elevated truck artery. Almost by chance—and just two days before its approval by the Board of Estimate—Villagers "learned that it provides, utterly unannounced to the public, for a sub-contract to Ebasco, *to make a community planning study of our neighborhood.*" Between the date when the planning commission announced that it would comply with the mayor's promise to undesignate the Village for renewal (January 17) and the date it actually did so (January 31), "there was quietly arranged this scheme for a new study of the West Village." According to information the committee received, Felt had been present at a meeting in Manhattan borough president Edward Dudley's office to arrange it: "*At the very time his Commission was preparing publicly to lift from us the threat of one study, another one was being prepared quietly. This is not reassuring.*" When asked directly, officials lied to the members of the community about the existence of such plans.[49]

The Villagers challenged Wagner that "at the very time your promise was in process of being carried out, other members of your administration were engaged in what appears to be a circumvention of this promise, and were doing so with precautions amounting to prevarication." The neighborhood committee was "both amazed and upset at an abrupt new threat which jeopardized the West Village. Both the nature of this threat and the manner in which it has arisen, fill us with foreboding." Village residents could not help but wonder at the absurdity of these "incredibly persistent schemes for tattering our community."[50]

The administration's conception of the West Village as model zoning project explains the unrelenting, underhanded measures that officials undertook to keep it on track. As it came to resemble instead a model debacle, due to the stubborn defense mounted by Jacobs and the committee, Felt worried that the entire citywide program would be undermined. Utilizing a public relations tactic pioneered by his predecessor Robert Moses, Felt drafted a statement of principles and sent copies to every conceivable institution and opinion maker in the city, including the general manager of the *New York Times* (as well as writers like Ada Louise Huxtable), chambers of commerce, advertising agencies, insurance, real estate, and law firms, clergy, universities, and foundations. For each he included a cover letter: "This is not being sent to you for the purpose of fanning a controversy. We accept the decision that the renewal study we recommended will not be made. However, we are gravely concerned by the fact that the basic issues which this report treats have been distorted and obscured by the heat and drama of controversy."[51]

When Wagner (more or less) finally told Felt that "the time has come to put the West Village urban renewal proposal to rest," he too did so in the interest of "even greater opportunities to serve the City through good planning." To drag out the current conflict "will only distract our energies and attention from the great tasks ahead. We have much to do in many parts of the city. We must recruit and mobilize the active support of the people for these great undertakings." He exhorted Felt to get over the defeat: "There is much to do together, let's get on with the job.[52]

The job at hand, however, was changing. As the West Village fight raged, Wagner's administration was simultaneously moving forward with the development of historic preservation statutes, and he even named prominent preservationist Harmon Goldstone to the planning commission.[53] A further evidence of shifting tides came with the appointment of the Committee for the Preservation of Structures of Historic and Esthetic Importance.[54] James Felt's relationship to these developments accentuated the tension between urban renewal and mounting preservation sentiment. After all, his new zoning resolution's underlying assumption was that everything which came before—and consequently the city as it currently stood—was wrong. Following its passage in December 1960, Felt would commit only to short-term "right to continue" for all prior "nonconforming" structures ("We have never held that this right may continue virtually in perpetuity").[55] Certainly no one in a Gilded Age preservation organization like the Municipal Art Society would weep for the eradication of industrial uses in residential districts, Felt's primary target. But in his more extreme postures, Felt argued that the preservationists' backward-looking focus was a general threat to the renewal ethos:

> In designating structures of historic or esthetic importance, we must distinguish between nostalgia or special group interest and true value to society. Sometimes these decisions will be painful. A charming old structure is not necessarily historic, yet most of us would not like to see it destroyed. Nevertheless, if such a structure precludes the development of an entire area, it must be cleared or moved in the best interests of the City. New York, unlike Venice, cannot afford to offer antiquity as one of its major products. The genius and strength of New York lies in its dynamic vitality and its continuing self-regeneration. To be sure we must cherish our past but we must not let it lure us to looking backwards instead of looking ahead.

At the same time, Felt warned that preservationists had as much as anyone to fear from an unregulated real estate industry. Making reference to the Allies' provisions to spare monuments, fine arts, and other cultural heritage during World War II, Felt commented "how ironic it is that we have no plan to protect our architectural and historic landmarks from becoming casualties of a peacetime real estate market."[56]

Mayor Wagner and his administration thus played an equivocal role in the emergence of New York's groundbreaking historic preservation laws. Three years before these were finally enacted, in the midsummer of 1962, Felt offered his resignation from the planning commission. The mayor insisted he stay on at least until the end of the year, "to get the West Side Urban Renewal Plan launched, and to get the newly-formed Housing Executive Committee, under his chairmanship, off to a good start." On December 18, 1962, Wagner "reluctantly" accepted Felt's resignation, praising him publicly: "I cannot refrain from commenting at this time on the great, and almost historic, contribution which Mr. Felt has made to planning and housing in this city. . . . Jack Felt is the ideal public servant . . . practical but yet thoroughly motivated by idealistic drives."[57] A few months later, Davies decided to leave the Housing and Redevelopment Board and return to the real estate company his father founded. The New York Times reported that "the decision [to abandon the West Village project] is understood to have been a factor in the resignation."[58] When Wagner decided not to seek reelection in 1965, and his city comptroller, Abraham Beame, was unable to keep city hall in Democratic hands, the once confident, formidable urban renewal order exited the stage of New York politics. Under John Lindsay's administration, the West Village was among the first neighborhoods to be offered blanket protection with districtwide landmark designation in 1969.

8 A Bitter End?
Self-Destruction by Democracy

The Collapse of the Urban Renewal Order in Britain

The demise of the urban renewal order was as universal as was its adoption. But the local variations on the endgame proved revealing, since the aftermaths differed markedly. In Britain, Harold Wilson led the Labour Party back to national power from 1964. But in the capital city, where the 1965 creation of the Greater London Council (GLC) expanded the electorate well beyond traditional Labour strongholds to encompass the entire suburbanized metropolis, that party alternated every few years with the Conservatives in controlling the new regional body, and planning became a major point of contention. As a result, the Greater London Development Plan drawn up from 1965 to 1969 was not approved until 1976. Meanwhile, preservation became an institutional force, beginning with the Civic Trust (founded in 1957 to counter the rural orientation of the 1895 National Trust), the Victorian Society (1959), and the establishment of Open Air Industrial Heritage museums (Iron Bridge, etc.). In 1967 the Labour government passed the Civic Amenities Act to facilitate the protection even of entire neighborhoods; the minister involved with its implementation, Wayland Kennet, wrote a handbook, *Preservation* (1972).[1]

In terms of the shift toward preservation, John Davis believes "the contrast between British Rail's gratuitous demolition of Hardwick's Euston Arch in 1962 and its inability to destroy Scott's St. Pancras in 1969 makes the point. By 1975 Simon Jenkins could feel confident that 'the fight for the relics of the pre-twentieth-century West End is almost won'; his judgment has since been largely vindicated."[2] Another poignant example was found at Covent Garden, an ancient food market that, like Les Halles in Paris or the Society Hill food distribution center in Philadelphia, was relocated to more modern trucking facilities outside the urban core (to Nine Elms in 1974). But unlike the other two examples, London's preservation movement saw the original market structures retained and adapted for the tourist economy. A more contentious issue was the proposal, prepared by a GLC planning team (together with the boroughs of Camden and Westminster) starting in 1965, to redevelop a surrounding ninety-six-acre area by clearing 60 percent of the neighborhood's structures, inserting road links, and relocating two thousand residents (figs. 8.1, 8.2). Perplexed by the aggressive GLC planners, one resident wrote that "these reckless fellows would certainly destroy most good urbane qualities the area possessed" and noted how ironic that the rede-

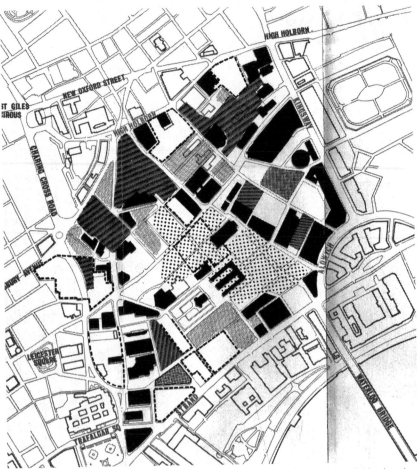

Figure 8.1 1968 London planning map appraising the entire Covent Garden neighborhood as needing redevelopment or other major fixes. (Covent Garden Planning Team, Covent Garden Area Draft Plan [Greater London Council, 1968]. With permission of City of London, London Metropolitan Archives.)

velopment plan brochure "is embellished with neighborhood shots showing old streets and traditional things that the plan's traffic and rebuilding scheme will actually eradicate."[3]

Citizen opposition greeted the plan's publication in 1968. One of the leaders of the group defending the Covent Garden and adjacent Soho districts, Cambridge architecture professor Nathan Silver, was coincidentally a former neighbor of Jane Jacobs in the West Village and a veteran of her neighborhood organizing. Observing the uncannily similar situation in 1972, he declared that "in London the

Covent Garden Community Association desperately needs someone like her."[4] According to Silver, Soho's neighborhood organizations had been dominated almost exclusively by young progressive professionals, such as himself and fellow architect Dickon Robinson, cofounders of the Soho Housing Association, or Ed Berman, a Harvard graduate who started a radical community theater company, Inter-Action.[5] The Covent Garden neighborhood by contrast retained a relatively engaged working-class community in its anti-renewal fight, as emphasized by Brian Anson, a Marxist planner with blue-collar roots, who defected from his position at the GLC in order to oppose its plans.[6] The plans produced an even higher profile (albeit less radical) resignation in protest in July 1972, when the GLC representative from the Conservative borough of Richmond-upon-Thames, Raine Legge (then Countess of Dartmouth, and later stepmother to Princess Diana) relinquished her seat on the Covent Garden task force because of her perception that "no individuals or bodies who represent the general public have supported us and I have felt increasingly that our proposals are out of tune with public opinion which fears that the area will become a faceless concrete jungle."[7] In 1973, following acrimonious hearings, Geoffrey Rippon, the Conservative secretary of the environment, designated much of the Covent Garden district as protected sites, and the redevelopment proposal gave way to revitalization measures.

Yet the social and economic pressures that underlay the urban renewal order, particularly the housing shortage, did not simply disappear behind historical markers, much to the chagrin of successive governments. The 1968 Seebohm report on social services noted the persistence of poverty; ongoing racial tensions were linked to deaths around Brick Lane in the 1960s and 1970s and during a 1976 riot at the Notting Hill carnival. In response to a sense of urban crisis, Labour and Conservatives alike had initially accelerated the redevelopment program over the course of the 1960s.[8] But the established urban renewal approach was rapidly losing its sheen, as tenant associations accused the government's housing policies of benefiting owners. And by 1969 a provocative new squatter movement had materialized, this round spearheaded by London's iconoclastic youth culture, with the occupation of the empty Piccadilly mansion next door to Queen Elizabeth's childhood home.[9]

The inclusion of grants for residential renovation in the 1969 Housing Act was indicative of a shift away from clearance. When Conservative Edward Heath became prime minister in 1970, one of his first acts was the creation of an omnibus Department of the Environment, incorporating many conservation authorities. David Eversley, strategic planning head for the Greater London Council under Conservative leader Edmund Plummer, wrote a critical 1973 examination entitled *The Planner in Society*, stressing "the changing role of a profession."[10] That same

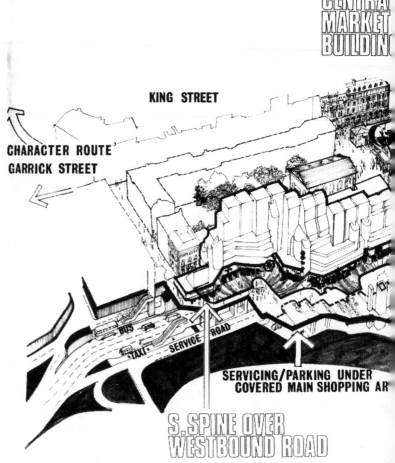

CONVERTED CENTRAL MARKET BUILDING

KING STREET

CHARACTER ROUTE GARRICK STREET

BUS

TAXI · SERVICE ROAD

SERVICING/PARKING UNDER COVERED MAIN SHOPPING AR

S. SPINE OVER WESTBOUND ROAD

Figure 8.2 Covent Garden redevelopment proposal including an expressway covered by a shopping center, parking, a conference center, and hotel towers. (Covent Garden Planning Team, *Covent Garden Area Draft Plan* [Greater London Council, 1968]. With permission of City of London, London Metropolitan Archives.)

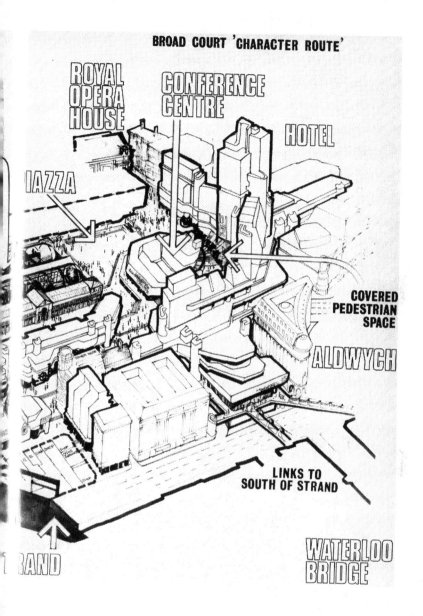

BROAD COURT 'CHARACTER ROUTE'

ROYAL OPERA HOUSE

CONFERENCE CENTRE

HOTEL

PIAZZA

COVERED PEDESTRIAN SPACE

ALDWYCH

LINKS TO SOUTH OF STRAND

STRAND

WATERLOO BRIDGE

Figure 8.3 A 1972 march of the Covent Garden Community Association and other residents opposed to the Greater London Council's redevelopment plans. In 1973, the Conservative cabinet secretary Geoffrey Rippon intervened to offer protection to the neighborhood. (Photo courtesy of Peter Baistow.)

Figure 8.4 This ironic 1976 street poster reflected growing resident opposition to urban renewal in London, as well as widespread British loss of faith in public planning agencies generally. (Source: Harald Bodenschatz, Volker Heise, and Jochen Korfmacher, *Schluss mit der Zerstörung? Stadterneuerung und städtische Opposition in West-Berlin, Amsterdam und London* [Gießen: Anabas, 1983].)

year, more extreme indictments of recent urban policy could be heard from David Harvey and Peter Hall and compared with historical perspectives like those collected in H. J. Dyos and Michael Wolff's *The Victorian City: Images and Realities*.[11] Labour's last go at national government for nearly twenty years was made under Prime Ministers Wilson (1974–76) and James Callaghan (1976–79), and included the passage of the Inner Urban Act of 1978, the Local Government Act 1974, and the Housing Act 1974, which shifted the focus from individual properties to neighborhood improvement (dubbed Housing Action Areas).[12]

Surveying the history of Britain since World War II, Kenneth O. Morgan laments how, "for most of these fifty-odd years, the British increasingly believed that they were badly led. Public figures suffered a collective loss of esteem." Public service of all kinds attracted far fewer young people than private pursuits. The prestige of academics and intellectuals diminished, as did the influence of patrician Keynesian planners and Tory paternalists who ruled (alternately) for nearly three decades after World War II. "The old enthusiasm for governments and the governing classes evaporated into a more cynical disillusion," Morgan concludes. "An older regime, based variously on deference, status, and structure, had been dismantled, but with no obvious replacement in view."[13] Despite unprecedented prosperity (or perhaps because of it), this fall from grace seemed as total as it was irreversible.

Anti-renewal in America: Empowerment or Obstruction?

Citizens across the United States registered their dissatisfaction with the reformist regimes that had enacted urban renewal. In Philadelphia, Richardson Dilworth resigned the mayoralty, halfway through his second term, to make an unsuccessful bid for governor in 1962, and city council president James Tate became Philadelphia's first Irish-American mayor. A *Philadelphia Bulletin* editorial described Tate's political style as "old-fashioned and non-elitist, shaped by personal loyalties and deals rather than ideas or ideals."[14] When Walter Phillips failed to unseat Tate in the Democratic primary the following year, the Young Turks' movement appeared to have run its course. "The city's mood, described as 'lively and confident' by Lewis Mumford in 1958, was declining to dank and demoralized."[15] Edmund Bacon stepped down from the City Planning Commission in 1970. In 1971, controversial Italian-American police commissioner Frank L. Rizzo was elected mayor on a law-and-order platform with racial overtones.[16] In Boston in 1967, populist Kevin White succeeded John F. Collins and only narrowly defeated Louise Day Hicks, who rode a wave of white working-class resentment over housing and school integration policies of liberal reformers.

Grassroots self-empowerment had been accompanied by federal legislative changes—congressional amendments to housing legislation in 1959 and 1965, and to the highway acts in 1962 and 1968—which revised the process of urban renewal to include more resident consultation and more physical rehabilitation. However, increasingly assertive citizen participation in urban planning was not universally welcome. As groups became more savvy and effective at obstructing proposals, unwanted projects could be deliberately bogged down, and eventually killed, through mandated hearings and court challenges—often exploiting the very legislative changes and program initiatives designed to encourage inclusion. Measures intended to defuse and incorporate opposition often, inversely, fanned it. Still, many U.S. urbanites came to believe that the sweeping powers granted to government agencies under the rubric of urban renewal had authorized a kind of undemocratic monster. Vigorous opposition, even gridlock, seemed warranted to check such tyrannical abuse of power.

Jane Jacobs became an archetype of the urban power shift. The *Village Voice* described her as "madonna misericordia to the West Village . . . who has probably bludgeoned more old songs, rallied more support, fought harder, caused more trouble, and made more enemies than any American woman since Margaret Sanger. . . . Overnight she became prophet and leader of a great neighborhood revival and, just as quickly, the scourge of nearly every city planner in the United States."[17] She was variously hailed in the press as "Madame Defarge, leading an aroused populace to the barricades," "a Jeanne d'Arc protecting the people of the city," and "the Barbara Frietchie of the slums." Often dismissive of her professional endeavors as an author, editor, activist and community organizer, many comparisons played on the mystique of an angry housewife: "If the lawyer's idea of aroused civic conscience is a run-away jury, then Jane Jacobs is the amateur's equivalent: a one-woman, runaway P.T.A. meeting."[18] But there was no denying her influence. One magazine feature noted that, less than one year since the publication of *Death and Life of Great American Cities*, when "her originality is only beginning to be felt . . . even critics of her book concede that it has permanently changed the climate of debate about the City." Perhaps, as detractors argued, many of her ideas had circulated in the profession for years. But Jacobs combined the one-two punch of a persuasive manifesto and a dramatic political victory to irrepressible effect (fig. 8.5). *Horizon* magazine editor Eric Larrabee wrote:

> Sooner or later, in any discussion of the American City today, the name of Jane Jacobs is bound to be mentioned. The reason is not far to seek. Last year a book was published challenging, in fact totally reversing, the assumptions on which orthodox city planning had so far been based. During the same year a group of private citizens in New York City—with a hitherto unbeat-

Figure 8.5 With her book under one arm and a phone balanced on her head, Jane Jacobs rallies citizens to topple city hall. Meanwhile, a developer carrying plans shores it up with moneybags. Supporters' balloons read "Victory in the West Village." This cartoon by Barbara Ninde Byfield appeared on a February 1962 block party invitation to celebrate residents' defeat of urban renewal proposals for that neighborhood. (Source: Jane Jacobs Papers, John J. Burns Library, Boston College. With appreciation to Glenna Lang and Marjory Wunsch.)

able alliance of public officials and real-estate speculators arrayed against them—fought to a standstill and ultimately defeated the so-called 'redevelopment' of their own neighborhood. Both the book and the battle, as it happens, owe most to the efforts of Mrs. Jacobs, a Greenwich Village housewife and architectural-magazine editor. She was chairman of the Save-the-West-Village campaign and ran it straight out of the book—and she wrote the book.[19]

As 1963 opened, New York journalists hailed Jane Jacobs as "that superb warrior for a better town," and even the society pages feted the West Village episode as a "dramatic example of what citizens can do to save a mindless city bent on suicide." Citing the defeat of West Village renewal and the Broome Street Expressway, in addition to Isaac Stern's crusade to preserve Carnegie Hall, "the saving of ancient trees in Tomkins Square . . . and the return of folk singing to Washington Square," *Cue* magazine declared that "battles can be won!" by citizens who "organize into pressure groups."[20]

Jacobs emerged as public intellectual of a particularly rigid stripe, whose professed core principle was "Don't compromise."[21] Jacobs and others in her neighborhood organization saw the renewal process as corrupt and disingenuous and refused to participate in it. This conviction led the group into an unremitting campaign to expose its opponents rather than find grounds for negotiation. Jacobs and other West Villagers feared any constructive suggestions on their part would be "converted into 'evidence' that the community was participating in urban renewal planning" and generally distract them from "from the overriding necessity at hand: killing the government plan."[22]

While increasingly successful at opposing outside plans, citizen groups like Jacobs' were perhaps less vocal for measures they supported, and practically none could yet point to any successful proposals of their own devising. Defensive battles often obscured the real point: that neighborhoods wanted to gain some control to pursue their own constructive programs. In the early 1960s, the New York traffic commissioner expressed a common criticism of the negative tactics deployed so effectively by Jacobs and the West Village neighborhood organization: "I have yet to hear of anything in New York that that group is for!" Indeed, that group deliberately chose to shelve its positive goals until after renewal plans were defeated, for fear they might be co-opted as tokens of community participation. Some community groups, however, did not wait for the dust to settle before devising counterproposals; they used them as rallying points against official plans. And others took control of the planning process in the wake of defensive victories.

Taking the Reins: Toronto's Anti-renewal Coalition Gains Power

Spared the worst excesses of urban renewal, Toronto enjoyed a political climate that offered sanctuary to refugees from developments in the cities of Europe and the United States; it also enabled Toronto to follow an alternate, middle course. German-born planner Hans Blumenfeld continued as an adviser to the Metro planning board after his mandatory retirement in 1961 and also became a lecturer in the University of Toronto's planning program. Yet when *Death and Life of Great American Cities* appeared in 1961, Blumenfeld published a surprising review that applauded Jacobs' opposition to slum clearance—though he continued to insist that a master plan and implementation through public ownership offered the best hope.[23] And from the comparative perspective of Jacobs herself, leaving behind the bitter divisions splintering U.S. urban politics by 1968, Toronto seemed on the cusp of a remarkable civic moment. As a broad reform movement emerged from neighborhood opposition, anti-urban-renewal protesters found themselves promoted from political outsiders to power brokers. With the movement building electoral momentum just as she arrived, the legendary New York activist enlisted as a supporter and even an adviser to a number of its key figures.

Jacobs viewed the budding reform movement in Toronto as an illustration and confirmation of her own ideas about power and governance in cities. In Jacobs' eyes, the undemocratic, unaccountable exercise of power had always been urban renewal planners' original sin. For her, Toronto became a reply to the urban crises south of the border. As she saw it, nearby Buffalo (and the American city in general) became a far more dangerous place due to the rift urban renewal policies generated between citizens and the state while undermining the physical basis of communities and neighborhood economies, thereby resulting in "frustration and an attendant violence that no police force can contain." Canadians, by contrast, still retained a civic optimism: "They aren't suspicious of their governments. They still have, in other words, a greater sense of trust, a greater stake in the neighborhoods where they live, a realization that what goes on in their cities can be influenced by them. It's this trust—of politicians and of each other—that makes cities safe; where people are mistrustful because they've been kicked around, they become apathetic."[24]

Jacobs was one of the early supporters of future Toronto mayor John Sewell, when he was still a radical young lawyer and grassroots activist working as a tenant organizer in Toronto's Trefann Court—an urban renewal area, which, aided in part by his intervention, was becoming increasingly controversial. In comparison with the scale of U.S. slum clearance and public housing projects, Canadians took a modest approach. The city's first public housing project, Regent Park in Cabbagetown, was actually approved through a voter referendum in 1947. But historian Sean Purdy nevertheless blames urban renewal and housing policies for exacerbating inequalities in metropolitan Toronto through stigmatization of public housing occupants. Residents in districts like Cabbagetown opposed and even mobilized against clearance throughout the 1940s and 1950s, albeit unsuccessfully. Citizen participation became detrimental to implementing plans only after about 1966, when opponents coalesced around new Toronto urban renewal projects proposed for Trefann Court, Don Mount, and Don Vale. Thereafter, New Left neighborhood organizers like Sewell and Karl Jaffary would find a potent political force by rallying residents of these renewal districts.[25]

Jacobs aided Sewell in his drive for redistricting so that the electoral influence of neighborhoods like Trefann Court would no longer be diluted by affluent districts like Rosedale, with whom they had been lumped under Toronto's long strip ward system. Jacobs testified in favor of new block wards, culminating in the province's redrawing of the city subdivisions for the 1969 election. This change then opened the way for Sewell's successful city council campaign for the new Ward 7 seat, during which he distributed leaflets advertising Jacobs' endorsement.[26]

When Sewell joined Toronto's city council, he took his place alongside a new slate of self-proclaimed reform aldermen elected citywide. The Spadina express-

Figure 8.6 Confronting Canada's urban renewal order: Jane Jacobs and two reformers on Toronto's city council led a protest against redevelopment at Sherbourne and Dundas Streets, April 5, 1973, tearing down construction fences to prevent demolition. Under Progressive Conservative mayor David Crombie, the city responded favorably to their disrupting the work crews through direct action. (Source: Jon Caulfield, "David Crombie's Housing Policy: Making Toronto Safe—Once More—for the Developers," in *The City Book: The Politics and Planning of Canada's Cities*, ed. James Lorimer and Evelyn Ross [Toronto: James Lorimer, 1974].)

way battle galvanized middle-class homeowners' organizations (British-inspired ratepayers associations) into a new political force, united under the banner of the Confederation of Resident and Ratepayer Associations (CORRA). By 1969, the reform label encompassed representatives from all the parties, stretching across the political spectrum, including both radical populists representing poor neighborhoods and bourgeois candidates endorsed by CORRA. Their common cause was a defense of neighborhoods and opposition to the Gardiner-style growth strategy of Metro planners. (While political scientist Warren Magnusson has termed this strategic consensus a "new urban conservatism," it is perhaps better thought of as "urban *conservation*"—less an ideology than pragmatic preservation.) New York residents may have exhibited similar impulses, but they never coalesced into such a formidable coalition. Though the reformers entered the new modernist Toronto city hall in 1969 as the minority on the city council, they represented a strong challenge to the political establishment. By 1972, there was a critical mass of reformers to attack the status quo ("the notion that planning issues were beyond politics") and replace the nonelected planning board with a more responsive citizen advisory panel.[27]

The reformers' greatest coup came in the election of December 1972, when thirty-seven-year-old David Crombie captured the mayoralty. Their charismatic winning candidate, however, hailed from the bourgeois wing of the reform movement. Generally a moderate, and loath to challenge his Progressive Conservative Party (which had long controlled the province, Metro, and usually the city as well), Crombie exposed the polarizing tensions within the reform coalition. Radical independents like Sewell resented him for shrinking from aggressive limits on the power of private developers.[28]

Jacobs provided succor to both the radicals and the moderates. Given the conspicuous anti-Spadina decree of Ontario premier Davis, the Progressive Conservative Party was tilting toward Jacobs' ideas even at the provincial level, and she was certainly also cozy with Mayor Crombie, commanding significant influence during his reformist administration. But she was also willing to truck with the radicals, as on the morning of April 5, 1973, when a demonstration—including Jacobs, reform aldermen Sewell and William Kilbourn and about eighty other citizens—assembled near the intersection of Sherbourne and Dundas Streets to protest the planned demolition of dilapidated row houses on that site (fig. 8.6). Since the law prohibited demolitions unless an area was fenced off, and since union agreements prevented the wrecking crew from replacing any damaged fences, Jacobs urged the group to halt the demolition by tearing down the required fences surrounding the houses—which is precisely what she and the others proceeded to do. Rather than committing political suicide by this act of vandalism, the aldermen galvanized the forces for preservation and bought enough time for the city to acquire the properties and develop an infill housing scheme.[29] Such outcomes—where destructive (literally) opposition tactics dovetail with constructive counterproposals, and New Left radicals cooperate with "red" Tories—appear even more remarkable when Toronto's post-urban-renewal reform movement is compared with that urban crisis Jacobs mentioned, unfolding south of the Canadian border.

Part IV Aftermath(s)
Ideological Polarization and Political Struggle after the Fall of the Urban Renewal Order

Keying off popular backlash, a circle of American policy intellectuals, based in Boston but influential in Washington, came increasingly to question the liberal project in cities by the mid 1960s. From the Joint Center for Urban Studies of Harvard and the Massachusetts Institute of Technology, figures including James Q. Wilson, Edward Banfield, Martin Anderson, and Daniel P. Moynihan staked out a terrain of skepticism that eventually attracted the label "neoconservative." Consequently, in addition to confronting a rash of anti-renewal protests and even race riots, the country's first cabinet secretary on urban affairs found not only his mandate but also his intellectual rationale seriously challenged before even taking office in 1966. His academic critics, all former liberals, foresaw at best a bleak future of harsh law-and-order prescriptions.

Yet theirs was not the only proposed alternative to the urban renewal order. The New Left appeared on U.S. college campuses in the early 1960s as a youthful impulse that included a rediscovery of poverty and various progressive politics generally submerged during the early cold war. And New Left criticisms infiltrated via social scientists into the training grounds of professional urbanists, first and foremost at the University of Pennsylvania, imparting a renewed, bottom-up social consciousness to questions of urban planning. Professor Paul Davidoff articulated a vision of neighborhood advocacy that inspired and radicalized a young cohort of planners. One of them, Denise Scott Brown, made early attempts to reconcile activism with urban design.

Neighborhood activists were not waiting around for theoretical frameworks or scholarly approval to realize that they might be their own best advocates in questions of urbanism. By the beginning of the 1960s, a number of New York City community groups had developed their own neighborhood plans, in contrast to the official ones from the city's planning commission. The most elaborate, and ultimately most successful, was a plan for affordable housing developed by residents of the West Village immediately after defeating the city's slum clearance proposal in 1962. The citizens produced a proposal that contravened nearly every practice of the urban renewal order. Their plan faced opposition from officials during the waning administration of Mayor Robert Wagner but eventually received a green light from a sympathetic Mayor John Lindsay in 1966.

After 1964, a vanguard of young urbanists started pouring into the neighborhood fray armed with New Left ideals, lending technical skills and professionals' legitimacy to community groups seeking to challenge urban renewal proposals from Cambridge to Harlem to South Philadelphia. In the latter case, Denise Scott Brown assisted the "the Main Street of black Philadelphia" to present itself as a neighborhood worthy of dignity rather than destruction. As a result, Edmund Bacon's last major unrealized contribution to a reimaged center city—the proposal to redevelop South Street—came to grief right on the doorstep of his flagship Society Hill project.

The flourishing partnership between New Left urbanists and community groups drew sustenance initially from private philanthropies, which provided seed grants for radical planners and architects to practice in poor communities. After 1964, such experiments relied on government support via the antipoverty initiatives of President Lyndon Johnson's administration. By 1966, advocacy planning had been incorporated into the major professional and educational organizations of the urbanist establishment, despite its radical repudiation of the technocratic expertise on which those institutions were founded. This perspective even achieved (relative) popular recognition by 1968 when the university student movement invoked community-based planning during campus sit-ins.

By 1968 the neoconservative camp was increasingly espousing an interpretation of U.S. cities as irredeemable, without hope of any effective government or intellectual response to their unraveling. That urban policy pessimism—expressed under the shorthand of urban crisis—became an important touchstone for conservative attacks on Great Society liberalism in general. Even before they found success at the ballot box in 1968, figures like Anderson and Moynihan shaped an urban policy for the Nixon campaign, emphasizing the withdrawal of federal engagement from cities. Thus, it would be the most cynical of responses that was empowered as the federal successor regime to the U.S. urban renewal order.

One former official in the Johnson administration's Department of Housing and Urban Development described the period as "the Waterloo of planning." The New Left urbanist vision of an alternative withered, a fate decided not by the results of grassroots engagements but rather via an electoral silent majority, taken by the President Richard Nixon's administration as a mandate for the top-down termination of Great Society urban programs upon which those experiments depended. Projects, careers, and whole neighborhoods that were invigorated during the heyday of New Left urbanism met disappointing fates by the early 1970s. Some, like the West Village housing plan in New York, were completed with difficulty and in a diminished form. Architects working with the Harlem community never witnessed the construction of any plans. Philadelphia's South Street neighborhood, after defeating highway and redevelopment proposals, found few public or private resources available for rehabilitation. The advocacy planners who assisted neighborhood groups subsequently found hardly any professional avenues in that direction and most disappeared into other specialties.

In Britain, New Left urbanist experiments mirrored their American counterparts. During the mid-1970s, a radical planner who resigned from the London planning department organized architecture students to assist Covent Garden residents advocating reuse of abandoned industrial buildings; the council even adopted a plan for one such site that grew out of the community group. But after 1979, the Thatcher administration's free-market ideology offered only the harshest rebuff to liberal and leftist alike: the complete dissolution of a multilevel urban renewal order, going so far as the abolition of London's municipal government. As in the United States, those who dreamed of a more sensitive version of urban renewal were left with none at all.

By contrast, Toronto in essence institutionalized many impulses of New Left urbanism, reconciling elements of the urban renewal order and its critics. In the mid-1970s, a new mayor and reform council undertook a massive core area study, aimed at protecting the central city while growing in a controlled way. Public authorities still executed large-scale, top-down, rapid redevelopments, such as the brownfield project that became the St. Lawrence Neighborhood. But even this provided a sharp break, applying a neo-traditional urbanism that rejected the high modernism of previous projects and reaffirmed the street patterns and mixed use of the existing city. Urban renewal would continue in Toronto, but the terms were completely transformed.

In Berlin, the old urban renewal order remained entrenched into the 1970s, with broad majorities welcoming a strong hand from planning authorities. While some German urbanists encouraged expanding resident participation, the same professionals expressly rejected the adversarial role of the Anglo-American advocacy planners. Despite some gestures toward preservation by architects in late 1960s, complete modernist redevelopment predominated in renewal areas. But the grass roots became more restive over the 1970s, as radical protests and squatters, particularly in Berlin's Kreuzberg neighborhood, demanded that officials attend to residents' preferences for older structures. Citizens collaborated with urbanists between 1978 and 1984 to rehabilitate dozens of apartment buildings as models of "gentle urban renewal," showcased in an international architecture exhibition sponsored by the city. Their reaffirmation of Berlin's traditional cityscape provided officials with a template for the citywide "critical reconstruction" of the restored German capital following its reunification in 1990. Thus, in a remarkable set of bookends, the violent ruptures which scarred that tumultuous city in the first half of the twentieth century contrasted with a comparatively stable transition subsequently. The cradle of modernist urban renewal evolved into a model of humane urbanism.

9 New Left Urbanism vs. Neocon Urban Crisis
Divergent Intellectual Responses in the United States

The Birth of Neoconservative Urbanism:
Boston Intellectuals Move Right

In the early spring of 1965, the presumptive U.S. urbanist in chief made a speaking trip to Boston. Robert Weaver was about to be nominated as the first secretary of the nation's new Department of Housing and Urban Development—in the process becoming the first African American to hold a cabinet-level post—after working on urban issues at the federal level since the Franklin Roosevelt administration.[1] At a moment when he should have represented the final consolidation of the urban renewal order, Weaver found himself assailed on dual fronts: by citizens in the streets and by intellectuals in the lecture hall. A large group of white residents from Charlestown and North Cambridge picketed his speech on the grounds that projects "enrich real estate speculators." In his Harvard address Weaver echoed the warnings of the Boston Housing Association ten years earlier, acknowledging the mounting protests: "Tearing down the houses occupied by the poor—and especially the poor who are non-white—and rebuilding for high-rent occupancy may accelerate the return of the middle class to central cities, but in time it generates widespread opposition to urban renewal." He conceded that "in retrospect, it seems obvious that urban renewal could never have been simultaneously the economic savior of the central city, an instrument for clearing slums, the means of attracting hordes of upper-middle-class families back into the central cities, and a tool for re-housing former slum dwellers in decent, safe, and sanitary housing." The incoming secretary sounded far from optimistic, and urban residents, ostensibly his core constituency, provided a less-than-supportive mandate.[2]

Just as vexing, the academicians in Cambridge, that wellspring of reformist urbanism since the 1930s, no longer offered automatic support. The popular revolt against urban renewal led urban policy intellectuals increasingly to question the entire liberal project in cities. The director of the Harvard-M.I.T. Joint Center for Urban Studies, James Q. Wilson, even asserted in January 1965 that "there is no urban problem in America except, perhaps, for the problem of urban aesthetics." Weaver (himself a Harvard graduate) responded that if Wilson really believed that there were no serious urban problems, then "the Joint Center might be merged with Harvard's Schools of Fine Arts and Architecture." Weaver attacked the Joint Center's publications as "intemperate and misleading," and he warned that "we are in danger of killing off our chance for living decently" if cynicism is substituted for more careful planning.[3]

Weaver worried about the intellectuals' abrupt opinion shift, driven to a great extent by researchers at the Joint Center, especially their analyses of the urban renewal order. As early as 1961, Joint Center sociologist Nathan Glazer questioned, with respect to the bland homogeneity of many renewal projects, whether it was possible for policymakers to prevent "what seventy percent of people think they want from becoming what ninety-nine percent actually obtain."[4] More thoroughly skeptical was political scientist Edward Banfield:

> American cities, accordingly, seldom make and never carry out comprehensive plans. Plan making is with us an idle exercise, for we neither agree upon the content of a "public interest" that ought to override private ones nor permit the centralization of authority needed to carry a plan into effect if one were made. There is much talk of the need for metropolitan-area planning but the talk can lead to nothing practical because there is no possibility of agreement on what the "general interest" of such an area requires concretely (whether, for example, it requires keeping the Negroes concentrated in the central city or spreading them out in the suburbs) and because, anyway, there does not exist in any area a government that could carry such plans into effect.[5]

The center's attentions—and its influence—shifted from city planning toward practical policymaking in Washington, under the leadership of James Q. Wilson and then, after 1966, Daniel Patrick Moynihan, with scholars of government including Glazer, Banfield, and Martin Anderson. In an era of fractious political controversy, this heralded a swing from the optimistic technocrat approach of planners toward more pessimistic political assessments, an emerging school of social theory eventually labeled "neoconservative."

Wilson became head of the Joint Center when founding director Martin Meyerson left for a deanship at the University of California at Berkeley in 1963.[6] Since his arrival at Harvard in 1959, Wilson's first books had shattered any lingering Progressive-era illusions about the discordant nature of race and politics in American cities.[7] At the Joint Center, Wilson collaborated with Banfield, who also arrived at Harvard in 1959, after working with Meyerson at the University of Chicago on the politics of planning for public housing.[8] In City Politics, Banfield and Wilson synthesized their empirical studies with the Joint Center's collected surveys of politics in thirty U.S. cities. They concluded that conflict-ridden interest group politics were unavoidable, despite the attempts of generations of idealistic reformers to create objective civil servants.[9] The skeptical notes of Wilson and Banfield became pointed political critique when M.I.T. industrial management student Martin Anderson's dissertation was published by the Joint Center in 1964 as The Federal Bulldozer.[10] This "critical analysis of urban renewal" from its inception in 1949 through the data of 1962 made a close examination of the economic costs and benefits of the program, concluding that vast expenditures had yielded very little progress.

Wilson moved the Joint Center into the heart of the storm around urban policy. His collection, Urban Renewal: The Record and the Controversy, asserted that the Joint Center, "like the two universities of which it is a part, takes no position on public issues, including urban renewal."[11] Nevertheless, Wilson cautioned those seeking to reconcile planning with civic democracy to be careful what they wished for, presenting sobering possibilities for renewal with any meaningful level of citizen participation. He warned that to undertake large-scale public works would inevitably be divisive in the absence of old-style urban political machines—precisely the ones destroyed by reformers who did not appreciate their effectiveness at integrating local and citywide interests. Those adversely affected by urban renewal, primarily the poor and/or minorities, inevitably opposed the projects. Idealistic reform mayors and expert planners had either to resign themselves to obstructionist citizen participation (and consequently slow progress) or else dispense with the ideal of democratic planning. Given the poor prospects of urban renewal, Wilson offered a bleak prognosis for urban America: "The central city may have to abandon the goal of recolonizing itself with a tax-paying, culture-loving, free-spending middle class and be content instead with serving as a slightly dilapidated way-station in which lower-income and minority groups find shelter and a minimal level of public services while working toward the day when they, too, can move out to a better life. That of course, is in great part the function that at least the older central cities of this country have always performed, and until we run out of lower classes (a day unfortunately far in the future), that may be the function they must continue to perform."[12]

A rhetoric of urban crisis expanded as Daniel P. Moynihan became director of the Joint Center in 1966, as evidenced in various affiliated projects.[13] The same year, M.I.T. published a collection—"with a mixed sense of crisis and confidence"—emphasizing the primacy of jobs and issues of urban work over physical planning or public services. Edited by Wilson's former Joint Center colleague Sam Bass Warner, Jr. (and including contributions from Marc Fried, John Dyckman, Gunnar Myrdal, and Jean Gottmann among others), Planning for a Nation of Cities was originally conceived at a conference encouraging "utopian

criticism and vision" with "a long view into America's urban future." However, Warner explained how this "distant vision" had dissolved behind "a high-temperature urban foreground," as volatile developments confronted the scholars: "the first summer of our labors was heralded by the Harlem Negro riots and the opening of President Johnson's 'War on Poverty,' the second summer closed with the Watts, California, riots and the establishment of a cabinet post for Housing and Urban Development."[14] Nor was that the last of the violent shocks for urbanists (and urbanites alike). A year later, following massive violence in Detroit and Newark, in an Emmy Award–winning documentary called "Summer '67: What We Learned" (which aired September 15, 1967 on NBC), television producer Fred Freed called upon Joint Center scholars to assess the causes of the disturbances. Then, in the spring of 1968, dozens of cities erupted in riots following Martin Luther King's assassination. By the time Secretary Robert Weaver found his staff barricaded in the H.U.D. offices because of unrest in the nation's capital city, the

Figure 9.1 A 1965 brochure from Harvard's design school (including this photomontage) reflected the growing urban crisis sensibility taking hold among Cambridge academics, particularly with the onset of urban riots. Harvard president Nathan Pusey diagnosed an urgent crisis in cities and the brochure elaborated: "Our cities are a disgrace and are growing worse. Elements hostile to man dominate our environments. We see disorder, filth and ugliness from every window. We do not control noise, smoke or congestion. Subjected to such pressures, decent human relationships erode into suspicion, hatred and violence. Whole segments of our population become alienated from our society. Slums spread faster than renewal." Such a negative view of cities was consistent with expressions decades earlier, including Harvard dean Sert's *Can Our Cities Survive?* (fig. 2.3), and the images were little changed since the time of Jacob Riis and Willy Römer (fig. 1.1). But the technocratic optimism that had recently spurred liberal urbanists at the Harvard and M.I.T. Joint Center for Urban Studies was increasingly scarce. (Courtesy of Special Collections, Graduate School of Design, Harvard University.)

crisis he had sensed brewing in Cambridge three years earlier had reached a desperate intensity, both in rhetoric and in reality.

A cultural crisis of conviction was precisely what James Q. Wilson perceived by 1968. In a series of articles appearing in the *New York Times Magazine*, just weeks after the King riots and simultaneously with the student occupation of Columbia University, Wilson displayed impatience with both the fixation on petty political scandals and the tolerance of antisocial behavior among rioters and antiwar demonstrators. Wilson provocatively suggested that neither corruption nor strong-arm police tactics were necessarily bad. His was a rough realism: Since violence and corruption are unavoidable elements of government, prudish middle-class moralism should not cloud one's ability to differentiate tolerable (even beneficial) from intolerable forms.[15]

Wilson suggested that specific examples of bribery, graft, and other forms of corruption be viewed within the context of other nonmonetary forms of compromise and persuasion accepted in democracy and that they be evaluated pragmatically rather than puritanically. He argued that the disintegration of old urban political machines had left the habits of corruption and petty greed without an institution able to integrate them for larger purposes, such as the provision of public utilities. Simultaneously, embourgeoisement of voter sentiment had made the now media-dependent candidates (formerly dependent on machine patronage) more vulnerable to even the hint of scandal. This resulted in charismatic candidates who hire bland, green administrators, rather than risking more experienced though ethically compromised staff.[16]

Regarding riots and other civil unrest, Wilson offered a cultural rather than a Marxist perspective, arguing, in effect, that "ideas have consequences." He predicted the rhetoric of discontent and resentment (especially over symbolic issues which are less easily resolved than more instrumental disputes) combined with permissiveness (a reluctance to use overwhelming government force to discourage the use of extralegal force) would lead to a growing incidence of expressive violence, even among the increasingly affluent. In response, he warned, the state must be willing to utilize force in order to maintain its monopoly on it, preventing contending factions within the polity from mobilizing violence.[17] His was a much messier, more Hobbesian worldview than that of the Joint Center's founders. Despair lay not far ahead.

The Birth of New Left Urbanism: Radicalizing the Philadelphia School

The popular revolt against the urban renewal order also yielded other new responses. At the opposite end of the ideological spectrum from the neoconservative urbanists in Cambridge, the most relevant ideas from the left emerged at the University of Pennsylvania's Graduate School of Fine Arts. Urbanists who studied and taught there in the 1950s were already riven by another divide, between advocates of social scientific methodologies and those who were concerned primarily with urban design questions. Denise Scott Brown, who arrived at the school in 1958, characterized this divide as analysts versus artists. But those debates were suddenly complicated by a newly aroused radical political sensibility and the more activist posture that accompanied it. "In an otherwise quiescent campus," Scott Brown recalled, by 1959 "something unusual was buzzing around the planning department"—something that would later be dubbed the New Left: "Here, long before it was visible in other places, was the elation that comes with the discovery and definition of a problem: poverty. The continued existence of poor people in America was a real discovery for students and faculty in the late 1950s. The social planning movement engulfed Penn's planning department."[18]

Scott Brown recalled a 1962 *New Yorker* article on poverty by James Baldwin ("page after page of diatribe against American society sat surrounded by *New Yorker*–style advertisements for luxuries and the good life") that "went like wildfire through our planning school." She observed this awakening as she finished her studies and began to teach in the school, noting how "social scientists became social activists; students chose projects in low-income, inner-city areas that we used to call 'the ghetto.'"[19]

That social planning movement found its systematic expression in Paul Davidoff, who came to the University of Pennsylvania in 1956 as a planning student and then became an instructor. Combining training from Yale Law School with a passion for social justice, Davidoff saw urban planning as a power struggle, a scramble for scarce resources. In particular, he envisioned the planning process as something analogous to the adversarial system of jurisprudence. Planners, he felt, only deluded themselves by thinking anyone could objectively identify and pursue some sort of abstract public interest. Instead, Davidoff saw only contending forces—and often grossly unequal ones. The poor and otherwise disenfranchised groups lacked a strong advocate in planning deliberations, and to rectify this, Davidoff imagined an urbanist analogue to the public defender—"advocacy planners"—who would function more like community organizers, helping citizens of modest means to voice their concerns (usually their opposition) about proposals sponsored by politically or economically powerful constituencies.

Davidoff crafted a theoretical framework for a more politicized approach to planning, publishing a set of highly influential articles over the early 1960s in the professional journals read by urbanists. Assisted by doctoral student (and later faculty member) Thomas Reiner, Davidoff honed his ideas teaching a course designed to democratize the process by which planning decisions were made, an approach articulated with the publication of an epochal 1962 article.[20] Then Davidoff's 1965 call for "Advocacy and Pluralism in Planning" made a strikingly relativistic contrast to the prescriptive confidence of practicing planners: "We know today, and perhaps it was always known, that there are no right solutions. Proper policy is that which the decision making unit declares to be proper."[21]

Davidoff rejected fine arts conventions in urbanist training. The design studio, overly concerned with aesthetics, was too conservative; he preferred to sensitize planning students to sources of social conflict like police brutality. Under Davidoff's banner, social-scientists-turned-planning-activists grew increasingly strident, and their position even threatened to marginalize the role of design-oriented faculty members (like Louis Kahn and Robert Venturi) in the School of Fine Arts.[22]

Scott Brown sympathized with both positions ("My New Brutalist background tied in equally well with Kahn and Gans"), but her hopes for a constructive synthesis of social scientific analyses and more inclusive, tolerant designs were dashed amid acrimony and polarization at the University of Pennsylvania. In opposition to her studio design classes, Davidoff ran an anti-studio class without any design whatsoever, exploring instead the problems of the Philadelphia police. Attacks on the studio institution, denounced as imperialist, eventually culminated in its abolition from the planning curriculum along with Scott Brown's departure from the university in 1965. While she recognized advocacy planners' criticisms as "excellent antidotes to overly-global thinking," she insisted on the necessity of "broad-scale, prototype thinking or middle and long-range planning and programming." She cautioned that, "by attacking all architects as proponents of shallowly-conceived beautification schemes, socially-minded planners are avoiding the reality: it is not the urban designers in planning commissions and agencies who block plans for social improvement of the cities, but far more powerful forces engrained in the social fabric itself."[23] That was a lesson she and other New Left planners soon experienced firsthand as they ventured out into restive urban communities.

10 The Anti-experts
Citizen Participation, Advocacy Planning, and the Urbanist Establishment

Grassroots Design:
The West Village Plan for Housing

Just as Paul Davidoff set forth his radical theoretical analysis of citizen participation in Philadelphia, pragmatic citizen groups in New York City found their own routes to something remarkably similar. On Manhattan's East Side, the Gramercy Neighbors successfully repulsed a slum clearance proposal, promoted by Robert Moses in 1956, by advocating for rehabilitation instead of demolition. After Moses shifted that scheme to a neighboring community, the Bellevue South Preservation Committee sought to replicate his defeat, and local architects, led by Mitchell Saradoff, drafted an elaborate counterproposal that emphasized infill construction with minimal clearance. (In spite of this, the city condemned the Bellevue neighborhood in 1964.) Residents affected by an East Village slum clearance proposal refused to be displaced and formed the Cooper Square Committee in 1959. The group developed an alternative plan over the 1960s, with consultation from M.I.T.-trained planner Walter Thabit.

The leading grassroots organizer for citizen planning, though, was Jane Jacobs, as demonstrated by a housing proposal she advocated in the West Village. By 1962 Jacobs had already made three distinct, consequential interventions into urban affairs: publishing her controversial *The Death and Life of Great American Cities* in 1961, organizing her neighborhood in opposition to a slum clearance proposal for the West Village during 1961 and 1962, and leading a citywide coalition to defeat the Lower Manhattan Expressway plan beginning in 1962. These dramatic strokes were of lasting importance for New York City, if not for urbanism generally. But all of them were reactive, defensive maneuvers against threats posed by unwelcome policies. In a letter congratulating Jacobs on her victories, Lewis Mumford warned her against "improvising the means of democratic expression each time, at a heavy cost," urging instead "a more permanent local organization" than such ad hoc opposition could supply.[1] Other city residents also sought more durable protections, and they were increasingly willing to take proactive, preventative actions against perceived threats to neighborhood stability. The historic preservation statutes being enacted by the mid-1960s offered some remedy, albeit in the form of relatively superficial—that is, exclusively architectural—protection. The time had come to offer some concrete alternatives to the urban renewal order on the social, economic, and political fronts, as well.

To enable residents not only to set their own priorities, but also to effectively advocate for them, Jacobs and her like-minded neighbors converted their ad hoc opposition group (the Committee to Save the West Village) into a permanent neighborhood association (the West Village Committee). The organization advocated relatively modest goals: garbage clean-up, tree planting, and property improvement. But tucked innocently within this list was a more ambitious aim: the creation of a working committee in 1962 to explore the possibilities for low-cost experimental housing.[2] This initiative announced the community group's intention to take neighborhood development into its own hands, challenging for dominance both private market forces like real estate speculation and those public agencies hitherto delegated the authority for making planning decisions.

To demonstrate that it was also capable of constructive citizenship, the committee proceeded to develop a proposal ("constructive plans, openly arrived at") for a housing development that challenged the assumptions of urban renewal and concretely demonstrated the viability of Jacobs' ideas on urbanism. These included an embrace of mixed uses, density, orientation toward the street and sidewalk, and other features at odds with the modernist principles enshrined in New York's new zoning codes. The committee pointedly adopted a set of inviolable principles, pledging to pursue housing alternatives without engaging in the standard operating procedures of urban renewal: Title I write-down, eminent domain, condemnation, and forced relocation.

The West Village neighborhood boasted residents with a variety of eclectic skills—from poets to longshoremen—to draw upon in support of its initiative (fig. 10.1). Jacobs herself was certainly well acquainted with the politics and considerations involved in planning, and in addition her husband was a practicing architect. Nevertheless, the West Village Committee eventually turned to the Chicago-based architectural firm of Perkins and Will to give form and practical design to the community's ideas. (Jacobs had lauded the firm for designs based on social function rather than aesthetic egotism.) The staff of the New York State Division of Housing and Community Renewal contributed consultation. Technical skills and professional expertise, not to mention other key resources like outside financing and official approval, were all necessary for the ultimate success of even a grassroots proposal. Yet the participatory process fundamental to the West Village Committee ensured that residents' goals and concerns were incorporated into the project from its inception. This was a direct challenge to the urban planning status quo.[3]

Figure 10.1 Community members meet in Jane Jacobs' kitchen around 1962, as an ad hoc neighborhood group, formed to stop urban renewal proposals, transformed into a permanent community organization. During the rest of the 1960s, the West Village Committee endeavored to translate its defensive successes into constructive initiatives to improve life in the area. Jane Jacobs is seated (perhaps posed) at left next to her son Ned; her husband, architect Robert Jacobs, is at far right next to publicist Rachelle Wall; MacMillan Press editor Stephen Zoll gestures at center; lawyer Martin Berger peers over his shoulder. (Unattributed photo from the Jacobs family collection.)

After a year of preparatory work, including "hundreds of hours" of neighborhood surveys, planning discussions and policy studies, the committee's proposal was unveiled on the front page of the *New York Times* in May 1963 (fig. 10.2). The plan for the West Village Houses envisioned a series of five-story walk-up apartment buildings whose orientation and scale meshed with older buildings, with mixed retail uses at street level. The construction sites were scattered along five small properties on the west side of Washington Street that opened up with the removal of the New York Central Railroad elevated freight line (a.k.a. the High Line). "These new houses are planned to fit intimately among existing structures, to fill out and complete the streets for which they are planned," a brochure promised. "They conform to the existing scale of the neighborhood and harmonize with its texture, enhancing, instead of disrupting, a highly successful and beloved neighborhood."

In an attempt to "combine humaneness and architectural beauty with what are called the social and economic realities of the 20th century," the committee

'Village' Group Designs Housing
To Preserve Character of Area

By ALEXANDER BURNHAM

The construction of 475 apartments in a series of five-story structures on vacant land in Greenwich Village was proposed yesterday to test new theories in urban housing.

The suggestion was made by the West Village Committee as [an] effort to sub- mi[tute] ing for the cur[rent] co[ncept of] urban housing as massive apart- m[ent] The committee, [a] vocal citizen co[mmittee] said the plan [is] co[nceived as] one to move mi[re than] [sa]ve the charac- ris[tics] [neigh]borhood. co[n] [said] that the plan uti[lize] to either pri- pa[rt] [fin]ancing. In the mo[st] it is proposed [fina]ncing and pri- th[e] [provi]ded by the In- fiv[e] [longshoremen's As- pl[e] la[nd] [unit]s to combine re[p] architectural [are called the otl ic realities of . Its intention C[o]

is described as putting "harmonious" housing into existing communities in place of the present "standardization and regimentation of urban society" through tall, massive and barracks-like projects.

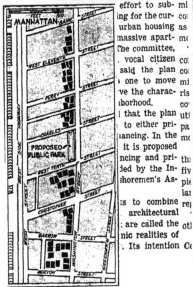

The New York Times   May 6, 1963
Shading shows sites urged for village housing test.

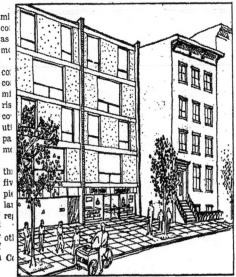

PLAN FOR WEST VILLAGE: Architect's sketch shows planned five-story units as they would appear integrated with existing brownstone. The architects for the project of the West Village Committee are Perkins & Wills.

Figure 10.2 The West Village Houses, a proposal in pointed contrast to typical housing redevelopments under urban renewal, debuted on the front page of the *New York Times* in May 1963. Devised by residents rather than planning officials, Jane Jacobs and her neighbors proposed a low-rise, modern ensemble across scattered sites, requiring no demolition or dislocation, featuring a mix of residential and commercial activities in structures that addressed the sidewalk and integrated with the surrounding cityscape. (From *The New York Times*, © May 6, 1963, *The New York Times*. All rights reserved. Used by permission and protected by the Copyright Laws of the United States. The printing, copying, redistribution, or retransmission of the Material without express written permission is prohibited.)

boasted that it could reduce construction costs by 60 percent while increasing the number of dwellings. The $8.5 million plan was to be funded by the state (90 percent) together with a union of port workers, the International Longshoremen's Association (10 percent). The scheme was radical in its modesty: no relocation, no elevator high-rises, no pedestrian superblocks. Most radically of all, the plan was commissioned by and derived from community laypersons, not the city's official planning agency. The proposal was, in short, a provocation, a grassroots alternative to the urban renewal order.[4]

New Left Urbanists Offer Anti-expertise: Harlem, Boston, and Philadelphia

Leftist urbanists in academic and professional planning circles rallied behind such grassroots developments, with Paul Davidoff's ideas providing the rationale. This shift was most evident in 1964. In Cambridge, Massachusetts, planning student Chester Hartman, sympathetic to Davidoff's critiques of the overly aesthetic focus of studio training, left the Harvard Graduate School of Design to pursue a Ph.D. studying slum clearance in Boston's West End. In 1964 Hartman became involved with several Boston-area community groups opposing the Inner Belt highway through Cambridge and urban renewal projects in Allston. He set up Urban Planning Aid, a pro bono advocacy planning practice with Lisa Peattie, Robert Goodman, and others. This "counter-planning force," in Hartman's words, assisted neighborhoods including Roxbury and the South End.[5]

Also in 1964, University of Pennsylvania-trained architect C. Richard Hatch organized the Architects Renewal Committee in Harlem (ARCH), a neighborhood-based advocacy planning firm led by young African-American urbanists (fig. 10.3). Hatch was soon joined by J. Max Bond, a Harvard-trained architect with previous experience in France and Ghana, and eventually the staff grew to over a dozen. The group's initial projects included advising tenants on their rights and surveying the neighborhood's housing stock, promoting both rehabilitation and infill housing. Davidoff sat on the ARCH board, a connection which the organization's publications made explicit: "We at ARCH believe strongly in the advocacy planning concept. We believe that neighborhood involvement coupled with technical sensitivity to community needs is essential to the planning process if it is to be at all relevant to Black and Spanish-speaking people" (fig. 10.4). One of ARCH's leaders, Arthur Symes, put it this way: "Architecture and planning are just too important to be omitted from the lives of people who happen to be poor."[6]

In Philadelphia, the ideas of advocacy planning found an outlet right near their source, as sympathetic students and teachers from the University of Pennsylvania's design school abetted anti-expressway neighborhood groups along

Figure 10.3 "Architecture and planning are just too important to be omitted from the lives of people who happen to be poor." C. Richard Hatch created the Architects Renewal Committee in Harlem (ARCH) in 1964–65 as a community-based advocacy planning firm led by young African-American urbanists. Funding came from foundations (the Taconic Fund, the Ford Foundation) and President Johnson's War on Poverty initiative. The group's initial projects included advising tenants on their rights and surveying the neighborhood's housing stock, promoting both rehabilitation and infill housing. (Source: *East Harlem Triangle Plan* [Architects' Renewal Committee in Harlem, August 1968].)

the proposed crosstown artery. Beginning in 1964, Thomas Reiner and planner Harriet Johnson began devoting planning classes to the plight of the South Street community.[7] Together with their students (including planning grad Louis Rosenberg), members of an American Institute of Architects workshop (including Allen Hinckey), and VISTA volunteers (including Mitchell Smith), they acted as a panel of advisory consultants to the residents and challenged the transportation projections of other academic experts.[8] By the end of 1967, his students and junior colleagues at the University of Pennsylvania had even convinced the expressway's originator, planning professor Robert Mitchell, that myopic methods of analysis had "neglect[ed] the social aspects" of the proposal. "Psychologically," Mitchell concluded after four summers of nationwide urban rioting, "the city cannot af-

Figure 10.4 The Afrocentric cityscape. ARCH urbanists declared that "neighborhood involvement coupled with technical sensitivity to community needs is essential to the planning process if it is to be at all relevant to Black and Spanish-speaking people." Rather than a proposal for dramatic redevelopment, their 1968 sketch of Manhattan's 125th Street corridor was rather a reaffirmation of the sidewalk public sphere in a minority neighborhood, precisely the sort of place targeted by conventional slum clearance schemes. (Source: *West Harlem Morningside: A Community Proposal* [Prepared by Architects' Renewal Committee in Harlem, Inc. and West Harlem Community Organization, Inc.; September 1968].)

ford at this time one more symbol of separation between the black community and City Hall."[9]

Mayor James Tate proved susceptible to the anti-highway pressures, though he remained noncommittal about the neighborhood's ultimate fate. A citizen group applied for urban renewal funds to revitalize, rather than raze, South Street. Early in 1968, community organizers approached Denise Scott Brown to help shift the neighborhood orientation from expressway opposition toward constructive rehabilitation. Scott Brown had left Pennsylvania to accept teaching positions on the West Coast, first at Berkeley then at U.C.L.A., and to immerse herself in the cities of the U.S. Sun Belt. In 1967, however, she married architect Robert Venturi and returned to Philadelphia to join his firm. While they waited for clients to appear, they taught courses together at Yale, including one focused on the ideas embodied by Las Vegas and American commercial vernacular urbanism. However, the couple was in fact subsisting primarily on the income from the Venturi family grocery store on South Street.[10] The Citizens Committee to Preserve and Develop the Crosstown Community (CCPDCC) soon provided Scott Brown's fledgling design firm with its first city planning commission (initially pro bono), and she in turn served as the lead urbanist for the expressway opposition. Scott Brown remembered: "The social planner who invited me to join the planning team said that although she didn't believe in architecture and thought that we should be tackling the social and economic problems of cities first, people were going to be pushed out of their houses onto the streets before we could ever deal with jobs or education. She added 'If you can like Las Vegas, we trust you not to neaten up South Street at the expense of its people.'"[11]

It was a belated recognition by the social planners she had sparred with at the University of Pennsylvania that even community activism could benefit from designers, provided they were adequately sensitized. For her part, Scott Brown had internalized much from the advocacy planning method of Davidoff and Reiner, acknowledging that "although it underrates both artistry and analysis, it is really the only moral method of planning and I have tried to follow it as a practitioner."[12] Even her influential studies of the aesthetics of Las Vegas and Levittown, she maintained, were "initiated in considerable measure through social concern."[13]

Learning from Las Vegas, written by Venturi, Scott Brown and fellow member of their firm Steven Izenour, represented a theoretical synthesis of the authors' design studio studies of the Las Vegas Strip, considered alongside recent professional projects including the South Street consultation. The Strip embodied "a complex order. It is not the easy, rigid order of the urban renewal project or the fashionable 'total design' of the megastructure."[14] The text manifested the dual-front debates of the University of Pennsylvania's fine arts faculty. On the one hand, the authors challenged an orthodox modernism that had "impoverished itself" by renouncing decoration applied onto structures and had ironically thereby "distorted the whole building into one big ornament."[15] On the other hand, they entreated social planners who might take the book's focus on vernacular commercial architecture as too aesthetic, declaring theirs was not "a criticism of those architects and academics who are developing new approaches to architecture through research in allied fields and in scientific methods. These too are in part a reaction to the same architecture we have criticized. We think the more directions that architecture takes at this point, the better. Ours does not exclude theirs and vice versa."[16]

The ideas that Scott Brown and Venturi developed in their teaching and writings advocated for an aesthetic vision that ran far beyond Philadelphia planning director Edmund Bacon's selective preservation. Not only had they cultivated an appreciation of the gaudy decadence of the Las Vegas Strip, but they also undertook a general aesthetic reappraisal of the ubiquitous if oft-maligned (at least among elite design circles) American suburb and Main Street. At the end of his 1966 treatise, *Complexity and Contradiction in Architecture*, Venturi invoked Gertrude Stein's observation that "Toledo [Ohio] was very beautiful" and then proceeded to prod the design establishment: "Is not Main Street almost all right? Indeed, is not the commercial strip of a Route 66 almost all right?"[17] In *Complexity and Contradiction*, Venturi called for an architecture that would accommodate more variety, juxtaposition and formal complexity than the rigid dogma of modernism (fig. 10.5). ("We have operated too long under the restrictions of unbending rectangular forms.") The work helped establish Venturi's reputation as an iconoclast in the halls of functionalist modernism, but he readily acknowledged that it was the foreign eye of Denise Scott Brown, especially her exposure to the commercial sensibilities of British pop art and even the late-colonial eclecticism of southern Africa, that enabled him to see the inherent logic of the American landscape. Here, finally, was the U.S. answer to the British Townscape perspective.[18]

Through the family grocery that Venturi inherited, the couple had a deep personal connection to the cultural and economic life of South Street. Suddenly, the South Street residents' initiative offered an opportunity to put their Main Street ideas into practice.[19] (South Street, they noted, "could, in fact, be called the Main Street of Philadelphia's center city black community.")[20] For Scott Brown, her husband, and their firm, South Street became crucial as "the first community project we undertook as practitioners not academics."[21] Thus, the project's success was as crucial for them as for the residents, given their precarious professional status: "We were unable to find other funds for our work—in one ironic week we were turned down on a funding request for the Las Vegas study because we were 'not socially concerned' and on the Crosstown Community because we were 'too political.'"[22]

The community group asked the designers to produce a plan for immediate rehabilitation of the area, in an attempt to raise property values and generally make South Street "a viable place to live again." Neighborhood committee leader

Figure 10.5 Typical Main Street, U.S.A.: the final plate from Robert Venturi's 1966 *Complexity and Contradiction in Architecture*, showing a visually busy Canal Street in New Orleans. The same photo was used by *Architectural Forum* editor Peter Blake two years earlier to decry the "deterioration of America's landscape" into chaos. In a polemical appropriation and transvaluation of that negative example, Venturi concluded with an appreciation of vernacular American urbanism: "Is not Main Street almost OK?" (© Wallace Litwin/The Burns Archive NY.)

George Dukes intended this strategy to "make the city's condemnation of the area too expensive and too socially explosive."[23] As Bacon did in Society Hill, the plan attempted to control real estate markets instrumentally, but in the South Street case it was a defense of the current residents *against* the city's planning apparatus, rather than an exercise of that authority. Under the circumstances, most of what Scott Brown and her team offered had to be symbolic: "The very first act, we suggested, should be to erect a banner over the street, paint one sign and rehabilitate one building, to show someone cares."[24] Her counterplan for the area was constantly forced to contend with the limitations of strained human and material resources in an embattled community: "The community vetoed one other scheme: some architects recommended getting donations of paint and painting all the side walls of houses where buildings had been demolished on the street. The community said 'If we had enough people with the ability to organize doing that, why would we waste their time on something so futile? We need them for other things such as banging on the mayor's door.' They also believed we should not waste community time on, for example, land use surveys because political activities were more important."[25]

Scott Brown's role proved to be more in the way of advocacy than planning, asserting with professional authority before various audiences that the neighborhood's architecture—and by extension the community—was worthy of preservation. While admitting the reality that the area's "fine, turn-of-the-century storefronts, preserved by a lack of pressure for change in the decaying economy, were badly deteriorated" (and often deliberately neglected in the face of a highway proposal), Scott Brown simultaneously exhorted the professional architecture and planning establishment to undertake an inversion of aesthetic values: "For all its decay and for all the evidence of social and individual distress, South Street is a lively, lovely piece of city, more capable of endearing itself to the imagination than the more famous but less vital Society Hill area bordering it."[26]

Like Bacon before her, Scott Brown had the primary role as an urban designer of propagating a vision, a way of seeing possibilities in the urban landscape. But her *Leitbild* was more tolerant of the messy conditions of urban complexity. Rather than the sanitation of the streetscape, she sought comparative justifications for its aesthetic dissonances (fig. 10.6). "The South Street corridor can become another Greenwich Village with the proper care," Scott Brown told a five-hundred-strong meeting in the Theater of the Living Arts. "A selective renovation . . . could renew the area as a commercial center and would bring tourists in to savor the historical symbolism and the architectural classics that abound here. Many of the homes, especially along Kater and Delhi streets, with their bright red, blue and pastel colors look now as though they were transplanted from the French Riviera."[27] Scott Brown (as Bacon did) found that her design sensibility was politically empowering, particularly as a tool for the important media battle, attracting national notice in an *American Heritage* beautification column, among others, as well as a good hometown angle: "At one point, the CCPDCC got good political coverage in the art section of a local daily, when no other section was sympathetic."[28]

A *Philadelphia Inquirer* society column announced "Advocacy Planners Put Hope in Ghetto." Its author was clearly smitten by Scott Brown's characterization of South Street's "intact chain of beautiful small 19th-century storefronts" as "unique, urbanistically eloquent in their relation to sidewalk and street, and by 'lucky' incident, preserved." Only a couple years after the completion of the colonial-perfectionist Society Hill project, the columnist tsk-tsk-ed at the

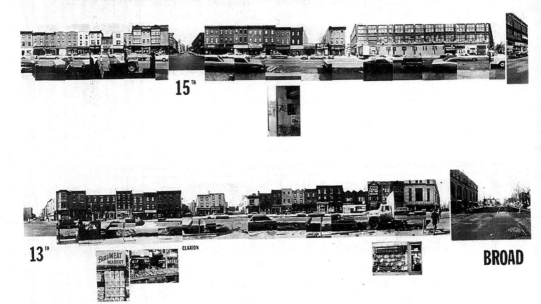

15ᵗʰ

13ᵗʰ   CLARION   BROAD

Figure 10.6 Almost OK. A streetscape survey of South Street in Philadelphia, inspired by pop artist Ed Ruscha's photographic study *Every Building on the Sunset Strip* (1966). When the so-called Main Street of Black Philadelphia was targeted for an expressway, an interracial opposition group organized. The Committee to Preserve and Protect the Crosstown Community commissioned the upstart firm of Robert Venturi and Denise Scott Brown in 1968 to advocate for the neighborhood, particularly in terms of combating negative perceptions of the existing cityscape. (Courtesy of Venturi, Scott Brown, and Associates, Inc.)

Depression-era plans that nearly "colonialized" South Street, "which would have been a barbarity, as any member of the Victorian Society of America can tell you." She enthused over the "conservative surgery" to "save the life of South Street," which deserved a "face-lift" (as did Market Street in the central business district). And this revival could conveniently occur "just in time to give it a major role in the Bicentennial celebration as a model thoroughfare of Negro culture, past and present."[29]

By the spring of 1970, this positive visualization approach had taken hold of media perceptions, and even demographics, as newspaper coverage of an open house organized by merchants of the South Street renaissance indicated: Reporters spotlighted the presence of artists and youth counterculture, echoing Scott Brown's comparisons with Greenwich Village.[30] By the end of 1970, pro bono law-

yer Robert Sugarman was assisting the neighborhood to pursue $2.3 million of federal urban renewal funds, and George Dukes, as chairman of the Project Area Committee, declared optimistically that the community had developed "ample plans for the crosstown area . . . adding 'We've been thinking while we've been fighting.'"[31]

Establishment Urbanism Experiments with the New Left Opposition

The assorted experiments in New Left urbanism flourished not only because of a shift in the Zeitgeist, but also thanks to the support of powerful patrons, at least for a time. Private philanthropies, particularly the Ford Foundation, provided early seed grants for the Architects Renewal Committee in Harlem and other urban neighborhood organizations. (ARCH also received crucial seed money from Stephen Currier's Taconic Fund.) And from 1964 onward, under various Great Society initiatives to tackle poverty, civil rights, and urban problems, federal funds supported the activities of numerous community organizers via the Labor Department's Office of Economic Opportunity (OEO) and the Model Cities program of the newly formed Department of Housing and Urban Development. For example, by 1966–67 ARCH was operating with an annual budget of over one hundred thousand dollars, with private philanthropic sources providing roughly half that total and the remainder coming from the OEO.[32] In many cases, these organizations were explicit in their embrace of advocacy planning to reconcile the "dominant forces affecting the quality of urban life: the growth of technocracy and the quest for participatory democracy."[33] When New York City elected the liberal Republican John Lindsay as a reform-oriented mayor in 1965, he championed measures to devolve power and accountability into "neighborhood city halls," and he lent his support to the West Village Houses in particular, helping the community group obtain permits from unsympathetic city officials. In the fall of 1967 New York Senator Jacob Javits convened congressional hearings, featuring testimony from Chester Hartman alongside Charles Abrams and Roger Starr, to focus on many of the increasingly problematic issues in urban planning, including citizen participation, environmental determinism, and what made the European outcomes so different.[34]

Just as New Left urbanism obtained powerful political patrons at the local and national levels, it also became ensconced in major professional institutions, as well. In the summer of 1964, a group of activism-oriented urbanists founded Planners for Equal Opportunity (PEO). Charter members included Paul Davidoff, Herbert Gans, Chester Hartman, Marshall Kaplan, and Walter Thabit. PEO immediately agitated professional organizations, training programs, and planning practitioners for greater inclusiveness.[35]

In 1964, the planning department at Brooklyn's Pratt Institute gave community advocacy its first permanent institutional role through a program, funded by the Rockefeller Brothers Fund, to consult residents in the Bedford-Stuyvesant neighborhood. By 1965, the University of Pennsylvania had abolished the traditional studio method from its planning curriculum. In 1966, Harvard University decided to incorporate advocacy planning into the Graduate School of Design and asked Chester Hartman to return as a faculty member to the program he had dropped out of in protest a couple years before. There Hartman set up the Urban Field Service, a student version of his pro bono firm, Urban Planning Aid.

In his 1971 *After the Planners*, M.I.T. planning professor Robert Goodman, who had practiced advocacy planning with Urban Planning Aid, condemned conventional renewal as liberal chicanery masking the disempowerment of citizens, ultimately concluding that socialism was the only response to the regressive effects of supposedly progressive planning. Similarly, Marshall Kaplan, who had trained at M.I.T. in the 1950s, came to describe himself as an advocate planner, convinced of the "marginal benefits of advocacy planning, given the political economy of scarcity we live in" as well as the "pluralism inherent in our cities and the tenuous nature of the planner's knowledge about what works and what does not work." Kaplan saw advocacy planning as critical to giving the poor a fair allocation of resources, and as a remedy for the "historic failure" of planners to involve affected groups.[36]

Thus, radical anti-planning advocacy, once defined in opposition to the urbanist establishment, was increasingly seen as mainstream, while traditional technocratic expertise in urban policy fell into disrepute. This paralleled, and even slightly anticipated, the eroding support for the foreign policy of Defense Secretary Robert McNamara, RAND Corporation whiz kids, and Washington's "best and brightest"—no surprise, then, that the student movement, so galvanized by antiwar sentiment, took up community planning as a complementary cause.[37] As sit-ins on campuses nationwide expressed grievances related to Vietnam, curricula, and governance, they also frequently included the plight of poor and minority residents of their college towns.[38] Advocacy planning, with its radical theoretical roots in graduate schools of fine arts, and its practical beginnings in mobilizing disparaged neighborhoods, had made its way into the moral consciousness of the collegiate bourgeoisie.

However, with popular support, as in other matters, a high-water mark can simultaneously signal the start of a receding tide. Any full account of the major social movements of the 1960s—student, antiwar, women's rights, and civil rights—must incorporate the potent conservative backlash that they engendered. Dramatic campus sit-ins, for example, hardened ideological lines and alienated many liberal faculty members from leftist students, while many whites took violent urban disturbances as a justification for abandoning any sympathy with the plight of poor blacks. Similarly, that political reaction shaped the fate of U.S. urbanism of all ideological stripes.

11 Nixon Urbanistes and "the Waterloo of Planning"

Neoconservative Urbanists + Silent Majority Backlash = the Urban Crisis Coalition

The M.I.T.-Harvard Joint Center for Urban Studies was founded in 1959 by urbanists who were liberal optimists about the possibilities for solving urban problems via social scientific analysis and modernist design. The center's opening was timely for providing credentialed expertise on questions of city planning and policy, just as Washington increasingly demanded such. The center's urbanists would advise administrations from Kennedy through Nixon. But in the mid-1960s the center's tone and leadership shifted—under political scientists like James Q. Wilson, Daniel P. Moynihan, and Edward Banfield—toward a profound skepticism about professional and policy fixes. By 1968, Banfield had concluded characteristically that the "government cannot solve the urban problem."[1] Nor did he express much confidence in the contributions of academic experts: "It's a national tragedy that people in decision-making roles turn over to intellectuals or computers the right to make their decisions. And it's bad for scholarship, too. A good professor is a bastard perverse enough to think what he thinks about is important, not what government thinks is important."[2] Banfield's dark reflections on "our urban crisis" became a touchstone for anti-statist conservatives.[3]

Stephan Thernstrom and Sam Bass Warner, Jr., were associated with the Joint Center as scholars of the urban past, consolidating the position in the late 1960s and early 1970s of a "new urban history" that trained social scientific analysis on the historical processes of urbanization and industrialization.[4] But each also actively engaged his scholarship with the ramifications of contemporary urban policy, and their work reflected the ideological developments of the period. A later retrospective by fellow historian Robert Wiebe described Warner's progression as one of rising anger, outrage, and indignation at the urban prospect—from the bewildering stratification process described in *Streetcar Suburbs* (1962), to the inhumane city (particularly for minorities) of *The Urban Wilderness* (1972), to a final renunciation of the Enlightenment heritage by *Province of Reason* (1984): "Planners monitored only by their own rationality threaten us with obliteration; individuals of conscience stand as our best hope."[5]

Thernstrom moved toward such an explicit break even earlier. Specifically, he received a grant to document and evaluate the efforts of Action for Boston Community Development (ABCD), a neighborhood antipoverty program launched in

1962 with "political support, civic respectability, professional competence and a good deal of money. Not only the top political leadership of Boston but the civic elite and key social-service professionals were eager to see this experiment succeed. Both the Ford Foundation and the federal government, in search of a new point of leverage from which to press for the reform of central city institutions, were happy to foot the bills."[6] Thernstrom's findings, if not his own political inclinations, were in keeping with the Joint Center's trend toward skepticism of liberal programs. His observations echoed James Q. Wilson's description of the double bind of urban renewal politics, in general, and Daniel P. Moynihan's criticisms of President Johnson's War on Poverty, in particular. The pressures for community control mired ABCD in too much neighborhood factionalism to produce satisfactory results.[7] He reserved the harshest judgment for professional urbanists who lent intellectual legitimacy to the program.

Declaring "The modern city is not a laboratory," Thernstrom amplified his conclusions into a broadside attack against social scientists, planners, and other experts meddling in cities: "The most sweeping conclusion suggested by this case study is the gloomy possibility that feasible new ideas on what can be done about city problems are exceedingly difficult to find, and that social-planning experts are not capable of providing them."[8] Thernstrom interpreted the ABCD experience to suggest that "the root problems of the modern metropolis are not technical but political, and that expertise is largely irrelevant to their solution."[9] Fundamental questions of "who gets what when and how," Thernstrom indicated, should be left to conventional political and market processes.[10]

Such was Thernstrom's judgment on a Boston program that Martin Meyerson helped frame—a classic example of the Joint Center's earlier hope for constructive urbanism through an alliance of academic planning and government power. As one of President Lyndon Johnson's urban advisers, Meyerson even proposed a national Urban Institute, modeled on the RAND Corporation. But from a vantage point at the other end of the 1960s, such a foreign policy analogy seemed as devastating as it was appropriate.[11] Nor was this merely an academic discussion. "Expert" urban proposals proved politically explosive at the grass roots, and while the fallout was not entirely predictable, it soon became clear that the country was drifting rightward. Richard Nixon's election in 1968 signaled the nationwide meltdown of a liberal political order in place since the New Deal.

Nixon's ascent may have marked an ideological changing of the guard, but the Joint Center continued to send envoys to Washington, just as it had done for the Kennedy and Johnson administrations. The transition of power provided as many opportunities for Joint Center urbanists as it foreclosed. Despite antipathies between Nixon and many intellectuals, the candidate's New York City law partner Leonard Garment brought Moynihan, now an emerging neoconservative, and Martin Anderson to Nixon's attention during the campaign.[12] By then a professor at Columbia University, Anderson was recruited as a speechwriter in 1966, at the earliest stages of Nixon's presidential bid, and he shaped a platform stressing minority entrepreneurship or "black capitalism." With his M.I.T. doctorate in industrial management and an influential urban renewal critique of the "federal bulldozer," Anderson became a key figure in both the campaign and subsequent administration, until his departure in 1971 (only to return to Republican politics during Reagan's campaigns), promoting research analysis and shaping a wide range of policy areas from the abolition of the draft to welfare reform.[13] Anderson staunchly defended the candidate against his detractors: "The antagonism of liberal intellectuals is based on ignorance. They always come to the *ad hominem* argument with Nixon. He represents a basic Republican philosophy of sincere concern for the individual. Liberals mouth this, but they don't care for the individual. Nixon is just as much an intellectual as the professors I knew at Dartmouth, M.I.T. and Columbia."[14]

Beginning during his time in the Johnson administration, Moynihan moved steadily in a neoconservative direction. As Johnson's assistant secretary of labor, Moynihan had produced a hotly debated working paper perceived as an attack on the black family. He defended his position, telling the Americans for Democratic Action that "liberals must divest themselves of the notion that the nation, especially the cities can be run from agencies in Washington. Liberals must somehow overcome the curious condescension which takes the form of sticking up for and explaining away anything, howsoever outrageous, which Negroes, individually or collectively, might do."[15] Likewise, Moynihan's subsequent book on the failures of the War on Poverty, *Maximum Feasible Misunderstanding*, appeared, at least to some, a deliberate attempt to curry favor with the incoming Nixon administration by voicing a critical review of its predecessor. Moynihan thus put himself in a position to offer insider experience without being seen as a Johnson holdover.[16]

But Moynihan brought enemies as well. Many minority leaders helped to block his appointment as H.U.D. secretary under Nixon, so the post went instead to Michigan governor George Romney.[17] Undeterred, Moynihan stepped down from the Joint Center in 1969 to serve as director of Nixon's new Urban Affairs Council and counselor to the President.[18] "As a professional social scientist," noted the *New York Times*, Moynihan "tried to bring to his colleagues in the White House an appreciation that careful statistical analysis of social problems was a crucial part of the policy-making process."[19] Nevertheless, his positions diverged from those of liberal scholars and urbanists.

When word leaked that Moynihan had recommended to Nixon that the President undertake "a period of 'benign neglect' on the racial issue," Moynihan found himself attacked. As he defended the large-scale City Beautiful vision of urbanism ("It is not to be traded in for anyone's idea of private gain or social welfare") before the 1969 convention of the American Institute of Architects, Moynihan was condemned as a racist by student groups who called for more radical responses to urban problems.[20]

Back in Cambridge, Moynihan was replaced as director of the Joint Center by M.I.T. political science professor Robert Wood.[21] Just returning from Washington as Moynihan was arriving there, Wood had worked on the Kennedy campaign and then served as assistant secretary of H.U.D. under Johnson, and even briefly in the cabinet after Secretary Weaver left for the presidency of Baruch College.[22] Wood tried to blunt the center's antipathy toward government urban programs and to challenge the rightward trend in the Nixon administration.[23] In response to "the President's continued isolation from social problems at home and the Administration's lack of attention to urban problems," six urbanists from the Joint Center came to Washington in May 1970 to inform Moynihan that "they could, in conscience, no longer offer formal or informal advice to the White House."[24] The group included former Johnson administration officials Wood and Charles Haar, a Harvard law professor who had been assistant secretary of H.U.D.[25]

A group of Harvard foreign policy experts had similarly broken publicly with Henry Kissinger over policies in Southeast Asia, specifically the expansion of war into Cambodia. Ironically, back at M.I.T. Wood found students denouncing him as a war criminal for his participation in the Johnson administration during the Vietnam conflict. These experiences, combined with his observations of the changing relationship between academics and politics over successive administrations, led Wood to fear that verifiable expertise was being obscured by campaign rhetoric and subjective ideology.[26] He and the Joint Center directed no explicit criticism at their former colleague Moynihan: "In fact, part of our purpose is to strengthen his voice and his hand in the Administration—to call attention to the effects of apparent indifference to city needs."[27]

Moynihan responded that "the United States does not now have an urban policy" and lauded Nixon for establishing the Urban Affairs Council "on January 23, 1969, as the first official act of his administration, to 'advise and assist' with respect to urban affairs, specifically 'in the development of a national urban policy.'" Moynihan was confident that "in recent years resources on a fairly considerable scale have flowed from Washington to the cities of the land and will clearly continue." But, he cautioned, "too many programs have produced too few results simply to accept a more or less straightforward extrapolation of past and present practices into an oversized but familiar future." Citing Nathan Glazer, he encouraged "effective decentralization," rejected "paragovernments designed to deal with special problems by evading or avoiding the jurisdiction of established local authorities," and suggested market-modeled incentive systems—"comparable to profit in private enterprise, prestige in intellectual activity, rank in military organization"—to attain urban goals.[28]

In an address to the American Jewish Committee, Moynihan renounced (apparently with sarcasm) his former "optimism about the use of social science knowledge in the management of public affairs." He criticized social scientists "for analyzing social ills without at the same time displaying a similar competence at offering solutions." Moynihan contended that the insistence that social scientists from Ivy League universities "somehow save the slums" was "no more than the nineteenth-century demand that cow colleges save the dirt farmer."[29]

Moynihan later wrote, "It has been said of urban planners that they have been traumatized by the realization that everything relates to everything. But this is so, and the perception of it can provide a powerful analytic tool."[30] Despite his attempt to put an optimistic gloss on what was essentially a condemnation of planning's incapacity, Moynihan's comments reflected a sense of crisis and despair that he and other advisers had done much to instill among urban policymakers.

Robert Wood concluded that the "neoconservative laments" of Moynihan, Banfield, and other policy intellectuals had checked the momentum of urban reform in favor of more politically palatable aims. The environment, he suggested, had far more middle-class appeal than "the conditions of the ghetto and the problems posed by the newest wave of urban immigrants."[31] Thus, when Nixon strategically declared in 1973 that the urban crisis had passed, he signaled an end to Washington's commitment to various urban renewal programs; in 1974 the administration ceased accepting applications for such funds.[32] The frenzy of U.S. federal urban policymaking that had culminated in the previous decade receded to what Wood judged as mere "blips on the screen, brief efforts to assert the nation's uncertain interest in its cities."[33]

M.I.T.-trained planner Marshall Kaplan emerged as a self-described urbanist in the late 1950s and advised a number of presidential task forces and commissions on urban problems during the 1960s. In the early 1970s, however, he confessed: "One need not look far for evidence, even if anecdotal, to show that the impact of the planning profession on the quality of urban life has been marginal at best and, at times, negative. Certainly, twenty years of federal planning assistance programs have not visibly built up the planning capacity of local governments or improved the quality of local life. Indeed, the prime beneficiaries of such aid seem to be, not local governments or local residents, but local and national consultants."[34] In attempting to "pinpoint the reasons for the impotence of the planning profession," Kaplan argued in his *Urban Planning in the 1960s: A Design for Irrelevancy* (1973): "I, for one, am convinced that a good part of the blame rests on the unwillingness of planners—and indeed of clients and constituents—to challenge ideas in common currency concerning professional goals, patterns of behavior and techniques."[35]

Together with then Joint Center director Bernard Frieden, Kaplan reported to President Ford in 1975 that "the gap between promise and performance" in the Model Cities program (which they had personally helped develop) was too "conspicuously large" and planners must go "back to the drawing board [in order to] really help American cities."[36] Such a negative verdict from the originators of a key liberal urban program reinforced the earlier critiques of neoconservatives like Moynihan and Banfield. Former H.U.D. assistant secretary Charles Haar coauthored the original Model Cities legislation; surveying the results a decade afterward from the Harvard law school, he declared it "the Waterloo of planning."[37]

Outflanked on the Right: New Left Urbanism Withers in the United States

By the early 1970s, experiments in New Left urbanism could be characterized, on the one hand, by the limitations of time and resources that reduced the adherents' ability to implement any proposals. On the other hand, well-organized communities, often allied with sympathetic young urbanists, were generally successful in opposing highway schemes and other redevelopments. There they benefited most from the meshing of technical expertise with grassroots political muscle. A contemporary study distinguished such collaborative resistance efforts "from the mere wielding of political force by a community group insofar as the opposed project is fought on a technical as well as political basis. Those opposing the project utilize the processes of both planning and community organization, with their attendant skills and expertise."[38] Ironically, professional planners and community groups could finally point to at least one area of complementary collaboration—opposing plans.

Advocacy planners, however, just like the public defenders Paul Davidoff envisioned them as, would have needed to rely on the commitment of public funding to sustain their activities on any permanent basis. Initially, such funds were available as a result of various Great Society programs. In 1973 President Nixon obliged the conservative critics of the urban renewal order by escalating his "benign neglect" into a general moratorium on public housing outlays and related urban spending, and by 1974 ending programs like Model Cities and the Office of Economic Opportunity. Some urban aid continued in the form of "block grants," but advocacy planning initiatives could no longer count on significant federal funds.

Meanwhile, at the local level, New York mayor John Lindsay had attacked top-down urban renewal for its lack of genuine citizen participations, and he campaigned in favor of developing planning and other authority to "neighborhood city halls." But while Lindsay did set up a comparable Urban Action Task Force in thirteen neighborhoods in 1967, resistance from the city council and other established seats of power hampered this initiative. They did not survive after he left office in 1973.[39]

The Fate of Jane Jacobs' American Experiment: West Village Houses

Even prior to those endpoints, grassroots urbanism faced formidable obstacles in the United States. Nowhere was this illustrated more poignantly than in the fate of the plan for housing proposed by the West Village neighborhood organization in 1963 (see figure 10.2). Over the course of the 1960s, Jane Jacobs and other residents of New York's West Village attempted to parlay their defensive victory against they city's slum clearance plans into positive actions to address their lingering concerns about affordable housing and to demonstrate their belief that government could play a role in stabilizing the neighborhood's real estate market. But in the wake of many bitter opposition battles, they failed to win the cooperation of officials necessary to bring such dreams to fruition. Their fields of victory, it soon became apparent, were plowed with salt.

New York's city planning officials immediately rejected the West Villagers' community-derived housing proposal as beyond the pale. Housing and Redevelopment Board director Frank Kristof declared: "Our overall reaction is that this is the most incredible proposal for housing that we have met since the adoption in 1879 of the old law 'dumbbell' tenement... buildings which are functionally obsolete before they have been produced." The administration's internal memos concluded that the Villagers' housing plan represented the neighborhood's "bizarre" attachment to its "obsolete" structures and "enshrined a principle to the point of a cliché." Some even suggested the architects at Perkins and Will "rate disbarral proceedings—or whatever is done to architects who act in a manner unbecoming of their profession." Five-story walk-ups, the city maintained, were "not only obsolete but unmarketable," and any loans granted to such a project (whether from banks or the city) were described as "reckless financial procedure."[40]

Ironically, the Villagers' earlier insistence on an amendment in the New Zoning Resolution, meant to prohibit high-rise development in their neighborhood, was now used to block the densities necessary to make the housing project financially viable. Furthermore, Jacobs was accused of violating her own convictions about functional segregation, lack of diversity, monotony, and mixed land use.

An internal city report questioned the plan's progressive credibility: "The most damning criticism that can be made of this entire proposal is . . . it is firmly rooted in protecting the status quo." Although the Village plan indicated with regret that the defeat of a British-style rent subsidy proposal by voters in November 1962 made it unfeasible to include any low-income housing in the project, that excuse was dismissed as an insincere mask: "The answer would be to have some of the units built by the Housing Authority—or is it that Mrs. Jacobs really is not enthusiastic about having low-income tenants in her pristine development?" At base, officials charged, Jacobs' seemingly radical ideas amounted to a conservative attempt by "vested interests within a community to avoid disturbing the existing residential pattern."[41]

The City Planning Commission rejected the residents' plan outright. Not only did it view the housing scheme as "not at all desirable or realistic," but the proposed location threatened to establish a precedent of "small residential parcels in a manufacturing district, thus circumventing the intent of the Zoning Resolution." Such housing might displace needed production and service jobs in the neighborhood, which could only be protected, they insisted, by means of "a more encompassing general urban renewal plan"—a pointed reference to the one the Villagers had recently defeated.[42]

Yet hopes for the West Village housing plan suddenly revived upon the election of John Lindsay, a long-time Jacobs ally, as mayor in November 1965. Lindsay offered the West Village Committee a written promise that he would facilitate the housing proposal. In July 1966, his administration gave officials notice of the sea change. While recognizing the City Planning Commission's objections, the new administration was decidedly in sympathy with the West Villagers' preferences. Directives from city hall suggested that the enthusiasm of residents and private developers for the neighborhood belied planning officials' hostility toward it.[43] The new mayor sent a clear signal that he wanted the community's plan implemented.

Lindsay forced city agencies to make an accommodation with the West Village housing plan—but that is not to say that they would ever be supportive. Sociologist Peter Melser conducted participant observation in the West Village during the time when the West Village Houses were being completed, allowing him to observe these anticlimactic developments. In a close analysis of the dynamics of the struggle for control of the neighborhood, Melser concluded that although the Villagers possessed an exceptional collection of talent and expertise, which allowed them to achieve influence at the highest political levels and to develop viable alternative plans, they were consistently hampered by the resistance of officials within city agencies who were uncooperative. The resulting delays and complications stretched the financial resources of the committee beyond its capacity, particularly as construction costs soared with the inflation of the 1970s. By the time the community's project was finally constructed in 1974, the design had been pared down to a bland shadow of its aspirations a decade earlier—and the project was nevertheless in bankruptcy (see fig. 11.1). In 1975, ownership (with control) passed into the hands of the foreclosing city agencies that the community had fought all along (and transferred subsequently to equally problematic outside investors). In short, the dream houses of Jacobs and the West Village Committee collapsed under market forces without the support (in fact, with the active resistance) of the city agencies.[44]

Ironically, by then it was also clear that Jacobs' critique of the urban renewal order, so controversial when her book popularized it over a decade earlier, was now the conventional wisdom. In 1974, none other than the sitting chair of the New York City Planning Commission, Lindsay-appointed lawyer John Zuccotti, spoke for many urbanists in declaring: "To a large extent, we are neo-Jacobeans."[45] Also in 1974, Random House asked Jacobs to read a draft of admirer Robert Caro's

Figure 11.1 Community planning compromises: a simplified design for the West Village Houses nearly a decade after originally proposed in 1963, scaled back as rising costs combined with stonewalling from city officials. The project finally broke ground with the support of Mayor John Lindsay. (With permission of the architect, Raymond Matz.)

Figure 11.2 The end of a community-designed experiment. The West Village Houses, as completed in 1974, featured less mixed use and more austere architecture than originally envisioned by the community. Shortly thereafter, the city foreclosed on the properties for bankruptcy, reselling them to outside investors. And yet by the end of the twentieth century, they offered some of the only middle-income housing in a rapidly gentrifying neighborhood, in keeping with the project's goal of moderating private market pressures. At the same time, the astronomical popularity of the West Village has given market validation to the urban *Leitbild* of Jane Jacobs' *Death and Life of Great American Cities*, so disparaged by critics like Edward Logue when she first articulated it. (Photo by the author.)

condemnatory biography of Robert Moses, *The Power Broker*, which became a bestseller.[46]

The ideological thrust of that critique was equivocal, both in Jacobs' particular case and in U.S. political culture generally. Jacobs herself personally evaded categorization, insisting: "Ideology is narrowing and limiting. Cities are not chaotic. They have an order of economic development, but they work without ideology. Ideology only prevents us from seeing the order."[47] But New Left sympathies—not surprising, perhaps, given her own arrests—were evident when, in response to the trial of eight political activists in Chicago, Jacobs joined other petitioners in September 1969 to oppose the anti-riot rider attached to the Civil Rights Act of 1968: "The effect of the 'Anti-Riot' Act is to subvert the First Amendment guarantee of free assembly by equating organized political protest with organized violence and premeditated incitement. In this decade, countless Americans have participated in organized demonstrations and protests—boycotts, freedom rides, community organizing, the peace movement. They have revitalized democratic politics."[48]

Jacobs confessed that her success as a political activist was more effective than her influence as a writer: "I'm not so modest—I know that it's possible for me, in this way, to have some power and get some things done; but it's an entirely different matter from writing. Writing doesn't get things done."[49] But a certain battle weariness, accompanied by a rightward shift, could be detected as well, in Jacobs' preoccupation with cultural and economic stagnation, and an increasing impulse toward devolution (arguing against New York City's 1898 consolidation, for example).[50] She confessed some surprising regrets to Susan Brownmiller in 1969: "I resent, to tell you the truth, the time I've had to spend on these civic battles. The new book was begun two years later than it should have been because of that expressway and the urban renewal fight in New York's West Village. It's a terrible imposition when the city threatens its citizens in such a way that they can't finish their work. Why, I know artists who aren't getting their pictures painted because of an expressway, poets who aren't getting their poems done."[51] She put her aversion to sustained community organizing more simply in a 1972 letter: "Fights like these are an outrageous imposition on the time and resources of citizens, who have much more constructive things to do with themselves." Jacobs' disillusionment spoke for many activists in the anti-urban-renewal movement.[52]

Advocacy Planning on South Street: The End of the Road?

Denise Scott Brown's efforts to valorize the community and architecture of South Street left some unconvinced. The *Philadelphia Daily News* maintained in 1971: "South Street dies a little more every day. . . . It is an urban hole. . . . It is a street of despair. . . . It is the bastard child of center city."[53] That year the administration of Mayor Frank Rizzo revived the crosstown redevelopment proposal in the guise of an elaborate redevelopment scheme, devised by architect Marvin Verman, featuring new apartments built over a tunneled expressway. Using a justification that appealed to the economic anxieties of the South Street community, this technically daring "Southbridge" design revived ideals of the urban renewal order ("responding to our urban problems on the scale they require") in the name of resisting the neighborhood's gentrification and guaranteeing affordable housing for the current residents. "If plans for [the expressway] are abandoned," its proponents warned in a reversal of the race moat argument, "the rehabilitation now occurring in center city would edge into and then past South Street—forcing out the present inhabitants."[54]

The Southbridge proposal received a mixed public response, reflecting some public relations success by the advocates of community preservation. The *Philadelphia Inquirer* reported, "Something kind of special has been happening quietly on South Street for the past two years. Artists and artisans have been moving into the section between Front and Seventh, producing and selling their creations in the old storefronts and living in the rear." One area real estate agent told the *Inquirer* that, while he was sympathetic to the Rizzo administration's urban renewal plan, he admired the commercial strip's ongoing resurrection into Philadelphia's Greenwich Village and "would not like to see the South Street Renaissance die in the cradle."[55]

Denise Scott Brown was unimpressed by the Southbridge scheme. She described urban design on a grand scale as "part of the enemy." Such design hubris, even when dressed as social reform, was inappropriate and even dangerous within the American political economy, because the highway department and the commercial marketplace—not welfare spending—were the most powerful actors. "Total design, Bauhaus-style, was intended to be accompanied by governmental and social commitment to social programs. In America today this is not so, and the Bauhaus ideals, as well as our more recent large-scale architectural urbanistic dreams, will be used as they were on South Street to betray rather than support the social concerns from which they sprang."[56]

In contrast, Scott Brown observed of her own proposals for the community, "our drawings and maps, although meager because of lack of funds, proved evocative; they were perhaps better than more explicit drawings since people could fill them with their own dreams."[57] Her own approach rejected all proponents of radically reforming the cityscape, be they technocratic transportation planners like Robert Mitchell, sanitizing urban aesthetes like Edmund Bacon, or socially progressive modernists like Verman. Her collaborations with Robert Venturi had made Scott Brown optimistic about the possibility of complex and tolerant design sensibility as a successor to dogmatic modernism (fig. 11.3).[58] Returning to the duality that haunted her at the University of Pennsylvania, Scott Brown suggested the moral and political implications of broader, "mannerist" urban ideas, as South Street made clear to her: "In this work, we learned what most planners and many architects find hard to accept: that there is a strong relation in architecture and urbanism between social concern and esthetic concern and that neither

Figure 11.3 Advocacy planning as affectionate design. Denise Scott Brown challenged the prescriptive modernist *Leitbild*, declaring that "the architect or planner cannot work 'from the inside' in the city unless he first learns to love it—for the life of its people *and* for the messy vitality of its body." As a consultant to anti-expressway community groups, she sought low-cost, non-destructive interventions that would recast the South Street neighborhood as desirable and worthy of preservation, in the case of this proposal literally reframing a vacant lot with a gateway arch and vest pocket park (circa 1970). Scott Brown favored modest, rough sketches "since people could fill them with their own dreams." Yet they had much in common with the British Townscape views. (Courtesy of Venturi, Scott Brown, and Associates, Inc.)

can be ignored. Indeed, the architect or planner cannot work 'from the inside' in the city unless he first learns to love it—for the life of its people *and* for the messy vitality of its body. Without this second love the first will be theoretical indeed. Weren't the worst devastations of Urban Renewal accomplished within a rhetoric that proclaimed 'the good of the people'?"[59]

Scott Brown had wedded the ethical and political impulse of the New Left advocacy planners with an aesthetic vision that affirmed a complex urbanism poised between sterile preservation and destructive redevelopment. The long-term consequences of that insight, however, were contingent on political developments in a country that, over the 1970s and 1980s, was reacting against urban aid and social programs generally. Whatever their professional conversions, U.S. city planners found their political and economic resources vastly diminished.

The Marginalization of New Left Urbanism

In the United States, advocacy planners could point to some lasting achievements, large and small: Mayor Lindsay endorsed Walter Thabit's Cooper Square alternative plan in 1968; it was officially adopted by the city in 1970. The Pratt Center's community work under Professor Ron Shiffman continued uninterrupted for decades. Other outcomes were more ambiguous: the Architects Renewal Committee in Harlem organized opposition to Columbia University's plans for redeveloping Morningside Park into a campus extension; the protests succeeded in stopping the project, though large-scale counterproposals that ARCH developed

Figure 11.4 From an expressway to a roller coaster. A girl peers into a vacant storefront on the 2100 block of South Street in 1975. While residents ultimately defeated the urban renewal proposal, abandonment and disinvestment plagued much of the neighborhood for years afterward, until private reinvestment flooded in during the 1990s and priced out long-term residents and businesses—a textbook case of the drought-flood cycle that Jane Jacobs diagnosed fifteen years earlier in American cities with no counterbalancing government policies. (Temple University Libraries, Urban Archives, Philadelphia, PA.)

were never constructed. The West Village Houses finally broke ground in 1974, but official foot-dragging and rising construction costs stripped the project down to bare bones. Bankrupt by the time the project was completed, the community organization lost control of the development it had planned as the city foreclosed and passed ownership to outside investors.

In Philadelphia, the South Street expressway proposal was eventually dropped. Denise Scott Brown's role as a consultant for the community's anti-crosstown fight consisted primarily of promoting appreciation for that neighborhood's messy vitality; in public forums she prevailed on policymakers to reenvision the community as something to be preserved rather than eradicated. Despite her fine arts training, she did so by executing hardly any design and very little planning. And though she debuted as an advocacy planner (what she called "the only moral method"), only two comparable opportunities surfaced subsequently, and her firm ultimately attracted recognition through designs for high-profile private clients like Ivy League universities and major cultural institutions.[60] Neighborhood groups, at least those in poor areas, simply did not command the resources to retain professional planners, particularly after the demise of liberal urban programs. The South Street area was saved from pro-highway planners but left with little assistance in the face of economic instability during subsequent years (fig. 11.4).

This political sea change had analogues in the urbanist establishment. Paul Davidoff left the University of Pennsylvania in 1965, teaching briefly at Hunter College before turning from 1969 onward to independent work on racial integration in suburbia. Chester Hartman, after vocally supporting the Harvard University student strike and criticizing the administration and his planning faculty colleagues, was fired in 1970 through an acrimonious process that rejected his teaching approach as "political strategy more than . . . city and regional planning." And what of Planners for Equal Opportunity's attempts to shift the professional establishment? Hartman remarked at the sudden demise of an institution "that had been an important force in planning issues . . . but which essentially had withered away by the early 1970s."[61] Advocates of New Left urbanism found themselves, after a brief moment at the center, at the margins once again. And U.S. city residents, having mobilized for a new kind of urban renewal with a more humane face, were left instead with little at all.

12 Softer Landings after the Fall Divergent Legacies of the Urban Renewal Order

"The Special Relationship" in Urbanism: Anglo-American Parallelism

In 1961 Harvard University urbanist Edward Banfield criticized the British planning tradition as elitist in its disregard for popular taste: "Arrogant officials may ignore the needs and wishes of ordinary citizens, and the ordinary citizens may respectfully acquiesce in their doing so, either because they think (as the British lower class does) that the gentleman knows best or (as the American middle class does) that the expert knows best."[1] But despite the advantages of such arrogance ("no dispute, no acrimony, no unworkable compromise, no stalemate"), planners simply failed to account for ordinary needs and wishes in pursuing the general welfare.

Such sentiments anticipated the populist appeal Banfield and other neoconservative urbanists had in Nixon's America. And he may have correctly diagnosed the paternalism inherent in the British planning establishment at the height of the urban renewal order. Yet a number of influential Britons were just then in process of undermining that elitism. Over the course of the 1950s, critics associated with the *Architectural Review*, urban sociologists studying London's renewal programs, and a young generation of architects influenced by popular culture all sought to stave off dogmatic slumbers by finding more direct ways of seeing the cityscape before them. In the process, they began to dislodge the dominant CIAM-influenced *Leitbild*.

Great Britain, not surprisingly, produced a variant of New Left urbanism. The nation harbored an indigenous radical tradition, vigorous scholarly critiques, and popular resistance to urban renewal. In addition, Britons closely observed U.S. developments. By 1964 King's Cross activist Theodore Roszak, editor of the independent weekly *Peace News*, exhorted readers to emulate the American resistance led by Jacobs and others: "If residents dug in their heels and refused to be budged, if they loudly and troublesomely demanded the right to renew their own neighborhoods I dare say the results could be astonishing. When the poor and the deprived ask the opportunity to rehabilitate themselves and back up the demand with organized non-violent resistance they are apt to be in a strong bargaining position." Roszak envisioned renewal projects organized around a kind of advocacy planning, with "semi-independent teams of planners and workers and their families each assigned a defined area of the slum to redesign and restore within the limits of the overall pattern."[2]

By the 1970s, community groups were poised to move beyond not-in-my-backyard opposition, and advocacy planning began taking hold in the United Kingdom just as its influence waned in U.S. cities. For example, residents opposed a massive redevelopment plan for London's Covent Garden neighborhood. A lead planner on that very redevelopment proposal, Brian Anson, with strong

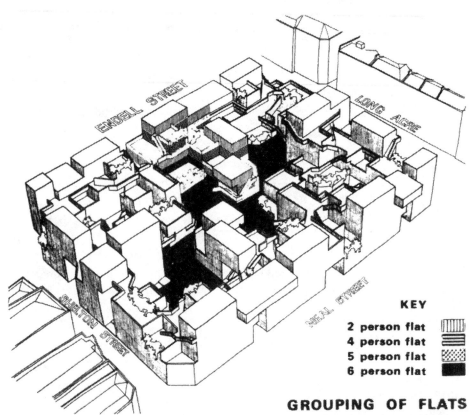

KEY

2 person flat	▥
4 person flat	▤
5 person flat	▨
6 person flat	■

GROUPING OF FLATS

Figure 12.1 This alternative redevelopment scheme for the Covent Garden area emerged from community design workshops led by radical architects, their students, and neighborhood residents during the mid-1970s. The Greater London Council had realized the proposal on the site of a former printing facility by the early 1980s. Neo-traditional design elements include massing of discrete units into a low-rise residential scale, within a conventional street pattern, and a sidewalk frontage orientation, while at the same time introducing interior quasi-public open spaces. (Source: Brian Anson, *I'll Fight You For It! Behind the Struggle for Covent Garden* [London: Cape, 1981], 262. With permission of City of London, London Metropolitan Archives.)

attachments to the working-class community, defected from the Greater London Council and organized residents to develop alternative plans for their neighborhood. He brought together locals with students from the Architectural Association to make counterproposals for reusing abandoned industrial buildings. After the national government intervened to stop the clearance scheme and provide historic preservation designations, the GLC incorporated some opposition group members into a citizen participation body, and in 1979 the redevelopment of a former printing factory closely followed the ideas developed by Covent Garden residents (fig. 12.1).[3]

Nevertheless, New Left urbanism in Britain also ultimately became a casualty of decidedly rightward political shifts—if slightly later than in the United States. Michael Ignatieff argues that "the failure of social democracy in Britain was, above all, an architectural failure—the vast acres of council flats were the most visible signs of Labour Party achievement, and they impressed neither their residents nor the middle-class voters whose taxes helped pay for them."[4] Of course, both parties collaborated in the erection of these tangible symbols of the postwar Keynesian consensus, and many of the most detestable projects were undertaken under Conservative governments. But Margaret Thatcher's libertarian ideological revolution of 1979 dramatically rejected her own party's progressive idea of "one-nation Toryism," and environmentally deterministic prescriptions were cast out of the political repertoire. By 1981, riots in the West Indian neighborhood of Brixton were viewed with resignation as symptomatic of an intractable, racially reinforced cycle of poverty. Following a brief fling with New Left urbanism, Britain's political establishment—like its transatlantic counterpart a decade earlier—found its successor to the urban renewal order in the pessimistic posture of urban crisis.

An Agreeable Political Climate: The Toronto Reform Movement and Canadian Exceptionalism

Canada, by contrast, proved remarkably hospitable to the urban ideas being cast out of theUnited States and United Kingdom, despite its geographic and ideological proximities, respectively. The fall of Canada's urban renewal order produced neither a conservative backlash, nor short-lived experiments in advocacy planning. Particularly in Toronto, an entire civic reform movement might be best understood as the large-scale institutionalization of New Left urbanism, encompassing consecutive municipal administrations that gained and held power throughout the 1970s.

Toronto in these years was a receptive importer of people and ideas, including such disparate urbanists as Jane Jacobs and Hans Blumenfeld. These two provide a revealing study in contrasts, as well as in something that might be called the

Toronto Effect. Blumenfeld was a committed socialist with an international perspective and held that planning was a universal, progressive undertaking. Indeed, he endorsed most urban renewal projects. As a politicized radical in an era of paranoid anticommunism, he found himself chronically stateless. However, he was embraced and promoted by the urbanist establishment, as when Martin Meyerson, director of the Harvard-M.I.T. Joint Center for Urban Studies, used influence in the Kennedy administration to secure Blumenfeld a visa.[5] As a practitioner, he had no trouble slipping into new positions and making extensive planning recommendations for Philadelphia and Toronto within months of arriving in those cities. Jacobs, on the other hand, placed a premium on local knowledge. Her most original insights as well as her most effective political power derived from her own neighborhood, a network of observations and personal associations built up slowly. Jacobs was estranged from the interconnected academic and planning establishments—at least until generational changes had set in by the 1970s. Her major public initiatives were defensive attempts to preserve the character of existing urban places.

Neither was a Torontonian before reaching the age of fifty, yet both were very welcome there and both left unmistakable marks on the city. Jacobs and Blumenfeld embodied contrary impulses. Blumenfeld was a socialist but also a believer in professional, objective planning, and as such he worked diligently for a pro-development metropolitan authority whose greatest aspiration was transportation efficiency as a means to capitalist growth. Jacobs idealized small-scale capitalism at the level of neighborhood stores and opposed the decentralization implicit in the Metro authority's vision. The city's unfinished highway system is a testament to both of them: Blumenfeld for the unfinished conception, Jacobs for its incompleteness.

Yet Jacobs and Blumenfeld, the anti-planning libertarian and the socialist planner, found themselves working together on Toronto's Harbourfront redevelopment project by 1974—a provincial initiative designed by Eberhard Zeidler, the German-Canadian who employed Jacobs' husband as an architect in his firm. This attested to the less acrimonious nature of Toronto politics, to be sure. But it also reflected the major political shifts of the Toronto reform movement, which was equal parts transformative (particularly in terms of the city's leadership and its *Leitbild* for future urban development) and inclusive (with respect to the process of politics and planning).

The most meteoric of the reformers on the city council was the young David Crombie, who first became an alderman in 1970 and then mayor three years later.[6] As a member of the Progressive Conservative Party's "red Tory" wing, he exhibited the nonpartisan character of Toronto politics, though his accessibility was exceptional. He even listed his home number in the telephone book as "Crombie, Mayor David," and "accepted the annoyance of 150 phone calls a week from strangers because he wanted to live in a city where the mayor was just another citizen."[7] Crombie's housing commissioner was Michael Dennis, a neighbor on Jane Jacobs' street. In 1974, she convinced Dennis to bypass the city planning department and employ Alan Littlewood, an architecture colleague of her husband, to develop plans for a new, 3,500-unit neighborhood on forty-five acres of old industrial lands bordering railroads and the Gardiner Expressway.[8]

The St. Lawrence Neighborhood, as it developed, stood in marked contrast to the West Village Houses that Jacobs and her neighbors initiated in New York. While the West Village Houses were the product of resident participation in the design and development of moderate-income housing in their own neighborhood, that project was delayed, diluted, and ultimately undermined by hostile New York city agencies. Toronto's St. Lawrence Neighborhood, by contrast, was closer in its outcome to Jacobs' ideal of social diversity and mixed use, although the design process was very different. Its large industrial site was not interwoven with an existing neighborhood, so resident participation was replaced by traditional top-down planning—though radical alderman John Sewell constantly pushed Mayor Crombie for greater public involvement in the process. As prominent Canadian journalist Robert Fulford said of these two Toronto mayors, "Crombie and Sewell were both careful and admiring students of Jane Jacobs' ideas, but they often disagreed on the way to apply them."[9]

For her part, Jacobs insisted that a familiar architect—explicitly not city planners—draft the St. Lawrence plans, and she coached Littlewood to adhere to traditional principles of density and mixed use, with street lines that blended into the existing cityscape. The design incorporated tiny streets of three-story row houses with fenced yards, as well as eight-story apartment buildings along a wide esplanade, all constructed of nondescript brick (figs. 12.2, 12.3). The project was certainly not glamorous, but when the St. Lawrence Neighborhood opened in 1979, just five years after its conception, it embodied the achievements of a progressive municipality committed to Jane Jacobs' ideas, unlike either the insensitive pro-growth planning of Metro Toronto from the Gardiner years, or New York's begrudging implementation of the West Village Houses. Sewell called it "the epitome of the new planning approach taken by the Reform Council."[10]

The Toronto reform movement that took control in 1972 made the reorientation of city planning both its campaign platform and primary objective. Some, including geographer James Lemon, interpreted the reform movement merely as a minor revision—driven solely by the self-interest of middle-class gentrifiers—to the golden age of Canadian comprehensive planning. In Lemon's view, the

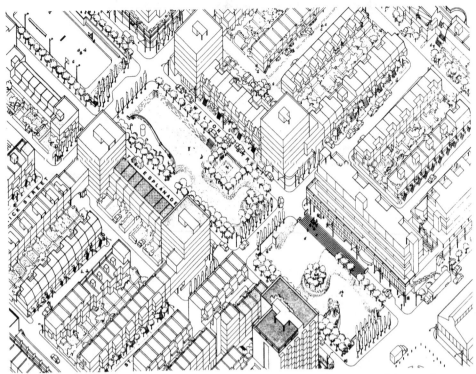

Figure 12.2 Urban renewal meets neo-traditional urbanism: Bird's-eye view of dense urban district envisioned by the City of Toronto's community and neighborhood planning division for St. Lawrence, a redevelopment of industrial sites near the Toronto waterfront in the shadow of the Gardiner Expressway. Upon the assumption of power by the anti-urban-renewal reform movement, the project became a district-scale experiment inspired by Jane Jacobs' urbanistic principles—and influenced by Jacobs' presence as a Toronto citizen—including high coverage of lot areas, buildings oriented toward the conventional city street grid, and other elements. (Source: *St. Lawrence Official Plan Proposals* [City of Toronto Planning Board, April 1976], p. 46. Image courtesy Toronto Public Library. Copyright permission: City of Toronto.)

movement offered no new solutions to the biggest problems, such as the loss of industrial jobs. And far from a radical break, it drew on many of the more constructive elements of earlier liberal precedents, such as the government provision of low-income housing. For Lemon, Jacobs was the importer of destructive American ideas into Canadian cities, namely, a misguided faith in those very uncontrolled market forces that comprehensive planning brought under control.[11]

Jacobs' writings indeed focused increasingly on the tension between "productive" urban markets and "parasitic" national governments. Her ideas also appealed as much to the libertarian right as the grassroots left. However, in the Toronto context, her urban vision was not simplistically anti-statist, but became a complement to a more aggressive public sector, primarily the local municipal one. Her initial role fighting as a political outsider quickly gave way to one of steering from well inside. Ironically, Jacobs became much more of an insider as an expatriate in Canada. Her paradoxes were shared by the reform movement, simultaneously radical and conservative, part bourgeois homeowners, part rabble-rousing grassroots organizers. But while in New York such intracommunal tensions, fanned by racism, fractured and polarized the city, in Toronto the disparate neighborhood constituencies allied into an electorally successful citywide movement. The political payoff, of course, was control of city hall. Furthermore, such a strategy—of storming and seizing the bastion of planning authority rather than discrediting and ultimately destroying such capacities—produced concretely effective, durable results upon the physical development of the city.

Conservative and progressive tensions always existed within the urban renewal coalition in both Canadian and American cities: technocratic planners ministering to both housing reformers and downtown business interests; old urban machines, white collar reformers, and New Left community organizers jostling for influence with city residents. In the United States, this volatile admixture

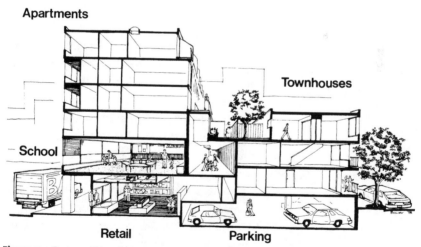

Figure 12.3 Cross section of a St. Lawrence neighborhood building along Crombie Park (named after reform mayor David Crombie), showing the mixed-use apartments, townhouses, schools and stores. (Source: *St. Lawrence, 1974–79* [City of Toronto Housing Department, 1979] p. 32. Image courtesy Toronto Public Library. Copyright permission: City of Toronto.)

was ultimately blown apart by a combination of its own design shortcomings, racial conflict, a broad cultural backlash, and even larger economic forces—all set within a context of geographic fragmentation and flight. Toronto never faced anything like the crisis of race relations that occurred in New York under John Lindsay (even as Gotham was largely spared the violent episodes of many other U.S. cities). But Canadians were not immune to the lure of the suburbs as an escape from urban challenges, either. There was in fact a very similar turn against urban renewal within cities across North America (and for that matter, in Europe). All the more remarkable, then, is the 1970s cohabitation that enabled reformers on Toronto City Council to reconcile—at times tensely, but for the better part of a decade—the affordable housing interests of working-class constituents with the preservation impulse of middle- and upper-class ones (and at times vice versa).[12]

Under Mayor Crombie, and then even more comprehensively under his successor's administration, an industrial policy to create jobs also found a place in the St. Lawrence plan. In 1978, John Sewell, the most radical of the reformers, became mayor of Toronto. Although he always retained an outsider activist's suspicion of government, he oversaw the completion of the St. Lawrence Neighborhood and sought to implement a kind of antitrust industrial policy—lifted directly from Jacobs' treatises on urban economics—which facilitated local, medium-scale civic capitalism. Precisely this sort of approach had eluded both Jacobs and her opponents in their attempts to reconcile the stagnating New York longshoremen's industry with the gentrifying West Village.[13]

Fans of Gardiner and Blumenfeld (such as Lemon) still take pride in the Toronto metropolitan planning apparatus they erected, which was contested and reformed but never dismantled, as the Greater London Council had been by Prime Minister Margaret Thatcher. Supporters of Sewell and Jacobs (like Fulford) revel in the neighborhood preservation and citizen participation movement that took control of city hall, democratized planning procedures, and got alternative projects built. In the 1970s, Toronto somehow offered all of these groups a locus of cohabitation, where all pointed with pride toward the city as an embodiment of their disparate principles. The St. Lawrence Neighborhood was just one of many large, concurrent public housing projects that exemplified a substantively different politics of planning—from Trefann Court to Sherbourne-Dundas—all undertaken with neo-Jacobsean approaches by Toronto's reform administrations. One could even find Jacobs and Blumenfeld collaborating on a waterfront development initiative. Through a constructive synthesis of many of the major planning impulses of the twentieth century, Torontonians defused the polarization which characterized their application in other communities.

Figure 12.4 Beyond individual projects, by the mid 1970s, Toronto's reform council was encouraging a wholesale shift from redevelopment toward an emphasis on residents' quality of life, with sensitivity to preserving neighborhood scale. To that end, it convened a task force of private citizens with "intimate knowledge" and a "personal interest" to reassess the needs of Toronto's core area. The group declared the area "is not a coloured abstraction on a map. It is the most vital centre in our Toronto community," and they pledged to maintain and enhance it. Indicative of the shift of emphasis, this photo, which opened the recommendation report, literally foregrounded the residential vernacular of older townhomes before the central business district that had risen along Yonge Street in the background. (Source: *Core Area Task Force, Report and Recommendations* [City of Toronto, Planning Board, 1974], introduction, p. 1. Image courtesy of Toronto Public Library.)

German Intellectual Deference and Backlash Evaded

Despite various transnational forces and links, German history seems periodically to follow its own unique route (a.k.a. *Sonderweg*) for better or for worse. This certainly turns out to be true of its post-urban-renewal era, when placed in transatlantic perspective. Throughout 1960s and well into the 1970s, West Germany's urban renewal order was not only firmly oriented toward an ambitious and aggressive program of modernist redevelopment, but broad political support also existed for that direction. Having overcome initial suspicions rooted in the deprivations of wartime planning, many residents were eager to inhabit new, modernized dwellings in functionally separated settings. Grassroots initiatives such as Bernard Werres' 1950 call on citizens to voice their opposition to plans in Dusseldorf—with the slogan "No, I don't like this city planning!"—were exceptional and ineffective.[14] Quiescence was characteristic in West Berlin, even among residents directly affected by redevelopment schemes, all of whom vacated without any legal pressure or formal eviction proceedings. Despite the lack of any advocacy for relocated tenants, civic opposition was simply absent.[15]

Likewise, visiting M.I.T. professor John Burchard, whose writings are silent on the fate of old neighborhoods (he favored modernist housing models like those exhibited at the 1957 international building exhibition in Berlin's Hansaviertel), saw German citizens in 1963 in complete sympathy with both the means and ends of urban renewal. He attributed this to a healthy political culture, including less anticommunist paranoia than in the United States. "Germans have been used for a long time to considerable state control of land and to serious restrictions on uninhibited private exploitation and development. Until the people of the United States understand that these are not slippery roads to the perdition of 'socialism,' beautiful and happy cities will become more and more difficult to make in America, or to preserve."[16] Particularly in the area of housing, Burchard admired the balance between public and private sector, as well as the German consumer's "good taste" in distinction to American suburbanites.[17]

Certainly, during the 1960s, some German urbanists (at least among the younger generation) shared with their colleagues abroad a gradual reaffirmation of old cityscapes. The first building in any official renewal area of West Berlin to be renovated, as opposed to demolished, was a designated historic property, Christenstraße 40, in Charlottenburg-Klausenerplatz, restored in 1967.[18] In 1968, activist architecture students as well as professional and academic sympathizers mounted a provocative exhibition at Berlin's Technical University, "Diagnosis of Construction in West Berlin," documenting with interviews and photographs the lamentable outcomes of urban renewal projects.[19]

The only significant apprehension that plagued German urbanists—one which was tied up with the complex process of postwar denazification—was whether the messy practice of democracy provided the clear vision necessary for good planning. As early as the February 1955 meeting of the German Association for Housing, City and Regional Planning (themed "The Master Plan Concerns Us

All"), Markus Kutter called planning an exercise of power that needed to make expertise more politically and democratically accountable.[20] Later, at a 1960 conference, Regensburg planning director Paul Schlienz, who had previously called for the clearance of every other apartment house in that city to create space "in accordance with the principles of contemporary planning," wondered aloud, "Just what is our model for the renewal of the cityscape? Shouldn't renewal begin with the individual and his attitudes? We lack the cultural foundation for building a clear will to plan."[21] Noting the similarities of terminology circa 1960 to those of the 1945 moment of collapse—discomfort with the "present instability in all areas of life," a longing for the "clear planning will" of the Nazi era, dissatisfaction with "democracy as master builder"—some historians see in German planners a chronic desperation to find any ideological basis for construction in the absence of discredited political justifications.[22]

The eminent German planner Rudolf Hillebrecht hoped to make planning democratically responsive via social scientific studies.[23] Hillebrecht shared with German sociologist Hans Paul Bahrdt a high esteem for Jane Jacobs. But if Jacobs was an instructive—albeit autodidact—urban sociologist, as Bahrdt claimed, she was no less an assertive political activist. Yet the relation among political resistance, urbanist intellectuals, and city planning would develop altogether differently in West Germany. Bahrdt's own willingness to engage urban sociology in the political process of planning landed him in front of the Bundestag, where he testified regarding the German Federal Republic's first urban planning act (or *Städtebauförderungsgesetz*, abbreviated StBauFG), passed in 1971.[24] Following other social scientists who drew attention to the fate of relocated families (Chester Hartman and Marc Fried in Boston; Michael Young and Peter Willmott in London), Bahrdt told the government that a constructive plan was one "which not only contains a conception of the future economic and social structure of a renewal area, that also evaluates the probability of realizing this vision and describes the phases of transition, but that also looks after the fate of those unjustly imperiled or inconvenienced by renewal measures." Bahrdt argued for the inclusion of what in the final legislation became provisions 8 (ongoing recorded resident participation), 4 (impact studies), and 9 (public design debate). Yet while these provisions theoretically strengthened the hand of residents in the planning process, a study one decade later concluded that the law had not substantially improved citizen participation.[25]

According to the social planning process Bahrdt had advocated, each urban renewal project was to codify an official document of resident objectives, and this "should function as a kind of protection when subsequent business pressures undermine the societal and sociopolitical goals." In his view, such a "social plan, fixed in writing, can have an important political function by systematically committing to a list of programmatic points, which the municipality cannot go back on later."[26] Ideally each social plan would even be ratified into law, though Bahrdt lamented that no such provision existed in the StBauFG as it stood. Thus, somewhat disappointed in the legislative outcome, he continued to hope for more legally binding participation mechanisms.

Yet while many were aware of the movement toward advocacy planning by the late 1960s, German urban social scientists consistently assumed a softer, more consensual disposition, one less willing to undermine official planners' top-down authority during a major period of urban redevelopment in that country. One example of this distancing posture is Bernhard Schäfers, a political scientist and sociologist with the University of Münster's Central Institute for Regional Planning, who welcomed the "possibilities for social planning" opened by the StBauFG.[27] Schäfers drew primarily on Habermas' Structural Transformation of the Public Sphere to conceptualize the planning process as a negotiation between planners and those affected. His case studies examined metropolitan reorganization in Nordrein-Westfalen, where "the idealistic conception of the public sphere, as the best forum for discussing decisions about the common good, proved to be illusory."[28] Yet for Schäfers this revealed not some thorny inherent quality of democratic planning (as per Paul Davidoff or even Edward Banfield), but just the pitfall of overly narrow self-interest, whereby "no one in the planned district was non-partisan enough to constitute the public sphere in the true interest of planning."[29] The politicized conflicts, he concluded, simply illustrated that the planning process was not yet fully developed.[30]

When Schäfers explicitly addressed the Anglo-American role of advocacy planner or community organizer, referring both to Paul Davidoff and to Karl Popper's "piecemeal engineering," he doubted that these models were directly applicable in Germany.[31] Instead, he interpreted his empirical studies to suggest that, in the face of growing responsibilities, planning agencies should not be constantly exposed to public pressures but rather insulated from them.[32] Schäfers concluded that planning reform was being pulled in three major directions—social revolutionary, liberal, and ad hoc advocacy—as well as a fourth impulse he termed educational. With a confidence in technical expertise implied by the last option, Schäfers and two fellow researchers at the University of Münster developed and published a proposal in 1969 promoting a more "social-science-oriented curriculum" for planners, based on their observation that social, economic and legal considerations were neglected in planners' training and planning practice.[33] Technocratic German urbanists clearly saw no Waterloo on their horizon.

Germany's 1971 federal planning legislation, while formally a dramatic step, represented an institutionalization of the status quo. Even Hans Paul Bahrdt's recommended amendments were moderate measures, which did not vilify planners or the planning process (compare with American urbanists on both the left and right). After the new law came into effect, Bahrdt declared that citizen empowerment (whether in citizen initiatives, citizen forums, renewal advisory councils, or district councils) could never replace "ongoing, trained, professional work on social planning. When corresponding citizen activities develop, their representatives will appreciate having social planning experts whose information they can utilize."[34]

To look at the beginning of the 1970s, one could conclude that the urban renewal order in West Germany was inextricably anchored in a particular political culture of nonconfrontational consensus, deference to authority, and confidence in technical expertise. In West Berlin a series of extensive highway and redevelopment projects were moving toward implementation in various neighborhoods. In the Kreuzberg district, planners designated an urban renewal area around Kottbusser Tor for the purposes of demolishing 84 percent of the existing housing, potentially displacing tens of thousands of residents (fig. 12.5).[35] At the center was the so-called New Kreuzberg Center, an enormous ten-story housing project erected between 1969 and 1974 (fig. 12.6).

Yet more disruptive challenges would subsequently accompany the political awakening of a generation that had few memories of war and little if any relationship to postwar housing crises. Following a decade during which citizens were little more than passive (often willing) subjects of neighborhood clearance, a number of citizen initiatives concerned with quality-of-life issues emerged across the country, notably the boycott of transit fare hikes in the summer of 1969 and the first appearance of squatters in the bourgeois district of Frankfurt's west end.[36] And despite Jane Jacobs' praise for the balanced approach of Hannover planner Rudolf Hillebrecht, residents of that city's Linden district successfully opposed redevelopment plans in 1972–73.[37] Scholars have connected these groundswells of political participation to the first major postwar recession, the "grand" coalition of the SPD and CDU, the 1968 student movement, and the so-called extraparliamentary opposition undermining official authority. Even the charismatic social democratic chancellor Willy Brandt urged Germans in 1969 to "dare to be more democratic." In West Berlin, the first concerted and politically potent confrontations between citizens and urban policymakers developed over the course of the 1970s, with grassroots initiatives in the Märkisches Viertel housing project as well as various older districts. Harald Bodenschatz has noted that "in contrast to the

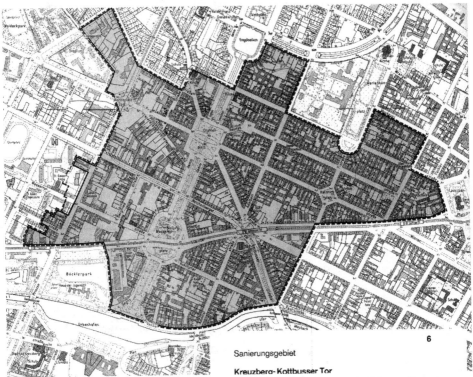

Sanierungsgebiet

Kreuzberg- Kottbusser Tor

Figure 12.5 Berlin city planning map depicting dense nineteenth-century building patterns in Kreuzberg and highlighting the extent of the neighborhood designated as an urban renewal area after 1965, including the X-shaped intersection at Kottbusser Tor in the center, and the large square Oranienplatz northwest of it along the diagonal arm. (Source: Bezirksmuseum Friedrichshain-Kreuzberg, Archiv. With permission from Senatsverwaltung für Stadtentwicklung, Berlin, Germany.)

1960s a broader civic opposition to urban renewal policy developed after about 1973 . . . dominated by organizations or individuals of the '68er movement and initially supported by some of the old neighborhoods and shop owners."[38]

In 1971, a Protestant priest in Kreuzberg began to organize public opposition to the dismantling of the neighborhood's social and physical integrity. Students and activists staffed a Kreuzberg storefront "Office of Urban Renewal and Social Work," distributing translated American writings from a decade earlier (including Gans' indictment of Boston urban renewal) in pamphlets polemically entitled *Urban Renewal—for Whom? Against Welfare State Opportunism and Corporate Planning.*[39] Over the following couple of years, a proposed eastern spur (*Osttangente*) of the urban freeway network provoked further resident activism in Kreuzberg (figs. 12.7, 12.8). Growing militancy in the district forced the city council to initiate the 1977–78 "Strategies for Kreuzberg" competition, which produced new concepts (if little implementation) in an attempt to reflect residents' values.[40] A final, radical resistance phase arrived in 1979 with the advent of politicized squatters, including calls for the illegal expropriation of apartments in the face of property owners' destructive neglect ("lieber instandbesetzen als kaputtbesitzen").[41] This movement coincided with a 1980 builder-financing scandal that brought down the Social Democrat–led city council, and Berlin's occupations soon peaked at 165 properties. But reaction soon followed, with a Christian Democratic government crackdown resulting in the accidental death (involving a bus) of one youth during a police action in the Schöneberg district in September 1981. Subsequent appeasement saw the legalization of a third of the squatters.[42] More important, what Roger Karapin called the "clear-cut renewal bloc" lost its influence in Berlin neighborhood planning (fig. 12.9).[43]

Figure 12.6 Berlin planners with a model of the New Kreuzberg Center, a major redevelopment project around the Kottbusser Tor area of Kreuzberg executed between 1969 and 1974. Its curvilinear form echoed Wagner and Taut's horseshoe project from the 1920s—albeit many-fold taller—and dropped onto central Berlin like Hilberseimer's Friedrichstadt proposal; see figs. 1.3 and 1.4. (Source: Bezirksmuseum Friedrichshain-Kreuzberg, Archiv.)

Figure 12.7 Photomontage of an eight-lane, multilevel freeway interchange at Oranienplatz projected for the Kreuzberg urban renewal area. Particularly in that neighborhood, Berlin's urban freeway proposals faced increasingly organized citizen opposition from 1972 onward and were eventually dropped. (Source: Bezirksmuseum Friedrichshain-Kreuzberg, Archiv. With permission from Senatsverwaltung für Stadtentwicklung, Berlin, Germany.)

In keeping with the German population's comparative support for modernist redevelopments, some of the most scandalous public reckonings with urban renewal's legacies in Berlin were concerned not with the nature of the program goals but rather with the quality of their execution. In 1982, just ten years after high-rise housing units for thirty-eight thousand were completed in the Märkischen Viertel district, the project was found to be in need of DM 50 million of structural repairs to facades and roofs.[44] Other embarrassing revelations emerged in the early 1980s, including the condemnation of the Britz-Süd housing project. All of a sudden, the renovation of recent renewal projects became—ironically—more pressing than slum clearance.[45]

In 1978, a series of articles in the *Berliner Morgenpost* by architect Josef Paul Kleihues and publisher Wolf Jobst Siedler convinced the Berlin council to host an international building exhibition (known by the German abbreviation IBA, and projected for 1984). By then design fashions were rapidly shifting away from the towers-in-parkland housing *Leitbild* of Walter Gropius and others who had garnered laurels at Berlin's last such exhibition, in 1957. This time the IBA had two concurrent foci, each led by a pioneer in the shift of Berlin architecture: With the motto "critical reconstruction of the city," Kleihues assembled new construction projects for war-destroyed areas like the southern Friedrichstadt and southern Tiergartenviertel. Meanwhile, under the banner of "gentle urban renewal," architect Hardt-Waltherr Hämer curated the division focusing on surviving old districts like Luisenstadt, incorporating the "Strategies for Kreuzberg" project.[46] Between 1968 and1974, Hämer had been among the first practicing architects to champion preservation and resident participation, turning the Klausenerplatz urban renewal area of Berlin's Charlottenburg district into an experiment for a new planning approach. Over the next decade (including building exhibitions in 1984 and 1989) the program's new buildings (Kleihues' division, known as IBA-Neubau) and refurbishments (Hämer's Altbau-IBA) effected the production of eight thousand new and renovated housing units, as well as the "transformation of a dozen empty industrial plants into 'culture factories,' the greening of interior courtyards, and the construction of parks."[47]

Figure 12.8 With signs depicting speculators and profiteers, Kreuzberg protesters in the mid-1970s attack urban renewal projects including the Kottbusser Tor redevelopment project and freeways through city neighborhoods, as well as expenditures for Berlin cultural sites like the former parliament building and the German opera house. (Source: Bezirksmuseum Friedrich-shain-Kreuzberg, Archiv. Used with permission of Jürgen Henschel.)

Figure 12.9 New paths for the future: district revitalization. A poster announcing the Berlin planning agency's 1977 public presentation of new strategies for Kreuzberg neighborhood renewal, emphasizing citizen participation in the process and highlighting the district's traditional streetscape, rather than modernist redevelopment plans. (Source: Bezirksmuseum Friedrichshain-Kreuzberg, Archiv. With permission from Senatsverwaltung für Stadtentwicklung, Berlin, Germany.)

In March 1983, the CDU-controlled city council adopted twelve principles of "gentle urban renewal." These emphasized citizen participation (1, 9), making planners accountable to residents (2), preservation of the neighborhood character (3, 6), gradualism (5), and reforms to landholding and financing practices (11). While primarily rhetorical rather than statutory, this resolution gave an official imprimatur to the goals of neighborhood advocates. Many of the principles were institutionalized by the districts or the city. Together with the IBA, these developments not only brought international attention to Berlin as a showplace for postmodern city building —a somewhat belated attempt by architecture and planning professionals to respond to the de facto popular referendum on the traditional urban form—but they also contributed to the public appreciation of the city as a valuable historical artifact. So did an omnibus 1987 exhibition for the 750th anniversary of Berlin's settlement curated by Kleihues.[48]

In contrast to their colleagues in the United States, German social scientists did not initially find their urban renewal critiques (or themselves) allied with any grassroots resistance movements during the 1960s, or with many planners, and so could do little to alter the accepted clearance procedures. (Compare with scholar-activists like Herbert Gans, Paul Davidoff, Denise Scott Brown, or Jane Jacobs, as well as influential policy shapers James Q. Wilson, Edward Banfield, Daniel P. Moynihan, and Martin Anderson—to pull from across the U.S. political spectrum.) Such developments largely had to await the arrival of the '68-er generation on the urban political scene, which took place over the course of the 1970s. Yet in a stark contrast to the anti-planning legacy of urban renewal opposition in the United States, the public sector did not emerge thoroughly discredited from the squatter episodes (though they may have helped bring down a Berlin mayoralty). An architectural community gradually awakening from dogmatic modernist urbanism played catch-up in response to the popular reaffirmation of the nineteenth-century neighborhood fabric (fig. 12.10). Postmodern approaches, epitomized by the Berlin IBA's "gentle urban renewal," were integrated into a still vital institutional planning apparatus by the mid 1980s.

These neo-traditional concepts then laid the foundation for the "critical reconstruction" of Berlin as a reunified—and self-consciously urbane—capital city a decade later. When Hans Stimmann became Berlin's planning director in 1991, he instituted a development framework for Berlin which would embody many of the ideas expounded by the IBA. The monumental *Planwerk Innenstadt*, a thirty-year plan presented in 1996 and accepted in 1999, is an anti-thesis to functionalism. It calls for the refocusing of residence and infrastructure investment on the metropolitan core, a heterogeneous mixture of functions, and reinstatement of the nineteenth-century block scale.[49]

Figure 12.10 A new/old *Leitbild*. The advocacy group Ökotop promoted the alternative rehabilitation of nineteenth-century tenements through such elements as green roofs and aqua-
culture. This Green utopian urban vision reflected the transvaluation of Berlin's traditional
cityscape by the end of the 1970s. (Courtesy of Detlef Surrey.)

Figure 12.11 Kreuzberg squatters and other area residents at a street festival on Berlin's Cuvrystraße in 1982. Radical agitation in that district put intense pressure on SPD and CDU city governments to handle such old neighborhoods with care. (Photo by Paul Glaser, all rights reserved.)

Perhaps the most notable contrast to the legacy of neighborhood preservation on South Street, and the American example generally, is the Berlin policy called Quartier Management. In the context of the German welfare state, planning officials now aggressively pursue neighborhood preservation in dynamic areas like Kreuzberg with the aim of maintaining not only physical but also social continuity.[50] In many respects, this program resembles the controversial American Model Cities experiments that proved so divisive during the 1960s. So, despite an initial aversion to politicized advocacy planning, and a reaction against urban renewal that came a decade later than in the United States, Germans in cities like Berlin became the true heirs of New Left urbanism.

Conclusion
First We Take Manhattan, Then We Take Berlin

This study provides a comparative perspective on concurrent developments in cities across Western Europe and North America. Each of the individual cases was certainly salient for distinct reasons, grounded in different urban and intellectual milieus: the unique dynamics among neighborhood activists living in New York in the 1960s, radical '68ers squatting in condemned districts of West Berlin, New Left student planners in racially charged Philadelphia, anti-modernist architectural feuilletonists in postwar London, local and national urban policy advisers from Boston's elite universities announcing an ambitious "great society" only to be followed immediately by a pessimistic "urban crisis," a citywide coalition of reformers in Toronto allying to take power and replace destructive urban renewal policies. Nevertheless, even where there were no overt transnational links, there were many less obvious ones causing these cities to follow similar courses. Neighborhoods slated for public redevelopment, like New York's West Village, Berlin's Kreuzberg, London's Covent Garden, or Philadelphia's South Street, became symbolic rallying points for residents and radical young urbanists. Many of these groups displayed a surprising degree of awareness of each other—while also being thoroughly rooted in their distinctive local environments. All of them illuminate some commonalities in the evolution of urban attitudes and policies.

Within the community of urbanists, in particular, the various episodes engendered at least three common effects:

1. A generational split between the first and second wave of a newly professionalized white-collar group (namely, city planners, urban-design-oriented architects, and other urbanists)
2. A search for new design methodology—citizen advocacy planning—that reconceived the planner as a facilitator serving the modest aspirations of residents rather than high architectural style or grand political programs
3. A revised *Leitbild*, and corresponding aesthetic vocabulary, that moved beyond the modernist ideal to embrace the value of the vernacular cityscape

Given the transatlantic scope of this study, there is an overriding irony in its conclusion that, even in the context of globalized forces and convergences, it is politics—and moreover the most local of political cultures—that ultimately

"Well, if you don't like it you don't have to look at it."

Figure 13.1 Kenneth Mahood cartoon from the British humor magazine *Punch*. The skyscraper alludes to the 1961 Upstream Building, London headquarters for the Shell petroleum corporation that boldly overtopped landmarks like Big Ben and Victoria Tower across the Westminster Bridge. (*Punch*, June 6, 1962: 858. Reproduced with permission of Punch Ltd., www.punch.co.uk.)

shapes our cities in a very material and social sense. By taking a transnational perspective on mid-twentieth-century U.S. urban history, this book identifies the transatlantic framework for postwar urbanism—both in the promulgation of modernist planning approaches and in the reaction *against* such liberal renewal programs (compare tables A1 and A2 in the appendix). However, all those ideas, like the individuals who bore them, ultimately functioned in specific political environments and institutions. Certainly, citizens across Europe and North America concurred in reaffirming traditional urban textures and rejecting wholesale redevelopment. But more provocative are the subsequent divergences. One convenient explanation is that, while discrediting the urban renewal establishment, the adversarial political cultures of Great Britain and the United States, by comparison with West Germany and Canada, left far more potent anti-statist residues, which continue to inhibit urban policy initiatives in those places. However, since national character and political culture are such abstract, intangible entities—although maybe no less real for being so—I have been content to suggest their presence indirectly, rather than attempt to conjure such elusive spirits into my analysis.

This story follows the fortunes of many liberal intellectuals concerned with the designs and policies affecting cities; it is chiefly concerned with people and institutions as agents of liberal urban reform. Yet one of its themes could perhaps best be summarized with a slogan of twentieth-century conservatism: ideas have consequences. Few of the actors in these pages shared anything like the worldview Richard Weaver expressed in his 1948 manifesto bearing that title. Still, the developments examined here plainly manifest the concrete, physical legacies of various intellectual debates. As William Carlos Williams (like many planners, a denizen of two distinct realms: art and science) once remarked, "We meet the past in every object it leaves behind. Not in ideas but in things." The political battles surrounding urban renewal left scars on the civic dreams of many urbanists, policymakers, and citizens. This is, then, also a story of the constraints on ideas, the limitations of planning. An age-old debate lurks in these waters. Simplistically one might distinguish latter-day idealists (primarily intellectual historians like Daniel Rodgers, but also planning historians like Robert Fishman and others concerned with the power of ideas and images) from the more materialist camp of urban social scientists (e.g., Manuel Castells, Harvey Molotch, John Mollenkopf, and David Harvey) that sees late twentieth-century planning and design as epiphenomenal to deindustrialization, stagflation, and the other shocks that doomed the golden age of liberal urban policy. Macroeconomic forces are doubtless important factors. But there have always been economic cycles in cities, and I have emphasized some distinctive elements in the specific professional and local political cultures that distinguish the period under study.

Some can certainly contend that there are large-scale economic forces more fundamental than the ideas or even the political developments explored here.[1] For my part, I confess being sympathetic to so-called urban regime analysis, one of the more fruitful theories, at least with respect to cities, that political scientists developed over the last generation. As pioneered in Clarence Stone's work on post–World War II Atlanta, the term "regime" refers to "a set of governing arrangements," and, among other relevant things, it conceives the forces of collaboration and fragmentation in tension—at times productively so. As Karen Mossberger explains: "The appeal of urban regime analysis has been its ability to explain urban politics by incorporating both political and economic influences, resolving prior debates over elitism, pluralism and economic determinism."[2] The implication above all is that urban actors regain some agency, with outcomes contingent (at least in part) upon their ideas and decisions. This conception thereby also provides a means to explain the diversity evident across even structurally similar cases, like the assorted cities of Western capitalist democracies. Accordingly, the international comparisons in this book suggest that national variations in urban policy outcomes are the product of something other than conditions of production alone.

The grassroots mobilization of urban constituencies around planning as an issue in city politics catalyzed the field of urbanism—and vice versa. Residents' feelings of neighborhood attachment and protectiveness received belated recognition from social scientists, complicating the picture of a period still often characterized in terms of either suburban out-migration or revanchist gentrification. During the 1950s, sociologists studying urban populations in London's East End or Boston's North and West Ends discovered the deleterious side effects of the urban renewal programs that urbanists (in some cases the very same researchers) shaped. In the early 1960s, the articulate, aggressive counterattack from Greenwich Village residents and activists epitomized organized neighborhood resistance. Later in the decade, young architects and planners helped residents challenge the plans of their mentors, and the repulse of redevelopment schemes became common in gentrifying areas like London's Soho and Covent Garden, or even the more racially charged neighborhood of South Street in Philadelphia. Community organizers and ratepayer advocates took over Toronto's city hall to reform planning by the mid-1970s. In West Berlin, where neighborhood protectiveness was not hitherto previously militant, a squatters' movement in the late 1970s distantly echoed the earlier renewal critics in Britain and America.

A political economy of design may seem overdrawn, but to understand liberalism's urban fate, the unraveling of these relationships of legitimation must be explained. Did failures of design, economics, or democracy kill urban renewal? Did renewal die of chronic economic ailments (what Jane Jacobs called its "internal contradictions") or just a political blunt trauma (the loss of its funded mandate)? Urban scholars are often sloppy in the way they describe the end of urban renewal and the dissipation of its momentum. In the case of the United States, historians usually either rearticulate the policy critiques of contemporaries like Herbert Gans and Jane Jacobs or use the national power shifts (Nixon's electoral silent majority) as a shorthand for its demise. Does it make sense to study design ideas alongside urban politics and policy? Did urban renewal reflect anything more than the idiosyncratic aesthetic preference of modernist planners, masquerading as social reform? Certainly, the extent to which abstract design can be said to have political content is questionable. Barbara Miller Lane emphasizes the politicized nature of architectural debate among the radical Bauhaus designers and their reactionary contemporaries in Weimar Germany. Meanwhile, architectural theorists like Aldo Rossi, Manfredo Tafuri, and Leon Krier attempt to untangle the conflation of ideology and design, asserting: "There exists neither authoritarian nor democratic architecture. There exists only authoritarian and democratic ways of producing and using architecture. . . . Architecture is not political, it can only be used politically."[3] Nevertheless, social reformers and modernist designers in Europe and North America clearly made common cause in the redevelopment of cities. They were united by a faith in environmental determinism, the belief that social problems inhered in city form. City planning allied aesthetics with politics; policy and design became interdependent.

Expert advisers and professionals formed the liaison between the spheres of politics and planning. City planners were riding a crest of professionalization by the mid-twentieth century, with the establishment of city planning commissions and dedicated training programs across the United States and Europe. They were but one part of a general Western trend of enshrining experts in complex social scientific questions. City and regional planning was just one dimension—spatial—of a comprehensive twentieth-century planning impulse, seen not only in the extreme Soviet collectivization schemes, but also very strongly in British postwar social and economic policy, and even, in diluted form, in New Deal initiatives like the National Resources Planning Board. The underlying unity of such programs was the Enlightenment and positivist assumption that previously thorny problems of the organization and allocation of resources (territory, labor, food, energy, capital) were soluble by human reason, particularly when administratively concentrated.

The politico-economic rationale for urban renewal was a microcosm of postwar Keynesian liberalism. Cities seemed mired in a depression despite sustained national growth. Government spending, it was thought, might halt the economic decline of neighborhoods and business districts. Disappearing industrial plants were not lamented by policymakers until much later, perhaps since the presence of manufacturing in the city was considered a nuisance by planning elites and others. Housing reformers like Edith Elmer Wood and Catherine Bauer were always concerned with questions of economics and poverty.[4] Only with the end of the urban renewal order did many planning and design professionals confront the complexity of economic viability (as opposed to idealized modernist form alone) or the volatile force of democratic political resistance—challenges from which the well-funded and administratively empowered planners from the worldwide Depression through the early cold war were largely insulated.

The unanswered question underlying most urbanists' assumptions, however, was the degree to which the market and the *demos* could in fact be molded or bent into some desirable form. This raises large theoretical and moral questions about the role of citizens within a statist vision. In the specific cases examined here, German planners were particularly explicit about their discomfort with discerning any clear planning will when mere democracy becomes the "master builder." In the United States planning officials invoked the specters of obstruction, mob scenes, even riots. Modernist urbanists everywhere decried the chaos of cities, with pointed aesthetic references to the orderly CIAM *Leitbild*. In reaction, an expressed tolerance for complexity and an appreciation for messy vernacular urbanism were characteristic of those who later championed more direct ways of seeing the cityscape and responding to residents' desires.

Planning, if broadly defined as Robert Fishman has done, is simply collective action for the common good.[5] New York's Robert Moses executed an unrivaled collection of public works through his singular will and influence; in comparison, most postwar liberals legitimized planning through an oligarchy of enlightened specialists. Jane Jacobs and her New Left allies, by contrast, wanted the means of planning to reside in the incremental interactions and microorganizations of neighbors and affinity groups. To them, urban renewal's greatest offense was not that it threatened to destroy vibrant communities, but that it was fundamentally tyrannical in its concentration of power and undemocratic in its application. Thus awakened to these dangers within their own vicinity, the West Village residents became harbingers of more widespread, later movements, and not only in their suspicions of liberal officialdom, but also in their devolutionary definition of all politics as local.

Jane Jacobs denied that critiques and protests like hers did anything to bring down the urban renewal program. She maintained instead that it was doomed to die of its "internal contradictions." One interpretation is that planning was a highly artificial imposition on the urban scene with little inherent logic, ultimately no more than a costly works program for planners. Keynesian policies and the postwar economic expansion offered stable streams of funding; consensus administrations provided the mandate. Later, planning simply foundered in their absence. Alternatively, one could argue that had planning proposals been better grounded in the workings of urban communities and economies, their support would have continued. This latter proposition is the implicit policy prescription of Jacobs' book. And it appears borne out by the sustained support for the sort of "gentle urban renewal" that was subsequently implemented in Toronto and Berlin from the 1970s onward.

In comparison with the longevity of some other programs rooted in the Great Depression, such as Social Security in the United States and the National Health Service in Britain, the urban renewal order hardly lasted more than about a decade and a half after its full implementation in those countries. Being out of step with the natural constituencies that could sustain urban liberalism—in fact, actively alienating them—spelled the end of such programs. It would have come as no surprise if the anti-statist and anti-urban elements of the population had rejected what was after all an enormous government program for cities. But instead, urban renewal's supposed beneficiaries became its most vocal opponents. Like Prohibition, which alienated urban working-class immigrants, urban renewal proved to be another example of urban reformers knocking out their own supports. Having been given a virtually free hand, the experts (in this case the planners and urbanists) were left to recognize not only the inherently irrational element of democracy (a theme since Walter Lippmann), but also the fallibility of their own expertise. An unprecedented, and perhaps irretrievable, mandate was squandered on attempts to impose a Leitbild dictated by functionalist modernism. In a rebuke to liberal technocrats, Stephan Thernstrom and other neoconservatives in the United States suggested that urban problems were not technical but political. However, the Leitbild of technocratic, modernist planners—their urban vision and the techniques for achieving it—became a major point of contention, and sparked major political shifts for New Yorkers, Torontonians, Londoners, Berliners and many others.

Just as problematic as the ends of the urban renewal order were its means. Robert Moses, and his many imitators across the United States, originally wrapped themselves in the mantle of progress, New Deal housing reform, and slum clearance. But Moses ultimately came to represent a kind of entrenched bureaucratic power, which liberal crusaders sought to reform by demanding more responsive public servants (which ironically, Moses had once personified). Jane Jacobs and her Greenwich Village allies held a substantially different conception of the locus of power and the nature of its exercise. In *The Death and Life of Great American Cities*, she theorized at length on the practice of democracy in an urban context. Most of her examples drew from the experiences of various Greenwich Village ad hoc committees (to preserve Washington Square or close it to traffic, to oppose street widening and, finally, the master plan), as well as the coalitions they mobilized. New York's three competing visions of urban democracy—embodied by Moses, Village activists, and elite New York liberals from the administration of Robert Wagner to that of John Lindsay—entailed contrasting tactics. Moses mobilized a vast and invisible network of patronage and mutual obligation (like the Tammany machines he displaced). The liberals attempted to outmaneuver Moses from within the city's (and state's) institutions, contracting alliances to tip the balance of power on various commissions and agencies—though generally they did not object to what he did so much as the way he did it.

The Villagers, in contrast, did not share any such assumptions. Their opposition was not just a matter of degree, but rather a rejection of the entire proposition of urban renewal. What's more, they screamed bloody murder. Their rhetoric and strategies were confrontational and inflammatory. Villagers adopted the tactic that the best defense was a good offense—they did not just resist the renewal plans; they attempted to get control and reshape them. Their ability to appropriate the process and redirect it, due both to the resources of their community and to its organized persistence, distinguishes the Villagers' resistance from the more widespread opposition to government projects that would later be called NIMBY-ism. While the Villagers shared with such impulses a suspicious disdain for the liberal technocratic experts, they differed in their idealization of an alternative grassroots democracy. Unfortunately, that goal proved the most elusive.

Urban liberalism in the United States split into a series of different social and ideological groups, of urban renewal ideologies and counterideologies which originated from multiple places: academe, politics, and the community at large. By the 1970s, the collapse of the liberal reform coalition (at both the local and federal levels), which many grassroots activists helped bring about, was ultimately so severe, the backlash taking with it so many political and economic resources, that few sustaining patrons remained for urban neighborhood organizations or the New Left urbanists of the advocacy planning movement. Ironically, the legacies of their anti-modernist radicalism endured primarily in the more conservative gentrification movements that followed. The South Street neighborhood, while physically preserved, has ceased to "the Main Street of black Philadelphia," and has instead become primarily the province of nationwide chain stores and young white professionals. Jane Jacobs' formerly unassuming West Village neighborhood now commands some of the highest real estate prices in the country. Thus, leftists may have helped to topple liberal urban renewal programs, but it was conservatives—in politics and the market—who often benefited. This helps explain the curious way Jacobs' texts and activism still garner approval across the political spectrum.

In the United States, following the bitter clashes around urban renewal and the collapse of the political coalition that underpinned it, the final decades of the twentieth century produced neither the kind of public housing and highway megaprojects of the immediate postwar years nor the type of imaginative neighborhood-government affordable housing partnership envisaged by New Left urbanists. Instead, it was confined to the modest freelance projects of nonprofit community development organizations, striving for neighborhood stability in the face of the volatile globalized forces that buffeted cities: deindustrialization and disinvestment alongside gentrification and office booms. If Jane Jacobs and other community-based defenders of city life proclaimed any sort of victory, it was a pyrrhic one: Certainly, top-down urban renewal was long since discredited as liberal reform; but a climate of fragmentation and backlash politics, not to mention exhausted public finances, left few resources for confronting ongoing urban challenges in the United States.[6]

Ideological fragmentation, however, was not the only road out of the urban renewal era, as suggested by the heartening examples in Canada and West Germany. There, as in the United States and United Kingdom, Jacobsean-style ideas inspired both left- and right-wing branches of an urban renewal opposition. However, particularly at the civic level, these factions continued to coexist and even to partner. Often it took the form of a loose complementarity—as when self-described red Tory Wolf Jobst Siedler made common cause with anarchist squatters to end slum clearance in Berlin. But there was often more formal cohesion, and substantive policymaking: Progressive Conservatives like David Crombie and leftist John Sewell shared a voting block on the Toronto council over the 1970s, and Berlin's Christian Democrats formed a coalition with the Alternative List in the early 1980s. In these cases the opposition to conventional urban renewal, even the ostensible collapse of the liberal center, made for cooperative political alignments rather than (or at least in addition to) divisiveness. The emergence of a new Leitbild of neo-traditional urbanism certainly provided cohesion for diverse policymakers. These examples are notable for how citizens managed to salvage and repurpose planning institutions from the ruins of a previous urban regime.

While the legacies of these common developments in urbanism diverged strikingly in each country—particularly in terms of electoral politics—the contrasts should also not be overdrawn, particularly in the long view. Just after London's successful episode of New Left urbanism in Covent Garden, grassroots planning was completely marginalized in the Docklands redevelopment, the signature redevelopment project under Margaret Thatcher, whose administration was even more hostile to leftist urbanism than Nixon's. Toronto's reform movement eventually dissipated back toward traditional party rule. And by the 1980s, preserving neighborhoods—not just architecturally, but by assuring affordability for a mix of income groups—was difficult all around; communities in London, Toronto, and New York all wrestled with the challenges of gentrification. (Recent real estate trends in Berlin are hard to compare, given the extreme distortions of unification and relocation of the federal government, but similar critiques of so-called neoliberalism abound there.) Nevertheless, each of these cities witnessed vigorous expressions of a more democratized urban politics through the advocacy planning initiatives of the 1960s and 1970s. Those experiments with New Left urbanism, some modest, others more ambitious, left behind tangible legacies in the built environment of these cities. Even more enduring, though, is the complicated ideological fallout produced with the collapse of the urban renewal order.

Appendix

Table A1. The transatlantic pillars of the urban renewal order, 1920–65

	TASTE: MAINSTREAM MODERNISM	EXPERTISE: PROFESSIONAL URBANISTS	RESOURCES ($$$): NATIONAL POLICY	POWER: CIVIC REFORM
Berlin	Horseshoe project (1921–28) CIAM Athens Charter (1933) International building exhibition (1957) Gropiusstadt housing (1962–75) New Kreuzberg Center (1969–74)	Office of *Stadtbaurat* (19th c.) Bauhaus school (1919–33) Gropius, Blumenfeld, and other exiles advise OMGUS (late 1940s) Hillebrecht influence (1957–59)	Foreign and domestic reconstruction finance (1945–) *Städtebauförderungsgesetz* (belatedly, in 1971)	*Groß-Berlin*: metropolitan government amalgamated (1920) "Red Berlin": Gustav Böß left-liberal mayoralty (1921–29) Cold War consensus, *Wirtschaftswunder* Key SPD *Bürgermeister*: Ernst Reuter (1948–53), Otto Suhr (1955–57), Willy Brandt (1957–66), Klaus Schütz (1967–77)
London	Festival of Britain (1951) Alton Estate public housing (1959) Barbican project (1955–71) Shell Oil's Upstream Building (1961)	Abercrombie's London plans (1943–44) MARS chapter of CIAM influential in LCC (1947–)	Redistribution of Industry Act (1945) New Towns Act (1946) Town and Country Planning Act (1947)	Morrison "machine" (1934–64) Greater London Council (1965)

Toronto	Regent Park houses (1947) Bulova Tower (1955) Don Mills new town (1953–59) City Hall (1958–65)	League for Social Reconstruction (1930s) Master plan (1943) CIAM's Tyrwhitt establishes University of Toronto planning program (1951) Metro Toronto Plan draft (1959)	Bruce Report (1934) Curtis Report (1944) National Housing Act (1944) Canadian Mortgage and Housing Corporation (1946)	Citizens' Housing and Planning Association (1944) Referendum for urban renewal (1947) Metro Toronto Council (1953)
Boston	Gropius house (1937) Prudential Building (1960–64) City Hall (1962–68)	CIAM's Gropius reforms Harvard Graduate School of Design (1936–53)		Hynes and Collins administrations (1947–68) Logue (Boston Redevelopment Authority, 1961–67)
New York	MoMA architecture exhibit (1932) World's fair (1939–40) Stuyvesant Town (1942–47) U.N. headquarters (1947–53) Lever Building (1951)	Hudnut reforms Columbia School of Architecture (1933–35)	Housing Acts (key: 1949, 1954, and 1968) Highway Act (1956) H.U.D. created (1965)	Moses (influence 1930s–1950s) Wagner administration (1954–65)
Philadelphia	PSFS Building (1929–32) Better Philadelphia Exhibition (1947) Penn Center (1953–70) Municipal Building (1962–65)	CIAM's Perkins reforms Penn Graduate School of Fine Arts (1951–71)		Clark and Dilworth administrations (1952–62) Bacon planning director (1949–70)

Table A2. The collapse of the urban renewal order, 1950–80

	TASTE: TOWARD PRESERVATION	EXPERTISE: PROFESSIONAL SELF-CRITIQUE	RESOURCES ($$$): POLICY CHANGES	POWER: GRASSROOTS SHIFTS
Berlin	Siedler condemns "assassination" of Berlin (1964) Kottbusser Tor redevelopment protested (1969–74)	Mitscherlich's "inhospitable cities" (1966) Bahrdt calls for urbanity and citizen participation (1961–71) Hämer's Klausenerplatz (1968–74) International building exhibition (1984)	*Relatively unchanged*	*Strategien für Kreuzberg* (1971–77) *Osttangente* freeway stopped (1974) Squatters' occupations (1979–) SPD city government collapses (1980) Twelve principles of "gentle urban renewal" adopted (1983)
London	Outcry over Euston Arch demolition (1962), Centre Point (1963–65), and Barbican projects (1971) Civic Amenities Act (1967)	"Townscape" movement (ca. 1947–) Smithsons and Team X (1953–59) Young and Willmott, East London study (1957) Greater London Development Plan (1973)	Callaghan faces economic "crisis" (1976–79) Thatcher becomes prime minister (1979) GLC dissolved (1986)	Piccadilly redevelopment stopped (1959) West Cross freeway stopped (1973) Covent Garden area redevelopment stopped (1973) Docklands privatizations (1977)

			Relatively unchanged	
Toronto	Dissatisfaction with high-rise over-development in city neighborhoods (1960s) Anti-demolition riot at Sherbourne and Dundas Streets (1973)	McLuhan criticizes automobile-oriented planning (1969) Core Area Task Force (1974)	Relatively unchanged	Spadina freeway revolt (1968–71) Reformers join council (1969) Crombie becomes mayor (1973) St. Lawrence neighborhood developed (1974–79)
Boston	Allston urban renewal opposed (1964) Dissatisfaction at City Hall Plaza (1967) Quincy Market refurbished (1967)	Gans, *Urban Villagers* (1962) Anderson, *Federal Bulldozer* (1964) Banfield, *Unheavenly City* (1970)		Inner Belt freeway stopped (1971) Anti-busing backlash (1967–)
New York	Jacobs, *Death and Life of Great American Cities* (1961) Outcry over demolition of Pennsylvania Station (1963)	Thabit's Planners for Equal Opportunity (1964) Hatch's Architects Renewal Committee in Harlem (1964) Shiffman's Pratt Center in Brooklyn (1964)	Historic Preservation Act (1966) Moynihan advises "benign neglect" to Nixon (1970) Nixon moratorium on aid to cities (1973) Model Cities program ended (1974)	Lower Manhattan Expressway stopped (1962–69) West Village Houses (1963–74) Historic preservation districts created (1965–69) Fiscal crisis (1970–75)
Philadelphia	Movement to designate Independence National Historical Park (1941–48) Society Hill renaissance (1957–65)	Davidoff's advocacy planning (ca. 1962) Kahn's Philadelphia school of architecture Venturi, *Complexity and Contradiction* (1966) Scott Brown on South Street (1968)	Community Development Block Grant program enacted (1974)	Crosstown freeway stopped (1971) Rizzo elected mayor (1971)

Notes

Introduction: The Final Frontier

1. Particularly, it seemed to him, "in intellectual, journalistic and some political circles." Daniel P. Moynihan, *Toward a National Urban Policy* (New York: Basic Books, 1970), ix.

2. Sam Bass Warner, Jr., *Streetcar Suburbs: The Process of Growth in Boston, 1870–1900* (Cambridge, MA: Harvard University Press, 1978), vi.

3. Kevin Lynch and Lloyd Rodwin, "A World of Cities," in "The Future Metropolis," ed. Lloyd Rodwin, special issue, *Daedalus: Journal of the American Academy of Arts and Sciences* 90, no. 1 (Winter 1961): 7–8.

4. Moynihan, *Toward a National Urban Policy*, 6.

5. Bagehot quoted in Michael Hebbert, *London: More by Fortune Than Design* (New York: John Wiley, 1998), 9.

6. Lyndon Johnson, commencement address at the University of Michigan, May 22, 1964, www.lbjlibrary.org/collections/selected-speeches/november-1963-1964/05-22-1964.html.

7. Charles Abrams, *The City Is the Frontier* (New York: Harper & Row, 1965).

8. See Jennifer S. Light, *From Warfare to Welfare: Defense Intellectuals and Urban Problems in Cold War America* (Baltimore: Johns Hopkins University Press, 2003).

9. Robert Fishman, "The Mumford-Jacobs Debate," *Planning History Studies* 10, no. 1–2 (1996): 7.

10. Mark Lilla, *The Reckless Mind: Intellectuals in Politics* (New York: New York Review Books, 2001); James C. Scott, *Seeing like a State: How Certain Schemes to Improve the Human Condition Have Failed* (New Haven: Yale University Press, 1998).

11. Jane Jacobs, "The Missing Link in City Redevelopment," *Architectural Forum* 104 (June 1956): 132–33; excerpted in Max Allen, ed., *Ideas That Matter: The Worlds of Jane Jacobs* (Owen Sound, ON: Ginger Press, 1997), 39–40.

12. Thomas Cochran, review of *The Historian and the City*, ed. Oscar Handlin and John Burchard, *Journal of Economic History* 24, no. 3 (September 1964): 401.

13. For a summary of urban history in first half of the twentieth century, see Blake McKelvey, "American Urban History Today," *American Historical Review* 57, no. 4 (July 1952): 919–29.

14. William Diamond, "On the Dangers of an Urban Interpretation of History," in *Historiography and Urbanization: Essays in American History in Honor of W. Stull Holt*, ed. E. F. Goldman (Baltimore: Johns Hopkins University Press, 1941), a reaction to Arthur M. Schlesinger, "The City in American History," *Mississippi Valley Historical Review* 27 (1940): 43–66; revised in Schlesinger, *Paths to the Present* (New York: Macmillan, 1949), 210–33. See also Schlesinger, *Rise of the City, 1878–1898* (New York: Macmillan, 1933); and Carl Bridenbaugh, *Cities in the Wilderness: The First Century of Urban Life in America, 1625–1742* (New York: Ronald Press, 1938).

15. Oscar Handlin adapted the Chicago school's urban sociology to historical studies of city immigration, including *Boston's Immigrants: A Study in Acculturation, 1790–1865* (Cambridge, MA: Harvard University Press, 1941), *The Uprooted* (New York: Grosset & Dunlap, 1951), and *The Newcomers: Negroes and Puerto Ricans in a Changing Metropolis* (Cambridge, MA: Harvard Univer-

sity Press, 1959). The Social Science Research Council promoted research on long-term trends in "the development of the city in society" and funded historians like David Pinkney, a scholar of Paris who urged the enlistment of historical analysis in the conception of contemporary urban problems by dragging the "theories and techniques of sociology and economics" into the archives of older European cities. David H. Pinkney, "Urban Studies and the Historian," *Social Forces* 28, no. 4 (May 1950): 423–29.

16. Richard Wade, *The Urban Frontier: The Rise of Western Cities, 1790–1830* (Cambridge, MA: Harvard University Press, 1959); *Frontier Cities* (1959); John W. Reps, *Town Planning in Frontier America* (Princeton: Princeton University Press, 1969), an abridgement of his 1965 *The Making of Urban America* (Princeton: Princeton University Press, 1965).

17. From Warner's review of *Nineteenth-Century Cities: Essays in the New Urban History*, ed. Stephan Thernstrom and Richard Sennett (New Haven: Yale University Press, 1969), *Journal of American History* 57, no. 3 (December 1970): 737. See also Oscar Handlin and John Burchard, eds., *The Historian and the City* (Cambridge, MA: Joint Center for Urban Studies, 1963); Sam B. Warner, Jr., *Streetcar Suburbs: The Process of Growth in Boston, 1870–1900* (Cambridge, MA: Joint Center for Urban Studies, 1962); and Stephan Thernstrom, *Poverty and Progress: Social Mobility in a Nineteenth-Century City* (Cambridge, MA: Joint Center for Urban Studies, 1964).

18. Key scholarly overviews of the history of urban planning are M. Christine Boyer, *Dreaming the Rational City: The Myth of American City Planning* (Cambridge, MA: MIT Press, 1983); and Peter Hall, *Cities of Tomorrow: An Intellectual History of Urban Planning and Design in the Twentieth Century* (Oxford: Blackwell Publishing, 1988)

19. Daniel T. Rodgers, *Atlantic Crossings: Social Politics in a Progressive Age* (Cambridge, MA: Harvard University Press, Belknap Press, 1998), 163.

20. James T. Kloppenberg, "In Retrospect: Louis Hartz's *The Liberal Tradition in America*," *Reviews in American History* 29 (2001): 469. See Rodgers, *Atlantic Crossings*; and James T. Kloppenberg, *Uncertain Victory: Social Democracy and Progressivism in European and American Thought, 1870–1920* (New York: Oxford University Press, 1986). It should be noted that Rodgers' transatlantic currents seem to flow only one way—westward—as, for example, "Their noses pressed against the glass of other nations' experience, American civic progressives brought home, one by one, devices for the more deliberate, conscious city building: the distinctive outlines of Second Empire Paris, the tools of Städtebau, even the British and continental European experiments in the social politics of shelter" (198).

21. The view of American liberalism as in opposition to socialism, common to Werner Sombart and Hartz, has been recently resurrected in Germany by Hans Vorländer, who sees a *Sonderweg* for both countries. See Klaus J. Hansen, "The Liberal Tradition in America: A German View," *Journal of American History* 87, no. 4 (March 2001): 1397–1408, for a discussion of Hans Vorländer, *Hegemonialer Liberalismus: Politisches Denken und politische Kultur in den USA, 1776–1920* (Frankfurt: Campus, 1997).

22. Nancy Cohen, *The Reconstruction of American Liberalism, 1865–1914* (Chapel Hill: University of North Carolina Press, 2002), charts the earliest phases of this shift; Theodore Lowi, *The End of Liberalism: Ideology, Policy and the Crisis of Public Authority* (New York: Norton, 1969), decries the end results.

23. Consider, for example, the intermodal and often regional public transportation authorities created in most major U.S. cities, including Boston and Chicago (both 1947), New York (1953), and Philadelphia (1963).

24. Gary Gerstle, "The Protean Character of American Liberalism," *American Historical Review* 99 (1994): 1043–73.

25. H. W. Brands, *The Strange Death of American Liberalism* (New Haven: Yale University Press, 2001).

26. See Gary Gerstle, "Race and the Myth of the Liberal Consensus," *Journal of American History* 82 (1995): 579–86, for an insightful discussion of Sugrue and Hirsch. Alan Brinkley, *The End of Reform: New Deal Liberalism in Recession and War* (New York: Alfred A. Knopf, 1995), argues that U.S. liberalism was in retreat already by 1937.

27. For example, Gareth Davies, "The Great Society after Johnson: The Case of Bilingual Education," *Journal of American History* 88, no. 4 (March 2002): 1405–29.

28. Jan Palmowski, *Urban Liberalism in Imperial Germany: Frankfurt am Main, 1866–1914* (New York: Oxford University Press, 1999).

29. For two very different perspectives on the same developments see Tristram Hunt, *Building Jerusalem: The Rise and Fall of the Victorian City* (New York: Metropolitan Books, 2005); and Patrick Joyce, *Rule of Freedom: Liberalism and the Modern City* (London: Verso, 2003).

30. J. Joseph Huthmacher, "Urban Liberalism and the Age of Reform," *Mississippi Valley Historical Review* 49, no. 2 (September 1962): 231; John Teaford, *The Unheralded Triumph: City Government in America, 1870–1900* (Baltimore: Johns Hopkins University Press, 1984). Robert Fishman sees this period as the golden age of what he calls the "metropolitanist" tradition of civic boosterism grounded in an "urban conversation"; see his introduction to *The American Planning Tradition: Culture and Policy*, ed. Robert Fishman (Baltimore: Johns Hopkins University Press; Washington DC: Wilson Center Press, 2000).

31. For architectural histories written with a keen awareness of social context, see the works of Gwendolyn Wright, including *Building the Dream: A Social History of Housing in America* (New York: Pantheon, 1981); and *USA: Modern Architectures in History* (London: Reaktion Books, 2008).

32. Henry Russell Hitchcock and Philip Johnson are credited with coining the term "International Style" for their 1932 exhibition on the modernist architectural movement at New York's Museum of Modern Art. See their catalog of the same name.

33. Mark Stevens of *Newsweek*, quoted in Douglas Martin, "An Architectural Milestone Loses Its Pedigree," *New York Times*, February 1, 2002, B1.

34. Steve Fraser and Gary Gerstle, eds., *The Rise and Fall of the New Deal Order, 1930–1980* (Princeton: Princeton University Press, 1990).

35. While urban historians have scarcely applied this approach, calls for—and examples of—the internationalization of U.S. history are by now well established, notably in Thomas Bender, ed., *Rethinking American History in a Global Age* (Berkeley: University of California Press, 2002); and Thomas Bender, *A Nation among Nations: America's Place in World History* (New York: Hill & Wang, 2006).

36. "Walter Gropius Dies: Founder of Bauhaus School of Architecture," *Philadelphia Inquirer*, July 6, 1969, 12; Rainer Haubrich, "Das Berliner Mietshaus," in *Berlin: Der Architekturführer*, ed. Rainer Haubrich, Hans W. Hoffmann, and Philipp Meuser (Berlin: Quadriga, 2001), 77. Haubrich estimates that the "rabid" practice of removing embellishments had defaced three-quarters of the older structures in East and West Berlin by the 1970s.

37. Sam Bass Warner, Jr., *The Urban Wilderness: A History of the American City* (New York: Harper & Row, 1972), 3.

Introduction to Part I

1. Influential antecedents include Giorgio Vasari's remodeling of Medici Florence, Georges-Eugène Haussmann's redevelopment of Paris under Napoleon III, the McMillan Commission's 1902 recommendations for Washington DC, and Daniel Burnham's 1909 plan commissioned by the Commercial Club of Chicago.

Chapter 1: Atlantic Crossings of the Urban Renewal Order

1. Robert Fishman, *Urban Utopias in the Twentieth Century: Ebenezer Howard, Frank Lloyd Wright, Le Corbusier* (New York: Basic Books, 1978).

2. Daniel T. Rodgers, *Atlantic Crossings: Social Politics in a Progressive Age* (Cambridge, MA: Harvard University Press, Belknap Press, 1998), 384–91.

3. Ronald V. Wiedenhoeft, *Berlin's Housing Revolution: German Reform in the 1920s* (Ann Arbor, MI: UMI Research Press, 1985). See also Helmut Gruber, *Red Vienna: Experiment in Working-Class Culture, 1919–1934* (New York: Oxford University Press, 1991); Eve Blau, *The Architecture of Red Vienna, 1919–1934* (Cambridge, MA: M.I.T. Press, 1999); and John Robert Mullin, "City Planning in Frankfurt, Germany, 1925–1932: A Study in Practical Utopianism," *Journal of Urban History* 4, no. 1 (November 1, 1977): 3–28.

4. John Burchard, *Voice of the Phoenix: Postwar Architecture in Germany* (Cambridge, MA: M.I.T. Press, 1966), 22.

5. Such attitudes were hardly unique to Berlin urbanists, but rather endemic to German culture in the period; see, for example, Harold Poor, "City versus Country: Anti-urbanism in the Weimar Republic," *Societas* 6 (1976): 177–92; Klaus Bergman, *Agrarromantik und Grossstadtfeindschaft* (Meisenheim am Glan: Anton Hain, 1970); and Friedrich Sengle, "Wunschbild Land und Schreckbild Stadt: Zu einem zentralen Thema der neueren deutschen Literatur," *Studium Generale* 16 (1963): 619–31.

6. Werner Hegemann, *Das steinerne Berlin: Geschichte der größten Mietkasernenstadt der Welt* (Berlin: Gustav Kiepenheuer, 1930). Hegemann, who was educated at the University of Pennsylvania (among other places), called for the rationalization of the city through the socialization of property. He lost his German citizenship in 1933 and went on to teach at Columbia University; a full study is Christiane Crasemann Collins, *Werner Hegemann and the Search for Universal Urbanism* (New York: W. W. Norton & Company, 2005). See also Martin Wagner, ed., *Das neue Berlin: Großstadtprobleme* (Berlin: 1929); Wagner would later teach with Walter Gropius at Harvard.

7. Keith D. Revell, *Building Gotham: Civic Culture and Public Policy in New York City, 1898–1938* (Baltimore: Johns Hopkins University Press, 2002), 185–226.

8. On early zoning, see Revell, *Building Gotham*, chap. 5; Patricia Burgess, *Planning for the Private Interest: Land-Use Controls and Residential Patterns in Columbus, Ohio, 1900–1970* (Columbus: Ohio State University Press, 1994); and S. J. Makielski, Jr., *The Politics of Zoning: The New York Experience* (New York: Columbia University Press, 1966).

9. As president of the CIAM from 1930 to 1947, van Eesteren was pivotal in formalizing the ideas of "the functional city" that underlay the 1934 Athens Charter. He also served as city planner for Amsterdam from 1929 to 1959. See "Eesteren, Cornelis [Cor] van," in *The Grove Dictionary of Art Online*, ed. L. Macy (accessed 30 May 2003). Hilberseimer later rejected his early approach to urbanism; see Ludwig Hilberseimer, *Berliner Architektur der 20er Jahre* (Mainz: Florian Kupferberg, 1967), 65.

10. Andrew Lees, *Cities Perceived: Urban Society in European and American Thought, 1820–1940* (New York: Columbia University Press, 1985), 311.

11. Description from Barbara Miller Lane, *Architecture and Politics in Germany 1918–1945* (Cambridge, MA: Harvard University Press, 1968), 5.

12. Harold Hammer-Schenk, "Alfred Hugenberg and Otto Kohtz: Projeckte für Berlin," in *Architektur als politische Kultur: Philosophia practica*, ed. Hermann Hipp and Ernst Seidl (Berlin: Reimer, 1996), 239–52, explores the Berlin proposals of American-inspired modernists during the Nazi regime. The role of American influences on German modernism is discussed by Michael Baumunk, "Die schnellste Stadt der Welt," in *Berlin, Berlin: Ausstellung zur Geschichte der Stadt*, ed. Gottfried Korff and Reinhard Rürup (Berlin: Nicolai, 1987).

13. Lane, *Architecture and Politics in Germany*, 3, 9, 216. Conservative architects associated with the Kampfbund für deutsche Kultur preferred the architecture of "around 1910."

14. Eric Mumford, *The CIAM Discourse on Urbanism, 1928–1960* (Cambridge, MA: M.I.T. Press, 2002).

15. To emphasize the transatlantic continuities on urban reconstruction, Friedhelm Fischer, "German Reconstruction as an International Activity," in *Rebuilding Europe's Bombed Cities*, ed. Jeffry M. Diefendorf (New York: Palgrave Macmillan, 1990), 133–34, cites Walter Gropius and Martin Wagner, "Program for City Reconstruction," *Architectural Forum* 79 (July 1943): 75–82; and the National Association of Real Estate Boards' *Post-war Cities* brochure (Chicago, 1945), which compared the effects of blight with bombing.

16. There is an ongoing discussion about the intentions and results of total war strategies during World War II. A recent collection, including an assessment of the air war's effect on Berlin by Peter Wapnewski ("Bomben auf die Reichshauptstadt 1943/44," 116–23), is Lothar Kettenacker, ed., *Ein Volk von Opfern? Die neue Debatte um den Bombenkrieg 1940–1945* (Berlin: Rowohlt, 2003).

17. Jeffry M. Diefendorf, *In the Wake of War: The Reconstruction of German Cities after World War II* (New York: Oxford University Press, 1993), 11. Rubble comparisons are extrapolated from Diefendorf's data on p. 15. In Berlin there were 55 million cubic meters; in Hamburg (the only city with as much as half of Berlin's total), 35.8 million cubic meters.

18. Bruce Kuklick, *American Policy and the Division of Germany: The Clash with Russia over Reparations* (Ithaca: Cornell University Press, 1972).

19. Thomas Schwartz, *America's Germany: John J. McCloy and the Federal Republic of Germany* (Cambridge, MA: Harvard University Press, 1991), portrays Germany as the "cockpit" of American postwar foreign policy.

20. Diefendorf, *In the Wake of War*, 246.

21. See Donald Fleming and Bernard Bailyn, eds., *The Intellectual Migration: Europe and America, 1930–1960* (Cambridge, MA: Harvard University Press, Belknap Press, 1969), including William H. Jordy's admiring appraisal, "The Aftermath of the Bauhaus in America: Gropius, Mies, and Breuer."

22. Jill Pearlman, "Joseph Hudnut and the Unlikely Beginnings of Post-modern Urbanism at the Harvard Bauhaus," *Planning Perspectives* 15, no. 3 (July 2000): 202. For a critical assessment of the imprint of Gropius on Harvard architects and beyond, see Klaus Herdeg, *The Decorated Diagram: Harvard Architecture and the Failure of the Bauhaus Legacy* (Cambridge, MA: M.I.T. Press, 1983).

23. Jeffry M. Diefendorf, "America and the Rebuilding of Urban Germany," in *American*

Policy and the Reconstruction of West Germany, 1945–1955, ed. Jeffry Diefendorf, Axel Frohn, and Hermann-Josef Rupieper (New York: Cambridge University Press, 1993), 332. See also Jeffry Diefendorf, "Berlin on the Charles, Cambridge on the Spree: Walter Gropius, Martin Wagner and the Rebuilding of Germany," in Kulturelle Wechselbeziehungen im Exil—Exile across Cultures, ed. Helmut Pfanner (Bonn: Bouvier, 1986), 343–58.

24. Fischer, "German Reconstruction as an International Activity," 140.

25. Blumenfeld accompanied the Philadelphia citizen's planning committee head Samuel Zisman. Diefendorf, "America and the Rebuilding of Urban Germany," 338ff. See also Blumenfeld's memoirs and collected essays: Life Begins at 65: The Not Entirely Candid Autobiography of a Drifter (Montreal: Harvest House, 1987); and Paul D. Spreiregen, ed., The Modern Metropolis: Its Origins, Growth, Characteristics, and Planning: Selected Essays (Cambridge, MA: M.I.T. Press, 1967).

26. This approach, articulated in a much-cited proposal conceived at the end of the war, Roland Rainer, Die gegliederte und aufgelockerte Stadt (Berlin: Deutsche Akademie für Städtebau Reichs- und Landesplanung 1945; a new, de-Nazified edition appeard in 1957), was dramatically demonstrated in two building exhibitions: Constructa 1951 and Interbau 1957.

27. Hans Bernhard Reichow, Die autogerechte Stadt: Ein Weg aus dem Verkehrs-Chaos [roughly, The automobile-ready city: A way out of the traffic chaos] (Ravensburg: Otto Maier, 1959).

28. Gerhard Rabeler, Wiederaufbau und Expansion westdeutscher Städte 1945–1960 im Spannungs-feld von Reformideen und Wirklichkeit (Bonn: Deutsches Nationalkomitee für Denkmalschutz, 1990).

29. Heidede Becker, "Vom kahlschlag zum behutsamen Umgang mit der alten Stadt," in Wohnen und Stadtpolitik im Umbruch: Perspektiven der Stadterneuerung nach 40 Jahren DDR, ed. Peter Marcuse and Fred Staufenbiel (Berlin: Akademie, 1991), 89.

30. "SPD setzt auf Städtebau," Bauwelt 22 (May 31, 1965): 613–14; on the CDU program see also Bauwelt 24 (June 14, 1965): 689–91; and Bauwelt 25 (June 12, 1965): 728–29.

31. Becker, "Vom kahlschlag zum behutsamen Umgang," 89.

32. Burchard, Voice of the Phoenix (n. 4 above), 166. Contrast his enthusiasm for the divided city: "Berlin's recovery is the most noticeable partly for ideological reasons and partly because there are still so many open lots to remind the visitor of 1945. There are such lots in Munich too but with no such dramatically juxtaposed new constructions. The Berlin result is noticeable on an absolute as well as on a relative scale" (4).

33. Mumford, CIAM Discourse, 127.

34. The myth of Rothenburg inviolate is dispelled by Diefendorf, In the Wake of War, 310.

35. Wilhelm Westecker, Wiedergeburt der deutschen Städte (Düsseldorf: Econ-Verlag, 1962).

36. Rabeler, Wiederaufbau, 168–69.

37. See, for example, a comparative study covering the period 1850–1950 by Dirk Schubert, Stadterneuerung in London und Hamburg: Eine Stadtgeschichte zwischen Modernisierung und Disziplinier-ung (Brunswick: Vieweg & Sohn, 1997).

38. For a contemporary discussion of the larger economic policy issues in immediate post-war Britain, see W. Arthur Lewis, The Principles of Economic Planning (London: Fabian Society, 1949).

39. Francis Sheppard, London: A History (Oxford: Oxford University Press, 1998), 349.

40. See E. Milner Holland, Report of the Committee on Housing in Greater London, Cmnd. 2605 (London: Her Majesty's Stationery Office, 1965).

41. Helen Meller, *Towns, Plans, and Society in Modern Britain* (Cambridge: Cambridge University Press, 1997), 78.

42. J. M. Richards, "Architectural Criticism in the Nineteen-Thirties," in *Concerning Architecture: Essays on Architectural Writers and Writing presented to Nikolaus Pevsner*, ed. John Summerson (London: Penguin, 1968), 253.

43. Wells Wintemute Coates had been tapped to lead the group by CIAM's secretary general, the Swiss art historian Siegfried Gideon. Mumford, *CIAM Discourse*, 77. See also John R. Gold, *The Experience of Modernism: Modern Architects and the Future City, 1928–1953* (New York: Taylor & Francis, 1998).

44. *Can Our Cities Survive? An ABC of Urban Problems, Their Analysis, Their Solutions, Based on the Proposals Formulated by the CIAM* (Cambridge, MA: Harvard University Press, 1942). The book, compiled by José (aka Josep) Lluis Sert at the group's request, was explicitly "based on the resolutions of the Fourth (1933) and Fifth (1937) Congresses of the CIAM" as well as the collaborative "researches and recommendations" of various members and subgroups, including Britain's MARS (xii).

45. Mumford, *CIAM Discourse*, 122–23.

46. Reginald Theodore Blomfield, *Modernismus: An Attack on Some of the More Extreme Tendencies of Modern Art* (New York: Macmillan & Co., 1934), v.

47. Mumford, *CIAM Discourse*, 73–76.

48. "For example, [Arthur] Ling is in the Town Planning Dept. of the LCC, [Gordon] Stephenson is chief technical officer to the Ministry of Town and Country Planning, where [William] Holford is technical advisor." Quoted in ibid., 169.

49. Helena Webster, "Modernism without Rhetoric," in *Modernism without Rhetoric: Essays on the Work of Alison and Peter Smithson* (London: Academy Editions, 1997), 17: "As a consequence [of austerity] many of the jobs for architects were in local government departments (after the war there was a marked movement of architects from private practice to public service, a net swing of 40 per cent among Royal Institute of British Architects members by 1948), which in London entailed working for the London County Council."

50. John Davis, "Modern London," in *The English Urban Landscape*, ed. Philip Waller (New York: Oxford University Press, 2000), 145: "The first victim was the holistic conception of the planned city that Abercrombie had bequeathed. . . . In the 1960s the planners turned their attention to the growing housing crisis."

51. Kenneth O. Morgan, *The People's Peace: British History since 1945* (Oxford: Oxford University Press, 1999), 554, cites deregulation of the housing market in the 1950s to explain the rise from 7 million owners in 1961 to 14.5 million in 1987, representing two-thirds of all occupants by 1996.

52. Nichola Bullock, *Building the Post-war World* (London: Routledge, 2002), 214.

53. Sheppard, *London*, 351.

54. Bullock, *Building the Post-war World*, 90, 213.

55. See Holland, *Report of the Committee on Housing in Greater London*.

56. Jane Jacobs, *The Death and Life of Great American Cities* (New York: Random House, 1961), 410.

57. James T. Lemon, *Liberal Dreams and Nature's Limits: Great Cities of North America since 1600* (Toronto: Oxford University Press, 1996), 272, 262.

58. See Richard Harris, "More American Than the United States: Housing in Urban Can-

ada in the Twentieth Century," *Journal of Urban History* 26, no. 4 (May 2000): 456–78. "In the United States, a substantial amount of public housing was built, with federal support, during the 1930s. In Canada, the first project was begun on local initiative only in 1949. A [Canadian] national program of construction did not begin until the 1950s or become significant until the 1960s" (469).

59. See Sean Purdy, "From Place of Hope to Outcast Space: Territorial Regulation and Tenant Resistance in Regent Park Housing Project, 1945–2000" (Ph.D. dissertation, Queen's University, 2003), chap. 1; and Kevin Brushett, "'People and Government Travelling Together': Community Organization, Urban Planning and the Politics of Post-war Reconstruction in Toronto, 1943–1953," *Urban History Review* 27, no. 2 (1999): 44–58.

60. Mumford, *CIAM Discourse*, 315. Tyrwhitt became a landscape architect in England in the 1920s (influenced by Sir Patrick Geddes, Frederick J. Osborn, and the Garden City movement), then studied planning at the Technical Hochschule Berlin "partly to see what had happened to the earlier town planning schemes under Hitler, and partly to experience life under a totalitarian regime." By the 1940s she was director of the planning program at London University, and she became involved with MARS (as a member in 1941, as assistant director in 1949) as it was becoming the focus of CIAM conferences. She collaborated with Siegfried Gideon. In 1948, she went to the New School for Social Research in New York, then briefly to Yale. After 1955, Tyrwhitt taught at Harvard, worked with Constantine Doxiadis, and consulted for the United Nations. (Ibid., 202, 246–47.)

61. Lemon, *Liberal Dreams*, 267.

62. Ibid., 257. See also John Bacher, *Keeping to the Marketplace: The Evolution of Canadian Housing Policy* (Montreal: McGill–Queen's University Press, 1993).

63. Robert Fulford, *Accidental City: The Transformation of Toronto* (Toronto: McFarlane, Walter & Ross, 1995), 51, 56.

64. According to his biographer, Gardiner, like Robert Moses, was loath to turn a modicum of his authority over to planning experts; he did, however, see planning as a politically expedient way to lend the veneer of objectivity to pro-growth policies. See T. Colton, *Big Daddy: Frederick Gardiner and the Building of Metropolitan Toronto* (Toronto: University of Toronto Press, 1980), 183.

65. See Spreiregen, *Modern Metropolis* (n. 25 above); Blumenfeld, *Life Begins at 65* (n. 25 above); and Charles Abrams, "Rich Country, Poor Cities," *New York Times*, July 16, 1967, 198, reviewing James Q. Wilson, Sam Bass Warner, Jr., and Blumenfeld.

66. Frank Smallwood, "Metro Toronto: A Decade Later," in *Taming Megalopolis*, ed. H. Wentworth Eldredge (New York: Praeger, 1967), 2:669–97.

67. Lemon, *Liberal Dreams*, 265. Smallwood notes that the master plan of the Metropolitan Toronto Planning Board was only drafted, never approved. Lemon maintains that "even so, the plan remained the guide for action."

68. Ibid., 274.

Chapter 2: Assembling the Four Pillars

1. The Amalgamated Clothing Workers and other unions in New York experimented with innovative financing for cooperative housing from the 1920s—though their buildings were still more traditional in style. See Gail Radford, *Modern Housing for America: Policy Struggles in the New Deal Era* (Chicago: University of Chicago Press, 1997), chap. 5.

2. Terence Riley and Stephen Perrella, *The International Style: Exhibition 15 at the Museum of Modern Art* (New York: Rizzoli/CBA, 1992), 192–200.

3. M. Jeffrey Hardwick, *Mall Maker: Victor Gruen, Architect of an American Dream* (Philadelphia: University of Pennsylvania Press, 2003). To understand shifting corporate and consumer tastes over the entire twentieth century in the context of commercial districts, consult Alison Isenberg, *Downtown America: A History of the Place and the People Who Made It* (Chicago: University of Chicago Press, 2004).

4. The uncannily ubiquitous American architect and critic Peter Blake devoted attention to this ideological shift—and much besides—in his memoir, *No Place like Utopia: Modern Architecture and the Company We Kept* (New York: W. W. Norton, 1996).

5. A recent collection considering such issues is Casey Nelson Blake, ed., *The Arts of Democracy: Art, Public Culture, and the State* (Philadelphia: University of Pennsylvania Press, 2007).

6. Louis Wirth, "Urbanism as a Way of Life," *American Journal of Sociology* 44, no. 1 (July 1938): 1–24; reprinted in Richard T. LeGates and Frederic Stout, eds., *The City Reader* (New York: Routledge, 1996), 197.

7. Regarding this terminology, comparative urban historians maintain that "the English *town planning* corresponds to the French neologism *urbanisme* and to the positive German word *Städtebau*," according to Paul M. Hohenberg and Lynn Hollen Lees, *The Making of Urban Europe, 1000–1994* (Harvard University Press, 1995), 390. The neologism may have been coined in Pierre Lavedan, *Qu'est-ce que c'est l'urbanisme* (1926). The *Oxford English Dictionary* notes the application of the word in this context by the *Times* on July 16, 1929: "In all the opening speeches, the newly coined word 'urbanism' was prominent. It denotes town-planning, [etc.]." For an optimistic application of the idea within Chicago school urban sociology, see Charles E. Merriam, "Urbanism," *American Journal of Sociology* 45 (1940): 720–30.

8. Eric Mumford, *The CIAM Discourse on Urbanism, 1928–1960* (Cambridge, MA: M.I.T. Press, 2002), 204.

9. Thomas Bender has often written incisively on this and other relevant topics, notably in *Intellect and Public Life: Essays on the Social History of Academic Intellectuals in the United States* (Baltimore: Johns Hopkins University Press, 1993).

10. A professional organization, the American City Planning Institute, was founded in 1917, and Harvard formed the first U.S. school of city planning in 1929. See Mel Scott, *American City Planning since 1890* (Berkeley: University of California Press, 1969), 117, 265.

11. Jill Pearlman, "Joseph Hudnut's Other Modernism at the 'Harvard Bauhaus,'" *Journal of the Society of Architectural Historians* 56, no. 4 (December 1997): 452–77.

12. On the arrival of modernism at Columbia and Harvard, see Jill E. Pearlman, "Joseph Hudnut and the Education of the Modern Architect" (Ph.D. dissertation, University of Chicago, 1993); and John R. Gold, *The Experience of Modernism: Modern Architects and the Future City, 1928–1953* (New York: Taylor & Francis, 1998).

13. On the migration of the Bauhaus see Hans Wingler, *Bauhaus: Weimar, Dessau, Berlin, Chicago* (1969); and Margret Kentgens-Craig, *The Bauhaus and America: First Contacts 1919–1936* (Cambridge, MA: M.I.T. Press, 1999). For Gropius in particular, see Reginald R. Isaacs, *Gropius: An Illustrated Biography of the Creator of the Bauhaus* (Boston: Little, Brown, 1991); Horst Claussen, *Walter Gropius: Grundzèuge seines Denkens* (New York: Olms, 1986); and Winfried Nerdinger, *Walter Gropius: Der Architekt* (Berlin : Gebr. Mann, 1985).

14. Guy Greer, ed., *The Problem of the Cities and Towns: Report of the Conference on Urban-*

ism, *Harvard University, March 5–6, 1942* (Cambridge, MA: Harvard University Press, 1942), 97–98.

15. Hudnut, for whose assistance Sert was "deeply indebted," provided a foreword which, while skeptical of perennial attempts to rationalize the city form, expressed confidence that CIAM's alliance of practical arts with "applications of science to economic and social problems" could provide remedies for the "frightful ills" afflicting contemporary cities (*Can Our Cities Survive? An ABC of Urban Problems, Their Analysis, Their Solutions, Based on the Proposals Formulated by the CIAM* [Cambridge, MA: Harvard University Press, 1942], iv). Lewis Mumford repeatedly refused to write an introduction to a book "without a single reference to the functions of government, group association or culture." See E. Mumford, *CIAM Discourse*, 132.

16. Jill Pearlman, "Joseph Hudnut and the Unlikely Beginnings of Post-modern Urbanism at the Harvard Bauhaus," *Planning Perspectives* 15, no. 3 (July 2000): 201. See also Anthony Alofsin, *The Struggle for Modernism: Architecture, Landscape Architecture, and City Planning at Harvard* (New York: W. W. Norton, 2002).

17. For a laudatory summary of the Perkins years, from the perspective of its alumni and emeriti, see Ann L. Strong and George E. Thomas, eds., *The Book of the School: 100 Years of the Graduate School of Fine Arts at the University of Pennsylvania* (Philadelphia: Graduate School of Fine Arts, 1990), 131–249.

18. See Martin Bulmer, *The Chicago School of Sociology: Institutionalization, Diversity, and the Rise of Sociological Research* (Chicago: University of Chicago Press, 1984). On Tugwell's planning ideas see his article "The Fourth Power," *Planning and Civic Comment* 5, no. 2 (April–June 1939): 1–31; and Michael V. Namorato, *Rexford Tugwell: A Biography* (New York: Praeger, 1988). On the University of Chicago during this period of ferment see Mary Ann Dzuback, *Robert M. Hutchins: Portrait of an Educator* (Chicago: University of Chicago Press, 1991).

19. William Grigsby and Chester Rapkin quoted in Strong and Thomas, *Book of the School*, 181; see also 168.

20. Herbert J. Gans, "Recreation Planning for Leisure Behavior: A Goal-Oriented Approach" (Ph.D. dissertation, University of Pennsylvania, 1957); Gans' Boston study was prepared for the Center for Community Studies from 1957 through 1959 and published as *The Urban Villagers: Group and Class in the Life of Italian-Americans* (New York: Free Press, 1962).

21. Meyerson's papers are at Van Pelt Library, University of Pennsylvania; see also Strong and Thomas, *Book of the School*, 166; and Martin Meyerson, Barbara Terrett, and Paul N. Ylvisaker, eds., *Metropolis in Ferment* (Philadelphia: Annals of the American Academy of Political and Social Science, 1957).

22. At the recommendation of a committee led by Edwin S. Burdell in 1956. See "History of the Department of Urban Studies and Planning," http://libraries.mit.edu/archives/mithistory/histories-offices/urbstud.html.

23. "Lloyd Rodwin, 80, M.I.T. Urban Studies Professor, Extended the Field of Planning to Social Sciences and the Third World," http://web.mit.edu/newsoffice/nr/1999/rodwin.html.

24. "Ford Grant Aids Urban Renewal; ACTION Receives $25,000 for Seminars—Rouse Heads Planning Body," *New York Times*, October 19, 1958, 78. See the ACTION summary volume, Martin Meyerson, Barbara Terrett, and William L. C. Wheaton, *Housing, People, and Cities* (New York: McGraw-Hill, 1962); and a subsequent ACTION-sponsored publication by Martin

Meyerson, with Jaqueline Tyrwhitt, Brian Falk, and Patricia Sekler, *Face of the Metropolis* (New York: Random House, 1963).

25. Serge Chermayeff and Christopher Alexander, *Community and Privacy: Toward a New Architecture of Humanism* (New York: Doubleday, 1963). See Lloyd Rodwin, *The Roles of the City Planner in the Community* (Cambridge, MA: Joint Center for Urban Studies, 1960); and Martin Meyerson, "Utopian Traditions and the Planning of Cities," in "The Future Metropolis," ed. Lloyd Rodwin, special issue, *Daedalus: Journal of the American Academy of Arts and Sciences* 90, no. 1 (Winter 1961): 180–93.

26. See, for example, the student-oriented surveys of the field such as by T. Lynn Smith and C. A. McMahan, *The Sociology of Urban Life: A Textbook with Readings* (New York: Dryden Press, 1951); or Paul K. Hatt and Albert J. Reiss, Jr., *Reader in Urban Sociology* (Glencoe, IL: Free Press, 1951). On the Chicago school of sociology see Robert Fishman, ed., *The American Planning Tradition: Culture and Policy* (Baltimore: Johns Hopkins University Press; Washington DC: Wilson Center Press, 2000); Robert E. L. Faris, *Chicago Sociology, 1920–1932* (Chicago: University of Chicago Press, 1970); Fred Matthews, *Quest for an American Sociology: Robert E. Park and the Chicago School* (Montreal: McGill-Queens University Press, 1977); and Bulmer, *Chicago School of Sociology*.

27. In his book *Land Use in Central Boston*, Harvard Sociological Studies, vol. 4 (Cambridge, MA: Harvard University Press, 1947), Walter Firey questioned the underpinnings of rational choice in economics with assertions that "Italians stay in the slums because their friends are there." James N. Morgan exclaimed with surprise in a review of *Land Use in Central Boston* in *American Economic Review* 38, no. 1 (March 1948): 201, that "at times Dr. Firey seems to be saying that the allocation of space is irrational." William Alonso's *Location and Land Use: Toward a General Theory of Land Rent* (Cambridge, MA: Joint Center for Urban Studies, 1964) was more conventional in its adaptation of J. H. von Thünen's agricultural land use theory to explain urban spatial distribution (including suburbanization). Using a centralized model and Philadelphia examples, Alonso posited straightforward optimization amid price pressures and locational disadvantages rather than irrationals like racism or stylistic obsolescence.

28. Richard L. Moier, *A Communications Theory of Urban Growth.* (Cambridge, MA: M.I.T. Press, 1962).

29. Kevin Lynch, *Image of the City* (Cambridge, MA: M.I.T. Press, 1960); Donald Appleyard, Kevin Lynch, and John R. Myer, *The View from the Road* (Cambridge, MA: Joint Center for Urban Studies, 1964).

30. See Robert C. Wood, *Whatever Possessed the President? Academic Experts and Presidential Policy, 1960–1988* (Amherst: University of Massachusetts Press, 1993), 63.

31. Lloyd Rodwin, ed., "The Future Metropolis," special issue, *Daedalus: Journal of the American Academy of Arts and Sciences* 90, no. 1 (Winter 1961); quotations are from Kevin Lynch and Lloyd Rodwin, "A World of Cities" (11); and Martin Meyerson, "Utopian Traditions and the Planning of Cities" (191–92).

32. See *Proceedings of Conference on the Training of Planners for Work in Developing Countries, Held at the M.I.T. Faculty Club and the Joint Center, December 14–15, 1963* (Cambridge, MA: Department of City and Regional Planning, 1964). The Venezualan activities ran from 1961 to 1969. See Lisa Peattie, *Planning: Rethinking Ciudad Guayana* (Ann Arbor: University of Michigan Press, 1987); Wilhelm von Moltke, *The Visual Design of Ciudad Guayana* (Cambridge, MA: Joint Center

for Urban Studies, 1965); Richard M. Soberman, *Transport Technology for Developing Regions: A Study of Road Transportation in Venezuela* (Cambridge, MA: M.I.T. Press, 1966); John Friedmann, *Regional Development Policy: A Case Study of Venezuela* (Cambridge, MA: M.I.T. Press, 1966); Lloyd Rodwin, *Planning Urban Growth and Regional Development: The Experience of the Guayana Program of Venezuela* (Cambridge, MA: Joint Center for Urban Studies, 1969); and Noel F. McGinn and Russell G. Davis, *Build a Mill, Build a City, Build a School: Industrialization, Urbanization, and Education in Ciudad Guayana* (Cambridge, MA: M.I.T. Press 1969).

33. Illustrative examples of locally oriented scholarhip from the Joint Center include Martha Derthick, *Report on the Politics of Boston, Massachusetts* (Cambridge, MA: Joint Center for Urban Studies, 1960). A decade later, Derthick prepared another report, *The Influence of Federal Grants: Public Assistance in Massachusetts* (Cambridge, MA: Harvard University Press, 1970). Lloyd Rodwin, *Housing and Economic Progress: A Study of the Housing Experiences of Boston's Middle-Income Families* (Cambridge, MA: Joint Center for Urban Studies, 1961). Richard S. Bolan, *A Program for Physical Planning in the Boston Metropolitan Area* (Cambridge, MA: Joint Center for Urban Studies, 1965); Richard S. Bolan and Donald S. Appleyard, *Physical Planning for the Boston Metropolitan Area* (Cambridge, MA: Joint Center for Urban Studies, 1965); Richard S. Bolan and John F. Kain, *Transportation Planning in the Boston Metropolitan Area* (Cambridge, MA: Joint Center for Urban Studies, 1966); Alexander Ganz, *Recommended Work for an Economic Development Program for the Boston Metropolitan Area* (Cambridge, MA: Joint Center for Urban Studies, 1965); William J. Curran, *Legal Consideration in the Establishment of a Health Information System in Greater Boston and the State of Massachusetts* (Washington, 1968); John H. Noble and Henry Wechsler, *Feasibility of Developing a Computer-Based Health and Welfare Information System for Metropolitan Boston* (Boston: Medical Foundation, 1968); *New Dimensions in Urban America: Implications for Municipal Administration and Personnel* (Cambridge, MA: Joint Center for Urban Studies, 1961). Other Joint Center research topics included Leon H. Mayhew's investigation, *Law and Equal Opportunity: A Study of the Massachusetts Commission against Discrimination* (Cambridge, MA: Harvard University Press, 1968); and Bernard Taper's survey, *The Arts in Boston* (Cambridge, MA: Harvard University Press, 1970).

34. Details from Stephan Thernstrom, *Poverty, Planning, and Politics in the New Boston: The Origins of ABCD* (New York: Basic Books, 1969), 13, 17, 19, 101. Meyerson's former colleagues at the University of Pennsylvania's Institute for Urban Studies, Herbert Gans and William Wheaton, consulted on the ABCD project.

35. Mark Gelfand, *A Nation of Cities: The Federal Government and Urban America, 1933–1965* (New York: Oxford University Press, 1975), 389.

36. Ibid., 307.

37. Wood, *Whatever Possessed the President?* 75.

38. Ibid., 172; see also 75–81 and a summary of the Townscape Panel Report from President Johnson's Natural Beauty Conference (May 1965) by Edmund Bacon, "Townscape: A Report to the President," in *Taming Megalopolis*, ed. H. Wentworth Eldredge (New York: Praeger, 1967), 1:270–74.

39. U.S. Department of Housing and Urban Development, *Building a Better America*, H.U.D. MP-1 (Washington DC: U.S. Govt. Printing Office, 1967), esp. chap. 1, "Career Opportunities: You and the City," 9–11.

40. John H. Mollenkopf, "How to Study Urban Political Power," in LeGates and Stout, *The*

City Reader (n. 4 above), 266. See also Mollenkopf, The Contested City (Princeton: Princeton University Press, 1983).

41. Joel Schwartz, The New York Approach: Robert Moses, Urban Liberals, and Redevelopment of the Inner City (Columbus: Ohio State University Press, 1993), 300.

42. The mechanics of such redevelopment (under Title I of the 1949 Housing Act) and its effects in implementation are well documented. See Jewel Bellush and Murray Hausknecht, eds., Urban Renewal: People, Politics and Planning (Garden City, NY: Doubleday, 1967).

43. A recent postrevisionist reconsideration of Moses and his significance is Hilary Ballon and Kenneth T. Jackson, eds., Robert Moses and the Modern City: The Transformation of New York (W. W. Norton, 2007). It qualifies the original negative revision of his legacy in Robert A. Caro, The Power Broker: Robert Moses and the Fall of New York (Knopf, 1974). Joel Schwartz, The New York Approach: Robert Moses, Urban Liberals, and Redevelopment of the Inner City (Columbus: Ohio State University Press, 1993), provides a broader perspective on the political environment in which Moses functioned.

44. Richard Plunz, A History of Housing in New York City (New York: Columbia University Press, 1990); Joshua Freeman, Working-Class New York: Life and Labor since World War II (New York: New Press, 2000).

45. John Sibley, "Model Slum Plan Beset by Delays; 'Pioneer' Project Drafted a Year Ago Not Yet Started," New York Times, May 28, 1961, 48.

46. Background drawn from Thomas H. O'Connor, Building a New Boston: Politics and Urban Renewal, 1950–1970 (Boston: Northeastern University Press, 1993); Lawrence W. Kennedy, Planning the City upon a Hill: Boston Since 1630 (Amherst: University of Massachusetts Press; 1994); and Charles H. Trout, Boston: The Great Depression and the New Deal (New York: Oxford University Press, 1977).

47. Also controversial at the time was the New York Streets project in the South End. A generation after the central artery was completed, Bostonians would undertake "the largest, most complex and technologically challenging highway project in American history"—at a cost of $14.6 billion!—in order to demolish it and replace it with a sunken roadway (figure and hyperbole from the Web site of the Massachusetts Turnpike Authority's Central Artery Tunnel project, www.bigdig.com).

48. On Logue see Lizabeth Cohen, Saving America's Cities: Ed Logue and the Struggle to Renew Urban America in the Suburban Age (New York: Farrar, Straus & Giroux, forthcoming).

49. Walter McQuade, "Boston: What Can a Sick City Do?" Fortune, June 1964; reprinted in James Q. Wilson, ed., Urban Renewal: The Record and the Controversy (Cambridge, MA: Joint Center for Urban Studies, 1966), 259–77.

50. The first American instance of this connotation cited by the Oxford English Dictionary appeared in Time, January 20, 1941, 77—"High Life in Philadelphia's Main Line Society"—though such a headline would presumably make little sense if the term were not already in common use.

51. See, for example, Baltzell's books: The Philadelphia Gentlemen: The Making of a National Upper Class (1958), American Business Aristocracy (1962), The Protestant Establishment: Aristocracy and Caste in America (1964), and Puritan Boston and Quaker Philadelphia: Two Protestant Ethics and the Spirit of Class Authority and Leadership (1979).

52. Philadelphia's upper class may well be the most studied American elite since Edith

Wharton stopped attending to New York's high society. This milieu was caricatured most famously (though from least personal experience) by Philip Barry's 1929 play The Philadelphia Story (and subsequent filmed versions). The social and psychological dimensions of this self-obsessed circle can still be glimpsed in the stories written by its denizens. Such portraits include Main Line: A Philadelphia Novel, by Livingston Biddle, Jr. (New York: J. Messner, 1950); and The Philadelphian, by Richard Pitts Powell (New York: Scribner 1956), which was adapted for the film The Young Philadelphians, starring Paul Newman.

53. Ed Bacon recalled the catalytic effect of Phillips' activism on young Philadelphians in Alexander Garvin, "Philadelphia's Planner: A Conversation with Edmund Bacon," Journal of Planning History 1, no. 1 (February 2002): 62.

54. James Reichley, The Art of Government: Reform and Organization Politics in Philadelphia (New York: Fund for the Republic, 1959). See also Joseph Clark, "Rally and Relapse," in Philadelphia: A 300 Year History, ed. Russell F. Weigley (New York: W. W. Norton, 1982); "Political Giant Joseph Clark Dead At 88," Philadelphia Inquirer, January 15, 1990, 1; "Joseph S. Clark Is Dead at 88; Ex-Mayor and Reformist Senator," New York Times, January 16, 1990, D26; and "Richardson Dilworth, 75, Dies; Twice Mayor of Philadelphia; A Combat Hero," New York Times, January 24, 1974, 40.

55. John F. Bauman, "Visions of a Post-war City: A Perspective on Urban Planning in Philadelphia and the Nation, 1942–1945," in Introduction to Planning History in the United States, ed. Donald A. Krueckeberg (New Brunswick: Rutgers University Press, 1983), 173.

56. Constance M. Greiff, Independence: The Creation of a National Park (Philadelphia: University of Pennsylvania Press, 1987), 70

57. For an overview of urban renewal in Philadelphia, see John F. Bauman, Public Housing, Race, and Renewal: Urban Planning in Philadelphia, 1920–1974 (Philadelphia: Temple University Press, 1987). On Philadelphia's political shifts, see Kirk R. Petshek, The Challenge of Urban Reform: Policies and Programs in Philadelphia (Philadelphia: Temple University Press, 1973).

58. Excerpt from Mitchell's unpublished memoir included in Strong and Thomas, Book of the School (n. 14 above), 162.

59. Mitchell recalled it originating when, "sometime late in 1945, Oskar Stonorov, Walter Phillips and Mitchell were sitting in a bar room of a Chicago hotel during a planning conference." Strong and Thomas, Book of the School, 162.

60. "Philadelphia Plans Again: Exhibition Designed by O. Stonorov and E. Bacon," Architectural Forum 86 (December 1947): 66–88; Ed Bacon, "Are Exhibitions Useful? A Postscript to the Philadelphia Show," Journal of the American Institute of Planners 14, no. 2 (June 1948): 23–28.

61. Garvin, "Philadelphia's Planner," 59.

62. Bacon claimed credit for the group's planning focus: "Because of my Flint experience, I directed the energy of a bunch of young people Walter got together as the first project to get us proper city planning for Philadelphia. By reason of my Flint experience, I had contacts with the national planning movement, and so I was able to arrange that the American Planning Society and the American Planning Officials and so forth all came to their annual meeting in Philadelphia." Ibid., 64.

63. See Nancy Kleniewski, "Neighborhood Decline and Downtown Renewal: The Politics of Redevelopment in Philadelphia, 1952–1962." (Ph.D. dissertation, Temple University, 1982).

64. Garvin, "Philadelphia's Planner," 63, 65–66.

65. See the admiring portrait of Clark and Bacon in Jeanne Lowe, *Cities in a Race with Time: Progress and Poverty in America's Renewing Cities* (New York: Random House, 1967).

66. Edmund N. Bacon, *Design of Cities* (New York: Viking Press, 1967), 7.

67. Quotes from Garvin, "Philadelphia's Planner," 72, 76; and Edmund N. Bacon, "The Need for an Image," in Strong and Thomas, *Book of the School*, 127

68. Madeline L. Cohen, "Postwar City Planning in Philadelphia: Edmund N. Bacon and the Design of Washington Square East" (Ph.D. dissertation, University of Pennsylvania, 1991), viii.

69. "The City: Under the Knife; or, All for Their Own Good," *Time*, November 6, 1964, 60–75.

70. Strong and Thomas, *Book of the School*, 156; and Emily T. Cooperman, "Perkins, George Holmes," *Philadelphia Architects and Buildings Database*, http://pab1.gsfa.upenn.edu/pab/app/ar_display.cfm?ShortId=23168.

71. On urban policy during the New Deal, see Gelfand, *A Nation of Cities* (n. 32 above).

72. See Martin Meyerson and Edward Banfield, *Politics, Planning, and the Public Interest: The Case of Public Housing in Chicago* (Glencoe, IL: Free Press, 1955).

73. Conceived as a blue-collar alternative to Society Hill for the retention of Philadelphia's working class, Eastwick was a "$78 million effort to build an unprecedented 'city-within-a-city'" that would "provide twenty-thousand jobs and homes for as many as sixty-thousand people." See Guian A. McKee, "Liberal Ends through Illiberal Means: Race, Urban Renewal, and Community in the Eastwick Section of Philadelphia, 1949–1990," *Journal of Urban History* 27, no. 5 (July 2001): 547–83.

Chapter 3: Aesthetic Critiques

1. Josef Wolff, "Fünf Jahre Städtebau der Nachkriegszeit," *Baum* 48 (1951): 42.

2. For an account of the sixth CIAM conference, held in 1947 in Bridgwater, England (including Richards' statements quoted above), see Eric Mumford, *The CIAM Discourse on Urbanism, 1928–1960* (Cambridge, MA: M.I.T. Press, 2002), 168–79.

3. Many young CIAM devotees in Britain would never forgive Pevsner and Richards for their "softness" toward insufficiently analytical ideas. See Joseph Rykwert, "Review of a Review," *Zodiac: International Magazine of Contemporary Architecture* 4 (1959): 15; and Reyner Banham, "Revenge of the Picturesque: English Architectural Polemics, 1945–1965," in *Concerning Architecture: Essays on Architectural Writers and Writing Presented to Nikolaus Pevsner*, ed. John Summerson (London: Penguin, 1968), 265.

4. Lionel Brett, "Attitudes to Landscape," *Architectural Review* 105, no. 630 (June 1949): 263–67.

5. Joan Ockman, ed., *Architecture Culture, 1943–1968: A Documentary Anthology* (New York: Rizzoli, 1993), 114. On the other hand, Ockman also noted the influence of Sweden's shift "against an overly rigid and formalistic" functionalism in favor of "*spontanietet*, signifying a more naturalist, informal way of working," adding: "Nowhere did this architecture find as warm a reception as in England" (43).

6. Robert Moses, "What Happened to Haussmann?" *Architectural Forum* 77 (July 1942): 57–66; "Rebuilding Britain," *Architectural Review* 93 (June 1943): 86–112.

7. J. M. Richards, "Regionalism Re-examined," *Architectural Review* 90 (July 1941): 40.

8. Ivor de Wolfe, "A Plea for an English Visual Philosophy Founded on the True Rock of Sir

Uvedale Price," *Architectural Review* 106 (December 1949): 362ff.; reprinted in Ockman, *Architecture Culture*, 115–19.

9. J. M. Richards et al., editors' introduction to "Man Made America," ed. J. M. Richards et al., special issue, *Architectural Review* 108, no. 648 (December 1950): 339–43. The issue featured a cover drawing by Saul Steinberg, "the most witty, perceptive and devastating critic in the world [without whom] the U.S. would possess no critic of the community art of townscape."

10. Richards et al., "Conclusion," in Richards et al., "Man Made America," 415. Incidentally, American anthropologist Anthony F. C. Wallace also criticized such projects in the early 1950s.

11. Ockman, *Architecture Culture*, 119. Kenneth Browne had become "Townscape" editor at the *Review* by the 1960s. Thomas Sharp applied the comparable term "civic design."

12. Cullen, an independent consultant after 1956, received the gold medal of the A.I.A. in 1976. On Gordon Cullen, see David Gosling, *Gordon Cullen: Visions of Urban Design* (London: Academy Group, 1996); as well as his own writings, Cullen, *Townscape* (London: Architectural Press, 1961); and Cullen, *Notation: The Observant Layman's Code for His Environment* (London: Alcan Industries, 1968).

13. Gordon Cullen, "Outdoor Publicity," *Architectural Review* 105, no. 629 (May 1949): 248–51; quoted in Gosling, *Gordon Cullen*, 31. Gosling sees Cullen's perspective anticipating that of *Learning from Las Vegas*, and in fact Denise Scott Brown and Gordon Cullen appeared together in a special issue of *Connections* (vol. 4 [Spring 1967]) on communication, interpreting cities as a "message system."

14. Nairn's books include *Britain's Changing Towns* (London: British Broadcasting Corporation, 1967), *Nairn's London* (Baltimore: Penguin Books, 1966), *The American Landscape: A Critical View* (New York: Random House, 1965), *Modern Buildings in London* (London: London Transport, 1964), and *Your England Revisited* (London: Hutchinson, 1964).

15. William H. Whyte, Jr., ed., *The Exploding Metropolis* (Berkeley: University of California Press, 1993), 184. The various *Architectural Review* articles and illustrations were also published as books: Ian Nairn, *Outrage: On the Disfigurement of Town and Countryside* (London: Architectural Press, 1959; reprint of June 1955 special number of *Architectural Review*); Nairn, *Counter-attack against Subtopia* (London: Architectural Press, 1957).

16. Rykwert, "Review of a Review," 13: "These facets of the surface of a planning policy occupy infinitely more space in the *Review* than any material on the sociological or speculative or even strictly technical aspects of the subject." Rykwert was also revolted by the *Review's* praise of Victorian-revival public houses in March 1955.

17. Alan Colquhoun, letter to the editor, *Architectural Review* 116, no. 691 (July 1954): 2.

18. John Burchard, *Voice of the Phoenix: Postwar Architecture in Germany* (Cambridge, MA: M.I.T. Press, 1966), vii.

19. Jane Jacobs, "Downtown Is for People," *Fortune* 57, no. 4 (April 1958), is accompanied by drawings by Cullen and captions by Nairn.

20. Jane Jacobs, foreword to *The Death and Life of Great American Cities* (New York: Random House, 1993), xiii.

21. Gerhard Rabeler, *Wiederaufbau und Expansion westdeutscher Städte 1945–1960 im Spannungsfeld von Reformideen und Wirklichkeit* (Bonn: Deutsches Nationalkomitee für Denkmalschutz, 1990), 175.

22. Ibid.

23. Ibid.

24. Harald Bodenschatz, *Platz frei für das Neue Berlin! Geschichte der Stadterneuerung in der "größten Mietskasernenstadt der Welt" seit 1871* (Berlin: Transit Buchverlag, 1987), 180.

25. Ibid., 181: "bindende nachbarschaftspflegende Kraft der geschlossenen Bauweise."

26. Quoted in Klaus von Beyme, Werner Durth, Niels Gutschow, Winfried Nerdinger, and Thomas Tofstedt, eds., *Neue Städte aus Ruinen: Deutscher Städtebau der Nachkriegszeit* (Munich: Prestel-Verlag, 1992), 30.

27. Martin Wagner, "Karl Friedrich Schinkel," *Bauwelt* 18 (May 3, 1965): 476–77; 19 (May 10, 1965): 514–15.

28. "Das Markgräfliche Palais in Karlsruhe," *Bauwelt* 24 (June 14, 1965): 695–700.

29. *Bauwelt* 23 (1964): 670. Other modernists, including John Burchard, also rejected its outcome.

30. Bodenschatz, *Platz frei*, 179.

31. Johann Friedrich Geist and Dieter Huhn, "Gebührt James Hobrecht ein Denkmal?" *Bauwelt* 24 (June 14, 1965): 704.

32. Ibid., 703.

33. Ibid., 701.

34. Julius Posener, "Stirbt die Stadt an der Stadtplanung?" *Stadtbauwelt: Beiträge zur Neuordnung von Stadt und Land* 6/*Bauwelt* 26/27 (June 28, 1965): 442–44, 454–58.

35. Walter Gropius, 1964 interview quoted in "Walter Gropius Dies: Founder of Bauhaus School of Architecture," *Philadelphia Inquirer*, July 6, 1969, 12. A best-selling memoir (adapted into a 1981 film) painted a scathing portrait of the youth culture that had taken root in Gropiusstadt by the mid 1970s; see Christiane F., *Wir Kinder vom Bahnhof Zoo* (Hamburg: Stern/Gruner+Jahr, 1979).

36. Edmund N. Bacon, *Design of Cities* (New York: Viking Press, 1967), 13.

37. Edmund N. Bacon, "The Future of Cities: Urbanity or Suburbanity," talk given at the University of California, Berkeley, September 26, 1963; quoted in Madeline L. Cohen, "Postwar City Planning in Philadelphia: Edmund N. Bacon and the Design of Washington Square East" (Ph.D. dissertation, University of Pennsylvania, 1991), 572–73.

38. Cohen, "Postwar City Planning," quotes extensively from 1988 interview tapes to highlight Bacon's "intention to change the social fabric of the neighborhood" (535–36), "to replace the people who were there with people who had the money and the urge to restore the buildings" (533), and to do so in such a way that avoided speculative development. In this "property-by-property redevelopment," a committee screened applicants for "total commitment to the emerging neighborhood" (552). This amounted to a handpicked socioeconomic reorganization of the area, under the banner of beautification and preservation. The committee's aesthetic litmus test—demanding that residents fix their homes up to restoration guidelines—was ultimately a financial one, since very few without money for repairs had the time to make up the difference with their own labor.

39. Bacon, quoted in Cohen, "Postwar City Planning," 534–35, 573.

40. Valerie Sue Halverson Pace, "Society Hill, Philadelphia: Historic Preservation and Urban Renewal in Washington Square East" (Ph.D. dissertation, University of Minnesota, 1976). Pace sees the Philadelphia renaissance as a success because citizens and government agencies worked together to meet the crisis of the central city.

41. Quoted in Pace, "Society Hill," 135.

42. Edmund Bacon, interviewed by Alexander Garvin at the Society for American City and Regional Planning History Conference, Philadelphia, November 1–4, 2001. The transcription is from my own notes and does not appear in the abridged published transcript.

43. Cohen, "Postwar City Planning," 602, based on a 1959 report of the Washington Square East Redevelopment Project.

44. Mumford, who was the oldest of Perkins' faculty, was at Penn from 1951 to 1956 and 1959 to 1961.

45. Ann L. Strong and George E. Thomas, eds., The Book of the School: 100 Years of the Graduate School of Fine Arts at the University of Pennsylvania (Philadelphia: Graduate School of Fine Arts, 1990), 160.

46. Quoted by Robert Wojtowicz in Strong and Thomas, Book of the School, 161.

47. Background from Robert Wojtowicz, "Lewis Mumford: A New Yorker in Philadelphia" (program essay for "Sticks, Stones, and Culture: A Symposium Celebrating the Centennial of Lewis Mumford's Birth," University of Pennsylvania, October 19, 1995, 14).

48. Ibid. Reaching an even larger audience, Mumford had expressed the endorsements of Philadelphia's renewal projects in his long-running New Yorker column, "The Sky Line," later republished in The Highway and the City (New York: Harcourt, Brace & World, 1963).

49. Lewis Mumford, The City in History: Its Origins, Its Transformations, and Its Prospects (New York: Harcourt, Brace & Co., 1989), graphic section IV, pl. 54.

50. For an overview of Kahn's career, see David B. Brownlee and David G. De Long, Louis I. Kahn: In the Realm of Architecture (New York: Universe Publishing, 1997). On Venturi, as well as the firm he founded with his wife, see David Brownlee, David G. De Long, and Kathryn B. Hiesinger, Out of the Ordinary: Robert Venturi, Denise Scott Brown and Associates, Architecture, Urbanism, Design (New Haven: Yale University Press, 2001).

51. Helena Webster, "Modernism without Rhetoric," in Modernism without Rhetoric: Essays on the Work of Alison and Peter Smithson (London: Academy Editions, 1997), 17.

52. Their own theorizing and analysis has played a large part in the Smithsons' self-promotion, from their CIAM polemics onward, which partly explains how they became Britain's most influential architects by the end of the 1950s, despite having built hardly any buildings.

53. Quoted in E. Mumford, CIAM Discourse, 203.

54. John R. Gold, The Experience of Modernism: Modern Architects and the Future City, 1928–1953 (New York: Taylor & Francis, 1998), 228.

55. E. Mumford, CIAM Discourse, 236.

56. David Robbins, ed., The Independent Group: Postwar Britain and the Aesthetics of Plenty (Cambridge, MA: M.I.T. Press, 1990).

57. Webster, Modernism without Rhetoric, 20, 24.

58. Peter Smithson, "The Idea of Architecture in the '50s," Architects' Journal 131 (January 1960): 124.

59. Webster, Modernism without Rhetoric, 32.

60. Denise Scott, e-mail communication with the author, March 8, 2010.

61. This account and quotes are drawn from E. Mumford, CIAM Discourse, 239, 244, 257–58. Alison Smithson complained that assistant director Jacqueline Tyrwhitt was "quite bossy" at CIAM conferences and that "the behavior of the middle generation . . . was basically the reason why the full force of my wrath descended upon them at Otterlo" (quoted in ibid., 256).

62. "CIAM: Resurrection Move Fails at Otterloo," *Architectural Review* 127, no. 756 (February 1960): 78–79.

63. E. Mumford, *CIAM Discourse*, 260–61.

64. Banham, "Revenge of the Picturesque" (n. 3 above), 265.

65. Alison Smithson, quoted in Jane B. Drew and E. Maxwell Fry, "Conversation on Brutalism," *Zodiac* 4 (1959): 73–74.

66. Webster, *Modernism without Rhetoric*, 32: "In the Smithsons' design [for Golden Lane] the *rue interieur* [of Le Corbusier] was replaced by 'streets in the air'—the Smithsons' own sociologically-based reinterpretation of the East End By-law street."

67. Sze Tsung Leong and Chuihua Judy Chung, *The Charged Void: Architecture/Alison and Peter Smithson* (New York: Monacelli, 2001), 86–95 and 200–205.

68. Gordon Cullen, "The Economist Buildings, St. James's," *Architectural Review* 137, no. 819 (February 1965): 114–24.

Chapter 4: Policy Objections

1. See Andrea Gabor, *Einstein's Wife: Work and Marriage in the Lives of Five Great Twentieth-Century Women* (New York: Viking, 1995), 180, 188–89.

2. Andrew Lees, *Cities Perceived: Urban Society in European and American Thought, 1820–1940* (New York: Columbia University Press, 1985), esp. chap. 10. Exceptions were a number of affirmative social scientific studies produced at the London School of Economics, including nine volumes of *The New Survey of London Life and Labour*, edited by Herbert Llewellyn Smith between 1928 and 1935.

3. Ruth Glass, "Urban Sociology in Great Britain: A Trend Report," *Current Sociology*, 4, no. 4 (1955): 5–76. Also Richard Hoggart, *The Uses of Literacy* (London: Chatto & Windus, 1957).

4. Counter to academic convention, he used the Orwellian gambit of a fictionalized future to satirize the effects of such policies. Michael D. Young, *The Rise of the Meritocracy, 1870–2033: An Essay on Education and Equality* (London: Thames & Hudson 1958). See also Young's political writings, including Young and Henry Noel Bunbury, *Will the War Make Us Poorer?* (London: Oxford University Press, 1943); Young, *What Is a Socialized Industry? A Discussion Pamphlet* (London: Fabian Publications and V. Gollancz, 1947); Young, *Labour's Plan for Plenty* (London: V. Gollancz, 1947); and Young, *Fifty Million Unemployed* (London: Labour Party, Transport House, 1952).

5. Peter Wilmott, review of *Urban Villagers*, by Herbert Gans, *Journal of the American Institute of Planners* 29, no. 3 (August 1963): 228.

6. Michael D. Young and Peter Willmott, *Family and Kinship in East London* (Routledge & Kegan Paul, 1957); Peter Willmott and Michael D. Young, *Family and Class in a London Suburb* (London: Routledge & Kegan Paul, 1960).

7. William C. Loring, Jr., Frank L. Sweetser, and Charles F. Ernst, *Community Organization for Citizen Participation in Urban Renewal*, Prepared by Housing Association of Metropolitan Boston for the Massachusetts Department of Commerce (Cambridge, MA: Cambridge Press, 1957), x.

8. Ibid., 211.

9. Ibid., 13.

10. Ibid., 15.

11. Chester Hartman, "The Housing of Relocated Families," *Journal of the American Institute of Planners* 30, no. 4 (November 1964): 266–86.

12. Chester Hartman, "Social Values and Housing Orientations," *Journal of Social Issues* 19 (April 1963): 113–31; Hartman, "The Limitations of Public Housing: Relocation Choices in a Working-Class Community," *Journal of the American Institute of Planners* 29 (November 1963): 283–96.

13. M. Fried and P. Gleicher, "Some Sources of Residential Satisfaction in an Urban Slum," *Journal of the American Institute of Planners* 27 (1961): 305–15; Marc Fried, "Grieving for a Lost Home: Psychological Costs of Relocation," in *The Urban Condition: People and Policy in the Metropolis*, ed. Leonard J. Duhl (New York: Basic Books, 1963); Fried, "Effects of Social Change on Mental Health," *American Journal of Orthopsychiatry* 34 (January 1964): 3–28; Fried, "Social Change and Working Class Orientations: The Case of Forced Relocation," in *Mobility and Mental Health*, ed. Mildred Kantor (New York: D. Van Nostrand, 1964).

14. Herbert Gans, *The Urban Villagers* (New York: Free Press, 1962). See also Gans, "The Human Implications of Current Redevelopment and Relocation Planning," *Journal of the American Institute of Planners* 25 (February 1959): 15–25. An exhibition on the topic was mounted at the Old State House museum in Boston from October 17, 1992, to April 30, 1994 (see the exhibition review by James R. Green in *Journal of American History* 80, no. 3 [December 1993]: 1024–1030), and produced a collection, *The Last Tenement: Confronting Community and Urban Renewal in Boston's West End*, ed. Sean M. Fisher and Carolyn Hughes (Boston: Bostonian Society, 1992), including Gans' essay "The Urban Village Revisited." Another subsequent study of the project is Edward J. Ford, Jr., "Benefit-Cost Analysis and Urban Renewal in the West End of Boston" (Ph. D. dissertation, Boston College, 1971).

15. Willmott reviewed Gans' work very favorably in *Journal of the American Institute of Planners* 29, no. 3 (August 1963): 228, hailing it alongside William F. Whyte's 1943 sociological classic about Boston's North End, *Street Corner Society: The Social Structure of an Italian Slum*.

16. Gerhard Rabeler, *Wiederaufbau und Expansion westdeutscher Städte 1945–1960 im Spannungsfeld von Reformideen und Wirklichkeit* (Bonn: Deutsches Nationalkomitee für Denkmalschutz, 1990), 76.

17. Wolfgang Hartenstein and Günter Schubert, *Mitlaufen oder Mitbestimmen: Untersuchung zum demokratischen Bewußtsein und zur politischen Tradition* (Frankfurt am Main: Europäische Verlaganstalt, 1961), foreword.

18. See Rudolf Hillebrecht's commentary, "Was der Städtebauer dazu sagt: Ein Nachwort," in Hartenstein and Schubert, *Mitlaufen oder Mitbestimmen*.

19. Wolfgang Hartenstein and Klaus Liepelt, *Man auf der Straße: Eine verkehrssoziologische Untersuchung* (Frankfurt am Main: Europäische Verl., 1961).

20. Alexander Mitscherlich, "Der Leitwert—Pflicht-Gehorsam: Ein Deutungsversuch," in Hartenstein and Schubert, *Mitlaufen oder Mitbestimmen*, 93.

21. Alexander Mitscherlich, *Die Unwirtlichkeit unserer Städte: Anstiftung zum Unfrieden* (Frankfurt am Main: Suhrkamp, 1965).

22. Quotes from Mitscherlich, *Unwirtlichkeit*, 124, 135–37, 143, 160.

23. Looking back over a decade of research, sociologists formed the core of selections for a collection edited by Wolfgang Pehnt, *Die Stadt in der Bundesrepublik Deutschland: Lebensbedingungen, Aufgaben, Planung* (Stuttgart: Reclam, 1974), including contributions from René König, Hans Paul Bahrdt, Lucius Burckhardt, Gerd Albers, Ulfert Herlyn, and Thomas Sieverts, among others. For the deeper roots of this development, see W. D. Smith, "The Emergence of German Urban Sciology, 1900–1910," *Journal of the History of Sociology* 1, no. 2 (1979): 1–16.

See also H. Korte, *Stadtsoziologie: Forschungsprobleme und Forschungsergebnisse der 70er Jahre* (Darmstadt, 1986).

24. Hans Paul Bahrdt , "Nachbarschaft oder Urbanität," *Bauwelt* 51–52 (1960): 1467–77.

25. Hans Paul Bahrdt, *Die moderne Großstadt: Soziologische Überlegungen zum Städtebau* (Reinbek bei Hamburg: Rowohlt, 1961), 100.

26. Habermas' original title was *Strukturwandel der Öffentlichkeit: Untersuchungen zu einer Kategorie der bürgerlichen Gesellschaft.* See Julian Nida-Rümelin, ed., *Philosophie der Gegenwart in Einzeldarstellungen* (Stuttgart: Alfred Kröner, 1991), 210ff.

27. Bahrdt wrote a dissertation for the influential sociologist Helmut Plessner in 1952, whereas Habermas produced a more philosophical dissertation, ultimately presented in Bonn in 1954. Later in the decade, Bahrdt and Habermas shared an interest in the sociology of workers. Compare J. Habermas, "Soziologische Notizen zum Verhältnis von Arbeit und Freizeit," in *Konkrete Vernunft: Festschrift für E. Rothaker* (Bonn: Bouvier, 1958)—cited by Bahrt in *Die moderne Großstadt*—and Bahrdt's work, together with Heinrich Popitz and others, on *Das Gesellschaftsbild des Arbeiters* (Tübingen: Siebeck, 1957).

28. In 1964, the same year that Habermas took up a chair at the University of Frankfurt as codirector of the Philosophy Seminar, Herbert Marcuse returned as a guest professor to the city where he had been a founding member of the Institute for Social Research and published *One-Dimensional Man: Studies in the Ideology of Advanced Industrial Society* (1964, though not translated into German until 1970), which was followed quickly by *Kultur und Geschichte* (1965). For his part, Habermas supplied *Antworten auf Herbert Marcuse* [Replies to Herbert Marcuse] in 1968.

29. In the original German Rudolf Hillebrecht, *Die Auswirkungen des wirtschaftlichen und sozialen Strukturwandels auf den Städtebau* (Köln: Westdeutscher Verlag, 1964).

30. Hans Oswald, *Die überschätzte Stadt: Ein Beitrag der Gemeindesoziologie zum Städtebau* (Olten: Walter, 1966), 9.

31. Heide Berndt, *Architektur als Ideologie* (Frankfurt am Main: Suhrkamp, 1968), 40.

32. Heide Berndt, *Das Gesellschaftsbild bei Stadtplanern* (Stuttgart: Kramer, 1968); recall that Bahrdt's 1957 work was entitled *Das Gesellschaftsbild des Arbeiters.*

33. Berndt, *Architektur als Ideologie*, 26.

34. Christian Norberg-Schulz, *Logik der Baukunst* (Berlin: Ullstein, 1965), 16. Norberg-Schulz sees Siegfried Gideon and Hans Sedlmayr as poles in the debate about whether modernist architecture is inherently dehumanizing; see also the preface by the sociologist Lucius Burckhardt.

Chapter 5: Outsider's Revolt

1. Catherine Bauer, "The Dreary Deadlock of Public Housing," *Architectural Forum* 106, no. 5 (May 1957): 140–42, 219–21; A. Scott Henderson, *Housing and the Democratic Ideal: The Life and Thought of Charles Abrams* (New York: Columbia University Press, 2000), 198–203.

2. For a comparison of Paul Goodman and Jane Jacobs, see John W. Dyckman, "The European Motherland of American Urban Romanticism," *Journal of the American Institute of Planners* 28, no. 4 (November 1962): 277–81.

3. Eric Mumford, "From CIAM to Collage City: Postwar European Urban Design and American Urban Design Education" (paper delivered at the conference "Urban Design: Practices, Pedagogies, Premises," Columbia University, New York, April 5–6, 2002). See also "The

Origins and Evolution of Urban Design: 1956–2006," special issue, *Harvard Design Magazine*, no. 24 (Spring/Summer 2006).

4. William H. Whyte, Jr., "Preface: C. D. Jackson meets Jane Jacobs," in *The Exploding Metropolis*, ed. William H. Whyte, Jr. (Berkeley: University of California Press, 1993).

5. Summary of Jacobs' talk at Museum of Modern Art on February 11, 1962, written by Sidney Frigand and Peter Lapham, City Planning Commissioner Goldstone Papers, New York City Municipal Archives, folder "West Village Housing."

6. Christopher Hume, "Let's Hope Jacobs Keeps Talking and That Movers and Shakers Listen," *Toronto Star*, September 7, 1991, G4, p. 378.

7. Ibid.

8. Jacobs' remarks were published in *Architectural Forum* 104 (June 1956): 132–33, as "The Missing Link in City Redevelopment," and excerpted in Max Allen, ed., *Ideas That Matter: The Worlds of Jane Jacobs* (Owen Sound, ON: Ginger Press, 1997), 39–40.

9. Lewis Mumford, letter to Jacobs (May 3, 1958), published in Allen, *Ideas That Matter*, 95.

10. Jane Jacobs, "Downtown Is for People," *Fortune* 57, no. 4 (April 1958): 133.

11. Author's interview with Jane Jacobs, Toronto, February 20, 2002.

12. Jane Jacobs, letter to Chadbourne Gilpatric, Rockefeller Foundation (July 1, 1958), published in Allen, *Ideas That Matter*, 47–48.

13. Jane Jacobs, *The Death and Life of Great American Cities* (New York: Random House, 1961), 270–90.

14. Ibid., 255.

15. Ibid., 305, 336. Jacobs is picking up on James Rouse, William Wheaton, and others; see Bauer, "Dreary Deadlock of Public Housing."

16. Letter from Robert Moses to Bennett Cerf at Random House (November 15, 1961), published in Allen, *Ideas That Matter*, 97.

17. Jane Jacobs, "How City Planners Hurt Cities," *Saturday Evening Post*, October 14, 1961.

18. Holmes Perkins, letter to Arnold Nicholson (October 17, 1961), Jane Jacobs Papers, Burns Library, Boston College, box 11, folder 6.

19. Quoted in Dennis O'Harrow, "Jacobin Revival," *American Society of Planning Officials Newsletter*, February 1962, reprinted in Allen, *Ideas That Matter*, 10.

20. Jane Jacobs, letter to Arnold Nicholson (October 17, 1961), Jacobs Papers, box 11, folder 6.

21. Dennis O'Harrow, "Jacobin Revival," *American Society of Planning Officials Newsletter*, February 1962; reprinted in Allen, *Ideas That Matter*, 9–10; Alfred Tronzo, quoted in William Allan, "City Planning Critic Gets Roasting Reply," *Pittsburgh Press*, February 22, 1962; reprinted in Allen, *Ideas That Matter*, 51–52; Roger Starr, "Adventure in Mooritania," *Newsletter of the Citizens' Housing and Planning Council of New York*, January 1962; reprinted in Allen, *Ideas That Matter*, 53–54.

22. Reprinted from *American City*, May 1962, in Allen, *Ideas That Matter*, 50–51.

23. Samuel R. Mozes, ed., *American Inst. of Planners, New York Chapter Newsletter*, November 1961–January 1962, Jacobs Papers, box 7, folder 3.

24. "Manahatta Plies Her Nails," *Town and Country Planning* 30, no. 5 (October 1962): 375.

25. Allan, "City Planning Critic Gets Roasting Reply," reprinted in Allen, *Ideas That Matter*, 51; reprinted from *American City*, May 1962, in Allen, *Ideas That Matter*, 50.

26. O'Harrow, "Jacobin Revival," 10.

27. Lewis Mumford, "Mother Jacobs' Home Remedies for Urban Cancer," *New Yorker*, December 1, 1962, 148–79.

28. Lewis Mumford, letter to University of California, Department of Political Science (October 18, 1961), published in Allen, *Ideas That Matter* (n. 8 above), 96.

29. O'Harrow, "Jacobin Revival," 10.

30. Robert Fishman, "The Mumford-Jacobs Debate," *Planning History Studies* 10, no. 1–2 (1996): 3–11.

31. Museum of Modern Art forum, February 11, 1963, summary written by Sidney Frigand and Peter Lapham, Goldstone Papers (n. 5 above), folder "West Village Housing."

32. Ibid.

33. Paul Mandel, "A Love Letter to London," *Observer*, undated clipping circa 1965, Jacobs Papers, box 7, folder 1.

34. The Smithsons explicitly anticipated Jacobs' renowned ideas about children and street life; see John R. Gold, *The Experience of Modernism: Modern Architects and the Future City, 1928–1953* (New York: Taylor & Francis, 1998), 225.

35. "Manahatta Plies Her Nails," 375.

36. See Ivor de Wolfe, "The Death and Life of Great American Citizens," *Architectural Review* 133, no. 792 (February 1963): 91–93; and Jane Jacobs, "Do Not Segregate Pedestrians and Automobiles," in *The Pedestrian in the City*, Architect's Year Book 11, ed. David Lewis, (London: Elek Books, 1965).

37. Arthur Ling, "Notes on Books," *Journal of the Royal Society of Arts* 114, no. 5120 (July 1966): 703.

38. Report of the meeting at the Royal Institute of British Architects, February 7, 1967, in *RIBA Journal* 74 (March 1967): 100.

39. Jane Jacobs, *Tod und Leben großer amerikanischer Städte*, trans. Eva Gärtner (Berlin: Ullstein, 1963).

40. Wolf Jobst Siedler, Elisabeth Niggemeyer, and Gina Angreß, *Die gemordete Stadt: Abgesang auf Putte und Straße, Platz und Baum* (Berlin: Herbig, 1964).

41. Elisabeth Niggemeyer, personal communication with the author, November 6, 2006.

42. "Stadtgespräch: Ein Gespräch mit dem Berliner Verleger und Publizisten Wolf Jobst Siedler geführt von Richard Schneider" (published transcript of television interview, January 8, 1986 [Berlin: Sender Freies Berlin, 1986]), 8–9.

43. Ibid.

44. Ibid.

45. Hans Paul Bahrdt, *Humaner Städtebau: Überlegungen zur Wohnungspolitik und Stadtplanung für eine nahe Zukunft* (Hamburg: Wegner, 1968). Quotations taken from (in order cited) pages 9, 11, 15, 218 n. 29, 160–61, 192, 197, and 204.

46. Ibid., 14, 27

47. John Burchard, *Voice of the Phoenix: Postwar Architecture in Germany* (Cambridge, MA: M.I.T. Press, 1966), 161. Hillebrecht is also discussed extensively in Jeffry M. Diefendorf, *In the Wake of War: The Reconstruction of German Cities after World War II* (New York: Oxford University Press, 1993).

48. Harald Bodenschatz, *Platz frei für das Neue Berlin! Geschichte der Stadterneuerung in der "größten Mietskasernenstadt der Welt" seit 1871* (Berlin: Transit Buchverlag, 1987), 171ff.

49. Rudolf Hillebrecht, "Von Ebenezer Howard zu Jane Jacobs—oder: War alles falsch?" *Stadtbauwelt* 8 (1965): 638–58.

50. Gerhard Rabeler, *Wiederaufbau und Expansion westdeutscher Städte 1945–1960 im Spannungsfeld von Reformideen und Wirklichkeit* (Bonn: Deutsches Nationalkomitee für Denkmalschutz, 1990), 76–77.

51. See Rudolf Hillebrecht, *Fundamente des Aufbaues: Organizatorische Grundlagen* (Hamburg: Phönix-Verl., 1948); as discussed in Diefendorf, *In the Wake of War*.

52. See discussion of Hillebrecht in chap. 4 under "Authoritarians in the 'Public Sphere': German Urbanists and the Problem of Democratic Planning."

53. Report of the meeting at the Royal Institute of British Architects, February 7, 1967, 98.

54. Jane Jacobs, letter to her husband and children (January 24, 1967), published in Allen, *Ideas That Matter* (n. 8 above), p. 87.

55. Diefendorf, *In the Wake of War*, 149.

56. Rabeler, *Wiederaufbau*, 175.

Introduction to Part III

1. On the 1966 election see Rick Perlstein, *Nixonland: The Rise of a President and the Fracturing of America* (New York: Scribner, 2008), chap. 7.

Chapter 6: The First Wave of Resistance

1. A photo of the ribbon tying ran in the *New York Daily Mirror*, and it was also covered by the *New York Times* ("Symbolic Ribbon Ties Off Washington Sq. as Hundreds Celebrate Ban on Traffic," November 2, 1958). On this episode see Robert Fishman, "Revolt of the Urbs: Robert Moses and His Critics," in *Robert Moses and the Modern City: The Transformation of New York*, ed. Hilary Ballon and Kenneth Jackson (New York: W. W. Norton, 2007), 129.

2. Kenneth T. Jackson, *Crabgrass Frontier: The Suburbanization of the United States* (Oxford University Press, 1985), 162.

3. Joseph A. Rodriguez, *City against Suburb: The Culture Wars in an American Metropolis* (New York: Praeger, 1999), 21–46.

4. See Mark H. Rose, *Interstate: Express Highway Politics, 1939–1989* (Knoxville: University of Tennessee Press, 1990); Owen D. Gutfreund, *Twentieth Century Sprawl: Highways and the Reshaping of the American Landscape* (New York: Oxford University Press, 2004); Zachary M. Schrag, "The Freeway Fight in Washington, D.C.: The Three Sisters Bridge in Three Administrations"; and Raymond A. Mohl, "Stop the Road: Freeway Revolts in American Cities," *Journal of Urban History* 30, no. 5 (July 1, 2004): 674–706. Mohl takes the San Francisco experience as a template for the factors contributing to effective roadway battles, with later cases such as the one in Baltimore benefiting from delay amid shifting legislation and public opinion; failures in southern cities like Miami are seen exceptions that prove his rules.

5. Edmund Bacon, as told to Jane Jacobs, quoted in Jacobs, *The Death and Life of Great American Cities* (New York: Random House, 1961), 358n.

6. John F. Bauman, "The Expressway 'Motorists Loved to Hate': Philadelphia and the First Era of Postwar Highway Planning, 1943–1956," *Pennsylvania Magazine of History and Biography* 115, no. 4 (1991): 518.

7. "Philadelphia Chinese Group Fights to Save Its Church," *New York Times*, April 10, 1966, 31. See also Stephen Metraux, "Waiting for the Wrecking Ball: Skid Row in Postindustrial Philadelphia," *Journal of Urban History* 25, no. 5 (1999): 690–715.

8. Stanhope S. Browne, chairman, Committee to Preserve Philadelphia's Historic Gateway, letter to *New York Times*, July 29, 1965, 26; "Expressway Route Fought by Residents of Old Philadelphia," *New York Times*, February 27, 1966, 28; "Philadelphia Road Plan Spurs Closer U.S. Ties with Cities," *New York Times*, May 29, 1967, 25; "U.S. Road Plans Periled by Rising Urban Hostility," *New York Times*, November 13, 1967, 1. See also the obituary of one of the leaders, "Frank Weise, 84, Architect; Fought Philadelphia Road Idea," *New York Times*, February 5, 2003, B8.

9. A characteristic letter to the editor took Boston's gash as a worst-case scenario, San Francisco's moratorium as the other extreme, and Philadelphia's depressed victory as the best compromise. Eleanor Stephens Johnson, "Depressed Expressway," *New York Times*, September 1, 1965, 36. See further coverage: Charles G. Bennett, "Mayor Is Revising Expressway Plan; He Will Propose Road That Runs below Surface," *New York Times*, October 29, 1965, 1; Christopher Tunnard, "Below-Ground Design For City Expressway," *New York Times*, June 1, 1965, 38; William E. Farrell, "New Study Asked for Expressway; Regional Plan Association Suggests Manhattan Road Be Put Underground," *New York Times*, July 10, 1965, 27.

10. Nancy Kleniewski, "Neighborhood Decline and Downtown Renewal: The Politics of Redevelopment in Philadelphia, 1952–1962" (Ph.D. dissertation, Temple University, 1982), highlights how the reform administrations shifted their focus away from slum clearance toward center city renewal, under the influence of the Greater Philadelphia Movement, just as areas like North Philadelphia were in greatest need of government assistance.

11. Details are found in Temple University, Urban Archives, *Philadelphia Evening Bulletin* Newsclipping Collection, files under "South Street" (box 219: "South–Southwestern") and "Crosstown" (box 52: "Cor–Cr").

12. Michelle Osborn, "The Crosstown Is Dead Long Live the Crosstown?" *Architectural Forum* 135 (October 1971): 39.

13. See Joseph Daughen and Peter Binzen, *The Wreck of the Penn Central* (Boston: Little, Brown & Co., 1971).

14. The quote is from Jacobs, *Death and Life*, 360–62; see also "Villagers Celebrate Victory on Traffic; Burn Car in Effigy," *New York Times*, June 13, 1959, 23. A detailed scholarly examination is Fishman, "Revolt of the Urbs," 122–29.

15. Jane Jacobs, "Downtown Planning" (address delivered at the Twenty-fourth Annual Meeting of the New York State Motorbus Association, New York City, November 10, 1958), Mayor Wagner Papers, New York City Municipal Archives, general correspondence, 1958, folder "Jacksona–Jamerz." See also Jacobs, *Death and Life*, 70.

16. Jacobs, *Death and Life*, 124–25. Also "Save Sidewalk Committee Formed, Eleven-Year-Old Sparks Village Civic Effort," *Villager*, March 10, 1960; reprinted in Max Allen, ed., *Ideas That Matter: The Worlds of Jane Jacobs* (Owen Sound, ON: Ginger Press, 1997), 67–68.

17. Letter from Herman Badillo to Mayor Wagner (August, 1962), Mayor Wagner Papers, subject files, folder "Housing—West Village, 1961–."

18. "Downtown Expressway Plan Killed," *New York Daily Report of Il Progresso Italo-Americano*, December 12, 1962, 1; Stephanie Gervis, "Political Powerhouse Kills Broome St. Expressway,"

Village Voice, December 13, 1962, 1; Jane Kramer, "All the Ranks and Rungs of Mrs. Jacobs' Ladder," *Village Voice*, December 20, 1962, 1; Robert B. Semple Jr., "New York's Little Italy Beats the Bulldozers," *National Observer*, December 24, 1962, 1.

19. Richard Seveso, "Mrs. Jacobs's Protest Results in Riot Charge," *New York Times*, April 18, 1968, 49.

20. Notice of benefit, May 27, 1968, published in Allen, *Ideas That Matter*, 73.

21. Jacobs had been arrested before, while demonstrating against the Vietnam War at the Whitehall Street draft induction center. On her legal defense, see Jacobs' November 1, 1968, letter to Richard Barnett of Kate, Gardner, Poor and Havens, Jane Jacobs Papers, Burns Library, Boston College, box 11, folder 6.

22. Brian Ladd, *Autophobia: Love and Hate in the Automotive Age* (Chicago: University of Chicago Press, 2008), 86. On the Buchanan report, in international context, see also Stephen Ward, "Cross-National Learning in the Formation of British Planning Policies, 1940–99: A Comparison of the Barlow, Buchanan and Rogers Reports," *Town Planning Review* 78, no. 3 (May 1, 2007): 378–83.

23. Mick Hamer, *Wheels within Wheels: A Study of the Road Lobby* (London: Routledge, 1987), 60–63.

24. Jane Jacobs, "Spadina Expressway," *Canadian Dimension* 6 (February/March 1970): 8.

25. See Hans Blumenfeld, *Life Begins at 65: The Not Entirely Candid Autobiography of a Drifter* (Montreal: Harvest House, 1987), 245–49; Darryl Newbury, *Stop Spadina: Citizens against an Expressway* (Mississauga: Commonact Press, 1989).

26. Jane Jacobs, "A City Getting Hooked on the Expressway Drug," *Globe and Mail*, November 1, 1969. Jacobs related her family's disbelief in "Spadina Expressway," 8: "They must certainly, we thought, have reflected upon the lesson of Los Angeles." See also J. Dingman, "Women: Social Critic," *Chatelaine* 42 (April 1969): 4: "She says it's a good place to live, but that in another fifteen years it probably won't be, because Toronto is going to destroy itself with expressways, as American cities such as Buffalo have done. 'For the time being, it's a splendid city,' she says. . . . Jacobs thinks Toronto has better public transportation now than it will in a few years." Many documents related to Jacobs' experiences in Toronto are reprinted in Allen, *Ideas That Matter*, 115–31.

27. Volker Roscher, ed., *Hans Blumenfeld, Stadtplaner—es sei denn, sie bauen eine humane Stadt: Autobiographie, 1892–1988* (Basel: Birkhäuser, 1993), 218–19. See also D. Nowlan and M. Nowlan, *The Bad Trip: The Untold Story of the Spadina Expressway* (Toronto: NewPress/Anansi, 1970).

28. "Jacobs Raps Expressway Plan," *Architecture Canada*, February 16, 1970, 1; Robert Fulford, *The Accidental City: The Transformation of Toronto* (Toronto: McFarlane, Walter & Ross, 1995), 76.

29. *Toronto Telegram*, April 7, 1970; reprinted in Allen, *Ideas That Matter*, 116.

30. Roscher, *Hans Blumenfeld*, 219.

Chapter 7: The Tide Shifts

1. Raymond A. Mohl, "Stop the Road: Freeway Revolts in American Cities," *Journal of Urban History* 30, no. 5 (July 1, 2004): 674–706.

2. An excellent study of grassroots neighborhood revitalization in cities including New York, Boston, Chicago, Atlanta, and Los Angeles is Alexander von Hoffman, *House by House,*

Block by Block: The Rebirth of America's Urban Neighborhoods (New York: Oxford University Press, 2003).

3. Quoted in Jewel Bellush and Murray Hausknecht, eds., *Urban Renewal: People, Politics and Planning* (Garden City, NY: Doubleday, 1967), 278.

4. John Sibley, "Model Slum Plan Beset by Delays; 'Pioneer' Project Drafted a Year Ago Not Yet Started," *New York Times*, May 28, 1961, 48.

5. James Felt, address delivered at the Sixty-ninth Annual Meeting of the Municipal Art Society, May 8, 1961, Mayor Wagner Papers, New York City Municipal Archives, departmental series: City Planning, box 16, folder 243.

6. New York City Planning Commission release, December 15, 1961, Mayor Wagner Papers, departmental series: City Planning, box 16, folder 243.

7. The designated section was bounded by West 11th Street, Hudson Street, Christopher Street, Washington Street, Morton Street, and West Street. City Planning Commission resolution appended to petition from Committee to Save the West Village, Mayor Wagner Papers, subject files, folder "Housing—West Village, 1961–."

8. New York City Planning Commission release, May 1, 1961, Mayor Wagner Papers, departmental series: City Planning, box 16, folder 243.

9. Quotes from J. Clarence Davies, letters to Mrs. John Norment, to Margaret Mills (both letters April 7, 1961), and to Joseph Oelhaf (April 10, 1961), Mayor Wagner Papers, subject files, folder "Housing—West Village, 1961–."

10. On the Gruen proposal, see Richard Plunz, *A History of Housing in New York City* (New York: Columbia University Press, 1990), 309.

11. Quotes from J. Clarence Davies, letters to Joseph Oelhaf and to Mitchell Brower (both letters April 10, 1961), Mayor Wagner Papers, subject files, folder: "Housing—West Village, 1961–."

12. "Picket to Bar Eviction," Associated Press photo clipping, May 22, 1960, Jane Jacobs Papers, Burns Library, Boston College, box 7, folder 3.

13. Eric Larrabee, "In Print: Jane Jacobs," *Horizon* 4, no. 6 (July 1962): 50.

14. Jane Jacobs, writing as chairman of the Committee to Save the West Village, to Mayor Wagner (March 27, 1961), Mayor Wagner Papers, subject files, folder "Housing—West Village 1961–").

15. Lewis Mumford, "Not Yet Too Late," *New Yorker*, December 7, 1963, 142.

16. Unidentified newspaper clipping, City Planning Commissioner Goldstone Papers, New York City Municipal Archives, folder "West Village Housing." See also "Zeckendorf Is Back—with Old Dreams and a Dowager's Money," *House and Home* 33, no. 3 (March 1968): 18.

17. Neighbors Committee statement and cover letter to Mayor Wagner, October 19, 1961, Mayor Wagner Papers, subject files, folder "Housing—West Village, 1961–."

18. Author's interview with John and Gerry Six, New York, June 1, 2002.

19. Rachele Wall, letter to Jack Lutsky (December 15, 1961); and Wall, telegram to Wagner (December 17, 1961), Mayor Wagner Papers, subject files, folder "Housing—West Village, 1961–."

20. See the reminiscence of Ned Jacobs, "Changing the World by Saving Place," *Alternatives Journal* 28, no. 3 (July 2002): 35.

21. "Negro Pupil Shift Fought in 'Village,'" *New York Times*, June 13, 1963, 15; "Village Pickets Protesting Shift of Negro Pupils" (P.S. 41 Education Committee flyer, September 1963); excerpted in Max Allen, ed., *Ideas That Matter: The Worlds of Jane Jacobs* (Owen Sound, ON: Ginger Press, 1997), 72; Stephanie Gervis Harrington, "Boycott Strips Schools, Over Half of Pupils Out," *Village Voice*, February 6, 1964.

22. Author's interview with John and Gerry Six, New York, June 1, 2002.

23. Joel Schwartz questions the substance of the Villagers' self-image, based on the collaboration during the late 1940s and early 1950s between the Greenwich Village Association and those, like Robert Moses, who sough to redevelop the area to the exclusion of low-income housing. He dismisses the subsequent resistance to these plans as a homeowners' revolt in reaction to overzealousness on Moses' part. See Schwartz, *The New York Approach: Robert Moses, Urban Liberals, and Redevelopment of the Inner City* (Columbus: Ohio State University Press, 1993).

24. Jane Jacobs, *The Death and Life of Great American Cities* (New York: Random House, 1961), 127.

25. William H. Whyte, Jr., ed., *The Exploding Metropolis* (Berkeley: University of California Press, 1993), xv.

26. Jacobs correspondence with *Architects' Journal* (November 22, 1962), published in Allen, *Ideas That Matter*, 4. An abbreviated version appeared as Jane Jacobs, "The How and Why of Planning," *Architects' Journal* 137, no. 3 (January 16, 1963): 126–27.

27. The petition accompanied a letter from Jane Jacobs to Mayor Wagner (March 27, 1961), Mayor Wagner Papers (n. 4 above), subject files, folder "Housing—West Village 1961–." See also John Sibley, "Planners Hailed on New Approach; Rehabilitation Draws Praise in Hearings on 4 Areas," *New York Times*, May 25, 1961, 37.

28. Priscilla Chapman, "City Critic in Favor of Old Neighborhoods," *New York Herald Tribune*, March 4, 1961; reprinted in Allen, *Ideas That Matter*, 49.

29. On April 27, 1961, Mayor Wagner was informed by his law department that he had been served in a suit from Jane Jacobs, Elizabeth Squire, Leon Seidel, et al., plaintiffs against the City of New York. The suit formalized Jacobs' assertion regarding the illegality of actions by the city's agencies. When New York Supreme Court ruled on *Jacobs v. City of New York*, its decision supported the Villagers' claims. Official communication, April 27, 1961, Mayor Wagner Papers, general correspondence, 1961, folder "JACO."

30. Jane Jacobs, letter to Mayor Wagner (March 27, 1961), Mayor Wagner Papers, subject files, folder "Housing—West Village 1961–." See also Sam Pope Brewer, "Citizens Housing Group Backs 'Village' Urban Renewal Study," *New York Times*, March 27, 1961, 33.

31. Official communication, April 27, 1961, Mayor Wagner Papers, general correspondence, 1961, folder "JACO."

32. Justice Hecht, "Jacobs v. City of N.Y." *New York Law Journal* 145, no. 95 (May 17, 1961): 14.

33. The petition is undated but was received at City Hall between May 17 and June 26, 1961. Mayor Wagner Papers, subject files, folder "Housing—West Village, 1961–."

34. Hortense Gabel, assistant to the mayor for housing, "Personal and Confidential," memo to Paul Screvane, deputy mayor, April 24, 1961, Mayor Wagner Papers, subject files, folder "Housing—West Village, 1961–."

35. Robert Wagner, letter to H. Marshall Scolnick (June 26, 1961), Mayor Wagner Papers, subject files, folder "Housing—West Village, 1961–."

36. Committee to Save the West Village, letter to Robert Wagner (July 1, 1961), Mayor Wagner Papers, subject files, folder "Housing—West Village, 1961–."

37. Press release, September 6, 1961, Mayor Wagner Papers, subject files, folder "Housing—West Village, 1961–."

38. Quoted from J. Clarence Davies, letters to Mrs. Renee Scheidel (April 7, 1961) and to Mitchell Brower (April 10, 1961), Mayor Wagner Papers, subject files, folder "Housing—West Village, 1961–."

39. Larrabee, "In Print: Jane Jacobs" (n. 12 above), 50.

40. "Villagers' Near-Riot Jars City Plan," *New York Herald Tribune*, October 19, 1961; reprinted in Allen, *Ideas That Matter*, 68.

41. Citizens Union, press release October 20, 1961, Mayor Wagner Papers, subject files, folder Housing—West Village 1961–."

42. "Report of the City Planning Commission on the Designation of the West Village Area as Appropriate for Urban Renewal and as Master Plan Section M-26," October 18, 1961, Mayor Wagner Papers, subject files, folder "Housing—West Village 1961–."

43. James Felt, letter to Deputy Mayor Paul Screvane (June 19, 1961), Mayor Wagner Papers, subject files, folder "Housing—West Village 1961–."

44. Jane Jacobs, letter to Mayor Wagner (March 27, 1961), Mayor Wagner Papers, subject files, folder "Housing—West Village 1961–."

45. Robert Wagner, letter to James Felt (January 12, 1962/December 17, 1961), Mayor Wagner Papers, subject files, folder "Housing—West Village 1961–."

46. Author's interview with Jane Jacobs, Toronto, February 20, 2002.

47. Robert Wagner's statement and James Felt's memo, October 17, 1961, Mayor Wagner Papers, subject files, folder "Housing—West Village 1961–."

48. Committee to Save the West Village, letter to Mayor Wagner (January 1, 1962/December 17, 1961), Mayor Wagner Papers, subject files, folder "Housing—West Village 1961–."

49. Committee to Save the West Village, letter to Mayor Wagner (April 9, 1962), Mayor Wagner Papers, subject files, folder "Housing—West Village 1961–."

50. Ibid.

51. Numerous examples of cover letter in Commission Chairman Felt Papers, New York City Municipal Archives, folder "West Village."

52. Robert Wagner, letter to James Felt, January 12, 1962, Mayor Wagner Papers, subject files, folder "Housing—West Village, 1961–."

53. Geoffrey Platt, letter to Robert Wagner (November 27, 1961), and press release, December 4, 1961, Mayor Wagner Papers, departmental series: City Planning, box 16, folder 243.

54. Noted in Wagner's release (December 3, 1961), Mayor Wagner Papers, departmental series: City Planning, box 16, folder 243.

55. James Felt, address delivered to the Metropolitan Association of Real Estate Boards, February 11, 1960, Mayor Wagner Papers, departmental series: City Planning, box 16, folder 243.

56. Felt, address to Municipal Arts Society (n. 4 above).

57. Mayor's release, December 18, 1962, Mayor Wagner Papers, departmental series: City Planning, box 16, folder 243.

58. Alexander Burnham, "Village Group Designs Housing to Preserve Character of Area," *New York Times*, May 6, 1963, 42.

Chapter 8: A Bitter End?

1. On Kennet's role in the preservation movement, see John Delafons, *Politics and Preservation: A Policy History of the Built Environment* (London: E & FN Spon, 1997). Delafons was himself deputy secretary at the Department of the Environment (among others) and involved with the listing of sites.

2. John Davis, "Modern London," in *The English Urban Landscape*, ed. Philip Waller (New York: Oxford University Press, 2000), 150.

3. Nathan Silver, "Jane Jacobs for Example," *Columbia Forum* 1, no. 3 (Summer 1972): 47–49.

4. Ibid.; Silver expressed "an ironic bit of comforting nostalgia that the situation we discussed in Covent Garden was much the same as had faced us residents of the West Village ten years ago."

5. Nathan Silver, interview with the author, London, September 24, 2003.

6. See Brian Anson, *I'll Fight You for It! Behind the Struggle for Covent Garden* (London: Jonathan Cape, 1981).

7. John Richardson, *Covent Garden Past* (Chichester: Phillimore & Co., 1996), 131. See also Terry Christensen, *Neighborhood Survival* (Dorchester: Prism, 1979); and Jim Monahan and Geraldine Pettersson, *Covent Garden: Putting the Record Straight* (London: Covent Garden Community Association, 1980).

8. Jim Yelling, "The Development of Residential Urban Renewal Policies in England: Planning for Modernization in the 1960s," *Planning Perspectives* 14, no. 1 (January 1, 1999): 1–18.

9. Kevin C. Kearns, "Intraurban Squatting in London," *Annals of the Association of American Geographers* 69, no. 4 (December 1979): 589–98; Ron Bailey, *The Squatters* (London: Penguin, 1973); Nick Wates and Christian Wolmar, eds., *Squatting: The Real Story* (London: Bay Leaf Books, 1980).

10. David Eversley, *Planner in Society: The Changing Role of a Profession* (London: Faber & Faber, 1973).

11. David Harvey, *Social Justice and the City* (London: Edward Arnold, 1973); Peter Hall, *The Containment of Urban England: The Planning System: Objectives, Operations, Impacts* (London: Allen & Unwin, 1973); H. J. Dyos and Michael Wolff, eds., *The Victorian City: Images and Realities* (London: Routledge & Kegan Paul, 1973), a collection featuring many New Urban historians; and the accompanying with the primary source collection: B. I. Coleman, ed., *The Idea of the City in Nineteenth-Century Britain* (London: Routledge & Kegan Paul, 1973).

12. Richard Rodger, "Slums and Suburbs: the Persistence of Residential Apartheid," in *The English Urban Landscape*, ed. Philip Waller (New York: Oxford University Press, 2000), 264.

13. Kenneth O. Morgan, *The People's Peace: British History since 1945* (Oxford: Oxford University Press, 1999), 563.

14. Michelle Osborn, "The Crosstown Is Dead Long Live the Crosstown?" *Architectural Forum* 135 (October 1971): 39.

15. Ibid.

16. Paulo Lyons, *The People of This Generation: The Rise and Fall of the New Left in Philadelphia* (Philadelphia: University of Pennsylvania Press, 2003), charts campus-based movements caught between "Philadelphia's pacifist Quaker tradition and the rising ethnic populism of . . . Frank Rizzo." See also S. A. Paolantonio, *Frank Rizzo: The Last Big Man in Big City America* (Philadelphia: Camino Books, 1994).

17. Jane Kramer, "All the Ranks and Rungs of Mrs. Jacobs' Ladder," *Village Voice*, December 20, 1962.

18. Eric Larrabee, "In Print: Jane Jacobs," *Horizon* 4, no. 6 (July 1962): 50.

19. Ibid.

20. Emory Lewis, "Rx for a Sick City: *Cue* Readers Suggest Some of the Ways Our Town, Seeming Bent on Destruction, Can Save Itself," *Cue*, March 16, 1963, clipping, Jane Jacobs Papers, Burns Library, Boston College, box 7, folder 1.

21. Larry Nathanson, "2nd Battle of Brooklyn," *New York Post*, January 11, 1962, 7.

22. Jane Jacobs, letter to the editor, *Columbia Forum*, Fall 1972; reprinted in Max Allen, ed., *Ideas That Matter: The Worlds of Jane Jacobs* (Owen Sound, ON: Ginger Press, 1997), 82.

23. Hans Blumenfeld, "The Good Neighborhood," *Adult Education* (Toronto) (May–June 1962): 264–70; reprinted in Paul D. Spreiregen, ed., *The Modern Metropolis: Its Origins, Growth, Characteristics, and Planning: Selected Essays* (Cambridge, , MA: M.I.T. Press, 1967), 180–89.

24. Christina Newman, "The Body Politic," *Chatelaine* 43 (November 1970): 14.

25. Sean Purdy, "'Ripped Off' by the System: Housing Policy, Poverty, and Territorial Stigmatization in Regent Park Housing Project, 1951–1999," *Labour* (Canada) 52 (2003): 45–108. On citizen participation and resistance to redevelopment projects, see Kevin Brushett, "Blots on the Face of the City: The Politics of Slum Housing and Urban Renewal in Toronto, 1940–1970" (Ph.D. thesis, Queen's University, 2001); and Brushett, "'People and Government Travelling Together': Community Organization, Urban Planning and the Politics of Post-war Reconstruction in Toronto, 1943–1953," *Urban History Review* 27, no 2 (1999): 44–58.

26. Sewell was elected together with another neighborhood advocate, Karl Jaffary. Sewell's campaign touted his work in Trefann Court, Don Mount, Regent Park, St. James Town, Sherbourne-Dundas, and elsewhere, calling for "meaningful participation" and "concerned about the way decisions are made and who makes them." Once on the council, Sewell transformed the Trefann Court redevelopment project, proposed by the City of Toronto Planning Board in 1956, into a process of community participation planning. Graham Fraser, *Fighting Back: Urban Renewal in Trefann Court* (Toronto: Hakkert, 1972), 168–69 and passim.

27. Magnusson divides the reform into "urban conservative" and "urban radical" wings. See Warren Magnusson, "Toronto," in *City Politics in Canada*, ed. W. Magnusson and A. Sancton (Toronto: University of Toronto Press, 1983), 115ff.; similarly, historical geographer and Torontonian James Lemon attributes the city's vigorous citizenship to British-inspired ratepayers associations, "protecting affluent and middle income neighborhoods from excessive development pressures." See Lemon, *Liberal Dreams and Nature's Limits: Great Cities of North America since 1600* (Toronto: Oxford University Press, 1996), 262. See also John Sewell, *Up against City Hall* (Toronto: James Lewis & Samuel, 1972); and J. Sewell, D. Crombie, W. Kilbourn, and K. Jaffary, *Inside City Hall: The Year of the Opposition* (Toronto: Hakkert, 1972). On the reform movement, Dimitrios Roussopoulos, ed., *The City and Radical Social Change* (Montreal: Black Rose Books, 1982), contains Bill Freeman, "John Sewell and the New Urban Reformers Come to Power," and M. Goldrick, "The Anatomy of Urban Reform in Toronto." See also F. Frisken, *City-Policy Making in Theory and Practice: The Case of Toronto's Downtown Plan* (London, ON: University of Western Ontario, 1988); Jon Caulfield, "Canadian Urban Reform and Local Conditions," *International Journal of Urban and Regional Research* 12 (3): 477–84; Caulfield, "Reform as a Chaotic Concept," *Urban History Review* 17, no 2: 107–11.

28. See Jon Caulfield, *The Tiny Perfect Mayor: David Crombie and Toronto's Reform Aldermen* (Toronto: Lorimer, 1974); and Caulfield, "David Crombie's Housing Policy: Making Toronto Safe—Once More—for the Developers," in *The City Book: The Politics and Planning of Canada's Cities*, ed. James Lorimer and Evelyn Ross (Toronto: James Lorimer, 1974), 138–47.

29. This story is frequently recounted by veterans of the reform movement; see, for example, Robert Fulford, *The Accidental City: The Transformation of Toronto* (Toronto: McFarlane, Walter & Ross, 1995), 82, where he concludes, "When the city builds a monument to Jacobs, it should probably go there."

Chapter 9: New Left Urbanism vs. Neocon Urban Crisis

1. A full biographical treatment is Wendell E. Pritchett, *Robert Clifton Weaver and the American City: The Life and Times of an Urban Reformer* (Chicago: University of Chicago Press, 2008).

2. Ben A. Franklin, "Weaver Asserts Disdain for the Poor Hinders Urban Renewal," *New York Times*, April 4, 1965, 79.

3. Ibid.

4. Lloyd Rodwin, ed., *The Future Metropolis* (New York: George Braziller, 1961), 12.

5. Edward C. Banfield, "The Political Implications of Metropolitan Growth," in Rodwin *Future Metropolis*, 93.

6. Ann L. Strong and George E. Thomas, eds., *The Book of the School: 100 Years of the Graduate School of Fine Arts at the University of Pennsylvania* (Philadelphia: Graduate School of Fine Arts, 1990), 166.

7. See James Q. Wilson, *Negro Politics: The Search for Leadership* (Glencoe, IL: Free Press 1960); Wilson, *The Amateur Democrat: Club Politics in Three Cities* (Chicago: University of Chicago Press, 1962); and Wilson, *Politics and Reform in American Cities* (New York: Holt, Rinehart and Winston, 1962).

8. Martin Meyerson and Edward C. Banfield, *Politics, Planning, and the Public Interest: The Case of Public Housing in Chicago* (Glencoe, IL: Free Press, 1955). In 1961 Banfield became the Henry Lee Shattuck Professor of Urban Government; see "Harvard Fills Urban Chair," *New York Times*, May 21, 1961, 44.

9. Edward C. Banfield and James Q. Wilson, *City Politics* (Cambridge, MA: Joint Center for Urban Studies, 1963).

10. Martin Anderson, *Federal Bulldozer: A Critical Analysis of Urban Renewal, 1949–1962* (Cambridge, MA: Joint Center for Urban Studies, 1964).

11. James Q. Wilson, ed., *Urban Renewal: The Record and the Controversy* (Cambridge, MA: Joint Center for Urban Studies, 1966), xvi. See esp. Wilson's contribution on the intractably political nature of the problem, "Planning and Politics: Citizen Participation in Urban Renewal," 407–21.

12. Wilson, *Urban Renewal*, 418.

13. See, for example, Raymond Vernon, *The Myth and Reality of Our Urban Problems* (Cambridge, MA: Harvard University Press, 1966); John K. Meyer, *Bibliography of the Urban Crisis: The Behavioral, Psychological, and Sociological Aspects of the Urban Crisis* (Chevy Chase, MD: National Institute of Mental Health, 1969). Reacting to "violence and disorders," Meyer surveys popular and academic literature between 1954 and 1968, reflecting a pronounced increase in attention to rioting around 1967 (and includes an index of authors, e.g., Moynihan.) Hunter College professors Jewel Bellush and Murray Hausknecht edited another collection of documents and

essays, *Urban Renewal: People, Politics and Planning* (Garden City, NY: Doubleday, 1967). Though less critical, Jeanne Lowe's *Cities in a Race with Time: Progress and Poverty in America's Renewing Cities* (New York: Random House, 1967) presented five admiring portraits of the efforts of Robert Moses in New York City, Mayors Dilworth and Clark and planner Edmund Bacon in Philadelphia, Richard Mellon and Mayor David Lawrence in Pittsburgh, Mayor Richard Lee in New Haven, and developers in Washington.

14. Sam Bass Warner, Jr., ed., *Planning for a Nation of Cities* (Cambridge, MA: M.I.T. Press, 1966), vi. The project emerged in conjunction with the 1964 Saint Louis Bicentennial. Warner, then at Washington University in Saint Louis, endorsed a minimum personal income and metropolitan reorganization. See the review by Charles Abrams, "Rich Country, Poor Cities," *New York Times*, July 16, 1967, 198, on Wilson, Warner, and Blumenfeld.

15. See Wilson's prolific output in 1968: James Q. Wilson, ed., *City Politics and Public Policy* (New York: Wiley, 1968); Wilson, ed., *Metropolitan Enigma: Inquiries into the Nature and Dimensions of America's Urban Crisis* (Washington DC: Task Force on Economic Growth and Opportunity, Chamber of Commerce of the U.S., 1967; republished, Cambridge, MA: Harvard University Press, 1968); Robert A. Goldwin, ed., *A Nation of Cities, Essays on America's Urban Problems: A Message by President Johnson and Essays by James Q. Wilson [and Others]* (Chicago: Rand McNally, 1968); and James Q. Wilson, *Varieties of Police Behavior: The Management of Law and Order in Eight Communities* (Cambridge, MA: Harvard University Press, 1968).

16. James Q. Wilson, "Corruption Is Not Always Scandalous; Corruption in Cities," *New York Times Sunday Magazine*, April 28, 1968, 54.

17. James Q. Wilson, "Why We Are Having a Wave of Violence," *New York Times Sunday Magazine*, May 19, 1968, 23.

18. Denise Scott Brown, "A Worm's Eye View of Recent Architectural History," *Architectural Record* 172, no. 2 (February 1984): 69–81. For recent scholarly interpretations of the various movements covered by the term New Left, see John McMillian and Paul Buhle, eds., *The New Left Revisited* (Philadelphia: Temple University Press, 2003); and Van Gosse, *Rethinking the New Left: An Interpretive History* (New York: Palgrave Macmillan, 2005).

19. Denise Scott Brown, "Rise and Fall of Community Architecture," in "Urban Concepts: Architectural Design Profile 83," ed. Andreas Papadakis, special issue, *Architectural Design* 60, no. 1–2 (1990): 33.

20. Paul Davidoff and Thomas A. Reiner, "A Choice Theory of Planning," *Journal of the American Institute of Planners* 28, no. 2 (May 1962): 103. See also Thomas A. Reiner's 1963 Ph.D. thesis in regional science, "Regional Allocation Criteria" (University of Pennsylvania), and his book *The Place of the Ideal Community in Urban Planning* (Philadelphia: University of Pennsylvania Press, 1963).

21. Paul Davidoff, "Advocacy and Pluralism in Planning," *Journal of the American Institute of Planners* 31 (November 1965): 186–97.

22. Barry Checkoway, "Paul Davidoff and Advocacy Planning in Retrospect," *Journal of the American Planning Association* 60, no. 2 (Spring 1994): 139–61.

23. Scott Brown, "Worm's Eye View," 14, 75.

Chapter 10: The Anti-experts

1. Lewis Mumford, letter to Jane Jacobs (January 4, 1963), published in *Ideas That Matter: The Worlds of Jane Jacobs*, ed. Max Allen (Owen Sound, ON: Ginger Press, 1997), 96.

2. "A Continuing Purpose," *West Village Committee Newsletter* 2, no. 1 (March 10, 1962): 1, in Bill Bowser personal papers, unprocessed collection, New York, NY.

3. Jane Jacobs, interviewed in *Mademoiselle*, October 1962; "Perkins & Will Architects Newsletter," November 1962, 10; "Articles of Association of the West Village Committee" (undated, probably February 1962), Jane Jacobs Papers, Burns Library, Boston College, box 27, folder 2; Jane Kramer, "All the Ranks and Rungs of Mrs. Jacobs' Ladder," *Village Voice*, December 20, 1962; Hugh Byfield and West Village Committee, letter to Wagner (April 9, 1962), Mayor Wagner Papers, New York City Municipal Archives, subject files, folder "Housing—West Village, 1961–."

4. West Village Plan for Housing brochure, Jacobs Papers, box 27, folder 2. Figures quoted in *New York Times*, May 6, 1963, 42.

5. Chester W. Hartman, *Between Eminence and Notoriety: Four Decades of Radical Urban Planning* (New Brunswick, NJ: Center for Urban Policy Research, 2001), 6, 18–20.

6. *East Harlem Triangle Plan* (Architects' Renewal Committee in Harlem, 1968), Avery Architectural and Fine Arts Library, Columbia University.

7. Temple University, Urban Archives, *Philadelphia Evening Bulletin* Newsclipping Collection, files under "South Street" (box 219: "South–Southwestern") and "Crosstown" (box 52: "Cor–Cr").

8. Michelle Osborn, "The Crosstown Is Dead Long Live the Crosstown?" and Denise Scott Brown, "An Alternate Proposal That Builds on the Character and Population of South Street," both in *Architectural Forum* 135 (October 1971): 40 and 42, respectively.

9. Mitchell's December 1967 recommendation to the mayor, quoted in Osborn, "Crosstown Is Dead," 40.

10. Andrea Gabor, *Einstein's Wife: Work and Marriage in the Lives of Five Great Twentieth-Century Women* (New York: Viking, 1995), 203.

11. Denise Scott Brown, "Rise and Fall of Community Architecture," in "Urban Concepts: Architectural Design Profile 83," ed. Andreas Papadakis, special issue, *Architectural Design* 60, no. 1–2 (1990): 34.

12. Denise Scott Brown, "Between Three Stools: A Personal View of Urban Design Practice and Pedagogy," in "Urban Concepts," 14.

13. Denise Scott Brown, "Paralipomena in Urban Design," in "Urban Concepts," 7.

14. Robert Venturi, Denise Scott Brown, and Steven Izenour, *Learning from Las Vegas* (Cambridge, MA: M.I.T. Press, 1972), 56.

15. Ibid., 72.

16. Ibid., xi.

17. Robert Venturi, *Complexity and Contradiction in Architecture* (New York: Museum of Modern Art, 1998), 104.

18. Ibid., 50; Gabor, *Einstein's Wife*, 195. The Townscape affinities emerge as Venturi pursues his thesis that "an architecture of complexity and accommodation does not forsake the whole," as when, for example, Times Square's "jarring inconsistencies of buildings and billboards are contained within the consistent order of the space itself," providing a vitality and validity comparable to those of Piazza San Marco, itself "not without its violent contradictions in scale, rhythm, and textures, not to mention the varying heights and styles of the surrounding buildings." The dynamism in complicated buildings or cityscapes is achieved precisely because "the eye does not want to be too easily or too quickly satisfied in its search for unity

within a whole." This element, he argued, is missing from "prim dreams of pure order, which, unfortunately, are imposed in the easy Gestalt unities of the urban renewal projects of establishment Modern architecture." Ultimately, Venturi concluded tentatively, "it is perhaps from the everyday landscape, vulgar and disdained, that we can draw the complex and contradictory order that is valid and vital for our architecture as an urbanistic whole." See 54, 104.

19. In *Complexity and Contradiction*, Venturi emphasized that unruly commercial (or "honky-tonk") "elements in our architecture and townscape are here to stay" and that "such a fate should be acceptable," since "Pop Art has demonstrated that these commonplace elements are often the main source of the occasional variety and vitality of our cities." He also suggested how this insight might be applied (44): "Cannot the architect and planner, by slight adjustments to the conventional elements of the townscape, existing or proposed, promote significant effects? . . . They can make us see the same things in a different way."

20. Scott Brown, "Alternate Proposal," 42; expanded in Venturi, Scott Brown, and Izenour, *Learning from Las Vegas*, 126–33.

21. Scott Brown, "Rise and Fall," 35.

22. Scott Brown, "Alternate Proposal," 44.

23. "Plans Outlined for South St. Minus Road," *Philadelphia Bulletin*, January 13, 1970, 20.

24. Scott Brown, "Rise and Fall," 35.

25. Ibid.

26. Scott Brown, "Alternate Proposal," 42, 44.

27. "Plans Outlined for South St. Minus Road," 20.

28. Scott Brown, "Alternate Proposal" (n. 7 above), 44. See also Elizabeth N. Layne, "A Question of Values," under "The Environment: Notes on the Continuing Battle," *American Heritage*, August 1970, 119.

29. Victoria Donohoe, "Advocacy Planners Put Hope in Ghetto," *Philadelphia Inquirer*, July 6, 1969, 6.

30. Katrina Dyke, "New South St. Previewed at Open House," *Philadelphia Bulletin*, March 9, 1970, 5.

31. *Philadelphia Bulletin*, December 7, 1970.

32. C. Richard Hatch, interview with the author by telephone, February 22, 2010.

33. Earl M. Blecher, *Advocacy Planning for Urban Development: With Analysis of Six Demonstration Programs* (New York: Praeger, 1971), 166.

34. U.S. Congress, Joint Economic Committee, Subcommittee on Urban Affairs, *Urban America: Goals and Problems: Hearings before the Subcommittee on Urban Affairs of the Joint Economic Committee*, 90th Cong., 1st sess., September 27, 28, October 2, 3, and 4, 1967 (U.S. Government Printing Office, 1967).

35. Walter Thabit, "A History of PEO: Planners for Equal Opportunity" (unpublished manuscript, Cornell University, City Planning Department, 1999).

36. Marshall Kaplan, *Urban Planning in the 1960s: A Design for Irrelevancy* (Cambridge, MA: M.I.T. Press, 1973), 61.

37. For a recent consideration of RAND and related topics, see Bruce Kuklick, *Blind Oracles: Intellectuals and War from Kennan to Kissinger* (Princeton: Princeton University Press, 2006).

38. During the 1968 Columbia University sit-in, students distributed flyers reading "Stop Columbia from taking over Harlem," according to Michael Kaufman, *1968* (New York: Roaring Press, 2009), 125.

Chapter 11: Nixon Urbanistes and "the Waterloo of Planning"

1. Edward Banfield, *Why Government Cannot Solve the Urban Problem* (Cambridge, MA: Joint Center for Urban Studies, 1968).

2. Edward Banfield, quoted in Theodore H. White, "The Action Intellectuals," *Life*, June 9, 1967.

3. See Edward Banfield, *The Unheavenly City: The Nature and Future of Our Urban Crisis* (Boston: Little, Brown, 1970).

4. See Stephan Thernstrom and Richard Sennett, eds., *Nineteenth-Century Cities: Essays in the New Urban History* (New Haven: Yale University Press, 1969); and Stephan Thernstrom, *The Other Bostonians: Poverty and Progress in the American Metropolis, 1880–1970* (Cambridge, MA: Harvard University Press: 1973).

5. Robert Wiebe, "The Urban Historian as Citizen: In Honor of Sam Bass Warner, Jr.," *Journal of Urban History* 22, no. 5 (July 1996): 630.

6. Stephan Thernstrom, *Poverty, Planning, and Politics in the New Boston: The Origins of ABCD* (New York: Basic Books, 1969), x.

7. Ibid., xi.

8. Ibid., 164–65.

9. Ibid., x.

10. Ibid., 175. ABCD planners, Thernstrom noted, "assumed that the chief obstacle to improving the lot of the poor was lack of knowledge rather than lack of will, imperfect understanding of the problem rather than resistances based on difference of opinion and interest. The planners' debt to Condorcet, their faith in the power of Reason, was very apparent; that they had learned what Hegel and Marx have to teach about conflict and power was doubtful."

11. Ibid., 181 n. 1; Thernstrom cited (without irony) Meyerson, Banfield, and Wilson to chasten those who had faith in urban experts: "The editorial writers who cheered the late 1967 news that Mayor Lindsay was retaining the RAND Corporation to recommend strategies for the governing of New York City could have profited from a consideration of [an] appraisal of how RAND and similar institutions have influenced American foreign policy."

12. Robert C. Wood, *Whatever Possessed the President? Academic Experts and Presidential Policy, 1960–1988* (Amherst: University of Massachusetts Press, 1993), 89.

13. Ibid., 91–104. Wood interviewed Anderson and remarks that "aside from presidential libraries, Anderson has the most complete and authoritative files for the presidential elections of 1968, 1976 and 1980 of which I am aware" (188 n. 9).

14. Richard Reeves, "Nixon's Men Are Smart but No Swingers," *New York Times Sunday Magazine*, September 29, 1968, 28.

15. John Herbers, "Emphasis on City; Revision of Federal Role in Urban Matters Likely," *New York Times*, December 12, 1968, 1.

16. Adam Walinsky, *New York Times Book Review*, February 2, 1969, 1, reviewing Daniel P. Moynihan, *Maximum Feasible Misunderstanding; Community Action in the War on Poverty* (New York: Macmillan–Free Press, 1969).

17. John Herbers, "Emphasis on City Problems Seen," *New York Times*, December 12, 1968, 1.

18. Robert B. Semple, Jr., "Moynihan, in Valedictory, Hails Nixon and Urges Support for His Proposals," *New York Times*, December 23, 1970, 54.

19. Ibid, 54.

20. Ada Louise Huxtable, "Student Architects Ask Aid to Combat Urban Plight," *New York Times*, June 27, 1969, 43. See also "Moynihan Critical of Cities' Designs," *New York Times*, June 24, 1969, 21.

21. "Wood to Head Unit for Urban Studies at Harvard Center," *New York Times*, January 9, 1969, 13; Robert Reinhold, "Johnson Idea Man Leaves with Hope; Wood, a Housing Authority, Heartened by Experience," *New York Times*, February 9, 1969, 61.

22. "Wood Replaces Weaver," *New York Times*, January 8, 1969, 2. Wood's own research interests in suburbs and New York City politics were something of an exception at the Joint Center. For Wood's views during his Washington tenure, see his "The Contributions of Political Science to the Study of Urbanism," in *Taming Megalopolis*, ed. H. Wentworth Eldredge (New York: Prager, 1967), 1:192–220.

23. John H. Fenton, "Boston Slum Cure Tied to Business; Antipoverty Head Asks Job and Housing Assistance," *New York Times*, April 27, 1969, 53.

24. Charles Haar, quoted in Jack Rosenthal, "6 Urbanists Denounce Nixon over War Spending; Say His Preoccupation with Asia Leaves Cities' Crisis 'Dangerously Unmet,'" *New York Times*, May 11, 1970, 22.

25. See Charles Haar, *Law and Land: Anglo-American Planning Practice* (Cambridge, MA: Joint Center for Urban Studies, 1964).

26. Wood, *Whatever Possessed the President?* passim.

27. Haar, quoted in Rosenthal, "6 Urbanists Denounce Nixon,", 22.

28. Daniel Moynihan, *Toward a National Urban Policy* (New York: Basic Books, 1970), 6–8.

29. Irving Spiegel, "Moynihan Says Social Science Finds Ills but Not Their Cures," *New York Times*, May 16, 1970, 29.

30. Moynihan, *Toward a National Urban Policy*, 6.

31. Wood, *Whatever Possessed the President?* 165; see also his response to Banfield's *Unheavenly City*: Robert Wood, *Necessary Majority: Middle America and the Urban Crisis* (New York: Columbia University Press, 1972).

32. "President Finds End of City Crisis, with Dip in Crime," *New York Times*, March 5, 1973. For a recent study of this shift, see Wendell Pritchett, "Which Urban Crisis? Regionalism, Race, and Urban Policy, 1960–1974," *Journal of Urban History* 34, no. 2 (2008): 266–85.

33. "In effect," he concluded, "Reagan could start with a fresh slate." Wood, *Whatever Possessed the President?* 156–57.

34. Marshall Kaplan, *Urban Planning in the 1960s: A Design for Irrelevancy* (Cambridge, MA: M.I.T. Press, 1973), v.

35. Ibid., vi.

36. Quoted in Wood, *Whatever Possessed the President?* 165.

37. Charles Haar, *Between the Idea and the Reality: A Study in the Origin, Fate, and Legacy of the Model Cities Program* (Boston: Little, Brown, 1975), 195.

38. Earl M. Blecher, *Advocacy Planning for Urban Development: With Analysis of Six Demonstration Programs* (New York: Praeger, 1971), 122–23.

39. John V. Lindsay, *The City* (New York: Norton, 1970), 114–21.

40. Frank S. Kristof, "The West Village Plan for Housing: Some Questions," Housing and Redevelopment Board interdepartmental memorandum, June 25, 1963; see also "Analysis and Comments on the West Village Plan for Housing," anonymous report, City Planning Commission Chairman Ballard Papers, New York City Municipal Archives, folder "West Village,

1964–1965." References strongly suggest that "Analysis and Comments on the West Village Plan for Housing" was prepared inside the City Planning Commission sometime after June 1963 and before the formal resubmission of the Village plan to that agency in July 1964.

41. Charles Grutzner, "State Voters Reject Subsidy Plan on Low-Income Family Housing," *New York Times*, November 7, 1962, 16. The twin goals of avoiding Title I subsidies and demolitions yet qualifying for Mitchell-Lama mortgage and tax exemption required a density slightly above that which the new zoning allowed, saddling "the plan with a built-in Gordian knot." See "Analysis and Comments on the West Village Plan for Housing."

42. Theodore Berlin, memo to Samuel Joroff, regarding field inspection survey, November 18, 1964; A. Leshan, memo to Chairman Ballard, October 28, 1964; Chairman Ballard, report of City Planning Commission findings to the Housing and Redevelopment Board, December 22, 1964, Ballard Papers, folder "West Village, 1964–1965.".

43. Donald H. Elliott, counsel to the mayor, memorandum to Chairman Ballard, cc'd to Lindsay (July 11, 1966), City Planning Commissioner Goldstone Papers, New York City Municipal Archives, folder "West Village Housing."

44. David K. Shipler, "'Village' Group Wins 8-Year Battle to Build 5-Story Walk-Up Apartments," *New York Times*, August 3, 1969, 35; Peter John Melser, "Confrontation over Control of Neighborhood Renewal: The Relationship between City Agencies and Local Residents in the Renewal of the West Village" (Ph.D. dissertation, City University of New York, 1979).

45. John Zuccotti, "How Does Jane Jacobs Rate Today?" *Planning*, June 1974, 23–27.

46. Jane Jacobs, letter to her mother (June 12, 1974), published in *Ideas That Matter: The Worlds of Jane Jacobs*, ed. Max Allen (Owen Sound, ON: Ginger Press, 1997), 98.

47. Jacobs is quoted in Susan Brownmiller, "Jane Jacobs: Civic Battler," *Vogue*, May 1969, 180.

48. Jacobs signed an open letter, "The Conspiracy," *New York Review of Books*, September 11, 1969; reprinted in Allen, *Ideas That Matter*, 180–81.

49. Jane Jacobs, "Social Uses of Power," in *The Writer's World*, ed. Elizabeth Janeway (New York: McGraw-Hill, 1969), 308.

50. Leticia Kent, "Jane Jacobs: Against Urban Renewal, for Urban Life," *New York Times Magazine*, May 25, 1969, 34.

51. Brownmiller, "Jane Jacobs," 180.

52. Jane Jacobs, letter to the editor of *Columbia Forum*, Fall 1972; reprinted in Allen, *Ideas That Matter*, 82.

53. *Philadelphia Daily News*, January 5, 1971.

54. Denise Scott Brown, "An Alternate Proposal That Builds on the Character and Population of South Street," *Architectural Forum* 135 (October 1971): 45.

55. Al Haas, "Ghost of X-Way Again Haunts South St.," *Philadelphia Inquirer*, March 26, 1972, B1.

56. Scott Brown, "Alternate Proposal," 44.

57. Ibid., 44.

58. They appropriated the historical antecedents of mannerist style and redefined the term as "breaking the rules." See "Team 10, Perspecta 10, and the Present State of Architectural Theory," *Journal of the American Institute of Planners* 33 (January 1967): 42–50.

59. Scott Brown, "An Alternate Proposal," 44.

60. Denise Scott Brown, "Between Three Stools: A Personal View of Urban Design Practice

and Pedagogy," in "Urban Concepts: Architectural Design Profile 83," ed. Andreas Papadakis, special issue, *Architectural Design* 60, no. 1–2 (1990): 14.

61. Chester W. Hartman, *Between Eminence and Notoriety: Four Decades of Radical Urban Planning* (New Brunswick, NJ: Center for Urban Policy Research, 2001), 29, 380.

Chapter 12: Softer Landings after the Fall

1. Edward Banfield, "The Political Implications of Metropolitan Growth," in *The Future Metropolis*, ed. Lloyd Rodwin (New York: George Braziller, 1961), 98.

2. Theodore Roszak, "Urban Renewal in America: A Better Way to Rebuild," clipping from October 9, 1964, Jane Jacobs Papers, Burns Library, Boston College, box 7, folder 2.

3. Brian Anson, *I'll Fight You for It: Behind the Struggle for Covent Garden* (London: Jonathan Cape, 1981).

4. Michael Ignatieff, paraphrased by Robert Fulford, *The Accidental City: The Transformation of Toronto* (Toronto: McFarlane, Walter & Ross, 1995), 74.

5. Volker Roscher, ed., *Hans Blumenfeld, Stadtplaner—es sei denn, sie bauen eine humane Stadt: Autobiographie, 1892–1988* (Basel: Birkhäuser, 1993), 229.

6. J. Caulfield *The Tiny Perfect Mayor: David Crombie and Toronto's Reform Aldermen* (Toronto: Lorimer, 1974).

7. Fulford, *Accidental City*, 65.

8. Ibid., 84.

9. Ibid., 87.

10. John Sewell, *The Shape of the City: Toronto Struggles with Modern Planning* (Toronto: University of Toronto Press, 1993), 191.

11. James T. Lemon, *Liberal Dreams and Nature's Limits: Great Cities of North America since 1600* (Toronto: Oxford University Press, 1996), 20–24. A full study of the cultural dynamics of this process is Jon Caulfield, *City Form and Everyday Life: Toronto's Gentrification and Critical Social Practice* (Toronto: University of Toronto Press, 1994).

12. See Richard Harris, "More American Than the United States: Housing in Urban Canada in the Twentieth Century," *Journal of Urban History* 26, no. 4 (May 2000), 456–78; and Harris, "Housing and Social Policy: An Historical Perspective on Canadian-American Differences: A Comment," *Urban Studies* 36, no. 7 (1999): 1169–75.

13. See Bill Freeman, "Toronto's Sewell and Urban Reform," in *The City and Radical Social Change*, ed. Dimitrios Roussopoulos (Montreal: Black Rose Books, 1981).

14. Clipping from *Baumeister*, vol. 47 (1950); reproduced in Gerhard Rabeler, *Wiederaufbau und Expansion westdeutscher Städte 1945–1960 im Spannungsfeld von Reformideen und Wirklichkeit* (Bonn: Deutsches Nationalkomitee für Denkmalschutz, 1990), 76.

15. Harald Bodenschatz, *Platz frei für das Neue Berlin! Geschichte der Stadterneuerung in der "größten Mietskasernenstadt der Welt" seit 1871* (Berlin: Transit Buchverlag, 1987), 76. Bodenschatz suggests the "absence of a tradition of conflict in other realms" made citizen participation unnecessary for Berlin renewal administrators.

16. John Burchard, *The Voice of the Phoenix: Postwar Architecture in Germany* (Cambridge, MA: M.I.T. Press, 1966), 160.

17. Ibid., 103. Burchard noted that Germans "are not so suspicious of the 'public domain' and that their land controls are more effective and less debated." In fact, long-term conceptual and legal cycles are visible in German planning statutes: In reaction against the absolutist

planning under baroque monarchs, protection of individual property rights was central to a liberal regime encoded in Prussian property law from 1794 through the long nineteenth century. By the turn of the twentieth century, the reaction underway against industrial city building had produced a reformist legal regime enacted around World War I and in effect until the implementation of the more moderate revision of 1986—though, again, that conceptual sea change preceded the statutory shift by about a decade. See Frank Steinfort, "Geschichtliche Entwicklung des Bau- und Planungsrehts," in Bau- und Planungsrecht: Raumordnungs- und Bauplanungsrecht, städtebauliche Sanierung und Entwicklung, Bauordnungsrecht, by Klaus Rabe, Frank Steinfort, and Detlef Heintz (Köln: Deutscher Gemeindeverlag, 1997), 2.

18. Bodenschatz, Platz frei, 178

19. Ibid., 184.

20. Rabeler, Wiederaufbau, 77.

21. Quoted in Klaus von Beyme, Werner Durth, Niels Gutschow, Winfried Nerdinger, and Thomas Tofstedt, eds., Neue Städte aus Ruinen: Deutscher Städtebau der Nachkriegszeit (Munich: Prestel-Verlag, 1992), 29.

22. Ibid., 29.

23. Hillebrecht received the findings of "traffic sociology" as a salutary contribution to democratic planning and found support in them for the proposition that Germany was in danger of repeating the mistakes of North American cities that had abandoned public rail transportation in the 1920s. See Wolfgang Hartenstein and Klaus Liepelt, Man auf der Straße: Eine verkehrssoziologische Untersuchung (Frankfurt am Main: Europäische Verl., 1961), 152.

24. The relationship between the StBauFG and prior (as well as subsequent) legislation is succinctly explained in Rabe, Steinfort, and Heintz, Bau- und Planungsrecht, 1–11 and 215–32.

25. J. Jessen, W. Siebel, et al., "8 Jahre Vorbereitende Untersuchungen nach §4 StBauFG: Nur ein Nachruf?" Stadtbauwelt 63 (1979): 242–49.

26. Hans Paul Bahrdt, "Die Bedeutung gesellschafts-politischer Ziele für die Institutionalierung der Sozialplanung," lecture at Institut für Städtebau Berlin der Deutschen Akademie für Städtebau und Landesplanung, 1974, quoted in Joachim Brech et al., Partizipation bei der Stadtplanung: Literatursammlung (Bonn: Bundesminister für Raumordnung, Bauwesen und Städtebau, 1976), 11.

27. Bernhard Schäfers, "Möglichkeiten der Sozialplanung nach dem Städtebauförderungsgesetz," Archiv für Kommunalwissenschaften 11, no. 2 (1972): 311–29. Similarly, see U. Herlyn, "Sanierungsbezogene Sozialplanung als Chance zur Partizipation," in Arbeitssituation, Lebenslage, und Konfliktpotential, ed. M. Osterland (Frankfurt: EVA, 1975), 213–32.

28. Bernhard Schäfers, Öffentlichkeits- und Interessenstrukturen in Planungsprozessen: Soziolog. Fallstudie am Beispiel einer kommunalen Neugliederung auf Kreisebene (Münster: Zentralinstitut für Raumplanung an d. Univ. Münster, 1970), 120.

29. Ibid., 121.

30. Ibid., 120 n. 1.

31. Bernhard Schäfers, Planung und Öffentlichkeit 3. soziologische Fallstudien: Kommunale Neugliederung, Flurbereinigung, Bauleitplanung (Düsseldorf: Bertelsmann, 1970), 196.

32. Ibid., 198.

33. Karl-Heinz David, Bernhard Schäfers, and Klaus Töpfer, Studie über Planerausbildung: Vorschlag zu e. sozialwiss. orientierten Raumplanerstudium (Bonn: Stadtbau-Verlag: 1970), 5.

34. Hans Paul Bahrdt, "Zweck, Inhalt und Durchführung von Sozialplänen bei Sanierungs-vorhaben," *Bauen konkret* 2 (1972): 16.

35. Roger Karapin, *Protest Politics in Germany: Movements on the Left and Right since the 1960s* (University Park: Pennsylvania State University Press, 2007), 64.

36. Ulfert Herlyn, "Die Bewohner im Wandel der Stadterneurung," in *Wohnen und Stadtpo-litik im Umbruch: Perspektiven der Stadterneurung nach 40 Jahren DDR*, ed. Peter Marcuse and Fred Staufenbiel (Berlin: Akademie, 1991), 174.

37. On Hannover as well as Berlin, see Karapin, *Protest Politics in Germany*, 61–116.

38. Notably "not—and this remains a central problem of the civic opposition until today—by the immigrants meanwhile living in the urban renewal areas." Bodenschatz, *Platz frei* (n. 15 above), 195.

39. *Sanierung—für wen? Gegen Sozialstaatsopportunismus und Konzernplanung* (Berlin: Büro für Stadtsanierung und soziale Arbeit Berlin-Kreuzberg, 1971).

40. See I. *Verfahren und Projektergebnisse; Stand: 1. Sept. 1979* (Berlin: Senatsverwaltung für Bau- und Wohnungswesen, 1979); and *Behutsame Stadterneurung in Kreuzberg: Schritt für Schritt* (Berlin: Gesellschaft der behutsamen Stadtereuerung, S.T.E.R.N., 1987).

41. Aside from antecedents in Frankfurt, a Berlin precedent was the occupation of the for-mer Bethanien Hospital convent in Kreuzberg during 1971–72, though this occupation was principally connected to the '68er student movement—as a symbolic response to the death of guerrilla activist Georg von Rauch—rather than a self-conscious protest against urban re-development policies. However, the local band Ton Steine Scherben, whose members took part in the activities, immortalized the episode in a song that became a battle cry for later squatters.

42. The movement was romanticized in the 1981 film *Schade, daß Beton nicht brennt*. Mar-git Mayer, "Hausbesetzer in New York und Berlin: Aktionen und Reaktionen," lecture at the Technical University, Berlin, 2001; Harry Böseke and Wolfgang Richter, eds., *Schlüsselgewalt : Lieber instandbesetzen als kaputtbesitzen* (Dortmund: Weltkreis, 1981); Harald Bodenschatz, Volker Heise, and Jochen Korfmacher, *Schluss mit der Zerstörung? Stadterneurung und städtische Opposition in Amsterdam, London und West-Berlin* (Gießen: Anabas, 1983).

43. Karapin, *Protest Politics in Germany*, 114.

44. Bodenschatz, *Platz frei*, 228ff. Also Hans Stimmann, ed., *Tendenzen der Stadterneurung: Entwicklung in Berlin, Erfahrungen europäischer Großstädte, Empfehlungen für Berlin* (Berlin: Senats-verwaltung für Bau- und Wohnungswesen, 1994), 49–51.

45. See R. Autzen et al., *Stadterneurung in Berlin: Sanierung und Zerstörung vor und neben der IBA* (Berlin: Ästhetik und Kommunikation, 1984).

46. For example, the Bauaustellung Berlin, GmbH, in alliance with indigenous resistance movements, helped stop the Kreuzberg-Süd renewal plans. Bodenschatz, *Platz frei*, 179.

47. Hans Wolfgang Hoffmann, "Die internationale Bauausstellung 1984/89," in *Berlin: Der Architekturführer*, ed. Rainer Haubrich, Hans W. Hoffmann, and Philipp Meuser (Berlin: Quad-riga, 2001), 221. See also, Bodenschatz, *Platz frei*, 202.

48. The exhibition in the Neuen Nationalgalerie, March 21 to May 28, 1987, was mounted by the IBA and produced a catalogue edited by Joseph Paul Kleihues, *750 Jahre Architektur und Städtebau in Berlin: Die internationale Bauausstellung im Kontext der Baugeschichte Berlins* (Stuttgart: Gerd Hatje, 1987).

49. While she emphasizes that an "expertocracy" still dominates decision making for Berlin, Elizabeth Strom notes in her examination of the postunification period that "preservation-oriented planning initiatives found in such West Berlin neighborhoods as Kreuzberg, emerging in response to top-down urban renewal policies, exerted an indirect influence on many of today's planning debates." See Elizabeth A. Strom, *Building the New Berlin: The Politics of Urban Development in Germany's Capital City* (New York: Lexington Books, 2001), 52. See Haubrich, Hoffmann, and Meuser, *Berlin: Der Architekturführer*, 250–51, 302–3. See also Harald Bodenschatz, "Von der Provokation zur Diskussion?" *Architektenkammer Berlin* 1997; Bodenschatz, "Planwerk Innenstadt Berlin: Eine Bestandsaufnahme," *Architektenkammer Berlin* 1997 (Berlin: Junius, 1997); and Bodenschatz, "Berlin—Potsdam—Brandenburg an der Havel: Annäherungen an den historischen Stadtgrundriß," *Architektur in Berlin: Jahrbuch 1998* (Hamburg: Architektenkammer Berlin, 1998).

50. Such local initiatives reflected a federal policy to promote "socially integrated cities" that was launched in 1999. Some scholars, including Margit Mayer and Werner Sewing, are critical of the program, though literature on it is only now emerging, primarily within the contemporary policy and planning community, for example, Gaby Grimm et al., *Quartiermanagement* (Edition Sigma, 2004); Herbert Schubert and Holger Spieckermann, *Standards des Quartiermanagements: Handlungsgrundlagen für die Steuerung einer integrierten Stadtteilentwicklung* (Köln: Fachhochschule Köln, 2010); and Joachim Schmidt, *Quartiersmanagement: Eine adäquate Antwort auf Prozesse der Desintegration in marginalisierten Stadtteilen?* (Munich: GRIN Verlag, 2007).

Conclusion: First We Take Manhattan, Then We Take Berlin

1. Nevertheless, historical studies of even such a large-scale economic process as deindustrialization tend to suggest the influence of public policies and local forces, as illustrated by the collection *Beyond the Ruins: the Meanings of Deindustrialization*, ed. Jefferson Cowie and Joseph Heathcott (Ithaca: Cornell University Press, 2003).

2. She continues: "Regime analysis depicts local actors as constrained by their environment (for example, by fiscal and economic necessity), but also capable of reshaping that environment through cross-sectoral governing arrangements. Regime typologies suggest that these arrangements vary not only because of differences in historical trends and local conditions, but because of the particular agendas and decisions of local political actors." Karen Mossberger, "Urban Regime Analysis," in *Theories of Urban Politics*, ed. Jonathan S. Davies and David L. Imbroscio (London: Sage, 2009), 40. See also Clarence N. Stone, *Regime Politics: Governing Atlanta, 1946–1988* (Lawrence: University Press of Kansas, 1989).

3. Leon Krier, quoted in Nan Ellin, *Postmodern Urbanism* (New York: Blackwell, 1996), 17.

4. Eugenie L. Birch, "Edith Elmer Wood and the Genesis of Liberal Housing Thought: 1910–1942" (Ph.D. dissertation, Columbia University, 1976); Birch, "Woman-Made America: The Case of Early Public Housing Policy," *Journal of the American Institute of Planners* 44 (April 1978): 130–44.

5. See the introduction to Robert Fishman, *The American Planning Tradition: Culture and Policy* (Baltimore: Johns Hopkins University Press; Washington DC: Wilson Center Press, 2000).

6. See Joshua Freeman, *Working-Class New York: Life and Labor since World War II* (New York: New Press, 2000); Vincent Cannato, *The Ungovernable City: John Lindsay and His Struggle to Save New York* (New York: Basic Books, 2001); Wendell Pritchett, *Brownsville, Brooklyn: Blacks, Jews, and the Changing Face of the Ghetto* (Chicago: University of Chicago Press, 2003); Jonathan Rie-

der, *Canarsie: The Jews and Italians of Brooklyn against Liberalism* (Cambridge, MA: Harvard University Press, 1985); and Ira Katznelson, *City Trenches: Urban Politics and the Patterning of Class in the United States* (Chicago: University of Chicago Press, 1981). A study of even earlier white grassroots revolts against the liberal consensus is Thomas Sugrue, *The Origins of the Urban Crisis: Race and Inequality in Postwar Detroit* (Princeton: Princeton University Press, 1996). The long-term political consequences are explored in Charles Brecher, Raymond Horton, et al., *Power Failure: New York City Politics since 1960* (New York: Oxford University Press, 1993); and John Mollenkopf, *A Phoenix in the Ashes: The Rise and Fall of the Koch Coalition in New York City* (Princeton: Princeton University Press, 1992).

Index

Page numbers in italics indicate illustrations or photographs; pages numbers followed by "n" indicate endnotes.

Bremen, 1965 housing and planning congress in, 32
Breuer, Marcel, 30
Bridenbaugh, Carl, *Cities in the Wilderness*, 4
Browne, Kenneth, 270n11
Brownmiller, Susan, 212
Bruce Report (1934), 40
Buchanan, Colin, *Traffic in Towns*, 139
Building exhibitions, Berlin (IBA), 226, 232, 233, 235, 260n26, 295n46
Bullock, Nichola, 39
Bunshaft, Gordon, 52
Burchard, John: German tours of, 32–33, 226, 293–94n17; Townscape movement viewed by, 88; *Voice of the Phoenix*, 260n32
Burgess, Ernest, 56
Burnham, Daniel, 49, 258n1
Byfield, Barbara Ninde, 169

Callaghan, James, 167
Canada, urban renewal in: comprehensive planning schemes, 40, 42–43; German exiles and, 10; political alliances and, 132, 241. *See also* Toronto, Canada
Canadian Mortgage and Housing Corporation, 42
Carl Mackley Houses, Philadelphia, 49
Caro, Robert, *The Power Broker*, 62, 210–11
Carver, Humphrey, "Housing Programme," 42
Cass, Samuel, 140
Cassidy, Harry, 40
Castells, Manuel, 241
Central Labor Council, 150
Cheek, Leslie, Jr., 111
Chermayeff, Serge, *Community and Privacy*, 57
Chicago, urban renewal in, 69
Chicago school of sociology: immigration studies and, 255n15; influence of, 56; Joint Center for Urban Studies and, 57; neighborhood succession models, 7; urbanism concept of, 7, 52, 102
Chicago World's Fair of 1893, 24
Churchill, Winston, 33, 38–39
CIAM (International Congresses for Modern Architecture): aesthetic influences in

Britain, 36, 37, 97–101, 217, 262n60, 269n3; aesthetic influences in Canada, 42–43, 44–45; aesthetic influences in United States, 50, 52, 53–54, 244; Athens Charter of 1933, 11, 29, 37, 97; criticism of, 69, 86, 88; demise of, 100; fascism and, 3; Hoddesdon conference, 1951, 97; international conferences, 76, 109, 261n44; leadership of, 261n43; modernism promoted by, 2, 11, 21, 25, 28, 30–31, 83; Smithsons' critique of, 97–101, 98–99, 109
Citizens Committee to Preserve and Develop the Crosstown Community (CCPDCC), 135, 194, 197
Citizens Housing and Planning Council, 153
Citizens Union, 155–56
City, The (documentary), 49–50
City Beautiful schemes, 24, 117, 205
City Center, New York, 64
City University of New York, 64
Civic Amenities Act of 1967 (Great Britain), 161
civic design, 74, 85, 96, 100, 102, 270n11
Civic Trust (London), 161–63
Civil Rights Act of 1968 (United States), 212
civil rights movement, 8
Clark, Joseph, Jr., 58, 68–69, 73, 287n13
Clay, Nanine, 111
Coates, Wells Wintemute, 261n43
Cochran, Thomas, 4
Cohen, Lizabeth, 267n48
cold war, 3–5, 8, 17, 29–32, 52, 60
Collins, John F., 20, 59, 65, 68, 167
Colquhoun, Alan, 88
Columbia University, 144, 183, 215–16, 289n38
Committee for the Preservation of Structures of Historic and Esthetic Importance, 159
Committee to Save the West Village, 151–60, 170, 188
communism, 8
Confederation of Resident and Ratepayer Associations (CORRA), 172
Conrads, Ulrich, 90
Constructa 1951 exhibition, 260n26

idea, 10, 11–12, 14, 17, 29, 37, 44–45, 66–67, 79, 84, 97–99, 98–99. *See also* modernism

Gabel, Hortense, 153

Galvin, John T., 65

Gans, Herbert, 235; Berndt influenced by, 107; influence of, 243; PEO group cofounded by, 200; at University of Pennsylvania, 102; urban renewal criticized by, 3, 7; *The Urban Villagers*, 56, 104, 230

Ganz, Alexander, 59

Garden City movement, 33–34, 34, 36, 49–50, 100, 107, 126, 262n60

Gardiner, Frederick, 46, 224, 262n64

Garment, Leonard, 204

Garnier, Tony, 11

Gates, Thomas, 69

Geddes, Patrick, 100, 262n60

Geist, Johann Friedrich, 91–92

Gelfand, Mark, 59–60

gentrification: in Brooklyn, 143; challenges of, 248; class and, 4; freeway proposals and, 129; in London, 242; Philadelphia's Society Hill and, 80, 93–94, 134; Philadelphia's South Street and, 212–13; racial issues, 112–13; in West Village, 130, 148–50, 224, 246–47

German Academy of City and Regional Planning, 104

Germany: critiques of decentralization and segregation, 79, 90–92; Dusseldorf, 226; early twentieth century, 21; Frankfurt, 17, 21, 32, 106–7; Hamburg, 105, 123, 125; Hannover, 32, 125, 126, 127, 229; Jacobs' reception in, 81, 121, 123, 125, 127; modernism in, 10, 226; Munich, 32; Münster, 30; Nazism in, 6, 8, 10, 17, 25, 28, 38, 125; politics in, 229–31, 241, 243, 244, 247, 295n41; 1960s federal initiatives, 31–32; post-urban-renewal era, 225–37; postwar city planning, 17; "public sphere" concept in, 91–92, 104–8, 293–94n17; urban planning act of 1971, 227, 228, 229; Weimar Republic, 25, 28, 243;

Wilhelmine era, 8, 14. *See also* Berlin, Germany, urban renewal in

Gerstle, Gary, 8, 9, 12

Gideon, Siegfried, 108, 261n43, 262n60

Gilpatric, Chadbourne, 80, 111

Glazer, Nathan, 151, 180, 205–6

Goecke, Theodor, 92

Gold, John R., 98

Goldstone, Harmon, 159

Goodman, Percival and Paul, *Communitas*, 109

Goodman, Robert, 191; *After the Planners*, 200

Gosling, David, *Gordon Cullen*, 270n13

Gottmann, Jean, 48, 181–82

Graysmith, Robert (cartoon by), 1

Great Britain: Jacobs' reception in, 81; Picturesque design tradition, 85–86, 100, 120; postwar nationalism of industries, 7; Victorian era, 7

Great Britain, urban renewal in: collapse of urban renewal order in, 161–67; Garden City movement, 33–34, 36; German exiles and, 10, 38; *laissez-faire* approach, 177, 219; MARS group, 35, 37–38, 55, 83–84, 86, 97, 262n60; modernism in, 35, 37–38; New Left urbanists, 177; parallels with United States, 217–19; politics and, 38–40, 103, 161, 163, 167, 219, 241, 247–48; postwar, 14, 33–40, 83–85; Smithsons' Independent Group, 79, 97–101, 119–20; Townscape movement, 3, 84–88, 97, 99, 100, 119–20, 195, 288–89n18. *See also* London, England, urban renewal in

Great Society programs, 2, 10, 60, 176–77, 199, 203, 207

Greater London Council (GLC), 40, 139, 161–63, 164–66, 219, 224

Greater London Development Plan, 139, 161

Greater Philadelphia Movement, 70, 74, 279n10

Greenbelt, Maryland, 49

Greenberg, Henry Clay, 153

Greenwich Village Association (New York), 138, 149, 152, 282n23

Grigsby, William, 77

and, 97, 100; utopianism of, 58; Voisin
plan (1925), 24; Wirth and, 52
League for Social Reconstruction, 40
Lee, Richard, 287n13
Lees, Andrew, 25
Legge, Raine, 163
Leitbild: Berlin proposals, 24, 232–33,
236; criticism of, 69, 245; definition of,
10; evolution of, 14, 239; functionalist
modernist, 28; MoMA exhibition and,
50; neo-traditional, 247; racial dynamics,
14; of Scott Brown, 197; zoning codes
and, 66–67
Lemon, James, 221–22, 285n27
Lever House, New York (Bunshaft), 52
Levitt and Sons developments, 11–12
Levittown, Pennsylvania, 102
liberalism: city politics context of, 8–10,
243–44, 246–47; definition of, 7; urban
renewal and, 4, 7–10, 175
Lilla, Mark, 3
Lindsay, John: Cooper Square redevelop-
ment, 215; neighborhood empowerment idea of, 200, 208; RAND Corporation consulted by, 290n11; West
Village given landmark designation
by, 160; West Village redevelopment
proposal and, 149, 152, 155, 176, 209,
246
Ling, Arthur, 261n48
Lippmann, Walter, 8, 245
Lipscomb, Alice, 135
Littlewood, Alan, 221
Local Government Act of 1974 (Great
Britain), 167
Locke, John, 7
Logue, Edward, 59, 68, 114, 115, 117, 119,
267n48
London, England, urban renewal in:
Abercrombie's master plan, 33–34, 36;
bungalow construction, 35; changing
views on, 79, 130–31; Covent Garden
neighborhood redevelopment proposals,
130–31, 161–63, 162, 164–66, 177,
218, 218–19, 239, 242, 247; Docklands
redevelopment, 247–48; early twentieth
century, 6; East End, 102–3, 242; Jacobs

and, 119–21; modernism and, 38–40,
240; Piccadilly redevelopment, 129,
139; postwar, 13, 17–18, 84–85; racial
tensions in, 163; Smithsons' designs,
100–101; social effects of, 80; squatters,
35, 163; Townscape movement, 3, 84–
88, 97, 99, 100, 119–20, 195, 288–89n18
London County Council (LCC), 38, 39, 40,
103
Loos, Adolf, 46
Lower Manhattan Expressway (planned), 64,
129, 134, 138, 187
Luce, Henry, 5
Lynch, Kevin, 57, 107, 111, 111
Lynd, Staughton, 151

Macmillan, Harold, 39
Magnusson, Warren, 172, 285n27
Mahood, Kenneth (cartoon by), 240
Mandel, Paul, 119
March, Werner, 90
Marcuse, Herbert, 107; One-Dimensional Man,
275n28
Marshall Plan, 29
Martin, Leslie, 38
Massachusetts Institute of Technology:
Center for Urban and Regional Studies,
53, 56, 57–59; Joint Center for Urban
Studies (with Harvard), 57–59, 60, 76,
175, 179–84, 202–7, 266n33
Matthew, Robert, 38
McHarg, Ian, 111
McLuhan, Marshall, 142
McNamara, Robert, 201
Mellon, Richard, 287n13
Melser, Peter, 209–10
Meyer's Court, Berlin, 18
Meyerson, Martin: Action for Boston
Community Development and, 59,
203; career of, 56–59, 180; as federal
policy advisor, 60; Jacobs and, 111; as
Joint Center director, 57, 203, 220; on
Philadelphia Planning Commission staff,
69; social analyses by, 7; Thernstrom's
reference to, 290n11; at University of
Pennsylvania, 76; "Utopian Traditions
and the Planning of Cities," 58

Parrish, Helen, 70
Passanante, William F., 137
Peace News, 217
Pearlman, Jill, 54
Peattie, Lisa, 191
Pei, I. M., 30, 73, 95, 111, 111, 117
Penn, William, 134
Penn Center, Philadelphia, 73, 74
Perkins, G. Holmes, 55, 74, 76, 95–96, 111,
   111, 114–15
Perkins and Will architectural firm, 191, 208
Pevsner, Nikolaus, 84, 100
Philadelphia, urban renewal in: advocacy
   planning in, 191–99; backlash against,
   in 1960s and 1970s, 14, 131, 133–36,
   167; Benjamin Franklin Parkway, 117;
   Better Philadelphia exhibition (1947),
   69–70, 71–72; Carl Mackley Houses,
   49; crosstown expressway proposal, 129,
   134–36, 136, 212–13; dismantling of
   initiatives, 15; early twentieth century, 6;
   Eastwick, 77, 103–4, 269n73; Gallery
   urban mall, 73; Penn Center, 73, 74;
   preservation and rehabilitation approach
   in, 79–80, 92–97, 109–10, 271n40;
   reform initiatives, 68–70, 71–73, 73–
   77; Schuylkill Expressway, 134; upper
   class and, 267–68n52; Young Turks
   movement in, 9, 20, 68–70, 131, 135,
   167. *See also* Society Hill, Philadelphia;
   South Street, Philadelphia
Philadelphia Citizens' Council on City
   Planning, 69, 76
Philadelphia City Hall, 74
Philadelphia City Planning Commission, 46,
   69–70, 73–74, 76
Philadelphia City Policy Committee, 68–69
Philadelphia Daily News, 212
Philadelphia Housing Association, 46,
   70, 76
Philadelphia Inquirer, 197–98, 213
Philadelphia Redevelopment Authority, 134
Philadelphia Savings Fund Society Building
   (Howe and Lescaze), 50
"Philadelphia School" of architecture,
   96–97
Philadelphia Story (film), 68

Phillips, Walter Massey, 68–69, 76, 135,
   167, 268n53
Pittsburgh, urban renewal in, 70
Planners for Equal Opportunity (PEO), 200,
   216
Planning for a Nation of Cities (collection),
   181–82
Plummer, Edmund, *The Planner in Society*,
   163
politics: in Canada, 132, 173, 220–24, 241,
   247, 248, 285nn26–27; contribution to
   demise of urban renewal, 242–47; in
   Germany, 229–31, 241, 243, 244, 247,
   295n41; grassroots mobilization and,
   242; in Great Britain, 38–40, 103, 161,
   163, 167, 219, 241, 247–48; importance
   of, 239, 241–44; liberalism and, 8–10,
   243–44, 246–47; machine, 9, 65, 131,
   181; in United States, 9, 131, 181, 241,
   244–47. *See also specific cities, names, and
   projects*
Pollock, Jackson, 52, 99
Popper, Karl, 228
Posener, Julius, 92
postmodernism, 108
Pratt Institute, 200, 215
professionalization, trend of, 19
Progressive Architecture, 96
Progressive era, urban policies in, 4, 5–6,
   9, 24
"public sphere" concept, 80, 91–92, 104–8,
   228, 293–94n17
Punch, 240
Purdy, Sean, 171
Pusey, Nathan, 183

Rabeler, Gerhard, 30, 90
racial issues: freeway proposals and, 129,
   135–36; gentrification and, 112–13,
   242; in London, 163, 219; neighborhood
   preservation and, 144, 148, 150, 191–99;
   in United States, 14, 112–13, 131–32,
   179, 181–85, 204–6, 224
Rafsky, William, 60, 134
Rainer, Roland, *Die gegliederte und aufgelockerte
   Stadt*, 260n26
Rand, Ayn, *The Fountainhead*, 52, 114

HISTORICAL

STUDIES OF

URBAN

AMERICA